Witch Doctor's Apprentice

Witch Doctor's Apprentice

Third Edition

Nicole Maxwell

WITH PHOTOGRAPHS

Library of the Mystic Arts
CITADEL PRESS
A Division of Carol Publishing Group
New York

First Citadel Press Edition 1990

A Citadel Press Book
Published by Carol Publishing Group

Editorial Offices
600 Madison Avenue
New York, NY 10022

Sales & Distribution Offices
120 Enterprise Avenue
Seacaucus, NJ 07094

In Canada: Musson Book Company
A division of General Publishing Co. Limited
Don Mills, Ontario

This edition of *Witch Doctor's Apprentice* is
published by arrangement with the author.

Queries regarding rights and permissions should be addressed to
Carol Publishing Group, 600 Madison Avenue, New York, NY 10022

Manufactured in the United States of America

10 9 8 7 6 5 4 3 2 1

Library of Congress Cataloging-in-Publication Data

Maxwell, Nicole.
    Witch doctor's apprentice / by Nicole Maxwell ; introduction by
Terence McKenna.
      p. cm. — (Library of the mystic arts)
    Includes index.
    ISBN 0-8065-1174-5 :
    1. Indians of South America—Medicine. 2. Materia medica,
Vegetable—Amazon Valley. 3. Amazon Valley—Description and travel.
I. Title. II. Series.
F2230.1.M4M3 1990
615'.321'09811—dc20
                                       90-2283
                                          CIP

Dedication

With heartfelt thanks, this book is dedicated
to Ruth Aley and Edward Holten-Schmidt,
who made it possible

Author's Note

In a very few instances, fictional names have been given to persons mentioned in this book. Otherwise, any resemblance to real people, living or dead, is no coincidence, but has been carefully striven for. They are my friends.

Introduction to the
Library of the Mystic Arts Edition

I FIRST READ Nicole Maxwell's *Witch Doctor's Apprentice* in 1976 but did not meet its author until early 1980. I had flown to Iquitos, Peru, from Lima to join my brother and several other botanists for the purpose of organizing a plant collecting expedition that would focus on authenticating reports of orally active DMT-based hallucinogens and obtaining samples of the plants involved.

"Nicole is here," my brother informed me in the first few minutes after I had tracked him down in a modest hotel on the Progreso, as the teeming business center of Iquitos is called. "This means that things will be a lot easier. She pretty well has the town wired."

I quickly found this to be true. Her name was respected at UNAP—the Universidad Nacional de Amazonas de Peru. And we found ourselves placed in touch with an excellent herbarium, with facilities for drying plants—an unbelievable luxury in the Amazonian climate. Nicole had worked years before for the Amazon Natural Drug Company, a small operation in Iquitos. Her old friend there, Adrianna Loyaza, proved to be invaluable in arranging for us to travel safely on the upper reaches of the Río Ampiyacu. Adrianna was part Witoto and spoke the language, and made a cassette tape message for us to play for her uncle, the headman at a village we wished to visit. It was Nicole who dreamed up the tape idea, and when we finally did play the tape for the old man, he was suitably impressed.

Nicole knew all sorts of people. Collectors, Indians, missionaries, tour operators and police—her years on the scene had given her an "in" nearly everywhere. When sitting with her in a restaurant in Iquitos, one felt as though one were accompanying one of the last of the Bourbons as the movers and shakers of the town stopped each in his turn to pay homage.

However, Nicole is far more than a mere habitué of café society; she is the only Caucasian that I have ever known who was able to convince me that after two weeks spent out in the Amazonian bush she was still actually enjoying herself. I have visited many of the places described in *Witch Doctor's Apprentice* and attest that Nicole's descriptions of hardships and danger are always masterfully and gracefully understated. That is precisely the opposite of most of the hairy-chested school of exploration reportage in which insignificant irritations are made to seem great tribulations.

But what is especially enduring and important about *Witch Doctor's Apprentice* is the way in which it presciently anticipates the importance of ethnomedicine and ethnopharmacology. In recent times the possibility of a plant-based cure for AIDS has been raised, and the global destruction of the rain forests has become page-one news. But in 1959, when Nicole made the journey to the Putomayo here described, Western medicine's appreciation of native healing was completely lacking. That is the conclusion of her entire odyssey, that the golden fleece of easy plant-based contraception was an unwelcome offering at the temple of mercantile pharmacology.

But during the fallow years of ethnopharmacology Nicole was not discouraged. She continued to build her collections of voucher specimens and data, which she has spent much of the past few years correlating. Vindication of the importance of plants and folk medical knowledge for the development of new approaches to health maintenance now seems assured. A rising global awareness of ecological crises and the toxification of the environment cannot fail to promote awareness of plants and natural products as traditional curative agents. One of the unsung pioneers in this effort has been Nicole Maxwell. Her book deserves to be read widely, as it gives a balanced picture of the river culture of the Peruvian Amazon poised on the brink of the irrevocable choices that will, no matter what course is taken, change forever the local way of life. Nicole's long career has been driven by a wish to participate in the preservation of the plant medicines that have been painstakingly garnered over many millennia. Such knowledge is not to be given up lightly, for it represents a way to partially alleviate human suffering. Her account of travel and exploration is a testament to a noble spirit and an idea whose time has come, that of the preservation of plants and folk knowledge with a proven potential in the treatment of human illness and disease.

TERENCE MCKENNA
Occidental, California
August 1989

Witch Doctor's Apprentice

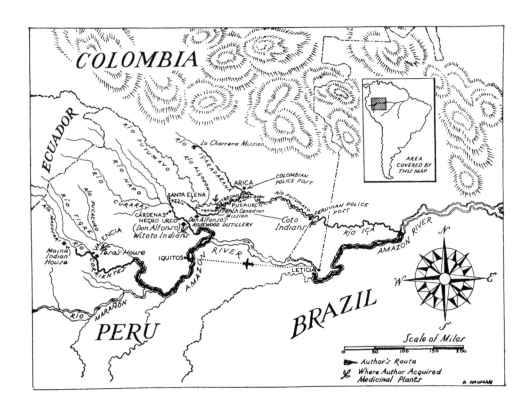

I

THE MOST frightening moment of my venture to collect medicinal herbs in the South American jungle was not when the Mainas caught me spying on a witch doctor ritual, nor during the terrible storm that nearly swamped our canoe on the Putumayo. It wasn't even when the jaguar came sniffing at my hammock the night I slept too far from my party. It was in New York before I left, at lunch with top scientists and executives of a pharmaceutical company.

I hate asking for money, even when I've already earned it. It took courage to ask distinguished botanists and pharmacologists to recommend a cash contribution toward a one-woman expedition up remote tributaries of the Amazon in search of medicinal plants whose properties are the cherished secrets of a few witch doctors.

Of course everyone knows that South American jungle tribes were the first to use the curare which is so important to modern surgical techniques. Many types of rauwolfia were employed by jungle shamans centuries before our medical men thought of tranquilizers. Quinine and all the other antimalarial drugs have their origin in the forests of the Amazon.

The pharmacists were familiar with all that. But I did tell them about some of the remedies I'd seen used or even used myself on some of the trips I had already made into the home areas of little-known tribes, remedies hinting at a vast reserve of vegetable medicines still unknown to science but potentially of enormous value. Surely it was time they were made available.

What would my route be? How long would the expedition take?

Those are the questions I hate. It is so hard to explain to people who know only civilization the uncertainties of the jungle. In areas at best sparsely inhabited by semi-civilized Indians, areas where there are no highways but rivers, where land travel means walking and transporting your supplies on the backs of men, you are literally at the mercy of the elements. You cannot wire ahead for manpower where there are no communications. You can't guess when a trail will be under water. You can never be sure a river won't be too full or too empty for navigation. I just made the best estimate I could.

I'd start on Río Napo and walk over to Río Putumayo. That's the big river which forms the border between Colombia and Peru before it empties into the Brazilian Amazon. If I hadn't by then found what I wanted, I would continue into the Colombian jungle. It might, with luck, be done in four months; it might take six. Actually, I was gone ten months, New York to New York.

The pharmacists were particularly interested in the plant juice which, taken by mouth, stops bleeding. I have known it ever since 1952 and try always to carry a bottle with me. I have seen it stop massive internal hemorrhages of women who had a bad time giving birth, and of a man crushed by a fallen tree. I've used it on myself externally; it has stopped the bleeding of any number of small cuts and scratches, and caused one rather bad cut on my right arm to heal rapidly and without scarring.

The gentlemen seemed less worried than I about my lack of training in the appropriate scientific fields. I told them that I'd been in medical school only about a year and a half and that my studies and research had been confined to physiology. They didn't seem to mind. "You just get the plants," they said. "Our botanists will identify them and our laboratories will do the research." The thing that did bother them was the idea of a woman's going alone.

"Do you think you're really strong enough?" one man asked, frowning dubiously. People always seem to think that a female explorer should be built like a lady wrestler. I suggested they consider the day's work a slender dancer like Margot Fonteyn can put in.

"But isn't it awfully dangerous for a white woman . . . you know . . . Indian men, and so forth ?"

I explained that a woman is really much safer among primitives than a man is. They aren't afraid she'll bring armies or oil companies; and they know she won't make passes at their women. As for the "White Queen of the Jungle" illusion, I told them about my Jívaro friends in Ecuador.

That was my first long jungle trip and I was lucky enough to get to a tribe of Jívaros who had never seen a white woman before. That's the tribe which is famous for decapitating their enemies and shrinking their heads to the size of an orange. Our arrival brought them crowding around, excited and noisy. They felt the material of my shirt, my blue jeans, my hat. I'm not quite five feet six, but not one of the men was as tall as I, although they were rather greater in circumference and had thicker wrists and ankles. Even in my baggy blue jeans they made me feel willowy. One man wanted to see if my hair would come off. Later I found out that they just couldn't believe it was hair; hair is something that's black (mine's brown) and coarse as a horse's mane. But at the time his investigations made me distinctly uneasy. A moment later, when a tough-looking warrior grabbed my wrist, it took all my self-control to stand still and look calm. But there were only four of us and at least forty of them, so I just stood there. He wet his forefinger, rubbed it vigorously on my wrist, examined both frowningly, and then held them out for the crowd's inspection, sputtering a stream of syllables that brought down the house.

Even my interpreter was rocking with laughter. I asked him to let me in on the joke. Wiping his eyes, he replied, "The Jívaro says, 'That isn't white paint; it doesn't come off. She's got skin like a fishbelly and eyes like a fish. Isn't she hideous?' "

No flattery was ever so sweet.

Or so useful. For I think it was that episode and my being a Fellow of the Royal Geographical Society of London that finally convinced the sponsors. You don't usually get F.R.G.S. after your name by riding the Staten Island ferry. It helped, too, that I'd done precensal studies of jungle Indians for the first Ecuadorian census in 1950, and had been made a founder of the Ecuadorian Institute of Geography and Ethnology. Nevertheless, when they telephoned a few days later to say that they'd decided to put up a thousand dollars toward my venture, plus a lavish supply of antibiotics, I was half stunned with gratitude.

That thousand just made the difference: It still wasn't going to be an expedition; you can't get Abercrombie & Fitched up in proper expeditionary style on what I had to spend, but you can get reasonably Army and Navy Stored.

Now I could make some of those plant medicines available to my own people. In the last few years, it had become an *idée fixe*. It was something that badly needed doing, and it was something I thought I could do—and have fun doing.

I made reservations on the pleasant and economical Chilean Line and started getting my kit together. Too much gear, the invariable sign of the amateur, can prove a serious handicap. For example, if you need eight bearers to carry your cargo on the walk from one river to another (say two or three days), you may find six without any trouble and then learn that no amount of money or persuasion or waiting will get you the other two. Six is all there are, and you either abandon some of your supplies or give up and go home. I had to keep reminding myself of that as I found first that tape recorders, then movie cameras, then a small portable freezer were beyond my means. A miniature freezer, kerosene-powered, would be wonderful for preserving things like the sap of a certain tree reported to be a miraculous rejuvenator. Unfortunately, the stuff, no matter what chemical preservatives you add, deteriorates in a few days and you are left with a stinking, gooey mess that would sicken a cockroach.

Oh, damn, you seldom find enough bearers. The sour grapes were pretty satisfying, except in the matter of armament. I never carry a big gun, it's too much trouble. But I've never gone into jungle without a pistol or a revolver. Now I had to choose between going armed and having enough trade goods. It wasn't easy. A good gun is expensive but a bad one is dangerous. Still, in all the trips I've made, I'd needed my gun only once when I foolishly got too far ahead of my party and ran into some undesirable characters . . . there isn't much law enforcement in jungle. That time it had been quite enough to hold my pistol quietly in my hand until they did decide to go away. But I've always needed all my trade goods, so I decided to go unarmed and trust my luck. It's never let me down yet and I've always had a superstitious feeling that it's really trusting my luck that has brought me through so many tricky situations.

I didn't have to buy sleeping equipment. Portable cots can be set up only when the ground is reasonably level. Tents, too, and it's often hard to find a place where the brush is open enough even for a pup tent. If you do, it blows down on you in the middle of a rainy night. I had my hammock. Not the Armed Forces' tropical hammock of slippery nylon with waterproof nylon roof and a zippered mosquito net. I used one of those for just one trip. It was not sociable. It couldn't be used for just sitting and chatting. Once I got into it, I had to zip it closed to keep out the bugs, and there was no place to dump cigarette ashes, no place to put my flashlight, gun, water bottle or valuables. Its slippery nylon ropes, unless tied with painful care, would undo themselves in the middle of the night. I always landed on the zipper and had to lie there trapped, smothering and humiliated until somebody came to unzip me.

Mine is the perfect hammock, shabby and mended though it may be. It is not made of cloth. I got it years ago from Ticuna Indians on the Colombian Amazon. They make them of chambira palm fiber patiently twisted into cord as supple as silk, but much tougher, then they weave the cord into a loose, knotless mesh that yields without pressure to every curve of the body. Mine is so big that I sleep crosswise in it, but it weighs only a couple of pounds and I know of nothing so relaxing.

Clothes were no problem, just blue jeans and long-sleeved shirts. I have used the same pair of mosquito boots for years, but boots are only for evening wear. In the daytime, moccasins are better or sneakers laced up over the ankles. High sneakers are the only thing for walking trails, low shoes stay behind in puddles, boots pick up pounds of mud and grow agonizingly fatiguing. Then, too, you have to wade through swamps and across little streams. Boots that are wet inside are impossible, but the water just squelches through sneakers, deliciously cool in the jungle heat. Snakes? One that can't strike above a boot isn't really trying. You don't see many anyway, and if you make enough noise, coming along a trail, they usually get out of your way.

My technical equipment consisted of one plant press, contributed by the pharmaceutical company. I don't know just what I'd expected, but it was surely something more impressive than a lattice-like rectangle of wood held together by two fabric straps which could be tightened to squeeze plants between the big sheets of thick blotting paper it contained.

It's the trade shopping that's fun. Big needles for sewing with thread of palm fiber, colored shirts, little mirrors, bright combs and pounds and pounds of beads. Those were routine. Safety pins combine the appeal of adornment with technology; ballpoint pens are useful for painless tattooing; red nail polish delights warriors—those were things I'd learned on previous trips.

This time my objectives were more serious. I needed something imaginative, a real witch doctor convincer, for my success or failure depended on my ability to conciliate them. Medicine is magic; magic is a witch doctor's business. Ordinarily, tribesmen may know an astonishing lot of plant secrets, but if the doctor doesn't sign the prescription, you don't get the medicine. Who wants to muscle in on the territory of the man who controls demons that cause sickness, the man who with an incantation and a gesture of the hand can send lightning to strike wherever he wishes.

I haunted novelty stores. I stared in windows full of gadgets that were not quite right. Then I woke one morning with a stunning inspiration. Glass eyes! Could anything be more magical? Really lifelike artificial eyes. Any witch doctor could make a reputation with one. They would be my clincher!

But where do you buy glass eyes? I went into several optometrist's shops along Fifth Avenue before I found one where a haughty young man admitted that they sometimes supplied "prostheses" for clients.

"Have you any dark brown ones?" I asked. "I'd like to see some samples."

He looked at me with a most peculiar expression. My eyes are blue. "No, we do not carry samples. They must be made to order."

"But, you see," I explained, "I need a dozen or so. Perhaps you could tell me about what they'd cost ?"

His own eyes glazed as he nervously named a sum more than double the price of a ticket to South America. He looked relieved when I left.

This was obviously not the way to buy glass eyes. I went home and consulted the telephone book. I found quite a few advertisements of companies that made artificial eyes, and chose one at random.

The voice that answered sounded friendly. Yes, he was Dr. Louis Herrman. No, he did not have a glass-eye factory, but he did make plastic ones to order.

"Oh, dear!" I said. "I've got to get a dozen or so, and I know they are terribly expensive, and I've very little money to spend. So I thought perhaps if I could find a factory, I might be able to get some imperfect ones, rejects or seconds or something that could be sold cheaply. You see, they have to be realistic enough only to impress Amazonian witch doctors."

"Would you mind trying to speak a little more distinctly?" he asked.

I said, "To impress witch doctors in the Amazon Basin. So if you do only custom-built jobs, perhaps you'd be kind enough to tell me if there is a factory anywhere that might have the sort of thing I'm looking for."

"Glass eyes . . . witch doctors . . . look," he said, "could you come on down and have lunch with me?"

With less than a week to pack and store the contents of a five room apartment, I had no time for eating. But when I saw him that afternoon, I wished I had gone. He was even more attractive than his voice—and he gave me twenty beautiful eyes. They were all dark brown except three. I guess Dr. Herrman thought I might meet a sentimental witch doctor, for he insisted that I have a sample to match my own. That created a problem. My eyes are apt to change from blue to gray and green when I'm angry. So he gave me three to match any mood I might be in.

CHAPTER

II

My ship sailed at midnight on November 30th, 1958. The sea, during the entire trip, was smooth as hand lotion. The ship was air-conditioned throughout from the first day we entered tropical waters. Each stateroom had a private bath. The food and service were excellent, the other passengers friendly and informal. It should have been very relaxing, but I had lost the knack of relaxation. I couldn't get to sleep. When after hours of tossing I did drop off, a recurring nightmare haunted me. It was always the same. I was packing. The apartment was full of friends who had come to help. I was trying to fit the antique Limoges dinner service, the electric iron, my precious stone head of Kuan Yin, assorted hardware, and the ancient Japanese and Chinese porcelain inherited from my father into a trunk too small for them. And all the time somebody was standing there in the door shouting, "Hurry! Hurry! The ship leaves in ten minutes!"

That always woke me. I'd remind myself that I was already on my way. Then I'd start to worry about that. After all, I had taken the pharmaceutical company's money, hadn't I? It was already spent. What if I couldn't deliver the goods? I knew that the Indians consider plant medicine magic, what the Witoto tribe calls *icaro*. I knew how jealously each tribe guards its *icaro* even from close friends who happen to belong to another group.

I was white. I was alien. I must have been out of my mind to believe I could pry out secrets whose very power, in tribal lore, could be canceled by a betrayal to an outsider. Secrets so many scientists had sought. I had met several highly qualified botanists, even a few well-qualified pharmacologists, who had returned with little to show from their expeditions. What possessed me to believe I could break the taboos of centuries? And what would happen if I returned empty-handed?

I would go on like that until the porthole showed gray and the getting-up gong sounded. Every morning I dragged myself down to breakfast more jittery, more fatigued than the day before. I began to notice an extra solicitousness on the part of the other passengers. My state was showing.

I decided that outdoor exercise might help. I hate calisthentics but ballet exercise is different. I'd studied ballet and knew from experience that ballet exercises are first-rate preparation for jungle treks. They improve your reflexes and sense of equilibrium. Jungle trails, however flat the terrain may look, are mostly uphill and down, and always slippery with mud or slick with wet, fallen leaves. When the only medical attention is weeks or months of travel away, any training which will help to avoid falls is important.

I decided to initiate a dance-exercise program and announce it at breakfast, partly so that the other passengers would not be startled, but mostly because I wanted to commit myself publicly to it so that it would be hard to weasel out after only a day or two. I even persuaded some of the other women aboard to join me. It would counteract the widening effect of the ship's good and abundant cuisine.

The first two days went with a certain éclat. The railings on the boat deck were just the right height for bar work, and we went through the entire routine, five positions of each. But the third day, I was alone up there. On the deck below, the women who had been so enthusiastic the first day painfully lowered themselves into deck chairs and refused to budge. I was ready to immobilize myself, too, but I couldn't admit it. And, besides, though my sense of balance might be improving, nothing else seemed to be benefiting except the morale of the crew gathered delightedly on the foredeck to watch. As for me, each day I was noticeably more tired and tense. Aching muscles did nothing to help me sleep and the discovery of how short-winded I was did nothing for my self-confidence on jungle trails. I'd got to the point where I talked like a telegram and couldn't finish a meal without dropping forks and spoons on the floor. Two Chilean doctors aboard, with the most exquisite tact, suggested I stop trying to knock myself out. Instead of exercise, they put me on tranquilizers. By the time we got to Lima, I had unwound.

All shipping for Lima docks at the port of Callao. The city proper is three or four miles inland but with expanding population the two towns have almost grown into each other. At Callao, maritime passengers go through customs. Going through customs was another worry that plagued me during the sleepless hours on ship. Peru has pretty stiff duties on things like radios and cameras and films—I had three small transistor radios which RCA Victor had given me to fascinate the savages, four cameras with elaborate flash equipment and enormous quantities of film. And what would the customs officers make of the box of artificial eyes?

This problem, at least, dissolved itself in its own stewing juices. A friend from the United Nations Technical Assistance Mission and a representative of the pharmaceutical company were waiting on the docks. Between them, they had already established my status as a scientific expedition. I swept through customs like a diplomat.

I never know quite how to answer when anyone asks me where home is. I just live wherever I happen to be, but that's somehow embarrassing to explain. Still, whenever I arrive in Lima I get the feeling of having come home. Perhaps it's because I know Lima better than I know any other city. I had to learn Lima and learn it thoroughly to write the English language guidebook for the Peruvian government's new Tourist Corporation back in 1947 and to assemble more material for another edition when I returned in 1951. That was a long time ago, and I have lived in other countries since, but for all its booming modernization, Lima never really changes.

Occasionally you meet a very chic woman who sets the mark of her own distinction on every new fashion she follows. She changes the length of her hemline, the shape of her hat, the way she does her hair without altering her own strikingly individual personality. That is the way Lima wears her changing social mores, her flowery avenues exploding into new residential or industrial developments and her surging new constructions. The personality of Lima is solidly based on four centuries and more of tradition. Lima was the first Spanish colonial capital of South America, the elegant city from which the viceroys, as deputies of the king of Spain, ruled the entire continent. The surface changes, though not so much as it might if the Spanish colonial motifs were not still cherished by modern Peruvian architects, but the city always feels the same.

Driving from Callao to Lima, I learned that the pharmaceutical company had a couple of chores for me before I could get off to Iquitos. Their publicity department had arranged press interviews and a radio broadcast. That was a blow. Anxious to get on to the Amazon, I had allowed for only a couple of days in Lima. With no time for visiting old and cherished friends, I simply hadn't the nerve to telephone anyone and say, "I'm back in Lima, but I haven't time to see you." So I had planned to sneak quietly through town and look up all my friends on the return trip.

I suppose I should have expected the interviews. The people of Lima are as curious as New Yorkers about the jungle and know it just about as well. Iquitos is scarcely more than three hours from Lima by air, and the state of Loreto, whose capital it is, is the largest in the Republic of Peru. But though its area is more than a quarter of a million square miles, official census statistics give it a population density of about one person for each ten square miles. Any place with no roads, no mail or telegraph service and only one good hotel is not apt to be frequented by Limenos. They are as intensely urban as New Yorkers, may visit Europe, the States and other capitals of South America, but within their own country their travel is mostly confined to the well-paved coastal strip with perhaps an occasional jaunt to the mountains to see the fabulous Inca ruins of Cuzco and Machu Picchu. They like to hear about the vast wilderness across the hills, but their voyages end where the pavement stops.

The press interviews were not difficult and I've become inured to the fact that newspaper photographs always make me look like Dracula's mother. But a thirty-minute radio interview in a language not my own was rather frightening. At Radio Nacional, an old friend, Pancho Pardo de Zela, was in charge. Pancho is a very suave character. He set about putting me at ease. Nothing to dither about, he assured me. Today we'd just put the interview on tape. Before it went on the air, he would edit it, cutting out any pauses if I froze, and erasing any serious mangling of the Spanish language. My Spanish is normally rapid and flowing, but in times of stress it sometimes backwaters. Now after a year in the States, I worried about being out of practice.

"When will it be broadcast?" I asked.

"Tomorrow morning and again Sunday morning."

Twice! I got twice as nervous. Pancho spent the first few minutes introducing me and then started asking how I traveled in jungle.

By boat—outboard-motor canoes whenever possible. I never walk if I don't have to, though it is sometimes necessary to take to the trail to get from one river to another. Trail is a nuisance because you need so much more personnel when all your gear has to be carried on the backs of men. Interpreters? I could pick up someone who knew Spanish and the Indian languages whenever I got to the near tribal areas.

What tribes? Witotos, Ocainas and Boras. I was mostly interested in the Witotos, possibly because I had had a chance some years before to spend a few days among them and knew that they had a considerable knowledge of jungle medicines. They are a big nation which originally resided between the Putumayo and Caqueta Rivers in Colombia. During the days of the rubber boom, the great rubber combines pressed thousands of them into service as *siringueros*, rubber gatherers. Now they are scattered, some in Colombia and some in Peru, and although almost all the groups have had some contact with civilization, the majority of them cling to ancient tribal customs and beliefs. They still live in the vast communal houses that are thatched to the ground, use palm-fiber hammocks for beds, favor polygamy, and at evening meetings of the men's secret societies teach the wisdom of their ancestors to the younger tribesmen. And some still practice *couvade*, an obstetrical system with a reverse twist common to many of the tribes of the Amazon, Basin. When an Indian woman feels her baby is about to be born, she simply has it. As soon as she has washed herself and her baby, the child's father takes to his hammock and remains there from three days to two weeks, depending on which tribe he belongs to. It is the mother's job to care for him tenderly, in addition to doing her regular work and nursing her new baby. The Amazon is a man's world.

In the old days, Witotos didn't bother with clothing. They used only paint and bracelets of fiber and seeds for adornment. The men wore only G-strings and on festive occasions added feather crowns and weird masks. Ritual cannibalism was practiced only when an enemy of great strength and courage had been killed. Then his brain was removed and ground to a pulp with various herbs and spices. The mixture was eaten in a solemn ceremony by the chief of the victorious tribe. Later he regurgitated it.

I had heard that although the Witotos in Peru had given up warfare and their more savage customs, there was still one small group in Colombia, not far from the Putumayo River, who still lived exactly as their ancestors did and forcibly repulsed any contact with whites or even civilized Indians of their own language group. These were the Witotos I wanted most to meet. Not so much because I thought it would be easier to get plant secrets from them, but just because I've always wanted to meet a cannibal. Especially one who wouldn't eat me. These boys wouldn't. I'm no strong, brave warrior.

I got through that part of the interview smoothly but began to founder when Pancho asked me about the religion and legends of the Witotos. They have a vague concept of an evolutionary process in the development of both men and plant life. I had been present at the Witoto festival of the pineapple in which the men chant its history. In the beginning, according to their litany, a hard, bitter-tasting, pineapple-shaped plant grew on the barks of trees. The ancestors of the tribe cut this away and planted it in the earth where it made roots. Every year they selected seeds from the largest plants and put them back into the earth. As the fruit grew larger its flavor improved, until finally, by selective planting, they had evolved the pineapple.

The story of animal evolution I had got second-hand from a man who had lived many years with the tribes and who admitted his interpretation might be erroneous. The Witotos have a separate language for religious concepts, and although they were apparently willing to teach it to him, they couldn't. They had no Spanish, and everyday Witoto has no words to express abstractions. However, for what it was worth, I tried to explain it as I had heard it to Pancho and his whirling, nervous tape recorder. In the beginning, the world had been a molten mass. It cooled and solidified and then the first animal life broke through the crusty surface in the shape of a little, wiggling tadpole. At that point I boggled. I couldn't think of the Spanish for tadpole. I asked Pancho in English. After all, though he speaks several languages perfectly, Spanish is his native tongue. But Pancho couldn't think of it either, so we just burbled for a while. Finally, we compromised on "infant frog, before it has legs" and then I went on to explain that this was the first animal which later developed, in the Witoto belief, into all other animals. But man, I had heard, came differently—in a whirlwind, spiraling down from heaven. Again, the old dogma of man's superiority to nature instead of his being a part of it.

Pancho must have had a date that evening, for when I heard the broadcast, he had not cut a single grammatical error, a single stammer, a single momentary blank. It was all there, including the tadpole business. And none of it sounded very bright. What's more, my voice came through with a deplorable cooing quality whenever I got nervous, which was most of the time. You could hear how hard I had tried to be charming. I hoped nobody I knew had been listening.

I have many friends in Lima, and with Christmas approaching I knew most of them would be in town. Lima may seem like home to me because the people have a tendency to stay put. You can return after any absence to find your friends living in the same houses and married to the same people. You may even be served by the same waiters in the same restaurants. I once dropped into the Bolivar at cocktail time after an absence of four years. The Bolivar Hotel is another of the stabilities of Lima. It has elegantly remained the center of Lima's downtown social life ever since it opened in 1924. Stopping there for a drink or tea saves telephoning to announce your arrival in town because the same people will be there and they will spread the word. That evening I sat down on one of the sofas that line the big circular lounge the regulars call the "snakepit" because its little round tables are usually filled by Limenos hissing the latest gossip. I asked the waiter to bring me a pisco collins. "Without sugar as usual, señorita?" he asked. After four years!

Now I hated having to rush away so soon. I had only time to notice that the mountains back of the city still turn to opals in the opaline dusk of Lima, that the policemen are as polite as ever, and that they still spell Irish stew "iristu" and milkshake "Milshe" (pronounced Millshay) on some menus, but that the news vender's sign, "All the Best and Prettiest American Magazines," was missing.

Iquitos is Peru's main Amazon port, the jumping-off place for many jungle ventures. It can be reached only by air. I have spent many a chilly gray dawn in Limatambo Airport brooding over the fact that every time I go to the jungle I'm ordered to get to the airport before it is light. All the airlines do it. They claim it's because the flights take three to four hours and the plane must complete its return trip before nightfall. I don't believe a word of it. I am convinced that all the Lima airline schedules are worked out by a sadistic insomniac who is determined that if he can't sleep, nobody shall. In the dreary, dawning hours when one's vitality is lowest, when the sick die and the wakeful worry, I'll bet the little monster gets a big bang out of spying on the passengers who huddle dispiritedly over little mounds of baggage waiting . . . waiting. . . . For, of course, the plane never leaves on time. That morning I got to the airport around five. I hadn't had a moment to visit with cherished friends, but now I had hours to wait in airports. I thought of phoning people from there . . . but who wants to receive social calls at that time of the morning? Not until nine o'clock were we told that the weather had cleared over the mountains and our plane could take off. I was so irritated I ate breakfast twice. And I don't even like breakfast.

The northeast flight to Iquitos is only 830 air miles from Lima, but it crosses three worlds. No matter how surly I may be feeling when I board the plane, I am always swept into a mood of awed exhilaration within minutes of the takeoff. First comes the narrow world of desert, the long coastal strip of sand like pale suede wrinkling and cracking into spiny foothills. An Andean foothill would be a fair-sized mountain in most countries. The plane gains altitude fast to enter the world of the Andes, a hostile world of sharp-angled rock jutting and thrusting into the sky. As the plane climbs—it takes over twenty thousand feet to clear the pass—there is no sign of life to be seen anywhere. No trees, no roads, no houses, only naked rock in strange shades of green and red and gray and purple, cut by fantastic gorges and abysmal valleys.

Gazing down, I wondered how big Peru really was. I don't mean how many miles it occupies on a well-scaled map, that's easy. But how many square miles of actual surface has it? If you could iron out all the wrinkles, those tremendous ridges of mountain ranges, the deep-creased valleys, if you could press them flat as a tablecloth, wouldn't it be one of the largest countries of the continent?

The letdown is long and slow and always, each time I've made the trip, blanketed by an unbroken layer of fluffy, white cloud, warm air currents from the Amazon Basin which condense on touching the cold of the Andes. Far below the plane, it looks soft and solid enough to stretch out on and go to sleep. But sooner or later, it thins and tears to show a bumpy, dark green mat of treetops, cut here and there by wide, slow rivers. The rivers twist and writhe like snakes with broken backs, bright silver where the sun strikes them, *café au lait* in the shadows of passing clouds This is the third world, the jungle stretching into the mists of the horizon. It is the biggest world of all.

We continued losing altitude until my ears popped, but I stared down at the wilderness in a trance. With never a clearing, the impenetrable solid mystery of foliage has a hypnotic effect. I could see a powdering of pink or gold or flame, tall trees bursting into bloom, or, perhaps, vines that were strangling them. And I wondered if civilized man had ever penetrated the shadows beneath, if Indians wandered there, if they used the magic I was seeking. Which of those trees, which vines, might hold a secret to cure the sick, to revolutionize some phase of the modern art of healing?

When at last we swooped low over a series of clearings, I couldn't quite believe them. But they were real man-made clearings. In some of them cows were pastured by shining little pools, in others there were straight lines of banana trees and little brown houses with shaggy brown-thatched roofs. We landed and stepped out of the plane into the moist, loam-scented air, the warm breath of the jungle.

CHAPTER

III

IQUITOS is a real city with taxis and buslines, radio stations and newspapers. And it is a real frontier town with its back against the jungle and the greatest river in the world coiling around its feet. I love its magnificent vistas, especially at dawn or sunset when a hint of cool, moving air rises from the Amazon and the wide, curving stretch of water reflects a gaudy sky. I love the houses of flowery, painted tiles which look as though they've been turned inside out with the wallpaper toward the street. And I love its people. Men and even little girls rise to offer you their seats in the bus. They greet strangers with pleasant respect on the narrow, back streets where wide, low roofs shade the sidewalks. But they will often say *Adiós* for Hello, which at first confused me considerably. They are friendly and relaxed, always unhurriedly happy to do anything within their power to help a stranger, for time is a relative concept—a distant relative.

The Hotel Turista, one of a government chain, is a modern building of heavy concrete fronting on the Malecón, the wide promenade along the high green bank of the river. Built in the days when the rubber boom made Iquitos one of Peru's richest cities, the Malecón has a clinging, dilapidated elegance and its wide balustrade is a comfortable perch from which to watch the changing moods of sky and water. White-clad men cluster here to enjoy the evening freshness, and girls with brown arms and pale dresses stroll by in pairs.

It was hot when I got to the hotel, but I decided against taking an air-conditioned room. New York had been icy and the ship's air-conditioning too efficient. I thought I'd better hurry to get acclimated. An emotional "jungle fever" added temper to the temperature in Iquitos, for the city was buzzing with embarrassed excitement. A rumor had spread like plague along the rivers of the whole area, terrifying the natives into panicky hostility. *Gringos* (Americans, English, any blond foreigners) were said to be prowling the forests and shooting their inhabitants, then melting their bodies down to extract the fat. This operation is known in Peru as *pishtaco*. Human fat, according to the story, is an essential ingredient of atomic weapons, and the United States had contracted for vast quantities to be sent from the local jungles.

Frightened river dwellers left their remote farms and banded together with armed sentinels posted day and night. Deep in the wilderness, *manguares*, the great tribal drums which telegraph tribal news through the jungle, sent throbbing signals in the shadowy wilderness. Indians and whites (almost anybody who has abandoned the tribal customs and learned to speak Spanish is called white in this part of the world) had joined forces, prepared to sell their lives dearly.

Close to the city, two sailors from a British ship had been warned away from the shore by a shouting mob of armed men when they went on a boating picnic. Antonio Wong (no gringo) was shot at while peacefully fishing from the aluminum speedboat he uses to show tourists native life along the rivers. The local newspapers daily demanded the arrest of anyone who spread this "criminal silliness," and three local radio stations scolded and reassured at regular intervals in several Indian tongues. But natives who can read are almost as rare as natives who have radios. The panic continued to spread.

In Iquitos, rumors flew back and forth. All missionaries were said to be in danger. We heard that a Canadian and two Americans had been badly beaten on the Amazon itself, another American had disappeared on the Curaray and there were rumors that four more had been killed on various other rivers. It took some time to prove these reports false. When all the checking up had been completed, the only casualty in the whole affair was not a foreigner but a frightened Indian who had come to seek refuge with civilized relatives living in the city. He fainted dead away when a tourist took a flash picture of him the night he got into town. When he revived, he explained that cameras are known to be gringo machines emitting "electricity" which hypnotizes the victim and robs him of his will. When he saw the flashbulb go off, he thought it was a new model equipped with lightning.

Fortunately, the governor of the Department of Loreto was a Peruvian navy admiral. All the admirals I have ever known were men who were adequate in emergencies. To quash the rumor before some serious incident occurred, the admiral planned a coordinated emergency operation employing the armed forces. Small army and police patrols worked through all the inhabited areas assuring the natives that they were under the governrnent's protection and that the rumors were nonsense. The navy's border-patrol gunboats, equipped with loudspeakers and interpreters, carried the word up and down the larger, more navigable rivers. In a surprisingly brief period of time, considering the vast area which had to be covered, the fear abated.

Actually, there is some remote, historical basis for the pishtaco legend. Dr. Ray Isbell, one of the missionaries from the University of Oklahoma's Institute of Linguistics, told me about it when he came through Iquitos with a family of Orejón Indians he was taking from the institute mission to their tribal headquarters on the Napo. They were uncommonly fat for Indians, and he was taking them home to prove that they had not been reduced to cracklings. Dr. Isbell said that back in the sixteenth century, lard was commonly used by the Spanish conquistadores to polish their armor and preserve it from rust. Unable to find pigs or any other suitable domestic animals in the New World, a few of the boys melted down some Indians to use their fat for this purpose. The Indians weren't Christians, they reasoned; maybe they weren't really human. That's not the sort of thing Indians forget.

I was delayed for a month in Iquitos, not by the panic but because it took so long to get word of my arrival to the friends who had offered to provide transportation for the first part of my trip. I'd known the Cárdenas family for six years and had had a wonderful time visiting their enormous plantation on the Napo River. Mr. Cárdenas, Don Alfonso, is an old jungle hand with properties on several rivers and interests in a number of jungle industries. When I arrived in Iquitos, Mrs. Cárdenas, Doña Juanita, had been for some months taking care of the farm on the Napo while Don Alfonso was even farther away building a rosewood oil distillery on a remote river. The letter I had written to tell them the date of my departure from New York was still sitting in their town house. They could not be reached by radio and telegraph, and since there is no postal service on jungle rivers, I had to wait for a boat to go up the Napo. But with the Christmas holidays approaching, nobody planned to leave town until well into the month of January. For Christmas and New Year's are celebrated handsomely in Iquitos. There are gala balls in all the clubs, there are parties everywhere, and there are the *Pastores*.

The Procession of the Pastores takes place in the poorer districts down by the great market. Its participants are mostly the less prosperous families of the city. To call the ceremony a children's pageant would be a little like describing the Vienna Boys' Choir as a children's glee club. The Procession of the Pastores may not be notable for its musical distinction, but it is an efficiently rehearsed and meticulously directed production. Yet it is far more significant than that: it is a touchingly genuine expression of faith and affection for the Infant Jesus, a manifestation of gratitude and joy at His birth.

The preparations begin months before Christmas when Señorita Enriqueta, a retired schoolteacher of advanced years, drills each child in his part, his song, his dance, his position in the company. At home, far into the night, mothers sew by the light of kerosene lamps, making costumes: the kings' costumes of shiny, cheap satin in stained-glass colors; the white robes for the little angels, their wings of white paper on frames of reed, and feathering the wings are hundreds of tiny slivers of white tissue, each meticulously attached at one end so that they flutter like real feathers. There are crowns of tinsel foil and wreaths of delicate paper flowers.

Just before Christmas Eve, after a flurry of housecleaning, altars are set up. In homes of the very poor, the altar may be nothing but a rickety table sitting on the uneven dirt floor and covered with a clean white cloth. The altar in the home of Señor Jesus Gonzales, a local merchant, is the most elaborate of all the altars and has been for generations, for it is a real altar probably dating back to colonial days. Paper flowers and light bulbs are twined in its ornate carving and at the base of large colored sculptures of the Virgin Mary, her Infant Son and St. Joseph.

The procession, followed by a happy crowd, starts just before dusk. At houses with little altars, the children, fifteen or twenty to a group, pause at wide-open windows to sing their songs. When they reach a house like the Gonzaleses', large enough to accommodate everybody, they pause at the door, waiting for the crowd to enter. The Gonzales family greets everybody gaily, finding chairs, offering seats on benches. I was a foreigner and a stranger, so, of course, I was received with special warmth and seated in a place of honor. The buzz of chatter stops as the children enter and form their tableau around the altar. Each child comes forward in turn to bow to the images and sing a little song of joyous welcome to the Infant. Then he resumes his place in the tableau. It was all done with professional timing, nobody showed the slightest stage fright, never a pause between performances. Even the tiniest girl, a little angel who didn't look a day over four, went through her act with blithe precision. Never any confusion, never a child who so much as bumped into another, even during the dancing.

The full performance at the Gonzaleses' house took well over an hour. Then the Pastores gathered again outside and the procession marched to the next altar to repeat the performance. Some of the audience, mostly relatives or friends of the children, stayed behind for a while to dance to the music of the guitar in the hands of Mr. Gonzales' nephew. Even the dancing is informal. Men dance with any woman who happens to be nearest, or two women together, or anybody who feels like it dances alone. It is a lovely, carefree fiesta. Soon word came that the Pastores performance was going on at another house and everybody rushed off to see it all again. It all goes on tirelessly until midnight, when everyone enters the tiny church in the market for midnight mass. When mass is over, they disperse to eat big Christmas dinners at home.

I made good use of the month I passed in Iquitos and gathered a lot of information on jungle medicine. I spent hours in bars buying *aguardiente* (local rum) for old jungle rats, in ice-cream parlors eating ice cream with missionaries and in the lounge of the hotel drinking soda pop with policemen. There is no Coca-Cola in Iquitos. I always present my credentials to the local authorities immediately after arriving—and the head of the Guardia Civil is for my work the most important of all.

The Peruvian Guardia Civil has outposts in many jungle areas and any *guardia* who serves a few years in the jungle learns a lot. Of course, they are too well disciplined to discuss any aspects of their work without the permission of their superiors. But once I ex-

plained my mission to the Comandante, he sent a number of
policemen to come to talk to me—always on their days off. The
slogan that "A *guardia* is never off duty" is no mere catchword.

Another source of information was the peddlers of jungle animals, alive or stuffed, who often came to the hotel to sell their wares
to tourists. I soon learned that most of the stuffed-animal venders
are townsmen, but some brought animals they had trapped themselves. Being Loretanos, they were always willing to sit down and
talk. Venders of live snakes are discouraged by the hotel manage-
ment, but I'd chase after them when I saw one walking down the
Malecón with a small boa constrictor in his arms or a venomous
snake in a rubber bag. Usually I would start the conversation with
the venders by taking their pictures. Then they could usually be
persuaded to have something cool to drink, but only after deliver-
ing their cargo to the dealers who make the purchases of jungle
wildlife for American or European zoos, one of the growing industries of Iquitos. Snakes are no more popular in bars and ice cream
parlors than in the lobby of the hotel.

Everyone had some first or second-hand knowledge of some
miraculous jungle remedy. A few of the prescriptions—gunpowder
in water, or kerosene by mouth for snakebites, the urine of a
newborn baby for bronchitis—I did not think would interest the
pharmaceutical company. But everyone was eager to help and some
of the leads sounded pretty promising. The trouble was that the
healing agents were always known as "some leaves ground up in
boiling water," "the root of some plant well mashed" or "the sap of
a tree or big vine . . . the Indians ran off into the woods and
brought it back." Always, the Indians had guarded their secret; no
one was ever able to be specific. Still, it later proved valuable to
know whether I should ask for a leaf or a root and which tribes had
remedies for what disease.

I accomplished a lot of trade-goods shopping, too, things you'd
never find in New York, such as shot and gunpowder for old
muzzle loaders, or for reloading spent cartridges. Ammunition,
once you've left town, is very costly if it can be had at all. I bought
dozens of yards of bright, cheap calico, tiny mirrors, fishhooks and
lines, hundreds of packs of cheap, black cigarettes. I laid in supplies
of food. Some of it was canned goods, but not much. Cans are
heavy and bulky and they hurt the bearers' backs while walking
trails. Lentils, which cook faster than beans, and rice and sugar,

oatmeal, instant coffee and powdered milk are my staples. I had brought with me a supply of "Multi-Purpose Food," a high-protein, high-vitamin-and-mineral preparation which had been generously provided by a nonprofit organization known as "Meals for Millions," who try to feed undernourished people in all parts of the world. After I got started, I regretted that I had brought only a modest half-dozen cans. It proved so helpful in nourishing the sick that I didn't dare use it for myself.

And I spent a lot of time looking for a witch. I knew there must be some about because the newspapers reported a police drive on unlicensed practitioners, but that only made it more difficult. I kept on asking questions and was finally given an address by a peddler, though I had to buy a hideous stuffed alligator before he'd tell me. From the beginning, I was dubious. The peddler's witch was a woman, and, as everyone in South America knows, all the best witches are men.

Zenobia didn't look much like a witch. A plump, rather pretty girl with a kinky permanent, she lived with her mother in a little house not far from the big market. Her ostensible profession was making artificial flowers. There are almost as many flower makers as laundresses in Iquitos, for there is a reed growing in the Amazon whose inner skin, properly dyed and worked, can be shaped into the most convincing artificial orchids. They are remarkably durable and have a peculiar ability to look new and fresh again if placed on ice when they begin to show signs of wear. But when I saw Zenobia's handiwork, I knew she must do something else for a living. The orchids she made were crude and clumsy and utterly unsalable. Nevertheless, I bought them. And ordered more and more—and threw them away—to have an excuse to visit her repeatedly. And I kept asking questions about plants. At first, Zenobia flatly denied any knowledge. Then she began to hint slyly that perhaps she did know a few plant cures. Finally one rainy morning, after I'd paid for a particularly hideous bunch of orchids, she invited me to come to the market with her. "There are old women," she said, "who bring certain plants to the market from the jungle to sell to those who understand them. I will take you there this morning and show you what to buy."

Eagerly, I started for the door. "Wait, señorita, the rain will stop in a moment." I looked out. It was still slashing down. I hastily put aside the idea of calling a taxi. Of course, Zenobia had no telephone

and, anyway, it wouldn't have been politic. Cabs cost five *soles*—
about twenty cents American. With the market only three blocks
away, even to suggest that we climb on a bus—which would have
cost two cents each—would have been to emphasize the fact that I
had money to throw away, to emphasize the difference between us.
People in Zenobia's circles think before spending pennies. And
haste is foreign.

I asked what plants we'd get, what they were good for. Zenobia
smiled mysteriously. "We will see," she said.

The rain thinned quickly as it always does. Downpours in Iquitos
seldom last more than a few minutes. While a storm is at its height,
people take shelter in doorways or under the wide overhang of the
low, tiled roofs. Nobody minds the lighter rains. It is so warm.
Soon the sun will be out again. Whatever has got wet will dry.

We started out in a thin sprinkling. Zenobia, chattering of everything except the one thing I was most interested in, led me past the
more modern part of the market, the big, ugly concrete building
where you buy meat and vegetables. We threaded our way through
the morning crowds around the stalls set up on narrow sidewalks
outside the Chinese stores. There are a lot of Chinese merchants in
Iquitos, but they sell no exotic Asiatic wares, just hardware and
rope, yard goods, cheap cosmetics and notions. Their shops are a
pinched and shabby edition of American dime stores.

We walked on to the head of the great concrete staircase leading
down to the shore of the river. I think this was the only time that I
have been able to go down that staircase without stopping to gaze
at the extraordinary vista from its top. It gives you a panoramic
view of a large bend in the Amazon, wide water edged by an
exuberance of jungle, spotted here and there by canoes or rafts
heavy-laden with produce. The thatched roofs of the little floating
houses, the clusters of native craft at the water's edge, are vivid with
heaped tropical fruit in reds and greens, yellows and purples. Massive stems of yellow-green bananas make decorative designs and
people clad in all the colors of the spectrum group, separate and
regroup in new kaleidoscopic patterns. This morning, even though
the sun came out as we approached, I was too eager to pause and
enjoy it. Those plants were almost within my grasp.

At the foot of the staircase, we turned right and cautiously picked
our way over the corduroy walk of great logs still slippery with wet.
Down at the muddy edge of the river, Zenobia led me to a small

group of canoes where women in bright calico blouses sat over heaps of herbs and roots. "This is my friend the Señorita Nicole from North America," Zenobia presented me formally. Each of the women put a limp hand on my shoulder in the old-fashioned *abrazo* and greeted me politely with "Adiós, señorita, I have much pleasure." Then we settled down to some courteously ferocious bargaining. I didn't even feel the heat of the blazing sun.

Obviously, I was supposed to know what I was doing, so I didn't dare ask questions in the presence of the women. Zenobia guided me tactfully. "Ay, Nicole, look what a lot of *patamono*, shall we get some? The *cuimbi* doesn't look so fresh, but maybe we ought to buy a little." Each purchase involved a lot of haggling and it was hours before we started back with a big basket full of odd-looking plants. As we climbed the stairs, I asked Zenobia to tell me what we'd bought, but she whispered, "Not here!" and started talking loudly about a movie she had seen the night before. At last we reached the privacy of her home. Slowly, tantalizingly, she laid the plants in little heaps on the table while I got out my notebook. Then with a lowered voice and a portentous air, she explained.

There was one you put in your bath water the fifth day of the new moon to change your luck. The little cloven root must be buried in the garden with a five-centavo piece to make your man generous with money. This little flower tucked inside your dress would make people believe anything you told them, and those pointed, fragrant leaves would get you your heart's desire. There were several others, including love charms of a most indelicate nature, but nothing I'd care to offer a reputable pharmaceutical company. I paid her, of course, and thanked her profusely, but when I started back to the hotel, I was feeling pretty glum. It had begun to rain again, too.

Maybe those pointed leaves had something after all. When I got back, the desk clerk told me a gentleman was waiting for me in the lounge. He was a thin man with a diffident smile, and when he told me his name, I recognized it as that of a distinguished agricultural engineer from a fine old Iquitos family. He said that he'd heard me on the radio. They'd interviewed me shortly after my arrival. It was really medicinal plants that I was most interested in, wasn't it?

That was bright of him. I'd answered lots of questions on that program, but I had said very little about plants because I didn't want every smarty in town to grab the nearest weed and come running to make a fast buck.

The engineer said he wanted to tell me about the properties of a shrub which grew wild near town. His mother had been ill for a long time with a heart condition too severe to permit her to fly to the capital for hospitalization. Iquitos' only communication with the coast is by air, and to cross the Andes planes must fly at a minimum of 20,000 feet. X-rays showed the señora's heart to be dangerously dilated; she'd never stand the trip. The old lady was bedridden for four months, then suddenly began to look and feel better. Neither the family nor the doctors could understand it, but her improvement continued. Her breathing was easier, her color was better, and her pulse grew steady and strong. In three weeks she was able to be up and about. New X-rays were made—two sets because the doctor thought there must be some mistake in the first ones. They showed the heart to be scarcely dilated at all, practically normal. The electrocardiograms, too, were within normal range. The doctor questioned her. The old lady, much embarrassed, finally confessed that she'd got discouraged. She'd dumped all her medication down the drain and let her old Indian cook take over. The cook had insisted she knew a plant that would "drive out the devil that stopped the señora's breath and made her weak." Three times a day, she gave the old lady a strong, hot infusion of the petals of some yellow flower. "And that's what cured me," the señora insisted.

That had been years ago. Since then a number of the engineer's friends with similar cardiac conditions had tried the brew and found it very helpful. He thought the plant should be sent abroad to a pharmaceutical company for investigation. Would I like a specimen?

I most certainly would. And rain or no rain, I was far too excited to stay in the hotel while he went to fetch it, or even in the jeep when we reached the boggy hollow by the Bellavista Road where the plants grow in profusion. We were drenched to the knees, wading through the tall, wet grass, and water poured into the sleeves of my raincoat as I tore branches from the tall shrubs.

I'd been given instructions on how to press plants, but they hadn't included the proper procedures for dealing with thick, woody stems and hard, knobby flowers like these. I did the best I could. I dried them tenderly with bath towels and carefully arranged them between the thick brown "blotters" of the specimen press, which were too stiff to accommodate themselves to such lumpy specimens. No matter how tight I pulled the straps on the lattice-like wooden rectangles of the press, you could see gaps along the stems and around the flowers which seemed as indestructible as big yellow ball bearings. I hoped they'd be all right, but I was so elated to have got a real medicinal plant at last that I didn't worry too much. I'd made a start.

❧ CHAPTER ❧

IV

A FEW DAYS later, we left. In the afternoon, my baggage was put aboard the boat: one footlocker, three big, rubber-coated duffel bags and one, even bigger, made of canvas and leather, the camera cases, a big box containing film and electronic flash equipment, and boxes of canned goods. Heaped in the hotel lobby waiting for Don Alfonso's Indians to cart it away, it looked like an immovable mound, but it quite disappeared among the cargo of the heavily laden giant canoe. After it had been stowed, we went to the Cárdenas house for dinner with the family. On her return to Iquitos, Doña Juanita had found her youngest, unmarried sister dangerously ill, so she had to stay in town to take care of her. I was disappointed. Juanita with her dimpled good nature and bustling energy is always fun to be with.

She is a pretty woman, curly-haired, plump but not too plump, considerably younger than her husband. Don Alfonso seems taller than he really is. Lean, as jungle hands usually are, he has such a soft voice and diffident manner of speech that you are apt to be fooled until you look at his profile with the jutting nose and strong chin. The conquistador ancestor who came to Peru as one of Pizarro's soldiers must have looked like him.

Juanita gave us all the things I like best for dinner. Even after six years, she remembered how much I like salad of fresh, crisp heart of palm, skillfully seasoned spare ribs, and, above all, *taco taco*, a native dish not considered elegant enough for the hotel or even for the local restaurants to serve. Made of plantains, boiled, then mashed and sauteed with crisp pork cracklings, it is delicious. And Juanita made a big pitcher of punch of *camucamu*, a native fruit about the size of a cranberry with a refreshingly tart flavor. After coffee, it was time to go.

It was a night of brilliant moonlight. Full moon is the ideal time to travel and not only for aesthetic reasons. The wide silver rivers curving between black walls of jungle are so luminous that every floating branch, every snag is etched, India ink on quicksilver, and the shimmery ripples over shallows and sandbanks are outlined in neon. Full moon, too, is always the time the weather is best. I would have hated to go through a storm in a boat as low in the water as ours. It was a really enormous dugout—what a giant tree it must have been—pushed by a powerful and noisy outboard motor. And it was so loaded with machinery, drums of gasoline, wooden boxes of tools and supplies for the farm that little ripples kept slopping over the edge and running down our necks.

We were eight people: Don Alfonso, six Witoto Indians from his farm and I. Two of the Indians were always on duty, one crouched aft over the tiller, another squatting on the prow to spy out the best channels and keeping a lookout for snags, shallows and flotsam which might foul the propeller. The rest of us were under a *pamacari*, a roof of palm thatch which shelters boats and cargo from rain, sun and the heavy dew of evening. We slept crosswise on the bottom of the boat, our heads pillowed on one edge, our feet propped on the other. But it wasn't too uncomfortable, for my alpaca wool blankets were thick and soft, pleasantly warm in the penetrating dampness that makes jungle nights chilly.

Everyone else, to judge by the really symphonic snoring, went to sleep at once, but I lay awake watching the moonlit water, the scalloped line of jungle like black lace appliqué on the edge of the luminous sky. I was back in the jungle, back on the wide, twisting rivers, on my way at last. I was too excited to sleep.

The next thing I knew it was morning. A cool, hazy morning that promised a hot and brilliant day. The jungle along the water's edge was disappointing, not nearly so wild as it had seemed at night. There were clearings, banana plantations, pastures, little thatched houses on stilts, and much of what had looked like jungle turned out to be *purma*, land which has once been cleared and which the jungle is reclaiming. We were on the Napo but still close to the Amazon, close to civilization. The Amazon is so much traveled it retains little of the quality of a virgin wilderness.

The Indians were making their morning toilet, leaning over the edge of the boat and sloshing water over their heads, dipping up more in gourds and garglingly washing their mouths. The boy at the tiller was a youngster of fifteen with a mouth split in a smile showing lots of beautiful white teeth in a broad, flat brown face. His name was Marcelino. Up in the prow, his brother Ayko, the youngest of those aboard, was lighting the little kerosene primus stove to make coffee. Don Alfonso, a solicitous host, asked me what I wanted for breakfast. "Whatever you're having," I answered. He explained that usually when traveling they just had two meals a day, one about noon and one about sundown. "But why is the boy making coffee now?" "Oh, of course, we have coffee and maybe a bit of plantain or bread to wake up with," he said, "but we don't call that a meal." I said it sounded fine to me.

It had been too dark to recognize anybody when we started out. Now I found that only two of the Witotos aboard were old acquaintances, Weebo and Mweeto, both men in their forties or fifties . . . it's hard to tell the age of Indians. Don Alfonso spent the morning trying to teach me a few useful words and phrases in Witoto. It was hard going. Some words like *makarita*—get going— and *mari*—good, or pretty—were easy enough, but mostly I found the softly guttural, half-swallowed consonants hard to reproduce without strangling and quite impossible to translate into phonetic spelling for my notebook. But the Indians loved it. Particularly Weebo and Mweeto, who felt they knew the Señora better than the others. My assault on their language kept them laughing all morning—even when I was silent.

They also laughed at my sissy drinking habits. Cocktails, pronounced "cocktelles," are apparently more popular before lunch than before dinner in this part of the world. When Ayko lighted the primus to heat up the big pot of chicken stew that Juanita had sent with us, Don Alfonso got out the pisco and the enamel cups. When I added water and lemon juice to mine (I just can't take the burning sensation of any strong liquor, except perhaps a very old fine cognac), Don Alfonso called to the Indians, "Look at the Señora! She makes her drink into lemonade!" They all thought that was very funny. Old jungle hands take their liquor straight.

When I awoke from my siesta the afternoon was pretty well worn out, and so was my happy morning mood. We seemed at last to be in real wilderness, but the water was so low that we had to keep to midstream where the current is harder to buck. Little ripples showing shallows near the edge make it impossible to cling to the shore as one usually does going upstream. Long sandspits, beaches they call them, made the bends of the twisting river even more exagge-rated, and our trip considerably longer, for they cut off a lot of *sacaritas*, little channels, which in high or even normal water give you short cuts around some of the curves. And to keep us farther away from the jungle, the beautiful vine-matted density of foliage began some distance behind the beaches where sharp-leafed wild cane had sprung from the usually inundated earth.

The sunset was disappointing, too. There were no clouds to make fire shadows in the sky. And my neck was stiff from sleeping with it bent against the little handbag containing toilet articles. It had been too hot to use blankets. And we didn't have "cocktelles" before dinner. And the chicken stew was all gone, so we ate a big fish that Don Alfonso had bought from some fisherman while I slept. It was good, but Ayko's cooking didn't compare with Juanita's. Jungle people just boil everything. After it was really dark, everyone went to sleep and snored some more. So to carry on my distempered pleasure, I remained awake to watch the moonlight and to wonder when I would have a chance to collect plant secrets. Attempts to draw the boatmen into discussions on the subject had met with discouraging blankness. But Don Alfonso said that at the farm I'd do better.

We arrived at four-thirty the next afternoon. A dozen Indian men in old khaki clothes were waiting at the "port." On the bank of the river, there is only a rickety shed for beached canoes and a thatched-roof house bearing the shield of the government and the announce-ment that this is the seat of the *Gobernador*. Gobernador is the title of the civil authority of the region and Don Alfonso is the gober-nador of this part of the Napo. It is his duty to register births and deaths, settle disputes among the inhabitants and send for the police if they should be needed.

The house of Negro Urco and the houses of the Indians are a good ten-minute walk over a well-kept trail through virgin jungle. As the men made ready to unload the boat, I asked Don Alfonso why he hadn't placed the residential section nearer the water. It couldn't be for fear of floods; this was rolling land, too high to be in danger of inundation. Every time a boat arrived it meant many man-hours of work to get the cargo over the trail to the house. "Seems like an awful waste of effort," I remarked.

Don Alfonso looked surprised. "But my Indians wouldn't have been happy there," he explained. "Witotos never have lived on the banks of the rivers, always they build their houses inland. When I brought the tribe from the Putumayo thirty years ago, I had to put them in a place where they'd feel at home."

Don Alfonso's solicitude for the well-being of his Indians is evident in a good many other ways. In fact, most of the other landowners consider the Cárdenas Indians to be outrageously over-privileged. They are given free medical care, well-constructed houses with wooden, not dirt, floors, and beds with proper bedding and good mosquito nets. They also have sanitary outhouses. ("For Indians—with all the outdoors right there!" one landowner jeered.) And culminating madness, when Mr. Cárdenas brought a gasoline-powered motor to supply electricity for his house, he also installed electric lights along the curving avenue between the double row of Indian dwellings, in the dwellings themselves, and even in the "clubhouses."

Don Alfonso has always been deeply interested in ancient tribal beliefs and customs. Since he has two clans of the tribe on his lands, he built them two Witoto-style clubhouses. Big dirt-floored circular buildings with walls of palm slats under towering thatched roofs, they stand at the end of the "avenue." They serve as cookhouses and dining rooms and are used for the occasional ritual dance fiestas which Don Alfonso encouraged. He also encourages the men's secret societies to meet in the clubhouses for evening gatherings at which the elders of the tribe impart their ancient wisdom to the younger men. But this is an uphill job. The younger Indians, born in Don Alfonso's civilization, consider such "classical" sessions rather a bore. They aren't much interested in ancient beliefs, and when it comes to parties, they'd just as soon dance rumbas to the music of the radio on the smooth wooden floors of their living quarters.

As I climbed the steps up to the big, L-shaped veranda of Don Alfonso's house, half a dozen Witoto girls in bright calico dresses gave me a friendly, giggling greeting. They remembered me, they said, from my previous visit. I felt I could be excused for not remembering them. They were all middle—or late—teenagers. Six years ago they were little girls. But I had no difficulty in recognizing old Ema. Ema is the Cárdenases' housekeeper, the oldest member of a reigning Witoto family. She's about seventy-five now, and her hair had turned gray since the last time I had seen her, but she seemed as quietly vigorous as ever and very glad to see me. She said she had thought of me often and always hoped that some day I would come back because I was different from most of the guests who came there. "Different? How?" I asked, waiting to hear how charming I was. "You different." She smiled. "When I have much trouble to cook something good, palm grubs maybe, or fine parrot stew, other people who come here, other women, they don't like. You I always remember eat everything, like everything. No trouble."

At that moment my bags arrived. It took endless self-control to make the chitchat required by etiquette—both Latin-American and Indian etiquette demand that greetings be lengthy affairs. The only real hardship of the trip had been going two days without a bath or change of clothes. The men, morning and evening, had stripped to their trunks and sloshed themselves with big gourds of water while I sat fuming in sticky modesty. Since we traveled day and night, there was no place for me to change clothes. For at least a day and a half, I'd been dreamily contemplating the luxury that awaited me in the cement-floored shower, the rapture of cold, rushing water. The hippopotamus and I have one thing in common—a tendency to sicken or run amuck if deprived too long of a chance to immerse our hides in water. I cut short the conversation and explained my plight to Ema. She was very understanding, for the Indians never pass a day without two baths. But she looked worried and explained that it hadn't rained for a week. The shower was supplied by a rain tank on the roof, and the water, having stood for so long, was not clean enough. If I cared to wait, she'd have them clean out the tank and refill it by hand from the bathhouse Doña Juanita had built about two yards from the residence.

I hadn't known about the bathhouse. Hastily, I assured Ema that what was good enough for Doña Juanita was good enough for me. So she sent ten-year-old Carlota with me to carry my things. Carlota explained that Doña Juanita had had them excavate an underground spring which never ran dry even in the longest dry season. The earth-filtered water was clear and clean, cool and abundant. I would love it. I would indeed.

The little house was built of *pona*, slats of split palm trunks under a tall, thatched roof. As Carlota opened the door and hung my towels and mesh clothing neatly on hooks in the wall, I saw two hairy gray spiders the size of butter plates. "Look!" I shouted, backing out again. "But they good," Carlota sounded surprised. "Eat bugs, eat mosquitoes, no bite people!" As far as I was concerned, they didn't have to bite. They could just scare me to death. But I didn't want to lose face by admitting it. I stood nervously in the half-open door while Carlota took off across the grassy field. Then I took a deep breath and hurled my sponge at the hirsute beasts. To my intense relief, they scuttled away down the drain, a foot-wide channel passing under the walls. I stripped, threw my dirty clothes in a corner, reached for the big, bright-colored enamel bowl which stood on the floor and went to work.

I remember the first dip-and-splash bath I'd ever had. That had been in a small country hotel in Indonesia and I had been surprised by its luxuriousness. Now as I stood on the *pona* platform and dipped bowl after bowl of clear water from the rectangular hardwood tank, as I felt the water's silky coolness pouring over my skin, I wondered why anybody in the tropics ever bothers with pipes and shower heads. Dip-and-splash baths make you feel so much cleaner. When you slosh a big bowlful over yourself, the water seems somehow much wetter than the water from a shower spray and between drips (for the greatest luxury, you must never hurry), while the water runs over your feet and between the slats of the floor foaming with soap into the drain channel, the faintest movement of air through the slatted walls chills you delicately. I sloshed ecstatically for half an hour. Cool water lavishly applied is my *icaro*, my magic.

When I emerged from the bathhouse, shouts and splashes sounded from the little lake under the palms. On the path to the residence, I was joined by two laughing Witoto girls. Dripping cotton dresses, the bathing suits of the jungle women, clung to their plump bodies and their long hair was slick with water. These people have a shampoo with every bath. I thought how different they are from the dour and dirty Indians of the mountains. Once I asked a mountain tribesman why he never bathed. He answered, "What happens, señora, when you peel the bark from a living tree? The tree dies. The life of the tree is conserved by its bark. With us it is the same."

I preferred my bark as it was now, rubbed down with menthol sharpened eau de cologne, dressed in a fresh, clean cotton skirt and a cool white blouse. I was feeling perfectly delicious—and, come to think of it, I must really have been, at least to the *isangos*. I picked up a lot of them as I went back through the tall grass and climbed the hill to the house. *Isango* is the local word for chigger, but the little fly is evil the world over. In the jungle, they lurk in the tall grass waiting for something edible to come along. When it does, they climb aboard and burrow under its skin and set up housekeeping to produce burning, itching welts. Alcohol applied locally is reputed to kill them, but all the chiggers I've ever had must have been confirmed alcoholics. It merely sharpened their appetites, and I had a bad time of it until somebody told me to try nail polish. That had been on a previous trip, and I had nothing but bright red polish with me. After I'd applied the treatment, I looked brilliantly contagious but it was worth it. The enamel seemed to asphyxiate the bugs instantly, and coating the bumps protected them so efficiently from being irritated by clothing that I have taken to using the nail-varnish treatment even on mosquito bites. Only now I am carefully supplied with the colorless kind.

Dinner was venison brought in that afternoon by one of the hunters. It was delicious and, like my chiggers, I ate largely. When we had finished, Indians began coming up on the porch to welcome us. They were dressed in their obvious best, the men in blue or white khaki trousers and clean white or turquoise shirts, the women in vivid cotton dresses with short waists and full skirts which had only the loosest connection with their anatomies. Their hair shone blackly. I noticed that the youngest women had short hair, cut none too stylishly, just hacked off square. Apparently they let it grow when they were reaching a marriageable age, for the older women all had long hair hanging around their shoulders. Most of the men's faces were tastefully decorated with red or black paint. Only the middle-aged or older men and women had tattooing, often an arched blue line of eyebrow, giving them a curiously surprised look.

Children clung to their mother's skirts and most of them burst into loud yowls when I tried to get acquainted. Strangers, white-skinned like me, are not a familiar sight. I thought music might warm the chilling atmosphere, so I brought out one of my little radios. I turned it on and twiddled the dial, but got nothing except a few crackling noises which proved the battery was all right. The RCA people had been dubious about how such small sets would work in the jungle. They were long-wave receptors and I would be far from any broadcasting station. What's more, the weather in the

Amazon Basin is notoriously bad for radio reception. They urged me to take one of their transistor shortwave sets instead, but these were too big and heavy. I wanted something I could fit into corners of my baggage.

Now I was awfully disappointed. "I guess it's just too small," I said. Don Alfonso admitted he knew nothing about radios but he did know that his shortwave set, now in Iquitos being repaired, didn't work very well without a large aerial. Since I didn't have one, he suggested we do it ourselves. "They're just wire, aren't they?" He got a spool of fine copper wire and we draped it over the rafters, then I connected it to a brass thing at the top of the little box, a sort of a rod which I suspected might be what this machine used for an antenna. Then when I turned the knob, we heard a tango coming from Radio Bogotá. Thereafter, whenever I used the radio, I carefully strung the wire all over the place. It wasn't until I got back to Iquitos that I learned we'd merely tied the wire to the handle. A satin ribbon would have had just as much effect. There had been nothing wrong with the radio before. I just hadn't given it time to warm up.

As the music grew louder, the children grouped around the radio to listen. The concert was a success with the older people for a little while, too, but this was Don Alfonso's homecoming and they wanted an impromptu fiesta. And what was a fiesta without dancing? Dancing, that is, to real, live music?

Some of the men lugged a big bass drum up the stairs. Someone else brought other drums and there were several bamboo pipes like primitive recorders. The music began. Sometimes they played mambos and rumbas, sometimes curiously primitive Witoto songs with a strongly marked rhythm. Everybody danced.

Don Alfonso led me out on the floor for the first dance. For the next one, he presented Don Gumercindo, the administrator of the farm, a small, Spanish-looking man with a quiet voice and a big smile. Then he, in turn, presented Antonio Siweni, Ema's nephew and hereditary chief of the tribe. Antonio wore a white shirt and immaculate white trousers, no paint at all, but a magnificent necklace of jaguar teeth. He was a good-looking Indian, taller than most, slender, with fine-cut aquiline features and slanted black eyes. Gumercindo and Antonio had apparently been assigned to me for the rest of the evening. They took turns, polite and silent. Like the others, they danced energetically at a stiff arm's-length distance. No cheek-to-cheek dancing at Negro Urco. And it was a good thing in that climate. The dry earth seemed to throw back at us the heat it had stored during the long, rainless days. My full skirt stuck to my legs and perspiration poured down my neck as we stomped and hopped around the porch.

Finally I told Don Alfonso I was really tired and begged him to excuse me. I said good night all around, solemnly shaking some thirty damp hands, and Ema led me to the bedroom she had prepared for me behind her own. She had hung my hammock between twin beds lining opposite walls. The hammock, Ema explained, was for siestas. At night, I'd use the bed she had made up for me. It had a headboard and footboard of some magnificent tropical wood and instead of springs there was a wooden platform under the straw-filled mattress. A hard bed, Ema said, makes a strong back. That was fine with me. I'd liked hard beds ever since childhood, when our ballet mistress had made us all take our rest periods lying flat on tables.

Ema said good night and I lay listening to the sounds of the party, which had loosened up considerably in the few minutes since I had removed my restraining influence. Drowsily, I thought, "Imagine me acting like a corset . . . and I've never worn even the lightest girdle in my life!"

V

Mornings at Negro Urco begin with the first light of day. I woke to a soft swishing sound and lay there wondering what it was. Then I dabbed nail varnish on the *isango* bites, pulled on some clothes and went to investigate. Two plump Indian girls were squatting to brush white powder from the cracks between the wide polished cedar planks of the porch floor. They had little brushes of hand-plaited straw and the skirts of their red calico dresses were wrapped tight across their sharply bent knees and tucked modestly between them. Scraping and giggling, "Good morning, señora," they moved across the floor in a sort of frog march. I asked what the white stuff was. "Last night, later, we play. Throw cornstarch." I remembered then. Around carnival time, I'd seen "carnival play." The Indians get great fun out of throwing water, mud or, if the budget allows, talcum or cornstarch and rubbing it well into each other's face and hair. Carnival was still a month away, but our arrival had given an excuse for this most hilarious of pastimes. I was glad they'd waited until I had gone to bed. It's no fun brushing cornstarch out of long hair.

Ema was standing in the door of the kitchen, a big, shadowy room on stilts tacked on to the far end of the porch. "Good morning, señora," she smiled, showing her long, even teeth—she still has all of them, "you like coffee now?" I wake up only by degrees in the morning, and I was still in the groping stage. I said gratefully, "As soon as I brush my teeth." Drinking, cooking and toothbrushing water is brought from a special well on a hill some distance from the house to fill big pots in the kitchen and on the porch. As I leaned over the railing brushing and foaming lavishly, three fat little brown boys followed by three fat brown puppies rushed to watch the fun. Toothbrushing is not an Indian custom. Instead, they wash their mouths repeatedly with clear water, and the more hygienically minded use the brushy ends of broken twigs, but not toothpaste.

In the dim kitchen, Victoria, Ema's one-eyed kitchen helper was squatting on the floor eating bees from a white enamel bowl. Hospitably, she offered me some. "Good," she said. "Ema fry them." I thanked her, but said that I could wait until breakfast time. Breakfast, I remembered, was apt to be any time from seven-thirty to ten o'clock. "You want some bananas?" Ema asked. She was squatted on a corner of the stove stirring something in a huge pot. The stove, greater in size than a billiard table, took up most of one wall. Like all jungle stoves, it was nothing but an earthen platform baked hard as adobe by many cookfires. This one was finer than most. It stood on a wooden table with tree-trunk legs, and the adobe was held together by other logs, peeled and shiny with years of use.

Pots hung on wires over a fire made of dry tree branches and three long, thick logs with a snapping fire where their ends had been burned away. High above the pots, two racks held meat and fish which were being slowly smoked because smoking or salt-and-sun drying are about the only ways you can preserve food when there's no refrigeration. Some of the meat was *choro*, woolly monkey. Their fuzzy hair singed off, decapitated bodies split and blackened with smoke, the small black fingers curled, they looked, I thought, rather gruesome. Ema told me they were only for kitchen use. "Don Alfonso no like monkey."

With a cup of strong, black coffee and a handful of *oritos*, tiny finger-sized bananas that are exceptionally sweet and delicate, I wandered back to the porch. The sweeping was finished and the girls had progressed to floor-scrubbing. Scrubbing is a part of the daily routine and Don Alfonso will stand for no easy once-over with a long-handled mop. The girls get down on hands and knees and scrub every floor in the house with cloths and buckets of water.

The coffee woke me up enough to begin enjoying the day. The fine white haze which had hidden everything beyond the porch railings was thinning, turning from pale smoke to pearl with a tinge of gold in the early sun. Gradually the landscape began to come through. First the orange trees around the house materialized, then, a little beyond, the luxuriant blackish green of the great mangos. In a moment the houses of the Indians appeared, neat, long rectangles on stilts under thatched roofs. In front of each entrance stood a gigantic wide-mouthed clay pot of water. Don Alfonso insists that they wash their bare feet before entering their living quarters.

To the east, I could see the deep, boggy hollow filled with tall ferns and swamp plants with big, shiny green leaves. I made a mental note to cut some of the feathery bamboos on the farther side of the bog. Bamboo sticks make good clothes hangers if you loop a string around their middle. Finally the mist evaporated and I could see, shining in the west, the little lake surrounded by palms, far below the house. And even farther, where the rolling land rose again, there was a vast stretch of some tall grass, silvery green in the sunlight. Later, I learned it was lemon grass, which the Cárdenas family exports for use in perfume manufacture. And beyond the lemon-grass field, the jungle again, tangled and vital. High above the mass below, I saw three tall palm trees whose foliage, like a bouquet of ostrich plumes, bent to one side, showing the direction of a wind so delicate I couldn't even feel it. The confused tweetings and twitterings of waking birds had thinned and separated into individual cries and melodies, some flute, some oboe, some harp, some pure bird music.

The "avenue," the little plaza between the big houses and the others, was quite empty except for some children and two short-haired mother dogs, each nursing a squirming cluster of fat puppies. Everybody, I supposed, had gone off somewhere to work. I wandered back into the kitchen. Ema was now in the washhouse, a balcony at the end of the kitchen, washing Don Alfonso's clothes. That gave me an idea. I got the things I'd worn on the trip.

Ema said, "Señora, I wash them for you." But I said no, I'd do them myself. I filled one of the big enamel washbasins, reached for the soap and squatted beside her. Ema's father had been one of the great witch doctors of all time. Don Alfonso had told me she knew a lot about medicine, jungle style, and as we rubbed and rinsed companionably, we talked. I asked a lot of questions about her family and the members of the tribe I'd missed the night before. Ema's brother, also a witch doctor, had died two years ago, she told me. He must have been nearly ninety. Most of the older generation whom I had known as the ancients of the tribe six years earlier were now buried in the little cemetery on the hill. They had been pretty rickety when I knew them, and though I was disappointed, it wasn't surprising. I didn't talk much about plants. I just told Ema that I was interested in them. It seemed a little early to pry for her secrets.

When I emerged to hang my washing on the line, Don Alfonso was holding sick call on the veranda. He gave shots of penicillin with streptomycin to a couple of children with heavy colds, vitamin shots to a woman who hadn't got her strength back as fast as he thought she should after having pneumonia. I asked why he didn't give all that medicine by mouth. "Psychology," he answered. "Now they know about injections, they don't feel I'm really trying unless I stick a needle into them."

When breakfast finally happens at Negro Urco, it is a hearty meal. We had fried eggs, long fingers of *yuca*, or manioc, a starchy tuber which is a staple food of the Amazon region, and some little fresh-caught fish with many tiny bones on which I almost choked. There was also sautéed toucan. The great-billed toucan is one of the most plentiful of the jungle birds and the meat is not badly flavored. But I find it hard to take at breakfast because its skin, at least when cooked, is a sort of royal blue. I didn't know why I should mind eating royal blue meat for breakfast but somehow I do. Later in the day, I don't object, though I prefer almost anything else. But not at breakfast.

This morning, remembering the warmth of the greeting from Ema, I stared at the bright blue leg on my plate and wondered if I could get by with telling her that blue foods were taboo for me. But just then she appeared with ripe and green plantains. "You don't like meat of toucan?" she asked, fixing me with a worried eye.

"I've already eaten so much—" I began. Disillusion darkened her face. "But I love toucan," I hastened to reassure her. "You know, Ema, I always like everything you cook."

She looked on, mollified, while I lifted my fork and sacrificed myself for science. After all, Ema *was* the daughter of a great witch doctor and awfully influential in the tribe. Ema beamed. "Is good. I tell hunters you get toucan every morning."

Don Alfonso was grinning as Ema returned to her kitchen. "Never mind," he said. "In a couple of days, I'll tell her I'm tired of toucan and she'll have to get us something else."

Breakfast finished with big cups of *ch'apo*, ripe plantains mashed in water in which they had boiled. Plantains are hard for the uninitiated to tell from ordinary bananas of large size. Green, they are hard and rather flavorless, and are served boiled or sliced and fried like potato chips as a substitute for bread; but when their meat is ripened to a warm yellow, it is sweet and soft with a sort of banana-dessert flavor whether fried or boiled.

After breakfast, I went out in back of the house where Paco and Chiriclay were breakfasting on rice spread on a stilted platform to dry in the sun. Chiriclay was a green-and-yellow parrot, a young one recently caught and wing-clipped, who didn't talk. But Paco, the great scarlet and blue macaw, had been there for more years than I have known the place. Ema hurried out with some bananas for me to give them.

"Don't they bite?" I asked.

"Chiriclay, maybe a little, but no can bite much, too young. No strong. Paco, no. Paco smart. Paco much gentleman. He talk good. How you, Paco?"

Paco just grabbed the banana and concentrated on eating

"Paco smart, smart. Say anything he want," Ema insisted. She told me that a few weeks ago she had gone hunting with her two dogs—Ema's advanced age had not blunted her passion for hunting—and stayed out until almost dark. When she got back, Paco sidled up to her, twisted his head knowingly, and said, "Mercedes took chicken."

Ema wondered how he'd learned to say that. But she paid no attention. When she started up the steps to the kitchen, Paco followed her. "Mercedes took chicken, Mercedes took chicken." He said it loudly and so insistently that Ema finally went back downstairs to look in the pen where she'd placed a fat, white hen bought from a neighbor the day before. The hen was missing. Calling herself a fool, she hurried over to where Mercedes lived with her family in a house some distance away. There she found her hen.

"Paco smart," Ema repeated. "Take care of house, take care of my chicken." Paco, the watch parrot, dropped the rest of the banana, spread his gorgeous red-and-blue wings, and strutted.

I heard drumlike thumping under the house and went to investigate. There in the shadow, a tall Indian, dressed only in shorts and a campaign hat, stood pounding rice in a wooden mortar with a heavy wooden pestle like an elongated dumbbell. When he lifted his head and grinned at me, I saw his eyes were thickly coated with white cataracts. He was blind.

"Is Señora, no?" he asked. "*Buenos días*, señora."

I said, "How did you know it was I?"

He laughed. "I hear you talk to Ema. I hear your shoes coming." I had on low moccasins. He was chatty. "Señora," he said, pounding rhythmically, 'in your country have machine to peel rice, no?"

I said, "Yes."

"Here me machine!" He threw back his head and guffawed delightedly, then repeated, "Me machine here. Me best machine!"

I told him that none of our machines could do as well as he. He was still laughing and repeating his witticism as I left. The ladder I'd noticed leaning against the porch railing had an Indian on every step. Up on the porch, Don Alfonso had opened the padlocked door to his "shop," a dim room with shelves and mysterious boxes. He was measuring white *tocuyo*, coarse muslin, into two-meter lengths. The Indians on the ladder had come to him for new sheets for their beds.

"But why do they stand on the ladder ?" I asked.

"Oh, I had that put up to keep them off the porch when it's rainy. Keeps the place from getting tracked up with mud. Now they've got the habit. They always use it when they want anything from the shop. Makes them keep in line, too."

A typical Cárdenas innovation.

After he'd measured and cut sheets for the last Indian, he brought out the pisco bottle and yelled to Ema that we'd soon be ready for lunch. Again my habit of putting water and lemon juice into good liquor caused much merriment among the watching Indians. While we were having "cocktelles" I saw a line of men coming up the hill. Along eight husky shoulders lay a peeled log about the size of a telegraph pole. The wood was blood-red. "That's *palo de sangre*," Don Alfonso explained. *Palo de sangre* is a wood too heavy to float in water and so hard that it often breaks saws. Don Alfonso had sent the Indians to the forest at dawn to fell a lot of tall, straight trees, peel the bark, and lop off the branches.

"Have to replace all the uprights in their houses again," Don Alfonso said. "They're rotten with termites. Champion termites we have here. That wood is so tough I don't think you could drive a nail into it. We tie our houses together with tough vines. Never use nails. But it took those termites only six years to finish the last set of uprights. I don't want the roofs falling in on my *cholos*." *Cholo* means mestizo, half-breed. Seems it's more polite to call a man a half-breed than an Indian.

Lunch was a repetition of breakfast except that there was venison instead of toucan and also a fine salad of heart of palms. Ema must have been impressed by my eating everything she cooked, for she was constantly worrying about the amount and type of food I consumed. During the morning I had seen two little boys close to the big house holding a white enamel bowl against the bark of an orange tree. I went to investigate. The bowl was half full of water whose surface was black with agitated bugs rather like large winged ants. One of the boys was brushing more insects into the bowl as they crawled in a black stream from a hole in the tree. He stopped to cram a handful into his mouth, then held the bowl out to me. "Serve yourself, señora," he said politely. "Is good."

Hastily, I looked up at the porch. Sure enough, there stood Ema. "Is good, señora," she called to me. "You eat."

Even though she hadn't cooked these for me, I didn't want her or the boys to carry tales about my spurning their generosity. It might be construed as a slight. Gingerly, I grabbed one by its wings. The wings came off. I shuddered. Pulling wings off flies was never my idea of fun. "Is all right," Ema called. "Wings fall off now. Wings have no taste. Better is body."

What could I do? By now, there was a crowd of children about me. So I picked up another insect, let the wings shuck off and popped it into my mouth, chewing quickly in case it could bite back. It had about the same flavor as sweet, watery orangeade. But at least I wouldn't be imagining its wings beating furiously in my stomach.

"You like?" Ema asked.

"Not bad," I answered, concentrating on taste rather than sight and thought. "But it has little flavor."

After lunch, Don Alfonso retired to his big hammock in the living room and I to mine in my bedroom. The siesta habit is sacred throughout South America and I'm in favor of it. I lay dreamy with pisco and lunch and listened. Nothing to be heard anywhere except the drone of bees. In the dim, screened interior of the house everybody slept.

Thunder woke me. Thunder means rain in the jungle. In minutes it was slashing down, hammering and bouncing on the dry earth around the house, and the heat was suddenly gone. It was so chilly I pulled on a sweater before I went out on the porch. Ema was sitting at the old-fashioned pedal-powered sewing machine. She was making trousers of blue denim.

"For Don Alfonso?" I asked. I'd noticed that from the moment he left town, he wore the same shapeless pants and shirts of rough cotton as the Indians. In fact, he explained rather apologetically, he never could wear anything decent on the farm. "My cholos have to have the same things I do. If they saw me in the kind of tropical suits I wear in town, they'd have to have them too, and I'd go broke on haberdashery."

These pants, Ema told me, were for her nephew Antonio. "I make clothes for everybody," she said proudly. "One, two other Witoto women also sew, but I make most."

I asked where Don Alfonso was. He had gone to settle a dispute between white settlers at a nearby *chacra*, a small farm. A man had come to report that a neighbor had borrowed his canoe and refused to return it. Don Alfonso had stormed out angrily. "I'll show that so-and-so. This is not the first time he's pulled this sort of thing. I've had trouble with him before. He knows perfectly well that canoes are not to be borrowed. A canoe represents weeks of work. Without his canoe, a man is the prisoner of his land. He cannot move without a boat. If this sort of thing were permitted, we'd have to moor our boats with padlocks! What a thing! Canoes! Who can afford locks? Either he gives back your canoe today, immediately, or he goes straight off to jail!"

"Alfonso mad," Ema giggled. "Spoil siesta."

It seemed like a good chance to settle down for a long woman-to-woman chat. I pulled a bench over by the sewing machine and began by asking more about various members of the family.

Ema was worried about a niece who was sick. The girl's name was Alexandrina, but it took some time for me to figure that out. In Ema's Witoto-accented Spanish, it sounded more like "Arehadarina." She was a girl whose parents had drowned when their canoe capsized on the Napo. Ema brought her to the big house when she was little and she had become a pet of the Cárdenas family. Alexandrina was twenty-five now, and still unmarried. She had been asked for by many young Witotos, but none of them had pleased her and Don Alfonso had not insisted. He did not approve of the ancient tribal custom by which a girl's parents gave her to a husband while she was still a child. Alexandrina's family was a noble one in the tribal hierarchy. It would have been unthinkable for her to marry an outsider.

When she was about twenty, Alexandrina's health had failed. The Cárdenases took her to Iquitos for examinations and it was found that she had several organs riddled with tuberculosis. Diagnosis had been rather slow because the lungs were not involved, but when the doctors determined her illness, they said there was no hope for her. Don Alfonso had been angry. "Nonsense," he said. "She's too young to die. My cholos do not die young. I will not let her." He brought Alexandrina back to Negro Urco and put her under Ema's careful supervision. But the girl continued to waste away.

"But, Ema," I said, "your father was the greatest witch doctor. You know much of his medicine. Can't you save her?"

Ema sighed. "With this, no. I try. But I am woman. I make the medicine, I sing the songs, songs of the icaro, songs of my father. But he man. I only woman." She lifted her head and pulled the cloth toward her, and the purr of the machine began again as her feet found the treadle.

That was the first time I noticed. Ema wore shoes! Wide brown sandals. She was the only Indian woman I had ever seen wearing shoes.

CHAPTER

VI

T HE NEXT DAY I got my first Witoto plant, the Keep Thin herb. An ancient tribal proverb says, "He who is thin lives long." Our medicos got around to this conclusion only a few decades ago, but the Witotos have believed it for centuries. Old Ema brought me the plant. She told me that her people gave it to children who are inclined to be pudgy. "Little fat one chew leaves. Get thin, stay thin. When big, is thin," she said.

"But what about fat people who are already big, grown up?" I asked. "Will it make them thin again?" I was panting with eagerness. My heart bleeds for people who have to diet.

Ema didn't know. "We have no fat people. All eat leaves when little. Now old, old. Not fat."

That was true enough. Despite her seventy-five years, I would have guessed her to be in her fifties for her gray hair. That was unusual. I have seen Indians who must have been at least seventy, but whose hair showed no signs of graying. I asked Ema about that. Did they dye their hair? Was there something they took to keep their hair black? She seemed to think that very funny and she laughed as she told me that Indians do not try to look younger than they are. "No care for face like Señora, no paint hair. We don't care. Here is what work woman can do make her good wife."

I had noticed that some women younger than she had faces terribly wrinkled and scrawny bodies with skin much too loose for them. I asked how she remained so young. "Is from family," Ema answered. "My family chiefs. My father witch doctor. My father's brother chief of all people. You look at people my family. Look at people not my family. You see. Different." And it was true, and

49

partially explained something that had been puzzling me. The Indians on the farm were of two quite distinct types. There were the ones like Ema, narrowly built with fine-cut, aquiline features and narrow heads and hands. All these, I learned, were of Ema's family. The others are much squatter, with round heads, broad, flattish features, and feet so flat you wonder how they can get them off the ground. The suction must be terrific.

That afternoon, I got another plant, one that should prove a great boon to humanity if ever the biochemists can suppress one obstacle to its popularity.

It was the day I put on a big show washing my hair. I was using my hairbrush to help dry it in the sun when a little boy came around the corner of the Cárdenas house. He started yelling something in Witoto and people came running from all directions. They gathered around, chattering, staring, giggling. My host and his family have black hair like the natives. Mine is long and the sun makes it reddish; I'd got it good and clean, so it was shining in the sun. They were fascinated. It took a long time to dry because all of them had to find out what my kind of hair felt like in their fingers. They also had to examine my hairbrush and try it out on each other.

When I started to pin it up, they had a jabbering consultation among themselves. I asked Antonio what they were saying. Antonio was an aristocrat, with a proud bearing that was impressive despite his much patched work clothes of faded khaki. He was Ema's nephew, the hereditary chief, and he spoke more Spanish than most of the Witotos. He had also been watching, but he was too dignified to do more than grin, and occasionally shoo some of the more daring children away.

"They say you no tie it up," he answered. "You wear loose like Witoto women. Look more good."

I said it was too hot that way. He translated and everybody nodded. They were all in a good mood, so I decided that if they could show such interest in my toilet, I could be personal, too, and ask them why the older Witotos have such magnificent teeth while few of the younger ones do. The women, especially. By the time they are the young-married set, most of them have nothing but gaps in front. Everybody started to talk at once, but Antonio stopped them. The secret was *yanamuco*, he explained. *Yanamuco* is a tree, and if you chew its leaves, now and then, your teeth will never decay.

Washing my hair was a new way to get a specimen, I thought, trying to repress my excitement. "Just what I need," I exclaimed, and showing off, I turned to two little naked, brown boys and said, "*Una yanamuco, ho. Guya cadi cooey. Una yanamuco. Makarita.*" That means, "Bring me a *yanamuco*, you. I want to eat. Bring *yanamuco*. Get going!" It was almost half my Witoto vocabulary and I was proud of it. The boys understood, too. They let out a hoot and ran off giggling. Everybody was laughing, but they always laughed when I tried to speak their language. Only this time the laughter didn't stop when I stopped talking. It got worse. Men stamped their feet and slapped their thighs. Women hugged themselves and rocked, shrieking.

In a moment, the boys were back again. When they handed me some branches with shiny green leaves, the laughter reached its peak. A couple of men collapsed with laughing, and rolled on the ground. Even Antonio was too far gone to speak. He grabbed the leaves out of my hand, making negative gestures.

I was puzzled. Must have a horrible taste, I thought. That's why the younger generation can't take it. I'll show them the *gringa's* no sissy! I stripped off a handful of leaves from one of the branches. Before I could get them to my mouth, Antonio gasped, "No, señora, no, no! Wait!" He took a deep breath and got himself well enough in hand to explain.

The leaves really do prevent caries, but a short time after you have chewed them, your teeth turn as black as shoe polish and stay that way for at least a week. Then the black slowly begins to wear off, and after a lengthy speckled period, the teeth are whiter than ever. Black teeth were fashionable in the old days, but the younger generation refuses to chew yanamuco.

What a joke on the Señora! Everybody started bellowing again. Me too this time. I knew something they did not know. I have two porcelain caps right in front, and yanamuco might not have affected them. Black teeth would be funny enough—but black and white? So I ran upstairs and put the branches in my press. If they could only isolate the anticaries factor! I was feeling pretty excited.

After that, we knew each other better. They no longer hovered outside in the darkness when I played my little portable radio at night, or perched half hidden in the branches of nearby trees. Now they settled on the steps, or came up to sit on the porch. And my plant collection began to grow in direct proportion to their confidence in me. By the time we left to go up the Napo to the Tamboryuco, they had brought me a half-dozen plants, all with unpronounceable names. The root to cure rheumatism had already been studied and the nettles to be rubbed on the site of any muscular pain didn't seem very appealing. It was the old histamine forming principle, only more so. The nettles make a terrible rash. Personally, I think itching is as bad as aching. Anyway, every drugstore is stocked with histamine-promoting unguents whose action is sufficiently controlled to cause no irritation.

Antonio brought me one of the plants one evening when we were sitting on the wide veranda. I saw him beckoning and went down the stairs. He had a little tuft of pale green leaves which he handed me as though it were something very valuable. This he explained, had saved his son José when he was only two. The boy had upset a full gasoline lantern, which exploded, burning his head and upper chest. Antonio's uncle, the great witch doctor, had run out into the woods and brought back the plant. When he put a poultice of the pounded leaves on the burned area, the child stopped crying and went to sleep. The burns healed with astonishing speed and the child grew up with never a scar. "You see him. Look good, no? Without my uncle's leaves, he now ugly, maybe dead."

I said yes, José was a handsome boy. The leaves must have much power. I thanked him effusively. But when I put them in my press, I was rather dubious. Sure, the boy was fine-looking. He had no scars. But he was fifteen now. It seemed very likely that the injury had been greatly exaggerated.

I should have known better. I should have known that anything Antonio offered would be exactly what he said it was. But it wasn't until a month or more later, on the Putumayo, that I realized the value of this specimen.

I showed the contents of my press to a mission-educated Ocaina woman named María, hoping to infect her with the collecting fever. When we came to Antonio's plant, her face lit up. "That leaf," she said, "that save me!" She told me that about eighteen months before, she had upset a pot of boiling stew, scalding her legs horribly. For a month, she'd been confined to bed. When an Indian woman stays in bed, it's serious.

One day an old woman from a neighboring clan came to visit. When she saw poor María's condition, she said she could cure her.

The woman went off into the brush and was gone until after dark, returning with a basketful of the leaves. As soon as the poultice was applied, María told me, the pain stopped. "Next day I walk," she said, beaming. "Now you look."

She showed me where her legs had been burned, from knee to instep. I couldn't see anything except smooth, brown skin, but we were sitting in her house where it was rather dark. I made her come out into the sun, put on my glasses, and examined the legs carefully. There were no traces of the accident. The skin was as smooth, as golden brown, in one place as in another. No sign of a scar. I felt I owed Antonio an apology.

The next two or three days at Negro Urco, it rained a lot and was so cool that I wore a sweater much of the time and one night needed two blankets on my bed. During sunny intervals, I wandered about chatting with any Indians who might be around, and taking pictures. I also chased butterflies because Gumercindo had made me a beautiful net. I'd brought along some nylon tulle to make head nets if the insects on the Putumayo were as bad as I'd been told. Gumercindo fastened a cone of nylon to a stiff wire loop and fixed it to a handle of smooth bamboo.

I found the fauna of Negro Urco somewhat confusing. There were birds as small and bright as butterflies, and butterflies as big as birds. And there were cockroaches the size of mice. They could fly, too, and I used a lot of self-control remaining impassive whenever one zoomed at me.

Every evening, after the radio concert, I'd hear Ema in the kitchen softly intoning a monotonous three-tone chant. Don Alfonso said she was still making icaro for the sick girl. I suppose it really was the Witoto equivalent of prayer, but that icaro, I thought, had a rather hopeless sound.

But Ema's worry about Alexandrina never interfered with the pleasure she derived from taking care of us, constantly looking after our needs and wishes. One evening before Don Alfonso had returned to the big house, Ema called me into her kitchen. "Cholo go fishing," Ema told me. "Bring back some for house. Come see."

The kitchen was quite dark. The electric power switch was never thrown until Don Alfonso had come back from his day's business. Ema squatted beside Victoria and Carlota, who were gutting fish. They were working by the yellow light of two kerosene lanterns, and the orange glow on their bloodied hands, their intent faces, gave a Rembrandt effect. There were some queer-looking fish still flopping in the far corner, black fish with strange spiny dorsal fins and curiously shaped heads. "What are those?" I asked.

"*Carachama*," Ema answered. "We no clean those now. Too many other kinds."

"But won't they spoil?"

Ema said no, these fish would stay alive over night, they were able to stay alive for a long time without water. Then I remembered hearing that in the Amazon and its tributaries were found a variety of lungfish, related to the curious Malayan ones which are said to be able to climb trees. I had read that these were among the precursors of the first amphibians and I examined them curiously.

"No touch," Ema warned me. "Spines can scratch, make poison."

She was working on a section of what appeared to have been an awfully long, narrow fish. It was a flattish cylinder, a good two feet long with reddish brown skin and reddish meat.

"What's that?" I asked. It was a section of electric eel. One of the men had speared it under the impression that he was getting a big fish. It had given him an awful jolt, Ema told me, chuckling. His arm was still numb when he brought his basket of fish to the house. At this, Victoria and Carlota burst out laughing.

"But I didn't know that they were good to eat," I exclaimed. "Ema, if you're going to cook it, may I have some?" I thought eating an electric eel would be something to talk about when I got back to the States. But Ema shook her head decidedly.

"You almost choke on bones of *bocachica*, little fish. This have much bones like small hair. How you choke on this?" The two girls rocked with laughter.

I began to wonder when we'd be getting on our way. The program was for me to accompany Don Alfonso and the large group of workmen he was taking to his almost-finished rosewood oil distillery on another river about halfway to the Putumayo. Don Alfonso told me it might be as much as another fortnight before we could leave. He was waiting for his son Augusto to arrive but Augusto wasn't going with us. I wondered just how much his unconfessed concern for Alexandrina was holding us up.

Meanwhile, Don Alfonso had ordered an old-style Witoto fiesta for me, on Thursday. It would be the fiesta of the *umari*—about the right time for it, Don Alfonso said. Most Witoto fiestas seem to be in honor of some fruit or other. The *umari* is a sweetly insipid fruit that I am not very fond of, though the local people love it.

Thursday was only two days away. That explained the buzzing of activity, the running to and fro, and the evening meetings within the big clubhouses of the men's societies. We walked down that evening and looked in the doorway. In the dim interior, a very old man with an umari in his hand asked questions which the younger men had to answer. Don Alfonso explained. "He points to the stem. 'What is the name for this?' The men answer. Then he points to the skin, the pulp nearest the skin, the pulp around the seeds, the little skin on the outside of the seeds, every imaginable part of the fruit. And the young men must know the answers, the sacred name and function of every part, the story of its origin. It's really a sort of botany lesson."

The women had plenty to do, too. They gather huge quantities of yuca to make the *masato. Masato* is the common tipple of most Amazonian tribes. A mildly alcoholic drink, I have seen it described in books as "a sort of native beer." Now that's a real euphemism. In fact, it is grounds for slander for any brewer's association. Actually, masato doesn't taste so bad. Anyone who can learn to like yogurt could learn to like *masato* if he didn't know how it was made. The process is so simple as to be practically foolproof, but I can describe it without the slightest fear of starting bootleg masato manufacture even among the thirstiest lushes on Skid Row.

Masato can be made from any starchy foodstuff, but in the jungle, the classic material is yuca. This is gathered by the women, peeled, boiled and mashed in big, deep trays of handsome native hardwoods. Then the real work begins. The women squat around the trays, gather double handfuls of the creamy pulp and stuff it into their mouths. Then they chew and chew and chew until the yuca has been so well mixed with saliva that it is in an almost liquid state. The women spew this back into the original mash, grab another handful and start all over. This part of the process is essential if the masato is to become alcoholic. For yùca contains no sugar at all, only starch, and salivary enzymes are needed to provide a fermenting agent. When the entire mash has been well salivated, it is allowed to ferment until it develops the proper tang.

When the masato is ready, it is served by the Indian women, who simply squeeze some of the fibrous mash into a bowl of water and present it to the drinker. I have often drunk it. I had to, for it is the first hospitality offered by any tribe as a gesture of friendship to a stranger. To refuse would be downright bad-mannered, even hostile. I can manage to get it down by holding firmly in my mind the fact that fermentation destroys all harmful bacteria. Actually, the water with which it is mixed is potentially far more dangerous, almost certainly more unsanitary than the mess itself. Even so, I am pretty certain I'll never become addicted to masato. I'd prefer a good, dry champagne any day.

I was happy to learn that the Cárdenas family had prohibited the classic masticated masato. They give their Indians sugar to use as the fermenting agent. They sold the idea only by telling them that it would save so much time and work lost on chewing. Hygiene doesn't impress the Witotos—even though they are personally immaculate and love to bathe frequently.

There are a lot of other time-consuming chores necessary for the preparation of a fiesta. The men have to go hunting to provide the meats to be smoked for the feast and the women must smoke them. There are fruits to be gathered in great quantity in order that the gift baskets of tough, bright green leaves may be decoratively filled. And there is the costuming.

Don Alfonso, for aesthetic reasons, allows only the youngest and prettiest girls to wear the old-style costume. I'm not even sure that it is technically a costume, for no clothing at all is involved, only paint, feathers, beads and their own smooth, brown skins. But they are certainly the best-dressed naked women I've ever seen. Their feet are painted black. From ankle to knee, they wear a fluff of white feathers, glued on. Thighs and buttocks are painted as far as the waist with elaborate symmetrical designs in black and ochre and white. The bronze skin showing here and there looks like another color painted on the ballet tights I thought they were wearing the first time I saw them. The naked backs are painted black, but in front the girls wear lavish necklaces reaching almost down to their knees. The necklaces are made of concentric strings of small red and white beads fixed to a stick which hangs across their chests below the collarbones, and they have so many strands that only the pointed tip of one small breast may occasionally poke through when the girls move. Chic is the word for these jungle debutantes.

Everyone was too busy and excited to talk to me, and I, too, was eager, for I wanted to take pictures. It seemed that Thursday would never come. When at last it did, the morning was rainy. I'd have been as lowering as the sky if it hadn't been for the arrival that noon of the *Oscar* and Don Alfonso's son, Augusto. That was heartening. It meant we'd soon be on our way. I was feeling a bit guilty about spending so much valuable time in the civilized luxury of Negro Urco.

I hadn't met Augusto before. He was a young man about twenty with a handsome, serious face. But the seriousness wasn't so evident that day. He hadn't been at the farm for several months, and he was busy greeting and joking with all the cholos who had been his friends since childhood. What's more, he had a new pet to show them. On the way upstream, the *lancha* had passed a young man with a boa constrictor that he was taking to Iquitos to sell. Augusto had bought it and he was as pleased as a boy with a new puppy. He named the snake Chavela. After he had shown it to everyone and I had taken its picture, he coiled the snake up in an old basket and set it in a warm corner of the kitchen. Ema and the kitchen staff took loving care of it.

The rain let up in midafternoon, but the sky remained uncertain. About five, the dancers appeared. I was terribly disappointed. I had hoped that some of the men might be persuaded to appear in G-strings and perhaps in feather headdresses, although Don Alfonso doubted they still had any. Instead, they were dressed in their best pants and shirts. Painted faces and an occasional necklace of animal teeth were the only touches of traditional elegance. But the girls looked lovely.

The men poured out of one of the clubhouses. Each had a basket of fruit on his back, and they marched down the "avenue" in a lock step with one arm on the shoulder of the man ahead. In his other hand, each Indian carried a bunch of bright green leaves. Don Alfonso couldn't explain the symbolism to me. "It's just the way they do it," he explained. Back and forth, up and down, they paraded to the music of a drum and bamboo pipes.

The women, during the first part of the affair, clustered on the sidelines watching. Augusto and I broke through their ranks, hopping back and forth, taking pictures. Augusto was the product of his father's attitude toward the cholos; there were no artificial barriers to their intimate friendliness.

Just as it got dark, everyone entered the clubhouse. The atmosphere was almost reverential, for the only light came from a half-dozen cook fires; apparently they didn't consider electricity proper to the celebration of the umari. But their dancing was far from subdued, even though there was nothing in their choreography to excite Broadway producers. They did the same stamping step they had performed while parading outside, only now the women got into the act. Arms locked, they stamped back and forth, a long line of women of all ages facing a long line of men. At intervals, they all gave a sudden, growling shout, shattering the air just as their ancestors' war cries must have torn through the jungle.

When I entered, with Augusto lugging my heavy strobe light batteries, two giggling girls rushed up and grabbed my arm. "You dance, señora," they shrieked, and before I knew it, I was in the front line of the chorus. Arms linked, we thumped and plodded back and forth, approaching the men, retiring, backward and forward. Sometimes they varied the pattern by forming circles and stamping first in one direction and then in another.

It was a stuffy evening. Inside the huge, shadowy circular hall, it was decidedly muggy. The dancing went on, but I soon realized that nobody else was putting out the effort that I was. Most of them, men and women, would dance awhile, then retire to the big earthenware pots of masato. Thus fortified, the women would lounge in hammocks hanging on the sidelines and the men would squat and eat the meat cooking over the little fires, or join a bull session with other squatters. After a while, they'd return to the chorus line. If they could, I said to myself, valiantly continuing to dance, I could.

But finally, hot and breathless, I found an excuse to pull away from the dance marathon by taking pictures. Oh, damn, I thought, why didn't I ever take the time for a good course in photography? My trouble is that I am a congenital amateur. As a photographer, I'm vague under even the best conditions, and the best of conditions these were not. The cholos, all pretty well masato'd by now, had quite forgotten about my being a stranger. That would make for very good pictures, but only if you could get them. Everybody seemed to be in a state of constant motion. It was too dark to use the viewfinder to focus, or even to see what I was pointing at. Augusto helped a lot, lugging the strobe light and holding his flashlight so that I could check my camera settings with the estimated distance of the subject. After I'd done that, the subject usually wasn't there any more. Or somebody would lurch in front of the camera or bump into me as the lens clicked. When, months later, I saw the developed film, I was astonished to find that I had quite a few decent pictures.

A couple of hours of this and I was exhausted. I slipped away, saying good night only to Ema, who sat smiling on the sidelines. She looked quietly ready to make a night of it, although I noticed that she would have nothing to do with the masato. On the porch, Don Alfonso was still bent over his account books. When I thanked him for the wonderful show, he answered, *"Perdone la pobreza, señora, usted merite mucho mejor."* Forgive the poverty, señora, you deserve much better. This traditional Spanish politeness which you hear much more in the provinces than in the big cities always makes me feel awkward. I never seem to find the right response.

Don Alfonso went on to tell me that in the old days the dances were really something to see, for the men wore handsome feathers and weird masks of wood and bark cloth. But, he explained, the old crowns had long ago been eaten by moths and however much the cholos had hunted, they wouldn't have been able to assemble sufficient plumage for new ones in the short time between my arrival and the day of the fiesta. As for the masks, they were a forgotten art, at least among his Indians. Now, if I'd excuse him, he must finish his accounts before we took off.

I asked if I should pack and be ready to leave in the morning.

Don Alfonso grinned. "You aren't in the United States, señora. Things here take their time. The cholos will dance and drink masato until daylight. Then they will sleep. It may even take them another day to sleep off the hangover. Perhaps we can leave by Sunday."

But Sunday was a day of sorrow. On Saturday, it had become obvious even to Don Alfonso that Alexandrina was dying. I had gone in to see her only once, the day after Ema had told me about her. "Arehadarina remember Señora from before visit," Ema had said. "Like now to see Señora." When I went into the little room, I couldn't recognize Alexandrina. I had vaguely remembered a plump, silent girl who had swept my room every morning, nothing like the emaciated woman who held out an arm like a broomstick when I spoke to her. I had stayed only a few minutes and had never gone back. The attempt to talk to a relative stranger had exhausted her, so that her head had fallen back on the pillow, and I'd run for Ema thinking Alexandrina might die then and there.

Saturday forenoon, Don Alfonso asked me if I wouldn't like to visit her again. Several Indian women were standing sadly around the wall. Alexandrina turned her head on the pillow when I greeted her, and I think she tried to smile. The still-full lips parted horribly over teeth that were now too big for such a small face. Her cheekbones looked as though they had been sharpened, and the hollows above and under them were cavernous. I put my hand on hers and said, "Try to get well, Alexandrina, everybody loves you here." Then I fled.

When I awoke from my siesta that afternoon, I heard the sound of little brooms. Nobody sweeps in the afternoon at Negro Urco. I lay half awake trying to think what it meant. I listened for voices, but there was only that swishing and the sound of somebody under the house sawing wood. Alexandrina! I remembered. I grabbed a dressing gown and hurried out to the porch. At Alexandrina's door, Carlota and Victoria squatted, their heads lowered, the tears dripping down on their little straw brooms. They were sweeping death from the room. Under the house, Gumercindo was making the coffin.

Since then, I sometimes have nightmares about the sound of sweeping, the sound of straw brooms brushing against a hardwood floor. I can't understand it. Alexandrina was scarcely an acquaintance, and though I felt sorry for her, her death was not unexpected. Not nearly so upsetting, nothing like the shock of a man's dying literally in my hands when I was trying to save him, that time in the Galapagos Islands. That was sudden, and it was at night, and I was all alone with him in a strange house in the strange and hostile islands. I'd sent everybody to try to get help and then he died and his wife came back up the walk screaming that she was going to kill herself and her child. That was the sort of death that should make nightmares, but it never has. I've never dreamed of it even once. So why should I dream of the soft swish of brooms, dream it as the sound of fear?

A little later, the men came for Alexandrina. Kinswomen had washed her, then wrapped her body around and around in the heaviest, most expensive *tocuyo*, five whole bolts of it, which Don Alfonso provided. They carried her to Antonio's house for the wailing. Antonio's family is the only family permitted to live in a Witoto-style house. Because of his exalted position as chief of the tribe, Antonio has been excepted by Don Alfonso from the rule of modern housing. The big circular house, a replica of the clubhouse, stands dignified and apart on a hill some distance from the others. They took Alexandrina there because she was of the noble clan, but had no close relatives. Even Ema was only her great-aunt.

I was curious about what was going on at Antonio's, but I noticed that Don Alfonso remained firmly planted on his own porch. I asked him about Witoto death ceremonies. "Oh, everybody stands around the body and the women yell," he said. "In the old days, they used to bury the body sitting in upright position under the house, but I've put a stop to that. Tomorrow, she'll have a Christian burial." Hesitantly, I asked if I shouldn't join them to present my last respects. "No, señora, it is not necessary."

His tone was the kind that ends a conversation. He did not wish to discuss Alexandrina's death, but he kept on talking to ease his grief. He buried it in a masterful professorial lecture on the Treaty of Ghent. History is Don Alfonso's greatest joy and diversion. He dragged masses of detail from his phenomenal memory about the influences of the Napoleonic victories on Britain's policy, brief sketches of the lives and characters of the American Commissioners, especially Henry Clay and Albert Gallatin, the reasons why the English got by with omitting a discussion of the fisheries question, the impressing of American seamen and the rights of neutral commerce. He also outlined theories about the economic and political stresses prevailing on the continent and in America at that time, their effect in causing and bringing to an end the War of 1812, and certain parallels in more recent history. I found it stupefying, but it seemed to cheer him. I prefer detective stories to combat depression, but Don Alfonso's drug is history.

CHAPTER

VII

Don ALFONSO and I went on up the Napo in an even bigger dugout, with more machinery and twenty Indians who were going to work in the rosewood oil distillery. Again, we traveled day and night, but now there was no moon. We were guided by a sharp-eyed Indian boy perched on the bow with a powerful flashlight. It was crowded and stuffy under the pamacari. We didn't even stop to bathe. I perspired sheer delight when, the next evening, we stopped at a little beach that marked the end of the trail to the Algodón.

My host had brought an Indian woman along to act as my personal maid, cook and bearer. Anadaraya was about sixty-five, a delicately made woman in a nondescript calico dress. Back in the days of the rubber boom, she had been a famous beauty. Men had fought over her favors—white men. It was a pity she spoke no Spanish. Since my Witoto was exclusively of the sell-me-this, get-me-that variety, we couldn't converse very freely about her past.

With someone who knows a few words of Spanish, I can fill out very satisfactorily with hand-waving. I had spent some time in Hawaii years ago and made a medium-serious study of Polynesian ritual dances. They have a language of the hand and arm, a vocabulary of motion which is astonishingly specific. No such thing exists in the Amazonian cultures as far as I know. In any case, I've forgotten all the finer points, but a sort of residue, the system on which the ritual meanings are based, has stayed with me. Now when I fall back on this hand-dancing, primitive people usually understand what I am trying to convey. I once won a bet by ordering two fried eggs and getting them.

Unfortunately, such abstractions as time are difficult to express. I couldn't get over to Anadaraya the idea that I was hand-asking about events that happened forty years ago. She just raised her eyebrows—hairless arches of blue tattooing—and tittered. All I could do was to wave away my own avid curiosity about her past. She probably wouldn't have been very confidential, anyway.

All the way, Anadaraya had squatted quietly in the boat, alert to hand me a match for my cigarette, to wash my cup the moment I'd finished drinking from it. When we landed, she hopped ashore, machete in hand, and ran off into the jungle. In a few minutes she returned with a bundle of green sticks and set to work. I watched, fascinated, while she stuck forked sticks into the earth, then fitted other sticks over them, close enough to make a table. Next she scooped up a lot of damp clay and plastered it on top. She had made a stove. She got some dry firewood from the place she had hidden it in the boat and in no time she had a fire going and was stewing a fillet of wild pig in a pot hung from a crosspiece braced on two other branched sticks. Dinner assured by an efficient jungle house-keeper, I went off to take a bath.

I have been leery of bathing in rivers ever since the night, years ago, that something nudged me underwater, and the next morning I saw four crocodiles on the bank. Actually, they were white crocs— only the black ones are supposed to bite people, but they impressed me disagreeably. Since then I've learned too much about *piranhas*, voracious little beasts which attack *en masse* and can strip the meat off a live cow in minutes, electric eels, water snakes and various other unpleasant water dwellers. These fishy enemies exist mostly in big, sluggish rivers. The Tamboryacu is a small, quick stream and I thought it would be safe enough. I had them swing the boat perpendicular to the shore and dropped off the stern into the lovely, cool, clean water. Even in that water, I felt personally drier. My clothes had been glued to me for twenty-four hours.

When I was dressed again, I discovered that half a dozen people had appeared and built fires on the sandspit opposite our moorings. Friendly, swarthy "white" men in tattered shorts and undershirts, they were hunters after wild pig and venison to smoke and sell in the market of Iquitos. We went across to get acquainted.

Now, for the first time, I got definite instructions on how to locate a medicinal plant I had heard about in the Ecuadorian jungle years before. Whenever I had gone back to the wilderness, I'd ask about it, but it was little known, and it sounded so very too-good-to-be-true that I had just about decided it was another rumor until I met Corporal Blas of the Peruvian Police in Iquitos. The plant was a do-it-yourself tooth extractor.

When I asked the corporal if he'd heard of it in his long years as a jungle cop, he said, "Sure, look!" He opened his mouth wide and pointed to the place where a large molar should have been. Eight years before, he and another policeman had been tracking a criminal through the forest. It was a case of abduction. The husband of the Indian woman who had been carried off had come along to help the police. In the middle of the first afternoon, the corporal got a terrible toothache. He didn't say anything about it until it was almost dark and they stopped to make camp. When he complained, the Indian said he could fix it so it would give him no more trouble. Borrowing a flashlight, he went off into the brush. When he came back, he brought a leaf in which he had put a gob of some brownish, sticky stuff and a few wisps of kapok. He told Blas to put a little of the brown goo on a bit of the kapok and wad it into the cavity of the tooth that hurt. But he warned him repeatedly not to let the resin touch another tooth.

Blas followed instructions. The minute the substance hit the exposed nerve, the pain stopped. "It just felt very, very cold," Blas told me. "But it never hurt again." The Indian told him to leave the application in place for twenty-four hours, then he could take it out.

Soon after that, the tooth began to break up. Tiny bits of it kept working out of his gum for the next month. There was never any discomfort, swelling or inflammation. The corporal thought all the root must have come out, all right. Some of the pieces looked like root canal—and if it hadn't been removed, he thought it would have made trouble before eight years had passed, wouldn't it? I thought so, too. Again, he opened his mouth, and again I peered. It looked just exactly like any perfectly healed extraction.

The Witotos had known nothing of such a plant, but one of their visitors one afternoon showed me the site of two extractions made with it. He had had no trouble afterward, either. But I was disappointed when I asked where he had gotten the medicine. He said it was from a tree that grew up on the Ucayali. That was a big river far south of the areas I would visit on this trip.

But I wasn't going to give up too easily. I asked everyone I met about the tooth plant. The question was routine in my interview. So now, chatting with the hunters, I asked them. Two of them opened their mouths and pointed. One had got rid of two bad molars that way. The other, one bad one and the good one next to it, because he'd been careless in applying the medication.

"And where did you get the medicine?" I asked, having shoved a flashlight down their throats. They said from Coto Indians just a couple of days below the trail on Río Algodón. They even told me the Coto name for it, but try as I would, I couldn't reproduce the gobbling sounds they made, let alone work out the phonetic spelling.

But I didn't care what they called it if only I could get my hands on it. The trail was right on my route. I'd meet the Cotos. The plant really existed. And come hell or whatever high water we would have to cross, I was going to get that plant. I had wanted it for so long.

I was so eager I asked whether we could start over the trail right now and spend the night in the camp Don Alfonso had built on the other side. It was only seven now; they said the walk took three hours. I was sure it was feasible, but everyone said I'd break my neck in the dark. And to gain what? The boats waiting on the other side wouldn't leave for a couple of days, not until all the cargo we'd brought had been carried over the trail on the backs of men. So why kill myself trying to get there tonight?

They thought the gringa couldn't take a three-hour trail at night, did they? And what if a party of Cotos passed on their way up or down the river and I missed them? Quietly, I shoved a supply of cigarettes into my pocket and put new batteries in my flashlight. It's a square one that hangs around my neck, leaving my hands free. These preparations made, I wandered off as though looking for the Ladies' Room.

It was a good trail, new and well blazed. Every few feet my light picked up a slashed tree or freshly severed seedling. No danger of getting lost. It was a lovely, cool night, the sky brilliantly powdered with stars that were soon blacked out by thick, vaulting branches. I'd been walking only a few minutes when I came to a bridge. Jungle bridges are just big tree trunks felled across a stream. I hate them even in daylight. The natives trot over them as though they were ten feet wide and had handrails and once in awhile I can manage that, too. That is, if the bridge isn't too slippery and if I can fight off the desire to look down. If I do, I'm done for. Even though the bridges may not be very high, I get the feeling that I'm looking straight down from a twenty-story window.

This bridge was unusually long and high. My light showed a fair-sized stream some fifteen feet below and the trunk was slick with mildew. Since there was nobody to see, I tried crawling. But it was too slippery even for that, so I straddled it and leapfrogged along on my haunches. I'd gone quite a distance when suddenly there was no more bridge in front of me. Just raw wood where the narrowing trunk had snapped off. And the river rushing on below. What's more, I was balancing in space with the bridge teetering under my weight.

I went into a fast reverse and backed up all the way to terra firma. Then I sat still until my heart stopped thudding. When I looked around, I saw that I had managed to get off the trail after all. The real trail—I could see the blazes quite clearly now—curved ahead a few hundred yards and then ended at another bridge. But I was no longer interested in nocturnal walking.

I went back to the boats. Nobody had missed me. But I didn't get any sleep that night. I still wanted those plants, and in my press.

The bearers with the first loads of machinery took off before it was really light, and before I was properly awake. Three hours over, and three hours back, they said. I would go along on the second trip, about noon. But noon came and no bearers returned. At one-thirty, I was too impatient to wait any longer. The man remaining with the boats could give the bag with my bedding and overnight gear to the first bearer who showed up. Anadaraya put my Nikon, extra lenses and film in the basket with her things, hoisted it to her back, and we took off.

It was a beautiful day for trail, sun and cloud, and not too hot. It was beautiful jungle for walking, no underbrush, just a deep carpet of dead leaves, infant trees trying to grow up fast to get to the sunlight before their energy gave out, and thick trunks of giant trees whose upper branches met and merged into a leafy roof. Leafless, ropy vines and cordlike roots dripped down from above.

I followed Anadaraya's duck-footed trot. All well-bred Witoto women of earlier generations walk with the big toes of their fan-shaped feet turned inward. I've been told that the custom dates back to their preclothing days when it made them seem more modest. After tripping a few times, I got back into my jungle step, lifting my feet high in order not to get caught in the roots that boobytrap jungle trails. Dark brown, thin as baling wire, and even stronger, they reach invisibly across dark brown leaves. The thin roots throw you; the thick ones hurt. Toes shod only in canvas shoes are pretty vulnerable to stubbing.

We'd been walking only about half an hour when it began to sprinkle, then to rain, then to pour. The trail turned from a wallow to a stream. We stopped for a five-minute breather at the end of the first hour. If you don't take a five- to ten-minute rest every hour or so, you don't last, especially on hilly trails like this, crossing the watershed between rivers. We sat on a log which was no wetter than we were and smoked cigarettes. The next rest period, my cigarettes were too wet to smoke, and the handkerchief in my other hip pocket was like a sponge. Four o'clock came and we still hadn't met the bearers who had promised to leave the Algodón camp at midmorning. But our three hours were up. Every time we began the descent from the top of another hill, I was sure we'd sight the Algodón at its bottom.

It was four-thirty before we heard men's voices coming toward us. Finally, we could distinguish the bearers slogging through the gray downpour. "How much farther to the Algodón?" I asked. An hour and a half. They'd been tired when they got there so they had taken a rest. They hadn't left until three. An hour and a half for them, but they were faster on trail than I am. And it would be dark by six. I began to worry.

We splashed on and over more little rivers, hurrying. I went under the bridges. After all, I couldn't get any wetter. And we couldn't waste time.

In the last dim moments of daylight, we smelled wood smoke. The camp! We slid down the hill, laughing with relief. Nelida, the wife of José Barton, one of the engineers at the rosewood oil distillery, immediately found for me some dry clothes, and a towel. When I went to bathe, Anadaraya bustled along to scrub my back and help me dress. Then she made another stove—there's a taboo about cooking over somebody else's fire—and started getting dinner. Even after bathing, I was dead tired, for it's hard going when you sink into knee-deep mud every step of of the way. I rested and watched Anadaraya, wondering if the Witotos have some geriatric plants we ought to know about. Anadaraya was sixty-five, she had carried a load all the way, yet she seemed as fresh and vigorous as if she had just got out of bed.

Nelida, as the wife of the engineer, was camp hostess. She fussed pleasantly making me comfortable. She was a white girl, not yet twenty, with a full oval face and the kind of fine-cut features that look faintly sulky in repose, but turn radiant whenever her interest is aroused. She introduced the other people. Her husband, Don José, was a good-looking, curly-haired man, about thirty, with a well-knit muscular figure and quick, nervous gestures. The other white man was Cárdenas' chief mechanic, Humberto Lozano, tall, thin, with a narrow face and narrow black eyes that looked as though he'd just finished smiling.

Nelida told me that Don Alfonso's cholos had built the camp and cut the trail under his direction. "How he knows these forests!" she exclaimed. "This is the only spot where the rivers come so close together. Even the official maps show the course of the Algodón all wrong. My husband says so. And from here, it's only twenty-four hours downstream to the distillery."

The camp was a string of *tambos*, palm-thatched shelters without walls, in a clearing hacked out of virgin jungle. At one end of the lane, the biggest tambo had a floor of pona and was reserved for the white chiefs. Next came a slightly smaller tambo, also pona-floored, which served the family of Julio Badillo, the mestizo overseer. At the far end, two other tambos, big but dirt-floored, had bunks built in them for the Indians, and there were two cookhouses. There were about a dozen people in all, personnel who had come upstream from Don Alfonso's oil distillery with boats to transport our cargo.

My hammock was still with my other possessions on the Napo. Nelida found me a clean sheet, a blanket and a mosquito net. There were no mosquitoes here, but she said I ought to use the net to keep off the vampire bats which abound throughout the Amazon Basin. I stretched out on the palm-slat floor, pulled up the blanket, listened briefly to the rain drowning out all other sounds of the jungle night, and slept like a baby.

At dawn, the rain stopped, but the little river was ten feet higher than it had been the night before. That meant good navigating, Lozano told me. They'd been a little worried about getting the heavy boats over the shallows. The first bearer arrived from the Napo just after I wakened. He brought my hammock and a lot of my personal gear wrapped in a waterproof poncho. Don Alfonso had sent him out with it at seven the night before, but being tired he had sensibly built himself a little shelter and had gone to sleep on the trail. With all the rain, I didn't blame him. When I opened my dressing case, I almost choked. The top of a bottle of ammonia had come loose and everything fumed—including the surprised bearer, who ran away in mortal fear of what other spirits might arise from my gear.

During the day, bearers shuttled cheerfully back and forth with incredible loads. Occasionally, it rained some more. In the Witoto quarters, women squatted, braiding long palm branches into thatch for pamacaris. I attempted rather awkwardly to help them, as much to amuse myself as to repress my eagerness to get going again in order to meet with Cotos who might have knowledge of the tooth-extractor plant.

Around noon, we heard a shout from the other side of the Algodón and a group of men appeared on the far bank. Don Alfonso, who had just come over the trail, sent a canoe to bring them across the river. I was waiting eagerly at the water's edge when they landed, but they weren't Cotos, only a white man named Rodríguez, his partner, Juan Gómez, and five peons. They had been marking rosewood trees in the forest, staking out their claim to the wood which they'd later cut and take down the river to sell to the Cárdenas distillery.

Don Alfonso invited his "clients" to join us in a prelunch pisco. They assented enthusiastically. It was a flowery pleasure to meet with such distinguished company in the vast, rude wilderness. It was a flowery pleasure to know a distinguished lady from the great distinguished country to the north. Then they brought out a couple of bottles of aguardiente to return our hospitality. Pisco and aguardiente make an explosive mixture. They drank their lunch while we ate.

When I woke from my siesta, there were several empty bottles strewn around the corner of the tambo where our guests were arguing vociferously. As I climbed out of my hammock, Rodríguez wobbled over. "It is a flowery pleasure, señora." He attempted a bow and sat down suddenly, but didn't stop talking. "Rodríguez at your orders. I am a gentleman. I am the prototype of a gentleman and my presence is for any lady a guarantee. You are safe while I am here, señora. I am exclusive. I am fond of exclusivity, is it not so?"

Nelida giggled. Rodriguez gave a quiet burp and went on. "I am so exclusive, nobody else shall ever have what I have. I have a lamp with six volts and, do you know, I allow nobody, save maybe your distinguished self, señora, to use that lamp. Nobody shall have my pants. Nobody shall have my shirt, my shoes. Save, maybe, the distinguished señora." He bowed more successfully from a sitting position. "It's the way I am. Exclusive. It's not that I am proud. We are all animals, is it not so? But mark me, señora, as a gentleman. I do not drink with peons. Now, Don Alfonso, he drinks with peons. Me, I am a gentleman, and when I say go, my peons go! When I say stand, my peons stand! I do not drink like Don Alfonso with peons!"

Gómez had been listening. He staggered over. "Where is my dear, noble friend, Don Alfonso? Why does my dear friend not protect his proud name from this unfortunate animal who is unfortunately my partner, who is drunk?"

Placatingly, Nelida explained that Don Alfonso and her husband, Don José, had gone back over the trail with the cholos to arrange the last portage. Lozano moved in quietly and sat down next to me. He was smiling but very alert.

Rodríguez glowered. "What's that you said ?" Gómez repeated it word for word.

"Drunk!" Rodriguez quavered as he lurched to his feet outraged. "Ungrateful animal!" For a moment, I thought he was going to cry. "You insult a gentleman like me in the presence of a distinguished foreigner. You make pigs' talk! Emasculated pigs!"

"I defend myself and the honor of Don Alfonso, my dear and noble friend!" Gómez swayed and regained his balance as Rodríguez suddenly swung on him.

"Calm yourselves, gentlemen." Lozano sprang into action in a way that was far from calm, but his voice was as soothing as he could make it under the circumstances. He toppled Gómez and hooked a long arm under Rodríguez's chin. "We are all friends here, gentlemen. Be calm. Be calm, amigos."

The excitement would probably have ended then if Gómez hadn't found a big stick by his hand when he fell. Grabbing it, he charged. Lozano had to loose Rodríguez to snatch the stick.

"Señora, your ammonia!" Lozano called, hanging on to the two grappling men. I snatched the bottle from the dressing case, which was fortunately at my feet. Then I hopped around the battlers with a saturated washcloth in my hand. I had no chance to use it during the next minute or two, but finally Lozano tipped Gómez over and threw himself and the struggling Rodríguez on top. He somehow managed to twist both Rodríguez's arms behind his back. I closed in and gassed both belligerents, holding the fuming cloth close to their faces. Ammonia is a great knockout drop. Choking and snorting, both Gómez and Rodríguez crawled to opposite corners of the *tambo*. They were both asleep before their eyes stopped watering.

Lozano, frowning, was examining the fleshy heel of his hand. "Look at that, señora," he exclaimed. "Somebody bit me! Wonder which one it was?" I poured iodine on the toothmarks. If neglected, the bite of a human can become quite as troublesome as any animal bite. I thought of Rodríguez's saying, "We're all animals." He had gone to a lot of trouble to prove it. Lozano must have read my mind.

"Look, señora," he said, "these aren't bad guys. It's just that they are all the time alone, way out in the woods. Meeting anybody, somebody they can talk to, gets them all excited. And a foreign lady, well, it made them want to show off, and the next thing they knew they were drunk. Alcohol is hard to get in the jungle, señora, if a jungle hand can get it at all. And none of them ever takes a drink alone. They drink to be sociable, and when they meet a friend, they make the most of it. So today, it was a 'flowery pleasure' for Rodríguez and Gómez."

I laughed and said, of course, I understood.

The last portage didn't get over the trail until long after dark. While Don Alfonso ate the dinner Anadaraya had kept hot for him, Nelida recounted the afternoon's fracas. Don Alfonso thought it was awfully funny. "Our gringa turns to chemical warfare!" he chortled. "These Americans and their technology!"

I protested that it had been Lozano's idea. Don Alfonso stopped laughing and looked smug. "That's why I left Lozano here with you. He's a good man. Never loses his head and always knows precisely what to do."

The two belligerents were still out cold when we climbed under our mosquito nets. When the camp stirred to life at the first hint of dawn, they and their peons were already gone. No doubt they hadn't felt much like saying a flowery farewell to the distinguished señora.

By noon, the cargo was stowed on two boats and a raft. The boats were the biggest canoes I had yet seen. Their sides had been built out and up with added lumber until they looked like giant lifeboats, but I was dismayed to see that the palm thatch the women had so industriously prepared was not for sheltering us from the elements. It was tenderly arranged, every last bit of it, over the big sacks of cement, boxes and bags of provisions and odd hunks of machinery. There didn't seem to be any room left for passengers, at least not for all thirty or more of us. But somehow everybody managed to scramble aboard. The only seat, a narrow bench almost hidden by bundles and bags, was reserved for Nelida, Don Alfonso and me. It was luxury compared to what the others had in the way of accommodations. Watching the way they folded and draped themselves in the most improbable positions with every evidence of complete content, I didn't dare feel uncomfortable and soon forgot that my back was cramped and my left foot had gone to sleep.

The Algodón is a small river, and the enchantment of the jungle rivers is in inverse proportion to their size. Narrow rivers are less apt to be inhabited. We passed no *purma*, no clearings, no houses, nothing but virgin jungle, great vine-drenched trees, giant ferns and fringe-leafed palms pushing eagerly on top of each other. Vegetation is far too flaccid a word for such exuberance; there's nothing passive and vegetable about it. It grows with a joyous vitality that is somehow contagious. I wonder if that doesn't contribute to the curiously ageless vigor of men and women who live among these forests.

The Algodón is narrow enough to allow intimacy with the beauty along its banks. I was so close that none of the details were blurred, and I marveled at the myriad shapes of leaves, the incredible variety and elegance of their designs. Even the delicate symmetry of their veins and sinews was right under my eyes. I could lift my hand and pick one here and there to examine it more closely. I wished I knew which leaves held the magic I was seeking.

Except where an occasional flamboyant lifted flaming branches to the sky, there were no big, garish splotches of color. I've seen that kind of jungle only on the painted walls of nightclubs. My jungle is more subtle. There are a thousand colors for leaves—and all of them green: black green and purple green, bronze and blue and yellow green, the green that is almost silver, and the pinkish green of very young and tender leaves.

Here and there, sparsely doled out, blossoms of every hue slashed or dotted or powdered fronds and deep curving branches, so tangled with verdure that I could never tell which leaf or bloom belonged to what. There were bushes with clusters of tiny mauve flowers, others bloomed waxy white or scarlet, and some dangled bunches of canoe-shaped blossoms whose orange petals had the texture of an orchid. I saw no true orchids, but now and again there were gorgeous red or white epiphytes or pinks. They grew at improbable angles on the branches of taller trees, branches furry with parasitic growths.

I stared and stared and wondered how so many people can talk and write about the deadly monotony of the jungle. Can they *all* be blind?

About three-thirty, Don Alfonso asked our indulgence to stop at a new clearing to see how it was progressing. To me, it was a desecration of the jungle. It belonged to the Vargas family, newcomers to the region, brought there by the news of Don Alfonso's distillery. The amount of land they had cleared in only three months showed what energetic settlers they were. In the center of the area, they had built two fair-sized tambos with split-palm floors on stilts high above the ground. A third tambo was in the process of being roofed. Don Horacio Vargas' wife, two daughters-in-law and the wives of his two peons sat on its new floor twisting palm leaves into thatch to put on the rafters already lashed into place above them. There was a new plantation of yuca and bananas in the still raw earth behind the house. To both sides, there were stretches so recently cleared that Don Horacio had not yet had time to burn the great trees toppled to make way for cultivation.

Vargas told us that several of his friends were bringing their families from Iquitos to settle along the Algodón. "Your distillery," he solemnly told Don Alfonso, "is a great thing for the progress of our country. It is initiative like yours that will some day conquer all our wilderness. If there were more men like you, sir, the state of Loreto would already be a fair and prosperous land with roads, with schools, with cities and industries where we now have only the jungle and the rivers."

I shuddered. I am not a misanthrope. I like nothing better than men, but they sure do mess up the scenery. Jungle scenery is an expensive luxury to a nation whose economy still has a long way to grow. But I was grateful that I was able to see the Algodón now and not ten years from now.

We took off under a blue-and-green sky with clouds turning from opalescent to incandescent. That evening, I saw one of the better tropical sunsets. Sunsets in this latitude are brief. But somehow a spectacular like that one, full of changing lights and colors, the sweep of the sky and its living, moving reflection in the water, is so full of incident that it doesn't seem short at all. By the time the stars showed and the water ran luminous between black walls of jungle, so much had happened, there had been so much to see, that I felt as though hours had passed.

I leaned my head back and watched the stars. My favorite constellation is the Little Dipper because it is the one I can recognize. It was above the line of forest to my left. Don Alfonso shouted over the roar of the noisy motor to ask if I had my blanket and the sheet of plastic shower curtain material I use for protection against rain. I howled back that they were in the bag at my feet. He said I'd better get them out. It seemed silly on such a beautiful night, but I did. Then I looked up again. The Little Dipper was way over on my right. Queer! Then, in a moment I realized that in the two or three minutes which had elapsed while I got the blanket, the river had twisted so sharply that we were going in exactly the opposite direction. I watched the constellations lope back and forth until my eyes were heavy and the roar of the motor which all day had made conversation impossible was now hypnotically soothing.

I don't know how long I'd slept when the rain started. I woke just enough to pull the blanket higher and to shove the plastic sheet around me and over my head. Then, chilled, cramped and wrapped like a mummy in damp plastic, I slept blissfully until morning.

The sun was hot and high by the time we got to the distillery. An excited young man was waiting on the bank for us. Don Alfonso introduced him as Carlos Otorola, the general manager. He had large, gentle black eyes, a crooked nose and curly black hair, which also grew here and there on his face in an attempt at a beard. He was delighted by our arrival. He could hardly wait to show us all he had accomplished, most especially the neat little farm where subsistence crops and a few vegetables looked very promising. He had reason to be proud of his work, for he was no old jungle hand but strictly a gifted amateur.

A member of an upper-class Lima family, Don Carlos had never been in the jungle until he had come to this part of Peru a year or so ago after finishing six years of study in France and Italy. "I just came to see what Loreto was like and maybe get a little hunting," he explained. "Don Alfonso showed me around and I remained to help him get things going. It's been great fun!"

The huge rectangular clearing was as neat as a tennis court. A space at the water's edge had been cleared for the shipments of rosewood logs and just behind were the mills which would grind the logs into chips. Behind the mills were the tall iron stills where the chips would be distilled and the fragrant oil extracted. The Cárdenas family exports its rosewood oil to the United States for use in only the finest perfumes, for it's pretty expensive to produce. Around five hundred pounds of raw wood are needed to make a single quart of the oil.

The next day I said goodbye to most of the Negro Urco contingent. Don Alfonso was sending Nelida and her husband, Don José Barton, along with me to see that I arrived safely at the mission settlement, Estrecho, on the Putumayo. He also offered six Witotos for bearers. I protested, aware that now of all times he needed all his personnel to finish the work on the distillery. But Peruvian hospitality pays no attention to that kind of protest. Finally, I admitted that I would welcome the opportunity to employ Coto bearers in order to pry out their tooth-pulling secret.

"Those rascals!" Don Alfonso exclaimed. "They like nothing less than work. And if you did get Coto bearers, you'd find half your gear missing when you finally got where you're going. They're awful thieves. Señora, no; while you're still in my territory you'll travel with the people I can guarantee. You'll be on your own soon enough!"

We settled for my taking the Bartons and four Witotos. Even Don Alfonso finally conceded that for my purposes it would be a good idea to pick up a couple of Coto bearers on the way. His people had never been over that trail, but the Cotos know it well. Still, I felt guilty about depriving him of Barton's services at such a critical time.

I made my adieus all around. When I tried again to thank Don Alfonso for his truly extraordinary hospitality, he laughed explosively. "*Vaya*, señora. Don't talk like a tourist. You should know that there's no question of hospitality between old jungle hands. You know we have to help each other. It's the law of the jungle."

Me an old jungle hand! I was never so flattered.

CHAPTER

VIII

Eᴀʀʟʏ ɪɴ the morning, after a day and a night downstream, we found several Coto families living in a couple of ramshackle huts on stilts across the river from where the trail began. They didn't look like people who would know much about anything. Their houses were dirty and dilapidated. The women, dressed only in necklaces and little skirts, were so timid that they withdrew to one room at the back of the house and peered at us through slits in the walls. All the men knew some Spanish. They had learned it at the mission of the Canadian Franciscan Fathers on the Putumayo, and were obviously impressed when I told them that I came from the same part of the world the Padres did. "Very big country, your country. Have much good things, Padre say." I settled down to make friends. It wasn't easy.

I started in by paying an exorbitant price for enough smoked tapir meat to provide a hearty breakfast for all of us. In jungle travel, you never pay for a night's lodging but often pay for the food you use.

Squatting on the floor we breakfasted. The meat was tough and rather tasteless. It was made even less appetizing by a slow rain of moribund insects from the roof. I have never seen anything like it before or since. Just as we started to eat, a cockroach fell from the thatch of the roof to the edge of my plate. I flicked it out. It crawled a couple of inches, turned on its back and died. Then a cricket hopped up, staggered and expired. Then two more cockroaches and a spider. Indians don't use insecticides; they accept insects as a normal part of life. My uneasiness increased as the insect morgue grew about me. Any comment might have been construed as criticism, and Barton and I were having a hard enough time selling them the idea of coming along with us. I just stopped eating . . .

At the mere mention of work, three of the five men who had greeted us remembered that they had things to do elsewhere. The two left were Alberto and Hilario. Alberto said he wouldn't mind, only who would look after his wives? Hilario said he had a cold. That was obviously true. I told him of the wonderful cold medicine I had straight from the country of the Padres. With that inducement, gifts of cigarettes and promises of lavish pay, we finally persuaded them to come along.

Alberto was smart and cocky. Hilario was misnamed. He was a stocky, flat-faced Indian in tattered khaki. His eyes drooped, his mouth drooped, and his spirit was chronically glum. But better glum than smart, I thought. I chose him to carry my camera equipment, impressing him with its importance. He must at all times stay close to me so that he'd be at hand if I wanted to take a picture. He puffed with pride, a better prey for my prying questions about plants.

The trail was like the Tamboryaco, dim and open, but this time it didn't rain. There were more palms, clumps of little ones and tall ones with hairy trunks and tops like feather dusters, great tree ferns elegant as lace. Often we would come to a mat of petals, pink, lavender, sometimes scarlet, on the brownish floor of the forest. But we never saw the flowers from which they fell. They were high on the top of the canopy of leaves above us, up where they could drink in the sun.

I knew that I wouldn't be able to work on Hilario about the plants while we were walking. The jungle trails are too narrow to walk abreast and, in any case, jungle Indians can't learn to walk by anyone's side. That's how you can always spot them when they come to a town like Iquitos. A whole family will walk down the wide pavements Indian file, talking over their shoulders to each other. Even if I had Hilario next to me, I had no breath to waste on talking, except when we stopped to take a pleasant rest or to take a picture.

We took a ten-minute rest every hour and a half because this was no three-hour trek. It was a full day's walk for anybody and I set a fast pace because I wanted to impress both my guides and bearers. A fast pace, that is, for me. The bearers, each with a seventy-pound load, took off like big cats let out of a cage. When they scrambled over a dead tree, a yard or more in diameter, which here and there had fallen across the trail, they moved with the effortless discipline of dancers in a modern ballet. They had the grace of muscles under perfect control, exquisite equilibrium with exquisite economy of effort.

The trail wound up and down over little hills. They were dry on top, but at the bottom of each hill there was always a rivulet to be crossed by a tree-trunk bridge. At first I made myself run across them, but after slipping off a couple of times with a resounding splash, I reverted to the old safe-and-sure. I pretended I wanted a drink of water as an excuse to walk under them. After the fourth or fifth drink in half an hour, even Hilario began to look skeptical.

Suddenly Hilario shouted. I couldn't understand what he said, but in the jungle when somebody shouts, you stop fast. Fortunately we were on an uphill grade, so I couldn't skid. There on the trail in front of me, right where my foot would have landed, was a small, slender snake, bright green on top, brilliant yellow underneath. *Loro machaco*, they call them, and they are venomous. I stood frozen while it wriggled across the path and out of sight behind some palms. Then I discovered that I was still standing on one foot. I guess I'd have had both feet off the ground if I'd known how.

Hiliario was sniffling àt my shoulder. The cold tablets weren't working as the literature promised. "Why you no kill?" he asked indignantly. 'Loro machaco bad. Very bad."

"With what?" I snapped. Walking trail, I never carry anything bigger than a cigarette case. "You think I'm going to try to crush a loro machaco by jumping on it with this?" I held out a sneaker-clad foot. Actually, I wouldn't have dared to move if I'd had an axe in one hand and a grenade in the other. I haven't met as many snakes as people expect you to in the jungle, but when I do, they can go their way and I'll go mine when they're well out of striking range. That may not be public-spirited, but I was never a girl to pick fights which I might lose, anyway not with dangerous animals.

"Why you no kill with stick?" Hilario insisted. There were a few broken branches lying here and there.

"Why you no kill with stick?" I snarled. And we plodded on, both sulking.

I was being foolish. This was no way to deal with an Indian, especially one you want to get something out of. But being frightened had made me cross. After we had walked a few minutes, I began to feel ashamed. Hilario with all that load of camera equipment was in no position to stoop down to pick up sticks or to chase snakes.

I gave him a pack of cigarettes. I took pictures of him. I told him how intelligent he had been not to risk damaging all the valuable equipment by chasing snakes through the brush. He looked a little mollified, I thought, but I wasn't sure.

A few minutes later, we were running down a very slippery slope. You have to run to keep your balance when they're that steep. Almost at the bottom, an invisible root caught my foot. Instinctively, I grabbed the Nikon with which I had been taking pictures and held it up as I fell. All the wind was knocked out of me and I just lay there. Hilario shouted, and Nelida, who was just ahead, came running back.

"José, José, the Señora is hurt!" she screamed.

Barton hurried over to me. I captured enough breath to talk. "No, it's all right."

"She's hurt very bad, José. Look at her face. White!" Nelida, too, was almost white.

"Just let me stay here a second," I pleaded. I was feeling my shoulder. I'd wrenched it badly when I held up the Nikon. I found it wasn't dislocated, but the pain was sickeningly sharp. They all looked so frightened that I got to my feet—I had to show them that I could walk. All I wanted to do was lie down, but we went on. Every step jarred agonizingly. I hooked my arm through the camera strap and the improvised sling helped a little. I kept waiting for it to stop hurting. It's just like a twisted ankle, I told myself. Hurts for a few minutes, then it gets better.

Nelida hovered about me. "Alberto says there's a tambo on the trail, just ahead. Several tambos. You can rest there. We'll be there soon, señora. It's close. Just over the next hill." That sounded hopeful.

I had the feeling that I had better get there in a hurry. The climb was steep and the pain was not easing at all. The earth, wavering like the surface of the sea, wasn't in the right place when I put my foot down. Trees telescoped in and out of focus, and suddenly in the middle of a jungle forest, I heard factory whistles shrilling. Then I realized the noise was caused by my trying to breathe. I could exhale easily, but when I tried to inhale, my larynx got tangled up with the rest of my equipment. I was acutely embarrassed, but I couldn't stop it. When I saw Nelida kneeling over me, I realized that I was no longer on my feet. She put both her arms out, and her hands on the back of my neck and began a strong, slow massage. My pipes stopped whistling and the scenery came back into focus. Soon, I managed to walk again, but I no longer tried to hurry.

Three tambos and a lean-to cookhouse stood together in a little clearing. They were unusually well built, the smallest tambo with a floor and part of a split-palm wall. I climbed into that one and asked Nelida to have someone hang my hammock.

"First a drink, a bath and dry clothes. Then I'll cure your shoulder," she said. She poured me a drink of my emergency pisco while one of the men fetched water in my collapsible canvas bucket. When I was clean and dry and agreeably anesthetized by another big slug of the brandy, Nelida made me sit on the floor while she kneaded my neck, my spinal column, and very gently my shoulder. It grew less sensitive under her hands.

Nelida's massage was much different from the usual; it was slower and went much deeper. While she worked, I asked her where she had learned it. "Oh, most women know how," she said, "otherwise, what would they do when their men get hurt? Even Indians know how to *sobar* injuries. They know it better than anyone. My mother learned from an Indian when my father hurt his back."

That reminded me of Hilario's sniffles. I called him over and gave him a couple more of the cold tablets. He said they were no good, so I gave him a drink of pisco. He liked that fine, but he was gloomier than ever, and it was obvious that his respect for the gringos had taken a series of blows. Later that afternoon, I finished it off.

Barton and some of the men had gone hunting to get meat for dinner, so I started questioning Hilario about the Coto treatment for toothache. My first questions were tentative, but so were Hilario's answers. He knew about the plant, obviously, but it took all my persuasion and the promise of another drink of pisco before he was willing to go after it.

He was away nearly an hour. I sat and castigated myself. I had waited so long for the toothache plant, why couldn't I have waited a little longer? Had I been previous again? Only witch doctors usually divulge the tribe's medical secrets, and they do so reluctantly. I had not been able to learn who was the Coto witch doctor, or how to get in touch with him. Had Hilario gone to him and reported that there was a snoopy *gringa* in the jungle?

But when he returned, triumphantly, he brought a small branch from the tree, for I had asked for leaves in order to identify the plant easily. However, he had only about a quarter of a teaspoon of the brown, sticky resin in the little bottle I had given him.

"I need more than that," I said. "I told you to fill the bottle."

"Is plenty," he answered, and the corners of his mouth turned down even further. "How many toothache you got? Is enough for all teeth."

Patiently, I explained that I did not now have a toothache. But I might get one later, and I wanted enough of the medicine with me for any emergencies. I also wanted enough to take back to my country for a large family which I invented to serve the moment's need.

Hilario was so surprised he stopped looking sour. "In your country is not this medicine?"

I said no, in my country is not.

His knobby brow wrinkled as he thought it over for a moment. Then he asked, "How they cure toothache?"

I said a doctor pulled the tooth out with pliers.

Hilario's mouth opened, and his eyes widened for the first time. "No hurt? No come down much blood?"

I said yes, much hurt. Much blood come down.

Hilario stared at me. Then he shook his head. *"Qué bárbaros! Qué malos!"*

What barbarians! What evil people! I'm sure he thought our doctors were pure sadists. He was so sorry for me that he went off and filled the whole bottle with his civilized medicine. Later, he gave me the tooth of a jaguar. He had never felt so sorry for anyone in his life.

I swallowed my country's pride easily, joyfully. What if I were a barbarian? I had my plant at last, and I could afford to be humble in front of Hilario.

Nelida continued to massage my shoulder every couple of hours. By the time we had eaten the big monkey her husband brought back for dinner, it had almost stopped hurting. In the morning, the shoulder was stiff, but there was no real pain. I felt ashamed and wondered if I hadn't been making a disproportionate fuss over a trivial accident. But Nelida said she'd work over it some more during the day and again in the evening even if it didn't hurt. Otherwise, it might make more trouble. "Get cold again," she called it.

When it grew dark, we heard strange voices speaking Coto. It's a peculiar language in which there seem to be only a few consonants, mostly guttural *k*'s and *g*'s and a few *b*'s floating stickily in a bubbling mess of vowels. Alberto greeted the Cotos joyously, and even Hilario lost some of his sluggishness. The two men and two women had just come from the Putumayo. The men wore only shorts and the women were dressed in *pampanillas* so muddy you couldn't tell the color. A *pampanilla* is a saronglike skirt of home-woven cotton, reaching only from calf to belt. They were nude from the waist up, like the women we'd seen at Alberto's house. The woman with an infant at her breast chose me as a roommate and hung her mosquito net next to my hammock. The four of them clustered about me, fingering my clothes, my hair and all my belongings. Their curiosity was endless and so intimate I almost lost my temper. But I didn't want to let Hilario down again. More of his sorrow for my lack of civilization I would not be able to take.

The men told us—they spoke almost fluent Spanish—that the trail to the Putumayo was almost impassable. Pure *tawampas*—swamps. The water came up to the women's shoulders and the bridges were all out of sight beneath the surface. "I fell off like this," one of the men shouted, and pantomimed a man teetering trying to keep his footing, then taking a dive, splashing and thrashing in water. Everyone laughed. I laughed so hard I jarred my shoulder. He repeated the performance and the boys found it even funnier the second time, and the third and the fourth and the fifth. The sixth time, the pantomimist landed rather hard and picked himself up with a scraped elbow, so he decided it was time to eat the bananas the women had roasted in the fire. The other Indians were disappointed that the show was over. For them, a thing that's comic once stays comic. The ideal audience.

Remembering Don Alfonso's warning that the Cotos, like so many Indians, have learned petty thievery along with the other gifts of modern civilization, I fell asleep hoping that when I awakened I wouldn't find that they had stolen silently away in the predawn darkness with most of my possessions. I needn't have worried. They were up before dawn, but there was nothing silent about it. The baby howled, the men gobbled, and the mother shook the floor of the shack as she stomped about gathering up her mosquito net and the sheet that she had used as a mattress.

The day was lovely. Plumes of steam rose from the forest, and the cool, moist scent of loam was clean to breathe. You could wash your hands in the big crystal drops in the cups of giant, heart-shaped leaves growing by the trail. Sometimes we walked through waves of delicate perfume drifting down from flowers too high to be visible. As we got to lower ground, lush vines clung to the great trunks, their big, elaborate leaves still shiny with dew. A New York florist, I thought, would lose his mind here; all that elegant, expensive verdure and nobody to sell it to.

All too soon, we got to the inundated section of the trail, and found that the Cotos had not exaggerated. For the next few hours, we walked in water almost never below our knees, and often up to our waists, sometimes above. I was glad I had lined the camera boxes with big waterproof sacks. The individual plastic bags for the cameras might not have been enough. There wasn't time to contemplate the beauty of it all now, I was too busy trying to keep my footing. It was slow going, for we had to test each step carefully. Ropy vines, fallen trees, little hollows and holes were invisible. Before us stretched only a vast brown sheet of water pierced by bushes and trees.

Barton made a staff for me from a thin, strong sapling. That helped me to keep my balance, but I was worried. The bearers were well out of sight somewhere ahead and Hilario was with them. How could we tell whether we were still on the trail? I couldn't see any indications of it. Barton laughed. "I can see it," he said. "You see that tree fern, there, just ahead? That's where it turns." He was right. Just as we turned past the tree fern, we came to a few yards of visible land and there in the mud were fresh footprints of men heavily laden. Over and over again, Barton was right in following the trail, but I still haven't figured out how he did it.

Breakfast had been only crackers and some coffee and chunks of *chancaca*, crude brown sugar, before we started out. I had told the bearers that we would eat during the first or second rest period; they must stop about nine-thirty and wait for us. That was a stupid thing to do. You never tell Indians to do anything at a certain hour. You say, pointing, "When the sun is there . . ." But they had taken off early and I'd been too sleepy to remember. Being hungry always makes me cross. My cigarettes were wet. We couldn't take a rest unless we sat down in a pool. And I was tired of pushing through water above my belt. It was after eleven with still no signs of bearers and they had the lunch. I was a martyr. I didn't cheer up until we heard a long "Hooo—" rather like the toot of an old-fashioned railroad train. That's the way people call in the jungles. It's a sound that carries a great distance.

The bearers were waiting at a dry place on a little hill where a couple of tambos stood. They were tired, too. The Cotos said they'd never seen the trail in such bad shape, wet, sometimes, but nothing like this. Lavishly, I opened tins of corned beef, salmon, sardines. To the Indians, canned goods are exotic delicacies. They seldom get them. I didn't have many and I had been hoarding them for emergencies. But I could afford to be prodigal now. The Cotos had told me about the mission store. They were round-eyed about the wonders it held. "Much kinds canned food, sugar, flashlights, beautiful cloth, fine clothes, even shoes!" The shopping center of the Putumayo. It certainly had no competition.

Soon the trail dived under water again, but never more than knee-deep now, and the stretches of dry land grew hearteningly longer and more frequent. A couple of hours more and we found ourselves on a bank, high as a cliff, bounding a wide, sluggish river that shimmered in the midday heat. The Putumayo at last! I gazed at it, slapping at the tiny, stinging gnats which suddenly attacked in swarming clouds. The river was very low. Mud flats at its edges looked indecently naked where they were not clothed with silvery green wild cane. Little ripples out in the middle of the river showed shallows. But I was very glad to see it. It was wide. And it was a river, a highway I could ride on instead of walking.

The path turned sharply to the right and continued along the bank. At every turn, I looked hopefully for the mission settlement, but there were always more woods ahead, spiny woods now, and one had to walk carefully or waste a lot of time unhooking clothes and sometimes skin from clutching thorns. The last hour seemed awfully long. It always does on trail, for, knowing you will soon arrive, you permit yourself to recognize how tired you are.

At last the trail came to an end. We were on top of a long slope. In the near foreground was a yuca plantation and beyond it a native house, thatched roof, no walls, on stilts. A bit further on we could see a long line of similar houses, ending at a prim, white church.

Behind the church was a little house, white as a box for a wedding present. That would be the priest's residence.

It looked like a deserted village. Not a soul was moving in the shadeless heat. Not even a dog barked as we trooped down the hill. The glaring tranquility, the stern tidiness, made us suddenly aware of our disreputable appearance, and we spoke in lowered voices. There was no one in the church. The big doors were closed. We straggled on to the priest's house and stood for a moment before it, timid as children. Then I knocked.

Pink and white and plump Père Victor, the priest, beamed at us hospitably, and threw wide the door. Even in the khakis he wore when not performing religious ceremonies, he looked like a priest. His lay-brother assistant, Frère Magloire, was all angles and energy. He had chosen the site and built the mission, much of it with his own hands. Nelida and I entered the house and stood uneasily, afraid to accept their offer of chairs. We were so soggy with mud that we were afraid of rubbing off on the furniture.

Both the priest and the lay brother were Franciscans from the Canadian French section, and spoke no English. Père Victor who had arrived from Canada only two months before, spoke no Spanish, so he beamed when I switched to French to explain who we were and what we were doing. But when he and Frère Magloire answered, I was lost. My French is the Parisian variety which I spoke as a child. It's a bit creaky now, but still fluent enough to make people think I'm French if I don't talk too much. Theirs was the archaic accent of the Canadian backwoods. They understood me perfectly, but I got about one word in ten when they spoke. We had to switch back to Spanish, with Frère Maloire interpreting for Père Victor.

Frère Magloire brought icy lemonade. Nelida, holding together a long rent in her skirt, perched on a wooden bench under the window, quietly sipping hers, but I was urged into a wooden rocking chair. It looked as though it could be easily cleaned, so I sat down. I had the feeling that our hosts were worried. Frère Magloire asked how many there were in our party. Looking out of the window to where they squatted, I counted the four Witotos, two Cotos, Nelida, Barton and I. That made nine. I felt apologetic about our being so many. They confessed that they weren't sure how to lodge us.

"The Indian houses would scarcely be suitable," Frère Magloire said. "You, madame, could go to the schoolmaster's house. It is very small, but we can lend you a cot. But the other lady and her husband and all the bearers, where can we find beds for them? We have so few visitors. It is a great pleasure, but how to make you all comfortable?"

Hastily, I reassured him. I had become so accustomed to having it taken for granted that I would have everything I might need that it hadn't occurred to me to mention it. I explained that we had come fully equipped with bedding, mosquito nets, even cookpots. All we lacked was a roof. In any case, my people would be leaving in the morning to return to the Algodón, and I'd be on my way, too, as soon as I could get transportation.

Both Père Victor and Frère Magloire beamed. It's my guess that we looked so indigent in our dirty clothes that the kindly Franciscans had thought they might have to incorporate us into their charitable works for life. Frère Magloire suggested that perhaps, since it was only for one night, we could all bunk in the house under construction, which would serve as a convent when the nuns arrived next month. Its roof, floors and walls were good.

"But the bathroom hasn't been put in yet," Père Victor exclaimed, distressed. "And there hasn't even been time to put screens in the windows!"

Nelida and I exchanged glances, but we were too polite to laugh. Screens yet! And bathrooms!

I assured them we would be perfectly happy there. Before I went to the convent-to-be, they let me use their shower. When I came out, Frère Magloire had prepared a meal for me, scrambled eggs, toast of bread he made himself—and miracle of miracles, a huge red tomato, icy cold from their kerosene-powered refrigerator. That was Christianity of the purest, for tomatoes will not grow in this part of the world. Père Victor had been given a half-dozen by a passing Peruvian Air Force pilot who was en route to a distant army base. I'd be willing to bet that these were the only tomatoes to arrive on the Putumayo in many years.

After eating, I was somewhat restored. Then Père Victor broke the bad news. The river was lower than it had been at any time in known history. All the rain which should have kept it navigable had carelessly been dumped in the wrong spot. How else to explain why the normally dry trail was so completely inundated while the river was so shallow that the only two boats to brave it had been stuck in the mud for the last four months? No supplies at all had reached the mission. Their little store was virtually empty! They had no canned food or kerosene or staples to sell me. What was more serious was the fact that I could not hire one of their motorboats because they hadn't enough gasoline to fill a cigarette lighter.

One worry after another. Another problem before the last had been solved. I lay awake that night in my hammock in the big convent, listening to the sleep of my companions. The interior partitions hadn't been erected yet. The building was like a huge, empty box under a corrugated iron roof and every snort, every deep breath, reverberated from walls to roof.

The lack of supplies was troublesome, but that didn't worry me too much. There were people living along the Putumayo and where there are people there must be food of some sort. I'd get along just as they did. But the lack of transportation . . . that was grave. Frère Magloire hadn't been able to suggest anything. It looked as though I might be stuck at the mission for an indefinite time. I was *not* going to wade back to the Algodón. I'd stay here and take my chances. That decision made, I went to sleep.

But not for long. A loud, wooden thumping woke me. It sounded like somebody beating on the door. Flashlight in hand, Barton crawled out from under his mosquito net and went to investigate. He threw open the big double front doors and his light shone in the face of a startled cow. Loudly, he shooed her away. The cow departed. We went to sleep again, but the cow's performance was repeated by her sisters a dozen times during the night. Barton made more noise than the cows. In the morning, we discovered that the attraction was the wooden ramp set up to make the door accessible until a stairway could be built. The cows came to lick from it the salt deposited by the perspiring feet of the bearers.

I put on a highly credible histrionic performance in the morning. I had to hide from Nelida and her husband my frantic worries about transportation and to keep from showing how forlorn I felt about having to say goodbye. If they had guessed, they would have made me go back to Don Alfonso and the distillery, which would have meant weeks of delay. So I pretended perfect confidence.

Nelida almost penetrated my front. "But we can't leave you here like this, señora," she objected. "How are you going to get away from here? Who will prepare your food while you are waiting? Who will take care of you?"

I made up a story about some boatmen from somewhere upstream who could probably take me, which convinced her and Barton that all would be well.

Gaily, I distributed tips and gifts to the Indians, who were happy because they had already managed to spend the money I had paid them before. I felt particularly grateful to Hilario. He had saved me the bother of seeking the Coto witch doctor who might not have been willing to give me the tooth-pulling plant. And Hilario would be safe from any retribution, for his doctor would never know that he had passed the tribal icaro to a gringa, who, although she may have flattered and bewitched the secret out of him, sent him happily back to his two wives with strings of beads for each of them. And she would go back to her country, where, in time, her people perhaps might not be so *bárbaros*, so *malos*, because of his small gift to their medical science.

As I watched them start back up the hill, I almost burst into tears. It wasn't only for the services I'd be lacking. I would miss their company even more.

Now I was really on my own.

CHAPTER

IX

THE TOUR of the mission which Frère Magloire gave me didn't take long. He showed me the sawmill he'd built in 1954 when he had finished clearing the land. "I made just a tambo to live in, and then the sawmill first, before everything else. Because, of course, if we are to have proper buildings we must cut the trees and saw them into planks." He recalled that there had been just one family of Indians, eight people, living on the mission grounds at the time. Now there were twenty-seven families, a hundred and seventy-five souls. "And more moving in, almost every month," he added happily.

He lingered over showing me the machine shop, running his knotty hands over his power tools as I might run my hand down the neck of a fine horse. Practically everything in the machine shop was the product of his vacation in 1955. It didn't sound as though it had been very restful. He returned to the Putumayo from his native Quebec Province with ten thousand pieces, all gifts he had solicited, and they ranged from a tractor to small tools. A lot of them came from members of his own family. He was one of sixteen children, thirteen of whom were still alive, and evidently as devout as he.

He'd had a lot of fun with the tractor. When he brought it up the river on a boat, Indians from miles around gathered to watch the yellow monster unloaded. Eagerly, they helped him make a gangway of big planks on logs large enough to bear the tractor's weight. The natives milled excitedly on the shore when he climbed into the driver's seat. But as the motor roared into action, they took off as one man for the woods and some of them didn't come back for two days.

I was particularly anxious to see the little store. Surely there must be something left. I was almost out of all edible and combustible provisions. Perhaps he thought I would want caviar and *pâté de foie gras*. As we walked toward the store, I assured him I would not be fussy, that even the lowliest can of sardines would be welcome. He shook his head sadly as he threw open the door. Behind the little counter, the shelves were bare except for a few bolts of tocuyo and a box of candles. I bought candles.

"Everybody comes here," Frère Magloire said. "They travel for days in their canoes to buy from us and now I must turn them away. You see, until we had the store, people along the river were at the mercy of the riverboat peddlers, and they are terrible profiteers. They charged many times the value of their merchandise and they got by with it because there was no competition. So I arranged with the bishopric to buy our stock at wholesale prices and ship it to us. We add only ten per cent to the cost. Our people can pay us in cash or products—hides, salt fish, anything we can use. It has stopped them from being exploited by those scoundrels. But now all we have is salt fish, caught and sun-dried here, and waiting to be shipped to the Amazon.

Salt fish is not my favorite food. But I promptly bought a good quantity. At least it's filling.

Frère Magloire with a sure sense of climax had saved the church for last. The walk to it took us through the first real garden I'd seen since leaving Iquitos, a garden of vivid-leaved crotons, red, gold and green, bordering beds of magnificent magenta coxcombs. I commented on its beauty.

"The natives still think we're crazy," Frère Magloire laughed. "They say, 'Yuca, yes, you plant, and plantains and bananas and pineapple, you plant and cultivate. But to plant, to spend so much work cultivating something you cannot even eat, that is madness.' When I tell them that I must have something to please my eyes as well as my stomach, they just stare at me and shake their heads."

Even in the first weary moments of our arrival the day before, I had been struck by the simplicity of the design and the perfect harmony of the church's proportions. Frère Magloire told me it had been designed by an architect lay brother, Frère Octave Dorien, who had spent a month's vacation at the mission. When we stepped inside, I just stood still and loved it. It was so flawlessly, so serenely right. Everything was painted white. The only adornment was a series of triangular lattices soaring airily to the high, peaked roof.

The line of the roof was repeated by tall windows with pointed tops.

Under a plaster image of St. Anthony holding the Infant Jesus, the altar was simply a rectangular wooden table covered by a white nainsook cloth with a band of crochet at each end. On it stood a pair of very plain silver candlesticks and above them a wooden cross not more than two feet tall, bearing the crucified Christ in silver bas-relief.

I wondered if the Franciscan vow of poverty had been uppermost in the architect's mind when he drew his design. Somehow I didn't think it had. Wouldn't that have created an atmosphere of austerity? There was nothing so severe in this. It was simple beauty, unadorned and unaffected.

At lunch with the two Franciscans, I told them that grateful as I was for their hospitality, I had no intention of becoming a permanent boarder. Nelida had prepared dinner for us over a cook fire in the clearing behind the convent. I intended to do the same. The only drawback was that I am an awful flop as a Camp Fire Girl. Any outdoor fire I build will not burn. Could they find some woman of the mission village who would help me out three times a day? I'd be happy to pay her.

They could and did. That evening, a slim, shy woman who looked more white than Indian appeared at the door to the convent. Her name was Zoila. Frère Magloire had sent her to cook for me. She would be glad to come every morning and evening, but at midday she would be working in her banana and yuca plot some distance from the village. Her eldest daughter, Delfina, would come to prepare lunch.

When Zoila built the fire I tried to get chummy, but her shyness was at first impenetrable. She seemed barely able to force herself to answer questions. I did elicit the fact that she was the widow of a man who had died a couple of years before. They had come from a small town on the Colombian Amazon many years before and settled not far from the mission. After her husband had died, she brought her six children to live where they would have the solace of religion and the chance of some schooling. In a sudden burst of confidence, she told me that she took Communion every Sunday. She had heard that Frère Magloire was trying to get someone to take me upstream to the trail that led to the "bad" Indians. Surely I wouldn't go before Sunday, would I?

Today was Tuesday. I told her that I would leave as soon as I possibly could. I hoped that it would be before Sunday.

"But you can't take Communion until Sunday." She looked very worried. "You wouldn't want to go on such a dangerous trip without first having Communion, would you, señora?"

I explained that my religion was different. I was a Protestant.

"But, then, you are not a Christian?" she asked, alarmed.

I said of course I was a Christian, a different sort of Christian.

That tore it. From then on she was so nervous that communication practically ceased. She and her daughter, a reedy girl of twelve, came regularly to boil my salt fish and the yuca I bought from them. They took conscientious care of me, but even though Frère Magloire tried to persuade them that I was not an infidel, they were decidedly leery. I could never get them to be chatty. If Zoila did know any of the native plant remedies, which I doubt, she would not tell me about them.

I spent four days at the mission trying to find transportation and slapping gnats. During the day there were two kinds of gnats, tiny ones whose bites caused minute but painful blisters, and the larger, black ones, who left little red dots wherever they landed. Both kinds worked voraciously from dawn to dusk. At night the mosquitoes took over. The chiggers were on twenty-four-hour duty.

I soon took to putting the repellent on thick enough to work like flypaper, otherwise the beasts just seemed to consider it an interesting condiment. I had learned not to scratch bites when I had lived in the Philippines, and had even developed a moderate immunity to many types of insects. Nothing of this sort had ever bothered me much before. But these—they came in clouds. They got into your nose and mouth. They had to be removed from your streaming eyes. Even the local people complained constantly and their arms and faces were pockmarked with tiny scars from bites which had been infected. This didn't add to their beauty.

Most of them were Indians who had come with their families to earn the money paid by the Franciscans for construction work or to put their children into the school for little boys. When the nuns came next month, there would be a school for little girls as well, though I got the impression that they all thought this was carrying culture too far.

The entire village came to call on me that evening. First a family, father, mother and six children of varying ages entered the door silently. The father stepped forward. "Juan Díaz. *Buenos noches,* señora," he said politely, offering me a damp hand to shake. Then they all squatted in a line against the wall and stared at me. I made polite remarks in Spanish while the parents stared blankly, the younger children tittered, and the baby at his mother's breast bawled loudly. Then the father walked over to my hammock and examined it. He fingered the blanket, turned away and felt the material of a shirt and a pair of blue jeans I'd hung on a nail, and said something I didn't understand. One of the children, a boy of about ten, interrupted, "He say he buy. How much?"

I explained that these were things I needed. Not for sale. Just then another family entered, and another. All squatted on the floor. All tried to buy everything I owned. When they found this impossible, they just sat and stared. It was getting pretty crowded when Frère Magloire bustled in. "All right, all right!" He made shooing motions with his hands. "You have greeted the Señora. Now you are friends. Now you go home and let her sleep. The Señora is tired."

As the last Indian reluctantly filed out, Frère Magloire grinned at me. "Better not to let more than one family in at a time," he advised. "They are good people, but awfully light-fingered. If there are too many for you to keep an eye on, you'll find a lot of things missing when they leave."

I had told him of my quest for plants. Frère Magloire had not been able to help much. "We don't fool around with that sort of thing," he told me. "Our headquarters sends us ample supplies of dependable medicines from home, things whose results have been scientifically tested." Now I told him that I hoped the evening visits might make it possible for me to get a few plants from the local people.

"I'm afraid they won't be much help," he said regretfully. "I don't think these people have any knowledge of medicinal herbs. I know that when one of them is sick or injured, they come running to me for treatment. They don't seem to be able to handle even common maladies like malaria themselves. I don't believe they know any medicine."

I didn't like to argue. Frère Magloire should certainly know better than I. But I wondered. Maybe the natives felt it would be rather gauche to show any knowledge of tribal lore amidst all this elegantly modern environment. Perhaps they felt a certain stigma attached to their pagan origins. *Nouveau riche* and *nouveau civilizé* have a lot in common. In any case, I got nothing from them, never a single plant, not even a hint of medical knowledge.

Nor could I interest them in paddling me upstream to El Encanto and the trail that led to the "bad" Indians. They were a Witoto group which had been discovered a few years before, a short distance off the trail that runs from El Encanto to a place called La Chorrera in Colombia. The Indians were still wild and lived exactly as they had before the whites came to the jungle. What's more, this tribal group had belligerently refused to have anything to do with either whites or civilized Indians of their own language group.

In the jungle when there's no way to continue traveling to the place you want, you have to take any possible means of transportation and just go as far as you can in the general direction of your goal. Then you start looking around for something else . . . or start out on your own two feet if you can find no other alternative. Boats and walking are the only means of travel. You won't find horses or mules. First of all because the trails are too narrow, too obstructed by low-hanging branches for even a pony to get through. And anyway, there are no animals once you're away from the well-settled areas. Livestock doesn't survive very well. Proper fodder is impossible to find in the forest, and, even on farms where fodder is planted, the vampire bats and many insect plagues make it hard to keep any domestic animal except pigs alive.

The third day of my visit at Estrecho, Frère Magloire found a solution to my travel problem. Carlos Wansi, a Yawas Indian who lived nearby, was willing to paddle me downstream to the mouth of the Igaraparaná. I could figure out later how to get up the Igaraparaná to La Chorrera and take to the trail from that end. There was a Colombian police post at the mouth of the Igaraparaná and a Catholic mission at La Chorrera. Wherever there are people, you can usually get cooperation.

Carlos Wansi came at dawn the next morning to carry my bags down to his canoe. He was a flat-faced Indian with an amiable look. For this trip, he had equipped his canoe with a brand new pamacari that looked rather like a perambulator hood and seemed disproportionately large. The boat itself looked small and about as stable as a floating leaf. I regarded it rather dubiously until I remembered that the Yawas are the most famous of South American rivermen. And Carlos himself looked steady enough to make up for an obviously "jealous" canoe. Jealous is the word they use in the Ecuadorian jungle to describe a craft that is easily upset. Could anything be more appropriate?

I love traveling by paddle even though it's many times slower than by motor. There is no racket to scare the animals away. You can hear the life of the water and the jungle. When we started out, the howler monkeys were roaring like a lot of jammed foghorns, and the waking birds, especially the parakeets, were shrill and raucous. Occasionally, a fish jumped or a big, white egret heron sailed low over the water, graceful as a Japanese print. Stretched on soft blankets in the shade of the pamacari, my back cushioned by the big rubber bag filled with clothes, I was as comfortable as Cleopatra barging down the Nile. Even the gnats weren't a nuisance, for Carlos kept to midriver to take advantage of the current and the insect pests' habit of staying close to land.

Carlos paddled steadily, three or four strokes on one side, then three or four strokes on the other. He sat in the unshaded prow, his potato-colored feet braced against the thwarts. They were queer-looking feet, wide and thick even for an Indian, and his bulbous toes made them look like some sort of tuberous vegetable. He was dressed in ragged khaki trousers and a shirt so patched that I couldn't be sure what the original color had been. Across the shoulders, even the patches on the patches were patched.

Carlos, chatty for an Indian, was obviously proud of his fairly good mission Spanish. He had been orphaned early in life and had grown up in the house of a mission priest. A couple of years ago, he had come here from Río Yaguas, which runs into the Putumayo far to the southeast, so that his children would be educated. He loved to talk about the boys' school, and he could hardly wait for the nuns to arrive to teach his daughters how to read and write and how to keep a clean, Christian home.

As he chatted, he often interrupted himself to say, "Look señora!" and he would point to a snake swimming in the water, its neck sticking out right-angled like a small periscope, or to macaws or parrots flying in pairs. Sometimes he'd say "Monkeys!" and point to a tree. I could see them only if they moved, but when they remained quiet, they were invisible among the leafy branches. Every time I asked, "Where? But where?" he was so disappointed that I soon learned to say I saw them whether I did or not.

Once he pointed to a decaying log lying vertical to the bank, one end in the water. "Look, señora, *taricayas!*" I had to look hard

before I saw five turtles sunning themselves. They were ranged in
order of size on the log, neat as a row of buttons, the largest closest
to the water. His shell must have been eighteen inches across. While
we watched, he plopped into the river, and the others, still in order
of size, followed him. It was an extremely orderly drill.

While it was still early in the morning, before the sun topped the
tall trees whose shadows were long on the water, we rounded a
bend and Carlos whispered, "Señora, señora . . . *tigre*!" I whispered
too. "Where?" Carlos was pointing right out into the river. I could
see only what looked like a bit of drifting wood. But it wasn't
drifting, it was cutting across current, headed for the shore. Then a
beautiful jaguar burst out of the water onto the muddy beach,
paused only an instant to shake himself, leapt and vanished into the
jungle. His coat was dark with water, but you could still see the
black rosettes in the wet yellow, and he looked big, big as a pony. In
all the times I had been in the jungle, I have never seen anything
more exciting. Previously my biggest thrill of that type had been a
tapir. I had never seen any of the big cats. I felt as though I had
been given a magnificent gift.

Carlos had a hunter's eye for animals, but he didn't know much
about plant medicine or magic. He remembered his tribe with
affection, but he didn't remember much of their customs. He had,
quite involuntarily, stopped being a primitive, no longer was endowed with the strange combination of superstition and wisdom,
of ignorance and insight, which always, much as I have seen it, awes
and astonishes me.

Late that afternoon, we rounded a bend and saw a house in a
little clearing. Carlos headed for it. "Here we sleep," he announced.

"You must be plenty tired, no, Carlos?" I asked.

"Tired, señora?" he countered. "Why tired?"

"You've been sitting out there in the strong sun paddling for at
least twelve hours."

Amazement wiped his face clean of any expression. Then his
brows knotted in bewilderment and he slowly shook his head. "But
just paddling, señora? Paddling never make anybody tired."

That hardwood paddle with its flat, diamond-shaped blade must
have weighed at least fifteen pounds.

Carlos shouted a greeting as we pulled into the shore and a
young couple in faded clothing came running out of the house to
welcome us warmly. Carlos hung my hammock on the porch. Like

most jungle houses built by white people, this one had two small rooms partitioned off at one end. All the rest was just a pona floor on stilts under a huge, thatched roof. The only furniture was hand-hewn benches and a table.

Our hosts were Amelia and Homero Rojas. He was a stocky, muscular Peruvian. Amelia was a plump woman with slanting eyes which showed a strong strain of Indian blood. They had come here three years ago from Iquitos to tame the wilderness, but now they were fed up with the Putumayo. Mr. Rojas told me they planned to move to another river as soon as they had harvested the jute he'd planted. They were happy to have someone to talk to. This was a lonely river. But it was not the loneliness that was driving them out. It was the gnats. Mr. Rojas said that they made working in the fields a torment. Mrs. Rojas added that it was difficult to do the daily washing of the family clothes—even the housework—because of the insects.

"And the children," she said, "they are always covered with bites and I'm always afraid they will scratch and make sores and then they will grow sick."

I hadn't seen any children. I asked where they were.

"They are timid," Mrs. Rojas laughed. "We are not used to having visitors and they are hiding."

Her husband stepped into a back room and emerged proudly leading a manly little boy of about five and a girl of about two. Solemnly, the children shook hands with me. Then they sat plumply on a bench and stared with eyes like shiny black olives.

I had hoped we might be able to buy some game or at least fresh fish, but they had none. Mr. Rojas had been too busy with his jute. He had no time for hunting or fishing. They were on a salt-fish diet, too. So Carlos got to work boiling up another batch of salt fish. As we sat down to the table, Mr. Rojas' head snapped up. "Listen!" he hissed. I heard a peculiar sort of chirping whistle. "*Tigre!*" It *was* a jaguar. I had heard them whistle like that before. I asked Mr. Rojas if they never growled or roared. He said no, the tigre makes only two noises, the whistling sound and a sort of snuffling snort. But the snuffling you hear only when he is very close. The whistle carries surprisingly far.

After dinner, I set my radio on the table and carefully strung that ludicrous aerial over the rafters. We got dance music from Bogotá and my hosts were enraptured. The children laughed with delight, and the boy, bolder now, climbed up to sit by my side. The family hadn't heard a radio for so long that they enjoyed even the longest-winded commercials. Even the children determinedly held up heavy eyelids until very late.

It was still dark when I was awakened by the barking of a dog. Carlos was coming up from the canoe where he had spent the night, and the Rojas watchdog objected. Every jungle house has at least one dog for hunting and to keep off the jungle marauders at night. Mrs. Rojas came running from the stove she was squatting over and yelled at the dog. She was already getting breakfast.

"This morning you will be our guest, señora. I want to give you a good breakfast to start the day."

I saw that she had a frying pan full of lard already over the fire. On the floor beside her stood the lard can. It was quite empty.

"No, señora," I protested. "You are too kind. You must not use the last of your lard on us. Who knows how long before you can buy more, before the river is navigable again and a trader comes along?"

"But you are guests in my house, are you not? Did we refuse last night to drink your coffee and smoke your cigarettes? *Vaya*, señora?"

"But that is no reason for you to throw your house out of the window," I answered. "Throw your house out of the window" is the common phrase used in Latin America to describe overwhelming and extravagant hospitality. And this really was. Any kind of fat is hard to come by in the jungle. Since it cannot be had locally, jungle diets are apt to be almost completely fat-deficient. After a while, even I, who normally dislike fried foods, find myself craving them. The bit of lard Mrs. Rojas had scraped from the bottom of the can had probably been carefully hoarded for some big event.

Smilingly, she went on dropping thin fingers of yuca and long slices of ripe plantains into the bubbling grease. When the plantains were a crisp, shining brown—they absorb fat like blotters—the frying pan was almost empty of lard. Into what little fat was left, she fried slices of sun-dried fish. It was a really big gesture and I was touched.

Saying goodbye, I persuaded them to accept a few packs of cigarettes and a can of instant coffee. Then I felt better. Coffee and cigarettes are luxuries, too, and I carried them in great quantity. The Rojases were still waving when our canoe rounded the bend. Friends we were who shared in time of need.

Before long, Carlos again whispered, "Señora . . . tigre!" It was another jaguar, as beautiful and as exciting as the other one I had seen. About noon, we passed a dwelling on a long, straight stretch of river. As we came near, a man ran out of the house and waved at us. "My cousin," Carlos said. They had a short, shouted conversation. Carlos apologized for not being able to visit because he was "on a commission" transporting a señora who came from the country of the Padres "to know the Putumayo."

The man ran back into the house, ran out again with something in his hand, jumped into a tiny canoe and came skittering after us with the speed of a water spider. He had brought us some fish roe, still hot in the dark green leaf packages in which it had been steamed. "Is good," he grinned. "I catch this morning, my woman cook now. Is very good. Señora, eat."

I gave Cousin a package of cigarettes and he enjoyed his smoke as much as we enjoyed the fish roe. I made Carlos stop paddling while he ate. Usually he would eat while he paddled, finishing the stroke on one side, tossing a bit of food into his mouth while shifting the paddle to the other side. It didn't even break the rhythm of his stroke. He paddled like a machine.

While he ate, Carlos explained to Cousin that he might not be able to stop over for a visit even when he was on the way back. He was in a hurry. He had to return in time to enter his children in school, for the new semester was beginning in eight days. The head of the family, he stated with considerable pomp, always escorts his children to school on the first day. Cousin was impressed. He treated Carlos with dignified respect thereafter, even when he said goodbye to us.

The day was hot, hotter than usual. The unaccustomed good food had made me sleepy. It was siesta time, anyway, so I slept for hours. When I awoke, it was much cooler, the wind was almost cold. Peering from the shady pamacari, I saw the sun still shone, but the clouds piling in the west had a curious look, solid, purplish, with a gaudy line of gold where the sun caught their edges. The wind was rising and above the flapping of the loose strands of palm on the pamacari there was another noise, distant but coming nearer, like the sound of a train approaching over a long railroad trestle. It was the sound of hard rain crashing down on the forest.

While I hurried to secure big sheets of plastic over the baggage, we rounded a bend and the rain like a dark curtain swept toward us.

I was drenched before I could get into my raincoat. But rain is only a nuisance on those big, wide rivers. It's the wind that's dangerous. Suddenly waves slammed at us from all directions, poured over the sides of the canoe. I grabbed a cooking pot and started bailing.

"Don't you think we ought to go ashore?" I shouted to Carlos.

"Where?" he shouted back.

I peered through the downpour. It was as opaque as rods of metal and almost as hard and cold. I could distinguish the shore quite close, but the jungle was dense, an impenetrable tangle of vines and branches almost all the way down to the leaping surface of the water. Nothing we could get through to solid land. Nothing we could tie a canoe to with any safety. One good wave would smash our canoe against branches that would as easily knock us into the water.

Carlos was paddling hard. "Pretty soon a house," he shouted, grinning over his shoulder.

I kept bailing, holding on to the thwarts as the canoe bucked like a bronco. I remembered what Frère Magloire had told me about the two policemen whose boat had overturned near here a year or so ago. They were both swimmers, but they hadn't wanted their canoe to be swept away and leave them stranded, so they held on, one on either side of the boat. Everything was under control until one man saw his companion's hand grow suddenly limp, then straighten convulsively as he disappeared under the water as though something were dragging him down.

"Something got him," Frère Magloire had said. "Not piranha. They don't work that way. It wouldn't have been a croc, either. An electric eel, most likely, or perhaps a big water snake. Some of those water boas are enormous."

I concentrated on bailing and tried not to think of the enemies below, growing hungrier from the lashing of the water. I admitted to myself that I was frightened. Sometimes that helps me to remain outwardly calm. The worst of the storm lasted only about twenty minutes. Then, as abruptly as it had risen, the wind died down and the rain thinned to a drizzle. Ahead on the bank, we could see now the big house which Carlos had referred to, standing in a half-overgrown clearing. We had been near it during the entire storm, but we hadn't been able to see it.

X

T HE HOUSE was dilapidated, but it had been a good house once. On stilts, with a thatched roof like a half-open book, it had railings all around, and even a couple of rooms walled off at one end. It looked like a white man's house, jungle white, of course, and the man waving at us from the "port," where a canoe was tied, wore the usual tattered khaki shirt and trousers, but his dark face had the high, roughly molded cheekbones, the slanting eyes of the Indian. He was Yori, a Muename from Colombia, who had learned Spanish while working rubber for a white *patrón*. He had come here a few years ago with his wife and built a house across the river, but this house was better. It had been built by a white settler, but the man was killed by a tigre. (Our tigre, I wondered, the beautiful creature we had seen this morning?) After that, the white man's family had moved away and Yori had taken over.

But it was lonely here, and Yori was full of sorrow. His wife was dead, maybe two years now. A witch had killed her with the coughing sickness. And only a fortnight ago, his oldest son had died. That was the witch's doing, too, and now the witch, the evil witch who lived *there* (Yori pointed to the woods), wanted to kill the other children. He had made them sick in the eyes, two days now. Soon they would be blind. Also they were sick in the stomach Could the Señora do something to cure them? They were hiding in one of the rooms because they were not use to strangers and they were timid. But would the Señora cure them?

I said I would see what I could do. But first I wanted to get into some dry clothes. The evening was chilly after the storm and I didn't want to catch a cold. Carlos brought a bucket of water and I bathed and changed behind a blanket hung across the end of the porch. When I came out clean, dry, eau-de-cologned and feeling much better, Carlos was in the kitchen, a shed tacked to the side of the house. Yori had sold us a big fish, caught only a half hour before our arrival, and we had yuca. Carlos was boiling the fish and yuca in a pot hung over an open fire in the big stove, the usual jungle stove, which consists of four logs enclosing a six-foot square of clay dried and hardened to adobe.

A girl of eight or nine edged through the door of a back room and stood blinking at me with inflamed eyelids while she tugged at her faded, outgrown dress. I said, "Good evening." She disappeared wordlessly, to emerge carrying her little brother, who might have been two or three. Behind her, she dragged by the hand a little boy about five. The larger boy's eyelids, like his sister's, were red and a bit swollen, but it was the baby who was really in bad shape. His lashes were matted with pus, and he howled as he rubbed his swollen lids.

I went to work on the girl first because I knew she wouldn't cry and frighten the others into thinking the application of an antibiotic ointment a painful operation. In jungle, I always carry a good stock of ophthalmic ointment because eye infections are the most common ailments. They have the advantage of being easiest to treat, too, for they are usually simple types that proper medication clears up dramatically. Only the baby screamed and fought. His father held him, but his sister had to grab his hands. He was such a strong little rascal that he almost gave me a black eye.

Yori had lit the usual jungle lamp, a butter can with a wick stuck through a cylinder of tin fixed on its top. I told him to save his kerosene. Who knew when he would be able to get more? I had been able to get candles at the mission store, so I lit one now and stuck it in the end of one of the two benches which were the only furniture. The family squatted on the floor to eat dinner, and I did, too. While we ate, we discussed the children's other symptoms. They were not appetizing, but the experience of having been the only woman in a medical school laboratory full of men who were interested in seeing how much I could take had cured me, permanently, of queasiness.

The children suffered from frequent nausea and abdominal discomfort. I had noticed how their round little bellies protruded. Could it be worms? I asked Yori. He stared at me in astonishment.

Of course, that was it! He'd been so upset ever since the witch had killed his son, so worried about the ghost tigre he heard prowling around the house at night, that such a simple solution just hadn't occurred to him. Now he remembered that the children had been just like this a couple of years ago. Then he had given them *oje*, a jungle vermifuge so well known that it's now in commercial production. "After take *oje*, much worm come out. Then all well. I give *oje* tomorrow."

We'd finished dinner. I stood up and stretched. Carlos took the dishes down to the river to wash and called good night from there. It was his bedtime. I sat on the bench against the railings; Yori had settled on the other against the wall behind which the children had retired. The candle on the bench's end was like a baby spotlight, sharpening the shadows around his mouth, his keen, deep-set eyes, exaggerating the flaring nostrils, gilding the edges of the unquiet hands.

"Tell me about the ghost tigre," I said.

"Is witch, bad man, who sending him. Is witch, living there." Again, he pointed to the jungle behind the house. "Is bad, bad. All time making evil spell with song, with drum. When wind coming from there, can hear drum, can hear song." We both listened for a moment, but there was only the croaking of frogs, the monotonous call of a night bird, and the rippling whisper of the river.

"Who is this witch?" I asked.

"Is old man of Ocaína tribe. Coming here much time ago. Making big house in jungle maybe one, maybe two-hour walk. He has stone, magic stone that is no stone, but he make of powdered heart of seven animal, jaguar, puma, howler monkey, hawk, viper, crocodile, boa constrictor. This stone he rubbing in hands, *so!*" Yori's head bent low over hands joined in a smoothing, caressing gesture. "Doing this with stone, saying much magic words, then he calling spirit of one animal. That animal come, go where witch pointing, look, smell, finding person witch name, making sick, killing. Also witch throwing stone like this." Yori made a big, throwing gesture that ended with a pointed finger, strangely frightening in the candlelight. "Then lightning striking man he name.

"Also has little stick making mark on paper." Yori twisted crouched over the bench to imitate a man writing with a pencil. "Mark is name of animal. He making mark, calling animal, spirit of that animal do what he say.

"So he kill my son. Now want to kill other children. Then he kill me. I know. Much night, I hear ghost tigre around house. I hear '*umppf* . . . *umppf*,' just like live tigre. Next morning maybe I find track, maybe no. Many times, I go hunting him, I no see. So I know is ghost tigre. No man can see ghost tigre."

"Was it the ghost tigre that killed the man who lived here before?" I asked.

"No, that real tigre, live tigre. Not like my son. Ghost tigre kill different."

"But how does the ghost tigre kill ?" I asked. "What happened to your son?"

It had started when his son's foot was burned by a coal from the fire. "I come home from hunt with wild pig. My son telling me 'Father, my foot is burn.' I look. Is little burn—here." Yori pointed a knotted finger at his instep.

"I tell him, 'My son, you stay in house. You no going to woods. Bad to cool burn in wet mud.' But he no obey. Next morning he say, 'Father, my foot big.' I look. Is big, big where ghost claw strike.

"I tell my son, 'Now if you going to woods and some thing chasing you, you cannot run. Now you stay in house.' I tell my daughter if he going, she tell me and I whip. But she is smaller, and she is woman, and she no tell. When I come late after start fish trap in little river, my son show me leg now big, big, to here.' Yori's hands made a tense frame below his knee and his eyes were lost in shadow.

"That night my son with fever. He no eating fish I bring. Morning I going to finish trap for fish before rain fill river. I coming back night. Leg of son is big, big. My daughter say son no go out. I think tomorrow I staying with him. But now he no eating fish, he no eating wild pig. Morning, he sleeping. I tell my daughter stay by him, I shoot macaw live in capinuri tree.

"Macaw giving good soup, strong soup, my son eat, he needing eat.

"I hunt too fast," Yori said. He jumped to his feet, arms crooked around an imaginary shotgun, head back, eyes searching imaginary branches. "Macaw fly other tree. I following. Fly again. I waiting much time, no moving. Then again see red, blue feathers in tree. I shoot."

He suddenly raised the imaginary gun and I jumped as the shadow jerked across my face.

"I come home. My daughter is not, my little son is not. I call. Then they running in house, with rush to tell me was only at river, washing clothes. My big son, my sick son, in his room, sleeps. I lift mosquito net. He is bad, bad. Leg is big, big, black. Belly is black." Yori sat again on the bench, hunched over as though his stomach hurt, and the candlelight made gullies between the tendons on his clenched hands. "Daughter say my son no going out, but I think he go. Now he wake and animal demon is in him. He making noises of animal demon. And when we no hold him, he jump, he hitting against floor, making all time noises of animal." Yori was crouching now, arms straightened to hold down a writhing body. "I say, 'My son, my son!' But he making noise of animal.

"I have to know what thing is got into him. I chew much tobacco and swallow my saliva until I am dizzy, dizzy like drunk. Then I can *see* what thing this is. I see my son walk through jungle. I see tigre walk after him. But my son not seeing. I seeing tigre leave path, making circle before my son, and waiting. My son walking on, no see. I seeing tigre crouching. My son near now. I seeing tigre spring." I flinched as Yori's clawed hands swooped forward and down to tear at his groin in a gesture of swift ferocity. "So I seeing ghost tigre striking my son. So I seeing ghost claws go into his leg, his belly, make black, make spoil.

"That night, my son die." Yori's hands dropped limply, emptily, and the shadows cut his face like scars.

We didn't say anything for a long time. The candle guttered, made little crackling sounds and went out. I lit my flashlight and Yori spoke again.

"Señora, what I do? My woman dead. I get another woman but only little time. She bad with my children, I send her away. She no like here anyway. No people. I can get no other woman. No women here. Nobody care for children. I go to woods, hunt meat. Children alone. Maybe animal hurt them. Maybe demon get them. How I save my children?"

I thought, poor guy. Poor, poor guy. No use at all to try to make an Indian understand that his son had died of septicemia from an infected burn. No Indian believes that sickness can be caused by anything except malicious magic. Any sickness of any kind has to be the result of witchcraft. Yori had narcotized himself with tobacco juice, and the resulting hallucinations had only set his previous convictions more firmly. I could think of only one solution.

"Yori," I told him solemnly, "you hate this place. You are not happy here. Your son dead, your wife dead . . . it is a bad, an evil place. You will leave it. I see this. Tomorrow, you will give your children the oje. The next day, they will rest and you will hunt. The day after that you will stay with them and smoke the meat you have shot for your journey. Then the next day, you will put your cookpots and your clothes and your children in your canoe. You will go upstream four days. When you see, on the right bank, white houses, you will stop, and there you will build your new house. Many families are there and you will find a wife. And there is a mission. There is a school where your children will be cared for when you are hunting. And there are padres who have a magic so strong . . . only good magic . . . that no witch, no demon can do anything against it. They are good and very strong. You will go there in five days. I see it. And you will be well and your children well and you will be happy."

I think I put it over.

Then I went and untied my hammock. Carlos had hung it at the farthest end of the porch. Now I placed it close to the wall of the children's room so that it would not be able to swing without bumping. I'd heard too much about things that went "*umppf . . . umppf*" around the house at night, and I did not believe they were ghosts.

Next morning, the children's eyes were noticeably better. I made Yori put the medicine in so that he would be sure he knew how to do it. Then I gave him a couple of tubes of the ointment and told him to listen carefully. He must apply the medicine, morning and evening, for five days after the children appeared to be cured.

"The medicine puts to sleep the demon that is feeding on their eyes. While the demon sleeps, it does not eat. It must sleep until it has starved to death. If you do not put the medicine on it twice every day, until it is good and dead, it will wake up again. And then when it wakes up, it will be so hungry that nothing will make it sleep. It will eat your children's eyes until they are blind." That was the nearest I could come to explaining antibiotic action in his terms. I made Yori repeat the directions after me, then again just before we left. He seemed pretty impressed.

After breakfast, I told him he really ought to give me some of his medicine in return. He agreed that was fair. There wasn't much growing near the house, but there was some good medicine a few hours away. He'd get it. I asked him to describe the plants. One was for curing warts. That didn't sound very exciting. The other two were plants I already had. And, anyway, I didn't dare keep Carlos waiting, getting his children into school was so important, so I settled for the plant that grew nearby.

Yori brought me a funny-looking weed, with spindly stems and feathery leaves. He explained that sometimes when the witch throws his stone at a person, a bit of it breaks off and remains in the victim "here" (hand over gall bladder), or "here" (hand over kidneys). It makes much pain. "You take morning, midday, night in boil water." His voice was as portentous as mine when I had told him about the ophthalmic ointment. The medicine would make little bits of stone come out when you urinate or defecate. When they come out, you are well.

When I got back to Iquitos, friends told me that Yori's plant is an infallible cure for gallstones and kidney stones. Imagine Yori's knowing that! I hoped the pharmaceutical people would appreciate it.

CHAPTER

XI

In MY BAGGAGE I had a small package and a letter which I had promised Don Alfonso to deliver to his friend Teniente Lingán, comandante of a Peruvian army post called Pucaurco, on the Putumayo. Carlos informed me that Pucaurco was only a half day away. We ought to reach it by noon.

"Is big buildings, many people, I think," he told me. "Maybe have store. Maybe Señora can buy many things no have got at Estrecho."

I tried to remember whether they had had a post exchange at the only jungle army station I had visited in 1948, way up on the Santiago River. I couldn't remember a store, but I did remember my arrival vividly. I had come in an open canoe of a member of the Jívaro tribe, for I had been visiting just across the border in Ecuador. It had been a very hard trip and I was, simply and accurately, a mess. It had been a shock to be courteously helped from the canoe by one of the most perfectly groomed young officers I had ever seen anywhere. He had led me up a graveled path, bordered by whitewashed stones, to a military post as immaculate as the young man's starched khakis. I had thanked God for the sudden downpour which half an hour earlier had drenched me and my leaky baggage, giving me an acceptable excuse for looking so bedraggled.

In the well-appointed guest quarters Teniente Taboada, comandante of the post and a recent graduate of the Peruvian equivalent of West Point, had lent me his own military academy dress whites, which happened to fit me to perfection. I don't think I have ever felt more elegant than I did that evening at dinner. The starched white tablecloth, the excellent food served by a smart, white-gloved soldier had seemed incredible against the backdrop of jungle. The night before, I had been camped on a riverbank with a bunch of savages who were still actively engaged in head-shrinking.

Now I decided if we were approaching another Peruvian military post, I had better get on with a thorough renovation. I wasn't going to be caught with my grooming down again. For the next hour, I manicured. I hung a blanket over the opening of the pamacari and squirmed into my only good pair of slacks and the last of the shirts which had been ironed. I'd been saving them ever since we left Negro Urco. Then I applied a careful makeup. I even tried to use face powder, but it turned to a gummy paste when it lit on the insect repellent.

Then I added a few more items to the list of things I intended to buy at Pucaurco. I had my dreams.

Pucaurco at last came into sight and I began to wonder. The big green buildings by the water's edge looked as though they badly needed another coat of paint, and the other constructions on the shore looked peculiarly unattractive. They had started as the usual jungle type, a pona house under a tall thatched roof, but sometime later they had been plastered with a coat of mud and painted. The local mud must have been the wrong kind for wattle-and-daub construction. Much of it had peeled off, and the houses looked as though they suffered from skin disease.

Comandante Lingán was a more reassuring sight. He had good features and with a bright smile he hospitably urged me up the hill to his house. I was happy to see it completely screened, though the screening was patched in many places. As we climbed the hill, I asked if they had a post exchange or a store of any kind. The lieutenant was sorry. They'd never had a PX and now the post was almost as low on supplies as everyone else and would remain so until the river was navigable again and the Quartermaster Department boats could get upstream. In personal emergencies, a plane could be sent for. Only yesterday, one had flown a sick man to the hospital in Iquitos. But the air force had no cargo planes in the area and could not undertake to solve supply problems.

The *Comandancia* where the lieutenant lived was a low, square building with two big rooms in front and kitchen and bath in the rear. Whoever designed it had been more concerned with ventilation than with privacy. The door opened on a living-dining room which occupied the whole face of the house. Behind it were the entrance to a narrow passageway and the bedroom, which was set apart only by a half-wall, less than waist-high, so that anyone in the living room was practically in the bedroom too. The low-hanging eaves of a galvanized iron roof made the interior shadowy enough to give the illusion of coolness.

Climbing the steps, the lieutenant shouted, "Leonora, we have a guest, a lady who is a friend of Don Alfonso Cárdenas."

There was a moment's silence, then a woman's voice called, "Make the Señora comfortable and beg her to excuse me while I dress. I'll be there in a minute."

Politely I looked everywhere except in the direction of the bedroom. The lieutenant said that I must spend the night with them. It was such a pleasure to see someone from the "outside."

In the morning, he would send me down to the mouth of the Igaraparaná in their fast motorboat. They still had plenty of gasoline and their boat would get me there in little more than two hours, though it was a day's trip by paddle. Now he would go to supervise the unloading of my baggage and he'd tell Carlos to come up so that I could pay him off.

I was sitting nervously listening to little rustles, a child's cry and a woman's soft-pitched admonitions at my back when Carlos trotted in. "Must go back quick, señora," he said apologetically. "Much hurry to get children into school." I thanked him for all his help, paid him, tipped him, and gave him a mirror from my handbag for his wife. He trotted happily back down the hill.

I waited some more. The room had the unmistakable appearance of army-furnished quarters anywhere in the world. In its center stood a serviceable oblong table of some dark wood, surrounded by the same type of uncompromising wooden chairs I remembered from my days as an air force wife. The only individual touches were a bright cotton hammock, two canvas beach chairs and a handsome shortwave radio set.

The lady of the house appeared leading her little daughter, a doll-faced child just old enough to walk. Señora Lingán was a young woman with very white skin and very black eyes emphasized by carefully applied eye pencil and mascara. She wore a crisp white blouse and black-and-green-striped slacks which would have been very smart if she had not been so overwhelmingly pregnant. She greeted me charmingly and introduced her daughter, whom she called Chinita. Peruvian children are taught politeness from the cradle. "Shake hands with the lady," Señora Lingán said. Obediently the baby stuck out a chubby hand, but when I took it she burst into howls of terror.

I'd been feeling pretty eager about lunch. The diet of salt fish was having a bad effect not only on my disposition but also upon my posture. I had to stand swaybacked, sticking my stomach out to keep my pants from falling down. My only belt had been lost or stolen in Estrecho, and any hips I ever had, had vanished quite completely. Now I remembered the delicious wild birds and the venison I had been served at Teniente Taboaga's camp, and I could scarcely conceal my avid interest when a little soldier spread the cloth and began to set the table.

Lunch was a big slab of salt fish. Not only was it salt fish, but salt fish with a most appalling odor. Frowningly the Señora sniffed it. "I think this end is all right," she said, and proceeded to serve us. Just then the striker brought in rice and beans. Hurriedly I told the Lingáns that I hadn't had either for such a long time. I loved rice, I loved beans, and I hoped they'd forgive me if I made a meal of them.

During lunch I learned that the lieutenant and the men on the post were from the highest mountain districts of Peru. The soldiers were draftees doing their year of compulsory military service. They didn't know how to hunt. They didn't know how to salt and sundry fish properly. And they couldn't even spend much time learning because they had been ordered to make a long military road, really a sort of supertrail, through virgin forest. They didn't even have time to do the subsistence farming which supplies most army posts with staples. The trail-cutting proved grueling for men used only to the cold, thin air of the mountains. They had had a lot of sickness until they got accustomed to the climate.

Siesta time upon us, the Lingáns hospitably offered me a third bed in their room. I declined. I was so used to my hammock, I explained, I really slept better in it than in a strange bed. Being mountain people, they thought this a bit queer, but Lieutenant Lingán obligingly hung it for me in a corner of the living room.

That evening, at dinner in the light of a single bare bulb hanging from the ceiling, I thought the Señora looked a bit peaked. Even the canned salmon they had opened in my honor didn't seem to tempt her. A couple of times her lips contracted oddly, but when I asked if she felt all right, she just smiled and said, "Oh, one is always a bit uncomfortable the last days before the baby comes."

"The last days. . . . But when do you expect to have the baby?" I asked.

"Oh, any time now. Really it was supposed to be due a couple of days ago. In fact"— her face suddenly paled—"I think it's coming tonight." Her narrow fingers gripped the edge of the table tightly as she rose. "Excuse me, please." Quickly she left the room.

Her husband dropped his napkin and followed her. What a time to be an uninvited house guest! How could they stand me? Fervently I hoped it was only that fish. It had smelled bad enough, but any upset it might cause shouldn't be too severe, for the lieutenant had eaten a large portion and he was obviously well. Dear God, I prayed, let it be that fish.

Chinita woke and whimpered. I approached the canvas hammock where she had been sleeping and made noises calculated to be soothing. She screamed. I retired to my chair. I was a great help. And if the baby should come tonight? Why, oh, why hadn't I learned any obstetrics during that year and a half at medical school? I'd never even seen a kitten born—and now only a half-wall separated me from a delivery bedroom.

The Lingáns came back looking relieved. "No baby tonight," the lieutenant said heartily.

Señora Lingán smiled. "Just a bit of colic, and it's gone now. Nothing like the pains I had when Chinita was born."

While we drank our coffee, she gave me a minute-by-minute account of Chinita's birth. It had occurred in a hospital, but it sounded pretty harrowing. With this baby so imminent, I asked, couldn't she have gone to the hospital in Iquitos when the plane came for the sick man?

"But then I'd have had to give birth all alone without my husband," she explained. "Of course, that's the way he wanted it. I even promised to go. I had everything packed and ready, but when the plane arrived, I just couldn't. I hid all the bags and went to the bedroom. José got awfully mad at me, but I wouldn't get aboard and he couldn't find the baggage. So I stayed." She smiled brilliantly.

"But how can you get the proper care here, so far away from civilization?" I asked. "Surely, there's no doctor or midwife on a post this size?"

They told me that they had an excellent *enfermero*, a noncommissioned officer who had been given an intensive medical course. "Ruiz is really good," the Lieutenant said. "He will probably handle it as well as anyone can."

Outside we could hear men talking and laughing. "That'll be our mascot out for his evening walk," Teniente Lingán said, rising. "Come, señora, have a look at him."

The mascot was a baby tapir named Claudio. About the size of a fat baby pony whose legs were too short, he had a comically shaped head which looked as though he had not been able to decide whether he had wanted to be an elephant or a pig and so had settled for a little of each. Most of the head was piggish, but he had a funny long nose like a rudimentary trunk. He was covered with silky brown hair striped with cream color along his fat sides.

Claudio, not at all timid, waddled up to the porch and happily ate the bananas we gave him. We were playing with him when Señora Lingán's voice sounded sharply. "José!" There was a gasp that sent both of us running back up the stairs. She was standing bent over the table with both hands gripping the back of a chair and the perspiration dripped down her face. The lieutenant put his arm around her and helped her quickly from the room.

I tried to not think about how the Señora must be feeling. I tried not to think about all the awful things that might happen. The jungle grew tall trees and lush plants, but it also spawned healthy bacteria. I went to the door to look out at it. I loved its dark massive strength, but tonight I feared that its vitality could be deadly. It could bring fever with the baby . . .

I tried to think of some way that I could be helpful. All I could remember was that in books and movies people always began by boiling lots of water . . . I felt helpless. I felt, for the first time, the oppressive loneliness of the jungle. Before, I had always loved its shelter. But tonight it was too remote.

When they came back the Señora was leaning heavily on her husband, but as they entered the room she pulled away. "No, José," she said with determination, "in Iquitos the doctor told me that as soon as the placenta broke I must start walking and walking. I can do it better alone." She started slowly pacing back and forth.

The lieutenant ran to the front porch and bellowed, "Guard! Soldiers of the Guard! Here! Run! On the double!"

A couple of short, dark soldiers ambled up and saluted. "Run!

Get the enfermero! Tell him the Señora's baby will be born!" This
time they ran.

I asked the Señora if there wasn't something I could do to help
her. Could I at least put fresh linen on her bed? She suddenly
remembered I was there. She thanked me, but there was nothing I
could do. "The enfermero has been sterilizing packs and bedding in
the baker's oven for days. Everything is ready. He and his assistant
will take care of everything."

The pains let up again. She sat down on a chair and asked if I
weren't tired. Wouldn't I like to retire to that bed which she had
prepared in her room? "A hammock may be all right for siestas, but
you need a bed for the night's rest," she insisted.

"No, señora." I flopped into my hammock feeling that I might
shriek if anybody tried to pull me out of it. "My hammock is my
home," I said. "I feel much gratitude, feel deeply, but here I will
stay."

"As you wish it, señora." She allowed herself to look relieved.

The enfermero and his assistant arrived. They were very neat,
alert young men, and they carried a huge roll of linens tightly tied in
a sheet. They seemed not a bit nervous.

"I knew the pack was already sterile," the enfermero said, "but I
didn't like to take chances, so I built the fire up again and gave it
another half hour at high temperature. That's what took us so
long."

The Señora retired to her room to rest for a while. The enfermero
questioned about the time intervals. The pains were still far apart.
Then he consulted his watch. "I think the baby will not be born
until one-forty or thereabouts," he told me.

We chatted. On the medical subjects I knew anything about, he
seemed thoroughly prepared. But he had never delivered a baby!

Again my fears returned. The enfermero's presence had calmed
me somewhat, but if he had never delivered a baby . . . "Wouldn't
some of the native medicine help us?" I asked nervously. "I mean,
I've heard of plants that the Indians take to have babies quickly and
safely. Maybe they're not available here, but couldn't we ask the
soldiers? They might be able to get . . ."

"No, señora," he said calmly. "Do not trouble yourself. We know
more than the witch doctors."

I wondered about that, but I felt reassured when he told me that
for the last two months, he had been rereading what he had learned

in school. Also he had talked by radio with the obstetrician the Señora had consulted in Iquitos. "I've already had our Iquitos command rout him out. He will be standing by at the radio station if anything unforeseen occurs and I need to consult with him."

I sank back in my hammock greatly relieved. Ruiz wasn't the boy to overlook a detail. I began to understand the Lingáns confidence in him.

Time passed with agonizing slowness. As the intervals between the pains shortened, the Señora seemed to suffer more. Now she stayed in her bedroom pacing in the dark. The enfermero and her husband walked with her, one on either side. At the worst moments, she would draw a long, shuddering breath, but she didn't whimper.

I cringed in my hammock. Since there was nothing I could do to help, I pretended I wasn't there at all.

Twelve o'clock came. She was on her feet a lot. One o'clock. She was leaning heavily on the men's arms, but she kept up that determined pacing. Finally she lay on the bed again, and I heard a flurry of activity. This time she didn't get up again.

I huddled in my hammock, not looking over the half-wall that separated us, bracing myself for screams that never came. Instead, there was a terrifying silence. Then the Señora groaned once, soft and long. "Ayyyyyyyyyyy." I heard someone grunt, heard a rustle of cloth, water being poured. The boiled water at last? Then came a baby's cry, strong and loud. I looked at my watch. One forty-seven. Ruiz, the novice obstetrician, had timed it accurately.

The lieutenant burst into the room. "It's a boy!" he shouted. I heard the Señora laugh.

"Is she all right?" I asked, wiping the perspiration out of my eyes.

The lieutenant ran out on the porch. "The Señora has given birth to a boy!" he bellowed into the dark. "I have a son!"

There was nobody there to hear him. He ran back to his wife. I heard a loud, smacking kiss.

"In a moment everything will be finished, señora," the lieutenant said, coming back into the living room, "then you will see my son. My first son. Now we must have music."

He turned on the radio and twiddled the dials madly. The only things he could bring in were a sermon from some Protestant mission and somebody in Canada broadcasting a cake recipe in English, though who'd be listening at two in the morning I couldn't imagine. It didn't bother the lieutenant. He brought out a pisco bottle, two thirds full.

"We must toast the new member of my family, my son, José Lingán, Junior, born the thirteenth of March at . . ." Dismay wiped the broad grin from his face. "Señora, we forgot to look at the time. I will never know the happy hour at which my first son was born.

Hastily I told him that I had checked it. The baby had cried at 1:47. His relief was quite disproportionate. I thought for a moment he was going to kiss me.

The Señora was by now propped up on a pillow looking as happy as her husband. She felt fine, she told us, not even tired, and she'd like a drink to celebrate. She took about a teaspoonful of pisco with the enfermero and his assistant who looked as pleased and proud as anybody as they bundled up masses of linen and left.

It was after four before the lieutenant or his wife could get sufficiently over their excitement to go to sleep. They were in far better shape than I was.

CHAPTER

XII

I HAD JUST drifted off to sleep when I was awakened by a banging on the screen door. The gray light of earliest morning showed the lieutenant in striped pajamas emerging groggily from the bedroom. A soldier at the door saluted. Was the Señora's luggage ready? The boat was waiting.

In the stress and strain of the night before, we had forgotten that the motorboat had been ordered for 6 A.M. to take me to Arica, the Colombian police post at the mouth of the Igaraparaná. It had to be back at Pucaurco by noon to attend to an errand up stream. Hastily, I shoved my hammock and overnight things into a bag and swallowed a cup of coffee. I tried to tell the Señora how much I admired her courage, how deeply I appreciated their hospitality at such a trying time. Mother and child were obviously doing very well. Sitting up in bed with the baby at her breast, the Señora was radiant.

The speed of the powerful motorboat after slow days of paddling was breathtaking. In barely two hours, we saw on the left (Colombian) bank a neat row of thatched huts and a larger low building of aluminum, shining silver in the sun. Two tall young men waited in the port to greet us. They were dressed in the gray-green uniforms and caps of the Colombian police, but each had a white bath towel draped over his cap and pinned under his chin. Counter-gnat measures. They looked like actors in a movie about the Foreign Legion, the taller one especially. He had just the profile, the square chin and the smoky-gray, heavy-lashed eyes for the part. He introduced himself and his companion. He was Corporal López, coman-

dante of the post. The sad-eyed young man with the thin face and a
softly hesitant voice was *Agente* Huertas.

I explained my mission. The corporal said I was in luck. A boatman named Alejandro who lived in Tarapacá, two days downstream,
was in La Chorrera now. He had gone up the Igaraparaná with part
of the supplies destined for the mission. A lot of cargo had been
lying in Arica for months awaiting transportation. Alejandro had
been able to carry only about a third of the stores on this trip. He
would return in a few days for another load and then I could travel
with him. After so many delays this sounded too good to be true.
As a matter of fact, it was, but I didn't know that at the time.

Meanwhile, the corporal and his wife would be happy to put me
up at their house. It was small, but they'd make room somehow.
Señora López was standing in the window when we climbed the
stairs to their house. She was wholesome looking, with curly blond
hair, and would have been really pretty if she had had any front
teeth. When she threw open the front door, my heart sank. Señora
López looked quite as pregnant as Señora Lingán had the morning
before.

The one bedroom was just big enough to hold two built-in
bunks, and the living room was so cramped that a narrow table
against one wall and the corporal's desk against the other left room
for only a couple of benches.

Wasn't there some other place, I asked, explaining that I
wouldn't think of imposing upon them. Perhaps the big aluminum
building at the end of the row of houses?

"Oh, there's lots of unoccupied space there," the corporal answered, "but it gets so hot I don't think that you could stand it. It
was sent prefabricated from Bogotá to be used as our administration and command headquarters. But when the sun shines down on
the uninsulated metal, it's unbearable. I had to bring my desk down
here to get any work done."

Airily I assured him that heat never bothers me. I'd be most
grateful if they'd let me have a room there. It didn't seem too bad
when we took my baggage in, just rather stuffy because all the
windows were closed. Of course, it was only about nine o'clock and
the early sun lurked behind a rapidly dissolving layer of clouds. A
narrow hallway led from the big room across the front of the
building to a pona cookhouse tacked on behind. On either side of
the hall was a doorless room, one of which held an iron cot with

strips of split palm laid lengthwise in place of springs on a mattress. That could be my bedroom, the corporal told me; I could stack my bags in the room across the way.

The partitions, like the walls, were aluminum. For windows there were hinged rectangles of aluminum in the outer walls. I moved toward one. "If I open this," I said, "and the window across the way, I'll have wonderful cross-ventilation."

"But there are no screens here," the corporal protested. "You'll never be able to stand the gnats. Around Arica, they're worse than anywhere on the river."

I looked skeptical.

"Really, señora," he went on. "About a year ago we heard that a very tough guy, an escaped murderer from the highlands, was on the Putumayo. I sent a patrol to pick him up. We kept him at the post, awaiting transportation, but he broke out at night and took off down the river. In the morning, we went after him I was in the searching party. Two days later we found him on a little beach. He'd gone off without a shirt and the bugs had got him good. We found him running around in little circles screaming, shouting, howling. From the waist up, he was a mass of swollen blisters. His mind was gone. He kept beating his arms, begging hysterically for us to save him.

"These stinging gnats can drive a man insane. No, señora, enough of these flying hellions can get in with the windows closed. You'd better try to get along without opening them."

A good story, I thought, told with imagination. Nevertheless, I unpacked my insect repellent first.

Now that I had a place to sleep, my thoughts turned to food. Of course, there was no place to buy any. I had a few cans of oatmeal left, a fair amount of instant coffee and a half a can of powdered milk. I could manage my own breakfasts in the cookhouse. But I wanted to save my remaining canned goods for the long trail to the home of the wild Witotos. I couldn't bank on being able to get more in La Chorrera. Hesitantly, I asked the corporal if he thought any of the families on the post would take a lunch-and-dinner boarder.

"My Señora and I would be very glad to have you eat with us," he answered.

I thanked him for his kindness, but privately decided to consult the Señora first. When I insisted on paying my way and suggested a sum I thought sounded fair, she was visibly delighted. "That would be splendid!" But a second thought wiped the smile off her face. "But, oh, dear, what can I cook for you? We haven't had any supplies for so long. There's no lard left, nor oil. No sugar, no flour, no rice or beans. All the hens have been eaten, so we can't offer you eggs. The hunting has been no good at all and the fishing worse. Señora, we've been getting along with nothing but salt fish and yuca and plantains. I'm afraid that you wouldn't be able to eat that sort of food."

I convinced her that I was, unhappily, accustomed to that diet. When she came to summon me for lunch, I was puzzled to find the table set for two instead of three. The corporal drew out a bench for me then seated himself at my side.

"But what about the Señora?" I asked.

"She serves us," he explained. "She will eat afterward."

I found the arrangement awkward and later I often urged her to sit at the table with us. There was room for three. But she always ate in the kitchen and they both seemed to consider it so perfectly natural that I wondered whether the corporal habitually ate in lonely splendor.

The corporal told me about the other members of his command. There were eight of them, all from the cool highlands around Bogotá, the capital of Colombia. Most of them were city boys, and since their tour of tropical duty was limited to a year and a half, they could hardly be expected to become expert jungle trackers and hunters in the allotted time.

"Actually," he explained, "it doesn't seem to matter too much. There is almost no crime in the area. Our principal duty is border patrol. And even though there are certainly not enough agentes to guard such a long frontier as our section of the Putumayo, it works out all right because there are very few attempts at violations of our laws."

Smuggling was no problem. There was nobody to sell smuggled goods to, no place to send them. The only communication with the more populated parts of Colombia was through the town of Leticia, down on the Amazon, and even Leticia had contact with the rest of the country only through the airlines.

Four of the agentes, as the Colombians call their policemen, had wives with them. The rest were shacked up with Indian girls from an Ocaina group living a half hour downstream.

But isn't that rather dangerous?" I asked. "Aren't the Indian girl's fathers and brothers apt to go on the warpath about it?" I was remembering the Peruvian some Jívaros had cut to bits on the Santiago River because he had taken a Jívaro woman to live with him.

The corporal laughed loudly. "Warpath! *Vaya*, señora! Old man Monje, the head of the clan, is tickled pink. It's very profitable for him to have a few of the daughters living with the whites. He never had it so good! When these guys are sent back to the capital, the first thing he'll do is try to make sure that their replacements will, ah, replace them in the shack as well as the barracks. Dangerous?" he snorted. "These Indians are civilized."

Sweet are the uses of civilization.

Eagerly I asked if there was a witch doctor in the Ocaina settlement. The corporal said there wasn't now. There had been an old man who knew "all that sort of stuff," but he had died years before the police had been stationed here.

"He was the one who magicked the lime tree," the corporal went on, "and maybe he did know something useful after all. Because that tree certainly is a wonder. Want to see it?"

We'd finished lunch, so he led me to the top of the cliff over the river and showed me a gnarled old lime tree whose thorny branches were so heavy with fruit that they had to be propped up with poles.

"Story is that the old geezer decided it would be convenient to have a tree that gave fruit all year round instead of only in season like all the others. That was back in the days before the police were here. When we moved in, the Indians went downstream. But old Monje told me about it. Seems the witch doctor and the other men of the tribe danced around the tree and sang songs to it. Then they sacrificed some sort of jungle animal and bathed the roots in its blood and God knows what else. But it's a funny thing. Look at that tree now! It's been constantly full of fruit, just like that, all the fourteen months I've been here, even when limes are supposed to be out of season and there's not another tree bearing anywhere on the whole river. They say it's always been like that, ever since they magicked it."

I stood there admiring the tree and slapping gnats. The midday sun was cruelly hot. I excused myself. After two nearly sleepless nights, I was exhausted. I found the air in the metal building stifling. I felt as though I were in the top part of a double boiler over a slow flame. Checking the knots of my hammock, I burned my hand on the wall, not badly enough to make a blister, but enough to hurt.

I couldn't remember ever having felt such heat. I had to keep my clothes on, for there was neither a door nor a curtain to shield me from the eyes of anyone who might walk down the corridor. I saw a desk with papers on it in the front of the building and I assumed that the men on duty used it at intervals. My shirt and blue jeans stuck to my sticky body. I could feel my brain melting and running down my neck. I wondered if they used this for a jail. Anybody locked here for a couple of hours would confess to anything or, like the poor murderer, escape and give himself to the gnats. Poor deliquescent delinquents. Poor deliquescent me. This was delirium or it would be pretty soon. The hell with the gnats . . . ! I had to get some air before I lost my mind.

I burned my hands again opening the windows. When I got the metal sections propped wide, I thought I felt a faint, sluggish breeze. But it was only the still air twisted and churned by a thousand tiny wings. Obviously, the corporal hadn't exaggerated. A mist of gnats swarmed through the windows. I hastily grabbed the repellent I had providentially unpacked and smeared it thickly over my face. Then I slept heavily.

When I woke I knew it must be late in the afternoon because I could hear the howler monkeys. They made an awful din. Thousands of them, I thought. Throughout most of the Amazon Basin, their ululation greets the dawn, goes on until the heat solidifies, then starts up again with the first presage of evening coolness. These were extremely conscientious howlers working overtime. It was as hot as it had been at midday. I lay there for a moment trying to think what their cry sounded like. One third wind in the trees, one third stormy surf and one third the sound you get opening a faucet when the water has been cut off.

Wide awake now, I instantly forgot all about the monkeys. I itched all over. I, too, had given myself as a feast for the gnats. My hands were covered with tiny spots. Idly, I began counting them, and got up to eighty-two on the back of my left hand without having started on the fingers. Then I gave up. Such statistics might be of documentary value but they were very bad psychology. The more you concentrate on bites, the more they sting. So I got up and went outside, first wrapping a towel around my head and neck. Throwing in the towel is an effective jungle counterattack.

A plump brown girl with slanting black eyes and a kinky permanent was climbing the notched log that served as a back stairway to the cookhouse, balancing a huge bucket on her head. Carefully she set it down, then turned to me and smiled, revealing very white teeth filed into neat, sharp points. They gave her the look of a shy, sweet-tempered shark. "Good afternoon, señora, she said. "Think maybe you want water for bath. Better you bathe here. Flies very bad now down by river."

I hadn't thought of being so intimate with the gnats. I would have returned from the river a punctured sieve. I thanked her from the bottom of my heart. Her name was María. She was Agente Huerta's girl and he had sent her to "attend" me. She prepared the meals for him in the cookhouse and she'd be glad to fix mine at the same time. When I explained my arrangements with the Lópezes, she seemed genuinely disappointed.

"Then, señora, I keep your water bucket full. Maybe you like I sweep your room mornings? Maybe you like I wash your clothes?"

I would indeed. Hurriedly, I dug out as much laundry as I thought I dared give her at one time. Then I gave her a few pesos.

She examined them wonderingly. "Why you give me money?"she asked.

I said it was to thank her for her trouble.

"You give me money to help you? What for? I help you anyway. No have to give money. I like to help." She didn't sound offended, just puzzled. I added to her perplexity by saying that was just the reason I would like to give some more money. Her permanent, I told her, would grow out in a few months and I would like her to get her next wave "in my name." That made everything all right.

The daily five o'clock assembly was finishing when, bathed and dressed, I stepped out the front door. All the policemen stood in line in front of the administration building while the corporal gave the next day's orders and an educational lecture on some phase of police work. Afterward, with proper ceremony, they lowered the flag. The morning and evening assemblies were about the only time one saw the entire post personnel together. Those not on guard or other assignments spent most of the day working on the plantations of yuca and plantains which furnished the post with food.

The corporal made introductions. The policemen were an assorted group in everything but age. They all appeared to be under thirty and they all made polite speeches of welcome. Then, as one man, they burst out, "Señora, what have you got to sell?"

I explained that I wasn't a peddler and told them of my mission. I thought one of them just might offer me a clue to another plant, but when I finished they looked at me blankly and said, "But surely you sell something, señora. You have so much baggage."

Just things I needed for the trip, I explained. However, they followed me inside. Would I sell them cigarettes? Would I sell them canned goods? Clothing? My boots? My radio? My wristwatch? Patiently I explained again and gave each man a pack of cigarettes. They accepted them eagerly and clamored for more, pulling wads of peso notes out of their pockets.

"But those are gifts," I said. "You can't pay me for them." They thanked me effusively but remained unconvinced.

"We've been out of cigarettes for months," a fair-skinned boy named Ayala told me. "Señora, you don't know how glad we will be to pay for as many as you'll let us have."

Again I told them that I needed all my supplies to exchange for medicinal plants I was seeking. I couldn't accept money. To do so would break the very laws they were here to enforce. I had no peddler's license—only a tourist visa which did not permit me to engage in any form of commerce. But if they knew of any medicinal plants . . .

They went away crestfallen. They knew nothing of jungle medicine. And they were men with four months' pay in their pockets and in all that time they hadn't been able to spend a centavo.

The sun was setting in a red shimmer when I went up to the Lópezes for dinner. The corporal stood outside his house, staring at the sky. "We'll have a big storm tonight," he said. "Can't see any clouds yet, but it's coming, and soon."

I asked how he knew.

"By the heat," he replied. "Whenever it's this hot, whenever there's no breeze and the sun is as violent as it was this afternoon, the people call it the *sol de agua*, the water sun. But how did you get along, señora? It must have been terrible in that metal building?"

"Oh, I slept all afternoon," I replied nonchalantly. I was determined to endure anything, even greedy gnats, except another accouchement. But it was a relief to learn that the afternoons might not always be that hot.

The whiplash speed of jungle storms never ceases to amaze me.

We were still picking at our salt fish when the storm struck. Thunder bowled across the sky, lightning hissed and crackled, and the rain made a noise like a thousand drums. I was sorry we didn't have a thermometer. I'd have enjoyed watching the mercury shrivel. The temperature must have dropped twenty degrees, dropped straight and fast as a rock falling off a roof.

In half an hour, the rain had steadied into a determined downpour with an I-can-go-on-like-this-all-night sound, so I ran for home. It was like plunging through a waterfall. The inside of the administration building wasn't much drier. Streams of water poured through the joints of the metal roof, and the storm blew waterspouts through the open windows. By flashlight, I slammed them shut, threw plastic sheets over my luggage, then investigated the bed. It was in the one dry corner of the room. Thankfully, I undressed, toweled myself, wrung out my clothes and climbed shivering under the blankets. My quarters now resembled an aluminum pot under a cold water faucet.

The next morning, one by one, the women of the post came to see me. They all looked somewhat alike, thin, bedraggled white women. Every single one of them had an empty gap where her front teeth had been. Their hair was scraggly and their clothing was invariably a faded, shabby dress, silt-colored from much washing in the muddy river, with men's trousers protruding oddly from beneath it.

And every one of them had come to beg me to sell her something, anything. They wanted to buy books in English, photographic film although they didn't have any cameras, things of no conceivable use to them. They were plaintively persistent, far more difficult to dissuade than the men had been, and I wondered how much of the night they had spent with their agentes scheming to separate me from the worldly possessions. They made me feel guilty. I had so much and they so little was the general idea they conveyed forcefully.

I had to keep reminding myself that I did not, in fact, have "so much." I had a mission to perform and I might not even have enough stores to get by if I kept on running into delays. After all, these women were at home. The rains had begun and the river was rising. Soon a boat would come along and they could get whatever they wanted. But where would I be then? Chasing wild Indians through the woods—if ever I were lucky enough to get out of my aluminum hotbox of a jail. I'd have nearly forty miles of trail to walk after leaving La Chorrera.

I gave them all the cigarettes I could spare. But with every new would-be customer, my luggage looked more mountainous. By the end of the day, I was thoroughly uncomfortable and out of sorts.

María was the only one who never asked for anything. When she brought my afternoon bath water, I asked her why the women wore dresses over their trousers. I could understand the trousers. They kept off the gnats. But why, I asked, didn't they just wear them with shirts?

María's back was toward me as she squatted, lowering the heavy bucket from her head. "Trousers uncovered not decent for women," she answered. Rising, she turned and her eyes fell on my blue jeans. She clapped both hands over her mouth and her dark face flushed darker. Then, wordless, she fled.

I didn't see her until the next morning. When I woke, she was standing in the doorless doorway of my room. "Good morning, señora," she said. "I hope you sleep well. I wait to tell you water is in kitchen."

"Why, María!" I exclaimed. "How nice you look!"

María, her face red but her head high, was wearing gray-green trousers and a man's shirt. She must have spent the night cutting an old uniform belonging to Huertas down to size. There was no sewing machine on the post, so she had to sew all the seams by hand. But she'd done a good fitting job.

"I think trousers very nice for women," she said gravely.

María is my idea of a lady, filed teeth or no.

CHAPTER

XIII

Sunday was the day I was waiting for, the day we were to visit the Ocainas. I dressed carefully, putting on my reddest shirt—all primitives love bright colors—and draped two of my gaudiest necklaces over it to act as bait. I tried to get a medieval turban effect with a towel so that it would fall gracefully into a snood to protect my neck from gnats. But it didn't work. After a number of attempts, I decided I'd be damned if I was going to be fashionable for those insects. I caked my face with repellent and wore the towel as a clumsy babushka.

There was no trail, so we went down the river in an unsteady little canoe which the corporal handled with alarming nonchalance. He wore his Foreign Legion cap jauntily, and I sat on my bare hands while frustrated gnats flew about us in a conference of war.

Pulling in at a large, neat clearing, we climbed the bank to a large, neat house on stilts. Inside there was a central hall with a number of doors opening from it into what appeared to be personal apartments. One of the doors bore a carefully lettered sign, "Please Knock Before Entering." Two treadle sewing machines, polished and shining, stood against the far wall.

Monje, the head of the family, must have been somewhere in the clearing, for he followed us as we entered the house. I turned quickly to greet him, but instead I swallowed a chuckling gasp. He wore a pink cotton hood. Then I remembered seeing other Indians with similar hoods to combat insects. Quickly he took off his pink cotton and I undid my terry-cloth white. Without our armor, we greeted each other politely.

Monje was a stocky, middle-aged Indian with puffy eyes. He

asked us to take seats on the benches lining the walls, then sent a little boy to summon the rest of the family. As the child passed in front of me, he startled me by turning to say, "With your permission, señora." The corporal was right again: these were civilized Indians!

The rest of the family appeared, half a dozen men and youths in well-pressed khaki, women in crisply ironed, light print dresses which were neither faded nor discolored and which actually fitted. Furtively I buttoned my shirt collar to hide the crude, gaudy necklaces I'd worn to impress the savages.

We sat and made very polite conversation. The younger members of the family spoke excellent Spanish. They had been sent to the mission school in La Chorrera. Everyone knew the Igaraparaná. They were sorry, but nobody was free to take me up there. Without a motor and gasoline, it meant sixteen days of upstream paddling, five days to a week to return. They were all terribly busy just now, trying to finish the construction of a new house and to prepare freshly cleared land for cultivation before the rains really set in.

One of the daughters-in-law rose and excused herself. It was time to treat her baby's eye again. I brightened and asked what seemed to be the matter. Just a little irritation. A gnat had flown into it and the baby had rubbed it.

"Have you a special remedy for it?" I asked hopefully.

"Boric acid solution," she said with pharmaceutical knowingness.

"But your people, don't they know medicines from the forest, plants that cure better than the white man's remedies?"

"I don't know, señora," she answered. All the other faces looked politely, woodenly blank.

I got it then. I was already defeated. Of course they'd already heard of my quest from the agentes living there, but they weren't giving. They had had too much fun poked at their beliefs by the only whites they knew intimately, the agentes who came and stayed eighteen months, and went away to be replaced by others who also found Indian magic ludicrous. That explained why I detected something sardonic in their courtesy. I was happy when Ayala came to take us to his house.

It lay some distance away, upstream and farther back from the river. The path took us through well-tended plantations and past an even bigger house which was about half built. Ayala's home was as small as the corporal's, just a little living-dining room, a bedroom and a cookhouse attached to one side. But the living-room walls were gaily papered with pages from *Life* magazine in Spanish. The display over the table featured an article on Harry Winston's diamond business with big photographs of some of his more splendid necklaces. It gave the room an air.

I liked Teresa. She was a gentle, serious-faced girl, obviously devoted to Ayala, and her courtesy didn't show the wariness I had felt in the others. Behind her reserve, I sensed a warmth, a friendliness that only needed encouragement. But sensing that she was too shy to be rushed, I didn't even mention plants.

Before leaving the post, I had put some bright combs for Teresa and some American cigarettes for Ayala into my handbag. I presented them now. Teresa was pleased with the effect of the scarlet combs in her heavy black hair, but Ayala was really delighted. His freckled face beamed as he told me that American cigarettes had always been the one extravagance he had allowed himself. They are expensive in Colombia and, of course, they are unobtainable on the Putumayo. As he eagerly stripped off the cellophane, he told me, "Until I came down here, señora, I never smoked anything else. The last time they raised the duty on them—I was in Bogotá then— I had to cut down on the amount I smoked, but that was still better than smoking black national tobacco. Real American cigarettes! This is wonderful, señora!"

Lunch was not salt fish, not even a fresh fish, but chicken! Teresa had killed one of the family's hens to give us a memorable lunch. Having eaten chicken made me feel optimistic. At least for a little while—until I got back to the post and the blow fell.

When we got out of the canoe, a woman squatting in the port washing clothes told us, with unbecoming gusto, that Alejandro, the boatman, had come and gone away again while we were at Ayala's.

"But where did he go? Back to La Chorrera?" I asked dismayed. She didn't know.

I pulled the hot terry-cloth towel off my head and started emoting all over the place. The one time I leave the post for a few hours I miss my only chance at escape. Stranded! Marooned in a double boiler full of ravening gnats!

And what about my work? What about uncounted thousands of sick who must languish on beds of pain until I came back with some miraculous remedy? What about the poor trusting pharmaceutical company waiting for those miraculous drugs? Worst of all, what about me? I threw my arms higher than my voice in large dramatic gestures.

I cannot remember often being as sorry for anyone as I was then for myself. Suddenly it occurred to me that my behavior was something less than gracious. My arms dropped and my face grew hotter. "Not that I don't appreciate how charming you've all been," I finished lamely.

The corporal's expression was quizzical. "Before you throw yourself to the piranhas, señora," he suggested, "shouldn't we ask the agente on duty just where Alejandro went? The law requires all transients to report their itinerary to the police, you know. Probably he ran down to Tarapacá to get gas. That's the only place on the river where he find any. It's a big Colombian army post."

And that was exactly what the boatman had done. What's more, the agente had told Alejandro that an anxious, and therefore profitable, passenger awaited him. Alejandro promised to return in five days. He would pick me up with the next load of the Padre's cargo.

Five days? That would be Friday. By Thursday I caught myself stopping to listen for the sound of a motor. That was silly. If Tarapacá were two days downstream, the return trip, bucking the current, must take at least twice as long. That meant a minimum of six days' travel. The sixth day brought no Alejandro. The seventh. The eighth. But, of course, I consoled myself, what riverman would arrive home after a long absence and start out again without taking a few days' rest in the bosom of his family. Surely I knew better than to expect such zeal from any sailor—particularly a tropical one.

But the ninth day came and the tenth, and it got harder and harder to keep on hoping. My one consolation was that if ever I got out of the post I could talk about the time I spent in a Colombian jail. For the corporal, after much hedging, admitted that the few prisoners they got were confined in the administration building to await transportation, though he wouldn't admit it until I pointed out that there was obviously no other place to put them. Someday, I thought, in a comfortable, air-conditioned, insectless bar, I shall be able to enjoy referring to my days as a jailbird.

The day after our lunch at Ayala's, Teresa came to visit me. I entertained her with a conducted tour through my belongings. She enjoyed it more than most tourists enjoy most sightseeing tours. For more than an hour, she happily fingered clothing, tried on necklaces, marveled at such mysterious, esoteric instruments as my hairbrush. I presented her with a lipstick and she was overjoyed. After every bag had been opened, camera cases and footlocker explored, she pointed to my plant press. "And what is that, señora?"

I almost said, "That, my pet, is what I've been waiting a long, hot hour and a half for you to ask!" Instead, I put on my best spider-to-fly manner and told her that my people, in the great country I lived in, wanted to learn from her people. We had many good medicines. We had sent many to her people, no? But every people has its own wisdom. We realized that her people knew many things my people did not know. My people had sent me to the Putumayo and other rivers in search of some of her people's wisdom.

"Already, I have learned much," I bragged. "Mostly from my friends the Witotos. They call themselves the wisest of all the tribes. Do the Ocainas know as much as the Witotos? Look, I will show you the things they gave me, they and the other Indians."

She pored over the specimens I had pressed with such care. I was proud of the way they looked. It showed how much I respected the native lore. I said, "I know that the agents, most of them, laugh at your medicine. But that is because they are people of little learning. Warriors are not necessarily wise men. Now the big chiefs in my country are different. They are learned men. And so they respect the wisdom of other learned men."

It seemed to be going over. Suddenly Teresa smiled. "This one, my people know it, too," she said, proudly pointing to the gall-bladder remedy Yori had given to me. "The brother of my mother's father knew much medicine. But he is dead."

I said that obviously the Ocainas had much knowledge and that I would love to take back some of their plants to my people. Teresa promised to bring me a couple of plants the next morning.

I waited eagerly. When she came, she brought some odd, wide dark-green leaves. "This one I know myself," she told me. "Is very good, señora. We take some leaf ground up in alcohol before the fiesta. You take this leaf and then drink and drink. You can get as drunk as you like, but the next day you will not be sick. You drink and not take the leaf first, you sick."

A hangover remedy! It wasn't quite what I'd expected of the demure young girl, but if it worked it should be worth a fortune! And I would be popular with all my friends back home.

Then she produced some rather spindly-looking weeds. "And

this very good for baby. You give a little bit of mashed leaves put them in baby's mouth as soon as he is born. That child no die. Will not die even when bigger. My mother, she had twelve children. Nobody ever die because she give us this when we born. All twelve now healthy. These two plants I know. Always we use."

I asked her if she knew any more. She shook her head sadly. No, my mother always take care if anybody sick."

At that moment, I blundered. "Teresa," I said, "why don't you ask your mother? I'll bet she knows all sorts of wonderful things. Here, look at these dress lengths." I turned to the heap of calico lying on the top of my foot locker. "This is the one you admired, the white with the yellow flowers. I want you to have it. It will remind you of how grateful I am for the wonderful lunch you gave us—and for the plants. And tell your mother that I'd like to give her one, too."

Teresa was delighted with the calico, but every time I mentioned her mother, she looked uncomfortable. It took a lot of argument to get her to promise that she would enlist the old lady's help.

The next day Teresa and her mother arrived. Teresa was far less friendly, her manner seemed frightened. The old lady was polite but cool. We chatted as the etiquette required, but it was difficult because Mama knew, or pretended to know, no Spanish. Teresa interpreted nervously. Mama had little interest in viewing my possessions, so I got out the calico and told her to take her choice. She examined the cloth minutely, suspiciously for a long time, then she chose a turquoise design.

But when we got to the subjects of plants, Mama knew nothing. She flatly denied that her people used any remedies other than those they'd learned from the missionaries. When I spoke of the wonders I'd heard her uncle performed, she merely said "Witchcraft" in a tone that practically brought the conversation to an end.

Shortly after that they left, but at the door Teresa paused to whisper, "I come back, maybe tomorrow." She came several times, but always accompanied by some member of the family. They were guarding their secrets. I knew better than to get Teresa into further trouble by trying to force the issue.

Meanwhile I tried various techniques for combating the heat and the gnats. It rained a lot, but nearly always at night or in the early morning. In the afternoons we had the sol de agua. I tried hanging my mosquito net over one open window and a sheet over the other.

But the gnats got around them and they kept out any languid breeze and finally I took to the woods during the heat of the day. The shadowy dimness gave me at least the illusion of coolness. Gnats like to stay close to the water's edge. If I went far enough into the jungle I might escape them entirely, but I might also never come back. For there were no trails and many an expert woodsman had been known to disappear permanently when he went too deep into the jungle. So I compromised by carrying my compass—feeling rather silly—and going only far enough to get away from the worst of the gnats.

But I was always tired and there was no place to sit down. The open spaces under the great trees are covered by more than just mud and wet leaves. Scorpions, centipedes and venomous spiders aren't too easy to see, but they are not too numerous here. Stinging ants are a different matter. "Ants in the pants" is a completely unfunny expression to anyone who has ever stretched out under a tree for a nap only to be awakened by an army of fire ants exploring the legs of her slacks. It's a traumatic experience.

The long days of waiting were not entirely without incident. One afternoon two men came paddling up to the post. They were on their way in the tiniest of canoes from the mouth of the Putumayo to some place far upstream, almost at the Ecuadorian border. "How long will it take you?" the corporal asked them. *"Quién sabe?"* they shrugged. "Who knows?"

There was entirely too much *quién sabe* in my life now. I had begun to hate that phrase. But these men had spent a night at Tarapacá. Eagerly, I asked them for news of Alejandro. They had never heard of him, of anybody who might be going up the Igaraparaná, but they did have one piece of news that set the post aquiver. The comandante at Tarapacá had received a radiogram that a *lancha*, a Peruvian trading boat, had left Iquitos weeks ago bound for the upper Putumayo. From its itinerary, it should reach Arica any day now.

From then on I was not alone in my listening. Any conversation was apt to be interrupted by a sudden gesture. *"Escuche!"* "Isn't that the sound of a motor?" Then somebody would sigh and say, "No, only the howler monkeys again." But the post was animated by a new excitement in making lists of purchases from the treasures the lancha might bring. They were like children waiting for Santa Claus.

When the great day arrived, we had plenty of warning. I was performing my usual sunny-morning chore, draping clothing and bedding over bushes in the sun. In the jungle, the cleanest clothes turn sour-smelling, spotted with mildew the color of rust, unless they are aired and dried every few days. Airing things at Arica presented a number of problems. First you had to tie or twist them around the branches in such a way that a sudden puff, or breeze would not blow them into the mud below. And once you had managed this, you couldn't go too far away for any sun hot enough to do real good might bring a brief, sudden downpour.

I was just finishing when I was startled to see Señora Beatriz, the corporal's wife, come lumbering around the corner of the house in high speed for anyone in her condition, shrieking, "Señora! Señora!" Her usually placid face was red, and she panted so heavily that for a moment I feared she might have the baby then and there. "Listen, señora," she gasped, "the lancha! You can hear the motor!"

I listened. Nothing. I bent my head and concentrated. Then, above the constant swish of the river and the buzz of gnats, I became aware of a rhythmic pulsing so faint, so distant, that it seemed little more than a vibration of the heavy air, something felt rather than heard. But it was there!

"Maybe it's Alejandro!" I exclaimed.

"No, no!" Señora Beatriz was very definite. "Alejandro has a very small motor. The sound is quite different. This is a big motor. It is the lancha!"

That was only the next best. But I did need supplies badly. "I'll get my list," I said. It was the list I'd started before I got to Estrecho. By now it had grown to mail-order catalogue proportions. "Have I time to dress before they get here?"

Señora Beatriz laughed. "Oh, it won't be here before evening. The river is so crooked that it comes quite close, then loops far away again three or four times before it reaches Arica. We'll hear the lancha and lose it again several times during the day."

She was right. The sun was setting when the lancha rounded the bend. It was a two-decker, actually I suppose not more than sixty or seventy feet long. But with a barge lashed to its side it looked majestic. Every lancha on these rivers has a barge, an *albarenga*, tied alongside to double its cargo capacity.

Everybody on the post stood on the banks waving and chattering with an animation I'd never seen in most of them before. The women looked entirely different. They had been busy with shampoos and curlers all afternoon and they had put on dresses so new that their bright colors hadn't yet been quenched by the mud of the river or by the terrible sun. Some had even applied lipstick. María, I thought, looked the nicest in a blue dress with a white band at the neck.

As usual, she stood a little apart from the others. I'd noticed that the other women were never very friendly with her. I gathered it was because of the Indian blood which, despite her filed teeth, she woodenly denied. Most of the white "wives" were poor drabs who had drifted here from God knows where, passing from agente to agente as new men came and their predecessors were transferred. They worked hard and served their men faithfully, but I guess their white blood was about the only thing they could pretend to feel superior about. So, like our poor "white trash," they made the most of it. But today was a day they had so long awaited and they were so happy that they were ready to be friendly with anyone. Today it was María who remained politely cool to their greetings.

The lancha edged to the shore and husky, brown-skinned deckhands jumped into knee-deep water to thrust the narrow gangplank firmly into the muddy bank. We all hurried down the slippery path. Everyone was too courteous to push or shove to be first aboard, but nobody was above a little fast footwork.

At the little shop amidships, there was disappointingly little to buy. People all along the river had been so avid for merchandise that a rationing system for essential commodities like sugar, lard and kerosene had been established, and thanks to that, everyone was able to buy a reasonable amount. "Luxuries" like sardines, corned beef or cheese in tins were in very short supply, but I was relieved to be able to stock up on oatmeal, powdered milk, flashlight batteries and a big tin of crackers.

On a back shelf amidst the bolts of dress goods, I spied a row of tall, shiny black rubber boots. What luck! My leather mosquito boots had proved quite inadequate for the puddles of Arica. Eagerly I asked for a pair, sized five. The obliging young man tending the shop slowly examined every pair, but sevens were the smallest.

"Never mind," I told him, "I'll just take the smallest you've got. It will be heaven to have dry feet again."

"But, señorita," he protested, "your feet will slide in them. You'll get blisters. I'll call Don Octavio. I think he has a couple of smaller pairs hidden away."

Don Octavio, owner of the *Otro Mago*, was a fat, smiling man, delighted to meet somebody he had heard talking over the radio in Iquitos. He made me feel like a celebrity. And he found some size five boots for me. A friend up the river had ordered some for his son. Don Octavio had brought along the size fives ordered, then thoughtfully added a pair of sixes, because with all the months that had elapsed, he was sure the boy's feet would have grown. They fit me perfectly. This pleased Don Octavio inordinately.

He was really getting a much bigger bang out of filling the needs of the river people than out of the money he was making. "What a trip!" he beamed. "If I didn't make rationing rules, they would have bought everything before I got half the way up the river."

"But wouldn't that be good business?" I asked. "You'd make the same money in much less time, and look at the saving on fuel."

Don Octavio was shocked. "And what about the poor people who have waited so long for Don Octavio to bring soap and clothes and something decent to eat?" He looked at me suspiciously. "You make the joke, señorita?" He laughed uproariously and I hastened to grin all over the face I wanted to save. Seeing my moderate bundle of purchases, Don Octavio boomed, "Is that all you've got?" I said yes, I'd have liked to buy more, but there was the rationing.

"No, señorita. The rationing is for the greedy ones. If I permit, they buy everything in the store to sell at a profit to their own neighbors. With you, it is different. You are not a *comerciante*. You are a foreigner and so entitled to consideration. And how do you think old Don Octavio would feel knowing that because of his rationing a foreign lady might be going hungry through the jungle? No, señorita. Choose what you will and then come have a beer with me."

This was indeed my lucky day. Over the beer, I confided to Don Octavio that there was one more thing that I needed. I had left the antenna, that ridiculous antenna, of my radio back in Pucaurco. The night of my arrival, I had tried all three of my little radios while I sat on my hard bed. None of them worked. I was sure it wasn't the batteries. Could he sell me some copper wire? I knew there was none in the shop, but didn't he have some for wiring in the motor?

He did and Don Octavio wound a good big roll of it for me. But he wouldn't let me pay for it. A little present, he insisted. And I needn't worry about spending the rest of my life in Arica. They'd return in a couple of weeks. If Alejandro hadn't reappeared, I could ride back to Iquitos on the *Otro Mago*. But now, señorita, it was time to take off.

I waved a long time though I knew that in the dark it was silly. I felt much more cheerful as I walked back up the hill in my fine new boots, my arms laden with loot. I had adequate supplies. I had definite prospects some day of getting out of my jail quarters. And I had met a fine man who cared for these jungle people.

Also I had my antenna. Everyone was so festive, maybe the Lópezes would like a concert. When I entered their home, the Señora greeted me exuberantly. "Tonight, señora, we will eat better. I have lard. Now I am cooking fried salt fish and fried yuca and fried plantains. And there's sugar for lemonade."

They were delighted with the radio. Carefully, fussily, I again tied the wire to the handle and the corporal helped me drape it around the room. When we turned it on, we heard fine, loud music.

"That's thanks to Don Octavio," I burbled. "If he hadn't been so kind about giving me some wire, I'd never have been able to use my radios again." Nobody had ever told me that no small radio will work in an aluminum building. "Tonight my luck is changing. Soon I will get out of your jail, Corporal López."

Two days later I was sprung.

XIV

T HE STEAMY quiet of late afternoon was suddenly torn by the roar of a motor too powerful to be Alejandro's, too swift for any lancha. A long, narrow open boat shot around the bend and swept toward our port. Hastily launched canoes took off from Monje's, bobbling and almost capsizing in the wake the boat kicked up. We ran down the path in time to see four bearded men jump ashore. They told us that they were a unit of the SEM. We all looked blank. *"Servicio de Erradicación de Malaria,"* the beard who seemed to be the boss explained. From what I could see through the brush, he was dark-eyed and handsome, in his early thirties. Gilberto Triana, chief of the Sector 3, Zone XX. They were fumigating all houses along the Colombian side of the Putumayo and its tributaries with DDT. Tomorrow they'd start work on the Igaraparaná, going all the way to La Chorrera. They'd do the Arica settlement on their return.

I was so desperately anxious to beg a ride that I grew tongue-tied. The corporal spoke up for me.

"Maybe you could give the Señora a lift. She's been waiting weeks for transportation to La Chorrera. She's collecting botanicals for pharmaceutical companies."

Triana eyed me dubiously. "It's not an easy trip for a woman. We have to stop to spray every house we come to. And this is an open boat. No protection from sun or rain. It's crowded, too, with all our technical equipment. And we have almost no supplies. We were up a side stream when the lancha passed so we weren't able to buy anything. We've had to live off the country the last few days."

Eagerly, I assured him that I was used to discomfort. I wouldn't mind. And I had stocked up on everything the lancha had to offer. I thought that I'd have enough to feed us all. "I have plenty of coffee, too," I added, remembering that Colombians are supposed to be great coffee addicts.

"*Bueno, señora.*" Señor Triana smiled. "If you could get this far from civilization on your own, you must be used to roughing it. We'll take off at six. Don't bring too much baggage. There just isn't room."

I thanked them excitedly, promised to bring only the minimum, and flew up the hill faster than I had moved in many a depressed, lethargic day. I wanted to get away before they changed their minds.

For once I did not detest packing. At first I was so excited by the prospect of escape that I found myself just picking things up and setting them down again. I had to calm down to make sense. I could leave all unessentials with the corporal until I returned. The Nikon with its extra lenses and the Contax would be sufficient cameras. A minimum of clothes, a few toilet articles and a couple of bath towels half filled one rubber bag. My hammock, mosquito net and one blanket filled another. Two small bundles would be easier to stow than one full bag. I hesitated over the medical supplies. All the little bottles in their little boxes took up a lot of room. I wasn't sick, hadn't been sick, didn't expect to get sick. And there was the mission at La Chorrera. Where there are the nuns, you can usually find expert medical care. I closed the footlocker on the medicines, set a couple of pots and some tin cups and plates by my bag and decided I was set to go.

That night, too excited to sleep, I kept remembering the time, years ago on another river, when I had caught pneumonia and dysentery. I was traveling by raft through uninhabited country, four days from even an Indian hut. I had no medicines and I'd never have got out alive but for the utterly improbable appearance of some international petroleum explorers.

They were going down the river in fast boats to rendezvous with a plane waiting to take them back to Lima. In the fading light, they almost didn't see me. It was early evening and my raft was already tied up to the bank. When they spotted me waving wildly, they waved back politely and kept going. Desperate, I crawled to the tail of the raft and started taking ballet positions. One more way ballet comes in handy. They swerved to see what on earth . . . ! In the dusk they could see only a trousered figure and they thought some poor guy had gone crazy. But they swerved. A fellow American was the last thing they had expected to see in one of the remoter jungle areas, and, least of all, a female hitchhiker. Their astonishment was as comic as my antics. But they flew me out to a hospital and saved my life. I swore then never again to travel without sufficient medical supplies.

So I got out of bed and put a good collection of antibiotics in a plaid plastic bag insulated with fiberglass which I had used for carrying cameras. But the medicines almost were left behind again when Señor Triana saw my baggage heaped alongside the boat.

"But, señora, we haven't got room!" he exclaimed. "The two rubber bags will fit all right, but those two big cartons and that plaid thing . . ."

"I'm perfectly willing to leave them, señor," I replied. "The cartons are nothing but the canned goods I got from the lancha and that plaid thing has medical supplies and some large-scaled maps of the region. I thought they might be useful. But I don't want to cause you any extra inconvenience."

"That's all food?" Triana beamed. "And medical supplies? All we've got is some sulfa and a lot of antimalarials. The maps will be a great help. We have none at all. We'll fit it all in somehow."

The boat was as full as it could be and still stay above water. Gasoline drums took up the most space; technical equipment occupied almost all the rest. Big compressed-air tanks for spraying looked like aqualungs. There were huge cans of powdered DDT . . . "That's the one thing we never run out of," Triana told me. Plastic-wrapped packages of papers and pamphlets and an extra motor in case of a breakdown. That boat was loaded!

The men themselves traveled light. They hadn't even brought cups or tin plates, just hammocks and a couple of changes of clothes. "We usually stop the night at a house of some sort," Señor Triana said, "and they usually lend us a few gourds. If not we can always cut big leaves. Nice and clean and no dishwashing."

I thanked my policemen who were up at this hour, frowned at my aluminum jail with its incarcerated gnats, who would no longer banquet on and off me, and stowed aboard. I was free. The motor zoomed into action around the bend of the Igaraparaná at a speed I had never known on a jungle river. I was so elated that I was full of talk. Though Triana and I crowded together on the only seat in the boat, the thirty-five-horsepower motor drowned out anything less than a bellow, and the wind snatched the words from my mouth. So I settled down to memorizing the names of the crew before I forgot Triana's brief introductions.

The tall, thin man at the tiller, who looked rather like a Texan, was Marco Antonio Jiménez, *Motorista*. Triana said he was the best mechanic he had ever known. José Ignacio Quintero, in charge of spraying, was the square-jawed young man lounging with every appearance of perfect comfort on the gasoline drums at our backs. I was uneasy about those gasoline drums. I wondered if I could smoke a cigarette without hearing my last, loud boom. But Triana lit one and so I decided it must be safer than it appeared. The cheerful round-faced boy squatting in the prow was Carlos Arturo Perdomo, listed as "Sailor," but later I learned he did anything from spraying houses to cooking our food.

The Igaraparaná, close to its mouth at least, is a medium-small river, wider than the Algodón but a mere rivulet compared to the Putumayo. The sun was still low and the lush forest shadowed the water so that the morning seemed fresh and cool. The wind of our passage blew away any gnats who might have been wafted out over the water for a last quick meal. It was a wonderful day to be getting away from Arica.

We reached the first house in about half an hour, though the corporal had told me it was hours upstream by paddle. It was the usual ramshackle pona construction on stilts with a couple of rooms walled off at the back. A surprised young Indian stood on the bank watching with unbelieving eyes the speed of our arrival. We all jumped ashore.

Triana explained our mission. The Indian just stared. "What's your name?" Triana asked. "Do you speak Spanish?"

The Indian said, "Yes, señor. I am Benito Torres."

Patiently Triana explained again. "Many months ago some white men came here in a boat almost as fast as ours. They asked how many people were in your family and they took samples of your blood on little pieces of glass. They gave you a white paper to keep and told you that soon other men would come to kill all the mosquitoes in your house. Remember?"

The Indian grinned. He remembered and at Triana's bidding went into one of the two rooms and emerged with a small white form bearing the seal of the SEM.

Triana nodded. "We are the men they told you about. We have machines to blow all over a white powder which will kill any mosquito which touches it."

Benito looked very happy. "Kill all gnats?"

"No," Triana answered. "It will kill only mosquitoes because they sleep on the walls in the daytime. It might kill a few gnats, but only if they touch the walls."

Gnats are a pretty fair example of perpetual motion. They sit down only on people, to read the menu and eat if satisfied. I know, I was their table d'hôte, special blueplate luncheon for too long. They seldom light on inanimate objects.

The Indian looked disappointed. "Better you make kill the gnats," he suggested. "Mosquitoes bite only night, people sleep. Not bad. Gnats bite daytime, very much. Very bad. Better you kill gnats."

Triana assured him that quite a few gnats would die. But, he explained, it was more important to kill the mosquitoes because their bite gave people malaria . . . fever.

Benito looked extremely skeptical.

"So now," Triana went on, "we will move out all furniture so my men can spray behind and under it. We must leave no place where mosquitoes can hide."

Benito nodded and called out something in his own language, which brought a shriveled old woman and a young boy running. They helped Quintero and Perdomo to drag out everything in the two rooms. It didn't take long. One table, two wooden boxes and two benches comprised their entire furnishings. Uncluttered is the word for jungle interiors.

Down at the water's edge, Perdomo and Quintero had shaken powdered DDT into a bucket of water and charged their sprayers. Now, the tanks strapped to their shoulders, they began spraying under the house first. A white vapor rose through the interstices of the slatted pona floor and I hastily went outside. When they had covered the underside of the house, they meticulously sprayed the walls and the roof, the undersides of benches and tables, even, to my astonishment, the back of a colored chromo of the Sacred Heart. They didn't stop until every square centimeter of surface was chalky.

While they worked, Triana filled out some forms and made notations on the Indian's card which he returned to him with strict instructions to guard it carefully until the next group, the doctors, came to make examinations and distribute antimalarial medication to those who needed it. By now Perdomo had stenciled in black on the front wall the magic letters DDT and the number one in a black circle.

We went back to the boat, but the labor of the two sprayers was not yet over. They had to recharge their tanks with air by laboriously using an old bicycle pump. The day was growing hot and they mopped their brows frequently. I seized the opportunity to ask Triana questions.

The fight against malaria was part of a world-wide program. UNICEF of the United Nations furnished vehicles, drugs and insecticides. Other expenses in each country are covered by the national treasury in collaboration with the U.S. Foreign Aid Program. Work in Colombia had begun a year before.

The first work in any area was geographical reconnaissance. One of those crews had made the initial visit to this area. Their survey provided estimates of the personnel, supplies and time which would be required for proper coverage of each sector, and determined, by blood tests, which areas were infected. After them came the fumigators such as our group. And these in turn would be followed by a medical crew who would examine all inhabitants and furnish antimalarial medicines to those who were infected. Their work, of course, had to be done last because until all the infectious mosquitoes were exterminated, any therapeutic measures would be of only temporary value. All the men in our party had been with the service since its initiation in Colombia and they all had found it an adventurous life. It was fun, Triana told me, at least this part of it. "But my office routine is dull. So I spend ten days of every month in Leticia on administrative duties and twenty on inspection tours like this one."

When the tanks had been pumped up and the men lifted them carefully into the boat, Triana explained that regulations required them to be kept always under ten pounds of air pressure so that they could be used as life preservers in case the boat capsized or someone went overboard.

This part of the river was thickly inhabited for jungle. We'd do a house, sprint upstream ten or fifteen minutes and find another. Getting out of the boat and into some shade so often made the heat of the sun hardly worth bothering about. It was not yet three o'clock when we reached a larger-than-usual house beside which stood a huge *maloca*. In the Colombian Amazon, a maloca is the traditional dirt-floored, round or oval Indian house whose walls are made of the same thatch as its roof. We had been warned that when we came to the maloca, we would have reached the end of the line. Beyond it there was no other dwelling for three or four days' paddling.

Señor Triana decided we would spend the night there. Or part of the night. We could never make it to the next houses in a day's journey, so it would be better to leave at moonrise, about two-thirty, he calculated, to start the long haul. That way we could hope to sleep the next night under a roof.

A maloca, I thought, might mean a tribal headquarters. At the very least it showed persistent respect for the old customs. It seemed promising. But there was nobody home except two women, one old, one young, dressed in neat, well-ironed cotton. The older one spoke a little Spanish. She told us that her husband was away. "My niece and her husband staying here. Her man, José, fishing. Coming back very soon," she said, regarding us distrustfully. "What you selling?"

Triana explained our mission and the others began emptying the two rooms of furniture. Auntie must have been a rich woman, judging by her possessions. To spray her room, they had to dismantle a real bed with head and footboard, though, of course, it had only pona slats in place of springs and mattress. In addition there were four big wooden trunks, padlocked, a serviceable treadle sewing machine and, wonder of wonders, a small, ancient Victrola. The turntable had long ago rusted into immobility, but, as Auntie proudly showed us, the crank could still be turned.

While the men worked over the house and the maloca, which was quite empty except for a couple of earthen pots, I tried to get acquainted. Auntie and niece accepted cigarettes, but maintained a deep-frozen reserve. The niece obviously understood never a word of Spanish and Auntie's conversation was limited to a "yes" or a "no." Her one unsolicited remark was, "You woman. You dress like man."

About five o'clock a canoe came round the bend, its single occupant paddling slowly, easily, until he lifted his head and saw our boat tied up in the port. Then his paddle churned the water like the entire Harvard crew in the last lap of a race. He jumped ashore

and ran toward the house. I called, "Good afternoon!" His ferocious scowl gave way to a look of astonishment when he heard the
voice of a woman. When Triana greeted him and explained our
business, he relaxed and became genial and chatty.

That evening, I remarked that José had looked pretty ferocious
until he found out how innocent our motives were. He had probably thought that the men were making passes at his young wife.
"Have any of you ever had trouble with the Indians on these trips?"
I asked. "Isn't this a pretty dangerous job sometimes?"

"Well, yes, señora," Triana said. "It is not without danger.
Jiménez was lost for four days in a place where the Indians were
bad."

Jiménez looked embarrassed. "Oh, I got lost for a while. Anybody is likely to sooner or later. It's just part of the job. Nothing
happened. We got out."

"But I'd like to hear about it," I insisted.

Jiménez frowned at the long, thin hands clasped between his
long, thin legs. He spoke slowly and hesitantly, as though he were
wondering why anyone would be interested.

SEM had been working on the tributaries of the Caqueta River,
an area so remote and difficult of access that it had been decided to
have the same crews do two phases of the program simultaneously.
They not only did the reconnaissance work of locating the houses
and taking blood samples to find out whether the region was
infected, but they also fumigated. From the base camp on the Mirití
River, Jiménez, Duque Flores and Theodulo Esterilla took off in a
canoe to find a group of Carijona Indians who had almost no
contact with civilization.

They had to find a tribal house near a big laguna. Finding the
entrance to the laguna had been easy. It looked like a fine, wide
waterway leading out of the river proper, but this was near the end
of a heavy rainy season. As they pushed their boat farther into the
channel, it narrowed and twisted between the branches of trees
whose trunks were hidden beneath the flooding waters. Finally they
emerged on a large lake. Watchfully, they paddled along its irregu-
lar border, searching always for an opening in the brush which
would indicate a path leading to a dwelling. For two days it rained
and stopped and rained again, but they found nothing.

Late in the afternoon of the third day, just as the rain stopped,
Duque squatting in the prow gave a shout. His outflung arm

pointed to a small bare patch of earth at the water's edge. A place to land at last!

They jumped ashore and wearily stretched cramped limbs, then set off to reconnoiter. Surely there must be a path nearby. But the day was fading under a gaudy sunset sky and the batteries of the flashlight were now totally dead. They spent the last minutes of light cutting palm leaves for a shelter and gathering wood for a fire. It was too wet to burn. But the three men felt, suddenly, lightheartedly optimistic. They were off that damned lake. They were on solid land. Tomorrow, some sign of habitation would surely turn up. But guard duty was even more important now, and the two who slept, slept with their machetes close at hand.

In the morning, casting through the forest near the bank, they found a trail, small, faint, half obliterated, but still a trail. Jiménez and Duque shouldered the heavy tanks, Esterilla put plastic bags of DDT in a bucket and tucked a bicycle pump under his arm and they set off. A trail meant people, and people, however savage, however hostile, meant houses to be sprayed. And food.

Hopefully they followed the track. The rain began again, making visibility poorer. This fourth day of hunger brought a dizzy weakness which made their loads staggeringly heavy and sometimes blurred their vision. Waveringly, they followed the faint track, lost it, found it again, and stumbled on. When at last Jiménez, who was ahead, saw a house, he thought he was hallucinating.

But it was a real house, with crude palm thatch to the ground and midget-sized doorways front and rear. Low doorways are sound strategy for warlike tribes. A man must enter crawling, and what could be more vulnerable to a war club or wooden spear than a man on hands and knees?

All three men shouted. "Ola!" "Amigos!" "Buenos días!" Silence. They shouted some more. Nothing happened. Esterilla squatted and peered through the doorway. "I think it is empty," he said. "No cookfires smoking."

One after another they slithered in. The dim light which filtered through doorways and chinks in the thatch showed no cookfires, no pots, only two palm-fiber hammocks and a crude basket sitting against a wall. Duque grabbed it. "Meat!" he exclaimed. In the basket lay part of a smoked leg of tapir. They slashed the tough black meat from the bone and ate it cold and, except for the smoking, raw. It wasn't nearly enough. They were still hungry when they finished, but searching turned up nothing else, so they settled down to sleep for a couple of hours.

When they awoke feeling better, they decided to find the Indians. But the trail ended at the house. The three men circled, looking for a footprint, a broken seedling, anything which might show the direction their unwitting hosts had taken. They found nothing until Esterilla suddenly gulped and pointed. Half hidden behind a tree, a savage stood watching them. Except for a short grass skirt, he was naked, and his face was painted with black stripes. Bright colored feathers were stuck through his earlobes, and in his hand he had an unpleasantly stout war club. But he was evidently alone.

The three men stretched their mouths in what they hoped would be recognized as welcoming smiles. *"Buenos días, amigo!"* they called, making friendly gestures. The Indian glowered. Then he began slowly to back away. Duque, tall, spare and fleet, darted around to cut off the savage's retreat. Jiménez tore off his shirt and tossed it at the Indian, calling, "For you! A gift!"

The Indian obviously knew no Spanish, but he seemed to understand the gesture. Cautiously, still poised for flight, he advanced and snatched the shirt from the bush on which it had fallen. He shook it out and looked wonderingly from it to the white men who were grinning like apes. It was a khaki shirt, badly snagged and soiled, but the Indian found it beautiful. Caution forgotten, he thrust his arms into the sleeves. He put it on backward. The tail hung to his knees and the collar swallowed up his chin. Quickly Esterilla snatched off his own shirt and put it on again to demonstrate how shirts are worn. The Indian grinned and fired a sputter of syllables in an unknown tongue as he followed suit. He couldn't seem to manage the buttons, so Jiménez quietly walked forward and did them up for him.

The Indian slowly rubbed a hand over the cloth, twisted his body within it, and broke into a large grin. Chattering, he led the whites toward his house. They were friends.

Near the back door stood a hollow tree. The Indian paused to beat out a booming rhythm on it with his war club before he ushered them inside. He darted back and drummed a long, syncopated message before he returned to squat on the dirt floor with his guests. He pointed questioningly at the silver tanks.

They tried to explain their work, but Spanish was no help, so they resorted to pantomime and sound effects. Jiménez charged a sprayer and blew a little DDT on the wall. Little Esterilla gave a masterful impersonation of a mosquito humming through the air, lighting on the powdery patch and dropping dead. The savage choked with laughter, but he seemed to catch on and allowed them to continue spraying. They were about half through when the rest of the tribe, summoned by drum telegraph, began to appear. Jiménez counted twenty-eight men, women and children in all.

They arrived in small groups. The men, short, swarthy, and muscular, were dressed like their host, whose name appeared to be Upi, Umbi or Umpi. It sounded different each time it was said. The women wore only girdles of tree bark which had been pounded until it was soft and supple. Their flat faces were unpainted but adorned with bright feathers stuck into little holes pierced in the wings of their nostrils. Some of them carried baskets of yuca on their backs. The children were naked.

The women remained timidly in the background and began preparations for cooking the yuca. They peeled it, then grated it on the hard-thorned sections of bark from the spiny palm. The men's reserve was conquered by their curiosity. They fingered the cloth of the white men's clothing and intently examined their technical equipment. A few had to be restrained from tasting the DDT powder. An old Indian of imposing bearing stepped forward and tapped himself on the chest. "Me chief," he told them in barely intelligible Spanish. Several times he told them his name, but they couldn't pronounce it. Umpi had apparently explained their mission, for the old chief indicated that they might continue their work.

The spraying finished, it was time to collect blood samples. Very carefully, the white men explained the process and its purpose to the chief. He nodded sagely, but didn't understand a word. They tried a demonstration; Jiménez let Duque puncture his skin and prepare a blood specimen on a glass side while the savages crowded around, watching in fascinated silence. When the men had finished, there was a burst of animated conversation. Every man had to examine the little glass slide. But when Jiménez tried to persuade them to follow his example, their friendliness vanished. Even Umpi drew back and regarded them with cold suspicion. To put white powder on walls was one thing. To take a man's blood and imprison it on a sliver of magic stuff as clear to the eye as a raindrop but as hard to the finger as rock, that was very different. Would a man's spirit be trapped with his blood? What kind of witchcraft were these strangers up to?

At that moment, the women created a diversion by bringing food. It was tasteless, but the still-famished men gorged gratefully. The savages withdrew to the other end of the house to eat, talking in low tones and throwing frequent, suspicious glances at the whites. Darkness had fallen and the light from the torch of oily wood flickered the walls with strange shadows. In its dull, unsteady glow, the painted faces and the bright feathers of the Indians looked more savage, more hostile than ever. When they had finished eating, they didn't return. The whites remained isolated in the corner where they had first thrown down their gear.

"We didn't exactly post guard that night," Jiménez said. "But we didn't sleep much either, and when one of us went outside for a minute, the others went, too."

Low-voiced conferences during the long dark hours brought them to a decision. They would not leave until they had completed their mission. They had never failed on a job yet. Their orders were to get blood samples, and blood samples they would get. They'd think up some way.

In the morning, the atmosphere had not improved. The savages pretended the whites weren't there. The women, grating their eternal yuca, didn't even look their way. It would be pretty embarrassing if when breakfast was served they weren't offered anything. To be passed up would mean almost as bad a loss of face as to beg food. It was time for a show of independence, so the three men walked out into the woods where Duque had noticed a *chonta* palm. The chonta's heart is crisp and delicately flavored; in the States, it can be bought in cans labeled Hearts of Palm at luxury stores. They found the tree and felled it. The heart of palm was thin fare for hungry men, but they lingered over it until they knew that the Indians would have finished eating. On their way back, they heard the booming of the tree drum, rhythmic and mysterious. They hurried on. It might mean trouble, but they had to know.

Cautiously they approached a group of shouting and wildly gesticulating Indians moving in a shuffling circle that looked like a curtain raiser for a war dance. Each man was either looking at or talking to something hidden in the center. At times the interweaving arguments of the Indians would reach an excited pitch, but underneath Jiménez could hear laughter.

After a long time, one of the Indians noticed their uninvited guests. The circle broke and in the center was an Indian laughing hilariously. With relief, Jiménez noticed that he was wearing pants and a shirt.

"It was real luck at last," Jiménez told me. "An Indian arrived who had lived with white people. He was a member of the tribe, but he had worked for years for some Peruvian rubber firm and he was back only to milk the trees in this area. He had been laughing at his unsophisticated relatives who thought we were there to extract their souls. So we paid him to talk them into giving us a drop of blood without their spirits. And then we paid him to guide us out of there. He showed us where the channel was hidden by the trees, and once we got into it, we were back at camp before night.

"So, you see, señora," Jiménez concluded as though he had taken up my time with a foolish yarn that certainly must have disappointed me, "nothing really happened. It was all just part of the job."

Triana obviously agreed with him, for he announced that we'd better stop talking and get some sleep. It was not quite dark, but we'd have to get up in a few hours. We all got into our hammocks.

Judging from the sounds of quiet breathing, falling instantly asleep was also part of the job. I wished I could learn that. I tried to go to sleep as they had, but it was just too early, so I got out my notebook and wrote up the day's events by flashlight. Checking the calendar, I discovered that tomorrow would be Easter. I was far behind schedule, but at last I was really on the final lap of the way to the wild Witotos and the discovery of unheard-of medical magic.

I thought of the story Jiménez had told me. The quiet way he accepted fatigue, hunger, even danger as all just part of the job. I resolved to be as dedicated as these men were and as philosophical, and to stop chafing at delays and discomfort or at least not to be so temperamental as I had been with the corporal a few days before. I lay awake a long time.

Such an Easter I hope never to have again.

By the afternoon of the following day, we were less than two days from the mission at La Chorrera. With the houses closer together, we had frequent chances to cool off or dry off as the case might be. At one of the houses I found a Witoto named Benito who had actually met the wild Indians I was so anxious to find.

He'd been accompanying the former head of the mission at La

Chorrera, old Padre Luis, who had been replaced by two younger men. They were hunting along the trail between La Chorrera and El Encanto. The third day they found footprints, many footprints, crossing the track. Following them for three hours, they came to the house of a group of Witotos dressed only in G-strings. Angry at the intrusion, they menaced the newcomers with war clubs. When Benito identified himself as a member of the tribe, they only grew angrier and accused him of being a spy for the whites, the evil whites who enslaved Indians.

"Padre Luis' beard what saved us," Benito told me. "Only the beard. The padre big man and beard white and bushy. Stick out above Indians' heads. They never see beard before. It frighten them. They let us go. But say we return they kill us for sure. The padre he want stay convert Witotos. I no want stay. Padre no listen to me. But they chase us with clubs all the way to the trail."

I tried to persuade Benito to take me to the savages, but he was horrified. "They kill us," he said. "They no like white men. Say white men make them slaves."

I insisted that the Witotos wouldn't think that of a woman. Well, maybe not, Benito said, but he was no woman. No promise of largess would persuade him to have any part in such a deal.

"You're not really serious about trying to make contact with those savages, are you?" Triana asked when we left Benito.

I said of course I was. That was why I had come to the jungle.

"You're either crazy or suicidal," Triana said. "The padres will never let you go."

I argued that I'd be perfectly safe among such people because they were not afraid of women. I cited the case of the Free Tribes Mission in eastern Bolivia where I had met some woman missionaries living with the Ayoré tribe which had killed five of their men. I also told him about the better-known but similar case of the missionaries who had been killed by the Aucas in Ecuador. The widow of one and the sister of another man they had killed are now living peacefully with the tribe.

"You're crazy," Triana repeated. "They'll kill you."

"Look," I told him rudely, "I've met a lot more wild tribes than you have and I know what I'm talking about."

That's not the sort of thing you say to any Latino. We ended the day sulking.

L<small>A CHORRERA</small> means the rapids. The river there is throttled by rocky cliffs. Thousands of tons of water foam and tumble down a long, uneven natural stairway of jagged stone to pour into a wide round basin that is the upper limit of navigation on the Igaraparaná. It makes a lovely roar.

I got there about nine in the morning. We'd spent the night at a house a half hour downstream in an area so thickly populated that the sprayers would have to work there all day. Triana had been kind enough to suggest that there was no point in my waiting around. He and Jiménez could run me up to the mission and come right back.

Padre Gregorio, a tall, thin priest with a very black beard above the very white habit of the Passionist Order, was waiting on the shore. He accompanied us to the rectangular white-painted adobe buildings of the mission set on a high bluff some distance from the water. Padre Plácido was waiting there with hot coffee ready for us. We drank it sitting in the neat, white kitchen. Padre Plácido's name became him. He was a plump, smiling young man whose beard looked even bushier because of his round face. They had both arrived from Barcelona only a few months before. It was great good fortune for them, they assured me, to be sent to such interesting work and to be sent together, for they had been friends since seminary days. That couldn't have been too long ago, I thought. Neither of them appeared to be over thirty.

Remembering Triana's reaction, I felt a bit wobbly about the matter of my visit to the savages. But I could never manage it without the padres' help. I began by asking about the trail to El Encanto. With all this rain, would it be under water?

Never, they said. It was a splendid trail, almost like a road. They'd seen part of it. It even had kilometer signs. It was much traveled and easy walking in any weather. No trail is easy walking as far as I am concerned, but this was no time to say so.

I told them of my plan and to my surprise they welcomed it with enthusiasm. Immediately they began considering what they could do to help. Padre Gregorio said, "We can get you reliable bearers, as many as you want for as long as you want."

"And we can give you supplies," Padre Plácido added. "True, we're rather badly off at the moment, but we'll take you through the storerooms and you can help yourself."

Thanking them, I mentioned that they obviously knew a lot about Indians for such newcomers. Most people unfamiliar with the tribes always think they are more dangerous to women than to men.

They explained that they had learned a lot about dealing with primitives from the Mother Superior at the Convent here. "Our nuns are an order founded early in this century for the express purpose of converting the heathens," they told me. "Our Reverenda Madre herself has gone into some quite hostile tribes in Colombia and Ecuador and made friends with them. That is the work of the *Orden de las Inmaculadas*. She, too, claims it's safer for a woman."

"The Inmaculadas . . . in Ecuador? She wasn't one of the three Inmaculadas who went in to the Salasaca Indians in Ecuador, was she?" I asked eagerly.

She was indeed.

I remembered the story well. I had heard about it when I lived in Quito. The Salasacas are not jungle Indians but a mountain tribe which lives in one of the most civilized and densely populated agricultural districts of the Ecuadorian highlands. But although surrounded by the white man's culture, they have for centuries refused to have any part of it.

They are a proud people. Legend has it that they originated in the highland plain around Lake Titicaca, between Peru and Bolivia, and were conquered by the armies of the Inca during the expansion of the Inca Empire. But they were valiant warriors and refused to stay conquered until the Inca applied the Empire's technique for dealing with recalcitrants. They transferred the entire nation of the Salasacas to a place so distant from their home that they would be among strangers and could no longer stir up rebellion among their neighbors. In order to maintain the health of the vanquished, the Inca transplanted them to an area whose climate and altitude were similar to their own. The Salasacas were sent to the Ecuadorian plateau.

The Spanish came, but the Salasacas never acknowledged their rule. Through the centuries, they have clung to their old traditions and they admit to no conqueror except the Inca. Even today they wear the black clothing they were supposed to have donned as mourning for the death of the Inca Atahualpa. And they have stubbornly barred all whites from their territory. Those rash enough to enter are first asked, then ordered, to leave. Then, if necessary, they are thrown out bodily. But since the Salasacas, left to themselves, have always been decent, orderly people, the Ecuadorian government has respected their tribal integrity. To such a degree, in fact, that when plans were made to push the Ambato-Quito highway through Salasaca territory, the Ecuadorian minister of public works gravely conferred with the Salasaca minister of public works.

The Reverenda Madre José de Arimateo was one of the Catholic missionaries who in 1945 braved the Salasacas. They entered quietly, two priests and three nuns, and for three months nursed the sick, taught children and tried to implant notions of hygiene in addition to their religious work. As they had promised, they withdrew at the end of three months. Little time passed before a delegation of Salasaca dignitaries arrived in Quito. They visited the minister of the interior. "We have come to the capital," they told him, "to buy the *madrecitas*."

In vain the minister told them that the nuns were not his to sell. They must consult the archbishop. The Indians didn't know about archbishops; they thought the minister was just trying to put up the price. So they went to the president. The president arranged a meeting with the archbishop and the Salasacas were astonished to learn that they could obtain the services of these valuable women free of charge. Gravely, ceremoniously, they expressed their thanks.

I had always wanted to meet one of those nuns. Actually I did meet three of the Inmaculadas while I was making precensal studies of jungle Indians for the first Ecuadorian census in 1950. I was riding down a mule trail one hot afternoon when I met three nuns in long, gray habits. They were walking at a good pace, and they held the folds of their voluminous skirts, heavy with clay mud, gathered in one hand. But the skirts still dragged so modestly low that I would never have known they were barefoot if I hadn't seen that each of them carried a pair of stout, high-laced shoes.

They were on their way from one mission to another and had been walking all day. I thought this trail heavy going even on a horse, for it was hilly country and the bottom of each hill was a morass. But the nuns looked fresh and cheerful, as though it were early morning instead of late afternoon, and they laughed aloud when I asked them why they didn't wear their shoes instead of carrying them. "We don't slip and slide so much barefoot," the oldest of the three told me. They went on their way still smiling.

The Mother Superior came to take me to the room the nuns had prepared for me in the convent. She was a small, slight woman with fine bones in her face. Her nose was delicately aquiline and her eyes, large and deep-set, were the reddish-brown color that so often goes with auburn hair. I wondered whether the hair hidden under the white coif and gray veil was auburn. But it was probably gray by now, for though she moved with a swift smoothness that was deceptive, she must have been well into her middle years.

My room was large, whitewashed, airy and cool. The first time I had visited a jungle convent, I had been surprised by the comparative luxury of the appointments and the quality of the food they served me. I soon learned that accommodations the nuns permit themselves are very different from what their guests enjoy. Their own quarters were Spartan, their food very simple, and the dishes from which they ate were coarse as their bedding. Every luxury that falls into their hands is lovingly saved for the pleasure of visitors.

The other four nuns came to meet me. All were Colombians from Medellín except one. She was the nun who did all the cooking, and she was an Otavalo Indian from Ecuador. They showed me through schoolrooms where big and little Indian girls rose and welcomed me politely, through the laundry rooms where Indian girls learned to wash and iron and through the dressmaking school where bigger girls worked at sewing machines. I saw the dormitories with neat rows of cots under bright bedspreads and the dining room where table manners, strange indeed to Indians, were patiently supervised.

My lunch was brought to a table in my room when we finished our tour. On pretty china, I was served delicious chicken soup, exquisitely seasoned chicken with rice and, wonder of wonders, green string beans from their own vegetable garden. That was the first green vegetable I'd eaten since leaving Iquitos and I had two helpings. The Indian nun who did the cooking was an artist.

After coffee, the Mother Superior came to ask me a favor. There was an Indian who was very sick. He'd been bitten by a snake more than a fortnight ago and they were afraid he was going to die. Would I examine him and tell her how he should be cared for?

I said that I would be happy to help in any way that I could. As we stepped into the hot sunshine, it suddenly occurred to me that at no time had I mentioned knowing anything at all about medicine. I stopped and stared at her.

"Reverenda Madre," I asked, "what made you think I might know what should be done for this Indian?"

Her eyebrows arched and she lifted one fine-boned, work-reddened hand. "But surely you must. It is what we prayed for. Our nursing nun got very sick and had to be sent away to a hospital. No one has come to replace her. She was as good as any doctor, but the rest of us, even the Padres, know nothing at all. So ever since we found José in such terrible condition, we have prayed constantly. Now you appear. Is it not clear that God in His great goodness has heard our prayers and sent you to save José?"

That really shook me. "But, Madrecita," I protested, "it is true that I went to medical school, but only for eighteen months. And I worked only in physiology—the study of the normal body. I've never worked with the sick at all. And it was so long ago! I know very little!"

The more I talked the more upset I got, but the Mother Superior only smiled radiantly. "How good God has been to us. He sent you because you had medical training. He has taken the matter into His hands. You will know what to do and you will find the way to cure José."

She spoke quietly but with such perfect conviction that the clenched feeling under my diaphragm relaxed a bit and I was able to enter the sickroom with at least an appearance of confidence. Two

Indian women were waiting outside the door, José's old mother and his thin young wife. Entering, I was almost overwhelmed by the stench. It was horrible. The still air was heavy with the odor of putrefaction, the odor of death.

The Mother Superior looked at me quickly. "I should have warned you," she whispered. "It's José's sick arm. It smells so dreadful that he's been having us change the dressing twice a day, even though the slightest movement, the faintest touch is agony to him. But he says he cannot stand the odor. It nauseates him."

The low-ceilinged room was dim enough to make it seem not too different from an Indian house. Big windows, any windows at all, are foreign to the natives and this room had only one long, narrow opening high under the rafters. The light that came through it fell on a white cot against the wall. A Witoto in his twenties lay on it. The bad arm, bandaged from fingers to shoulder and folded in a clean white bedspread, made a greater bulk than the emaciated body under the spotless sheet. José's face was all cheekbones and tight-stretched skin with an ugly grayish color under the brown. His eyes, in deep, hollow sockets, showed a yellow line of eyeball through the slitted lids, and he lay motionless. I thought he was unconscious until the Mother Superior spoke.

"José! Look, José! Here is a Señora who has come from very far. She has the medicines of the white people and she is going to make you well again."

With visible effort, José rolled his head on the pillow and through fever-cracked lips mumbled, *"Buenos días, señora."* I put my hand on his forehead. It was dry and very hot.

"Have you been watching his temperature?" I asked.

The Mother Superior said she couldn't. Their thermometer was broken. I had a spare which I could give them. I ran to my room to get it and while there picked up my entire medical kit, hoping that the sight of all those bottles might raise the boy's morale. I found his temperature a shade over 104°. When I took the thermometer out of his mouth, he said, "Body hurt. Arm hurt, smell. You change cloth, please?"

José's wife was sent to the kitchen for boiled water to soak off the dressings and the Mother Superior gave me the case history. A bit more than a fortnight ago José had gone hunting. He noticed a cave in the rocks and, investigating, a snake struck his hand. By the time he got his arm out of the hole again, there were three sets of puncture marks at the base of his palm. He got home all right, though the pain was very bad, and his people applied native remedies. After a couple of days, he seemed better but the hand would not heal. It was painful and swollen. Then the wrist and arm began to swell.

Word was brought to the nuns and they paddled four hours downstream to visit him. Finding him sick and feverish, they gave him one shot (400,000 units) of penicillin. They returned, confident that he would get better. Word came four days later that he was worse. The madres returned and gave him another shot of penicillin. A few days later, he was brought to the mission on a stretcher. He had been there two weeks now and though they had given him several more shots of penicillin, he had grown steadily worse.

I thought I understood it now. The crucial period for the action of snake venom is supposed to be the first twenty-four to thirty-six hours. Anyone who can survive the poison that long will usually recover unless an infection from the snake's fangs sets in. Such infections are dangerous and that is why all first-aid courses emphasize the necessity of careful, deep disinfection at the site of the punctures.

José was no longer suffering from the snake venom, but he had developed a galloping septicemia. The native remedy his people had given him probably curtailed the effects of the poison. But they had obviously used no disinfectant. The small doses of penicillin may have made the infection much more virulent as the invading bacteria become penicillin-resistant. I thanked God that I had brought other types of antibiotics. I hoped the infection wouldn't be resistant to the ones I had, for José was in critical condition.

"Have you given him a lot of fluids?" I asked.

"Oh, no!" the Mother Superior replied. "He won't drink any water at all. His people believe it's fatal to drink water after a snake has bitten them. He didn't take broth and soup after the first week. He can't keep it down."

I looked at her aghast. Weeks of fever and no liquids. Of course he was terribly dehydrated. I couldn't see why his pulse, though fast, was still strong, why he hadn't gone into irreversible shock long before this. I asked for lemons and sugar to be sent with the boiled water. When they came, I filled a half-pint cup with well-sugared lemonade. Then I got out two capsules representing 250 mg. each of mixed antibiotics and another of vitamins in therapeutic dosage. He looked apprehensive when I handed them to him.

"You must swallow the capsule with all that is in this cup," I told him. "I know that you cannot drink water, but this is not water. This is medicine. The capsules you must take with the lemon because lemon makes the medicine strong. Lemon cures much sickness. You know that, don't you?" I took a chance there. But I knew that many tribes have great faith in the medicinal value of lemon juice.

José obeyed, swallowing the capsules and sipping the lemonade. He was about halfway through it when he suddenly put down the cup.

"I cannot. I am going to throw up."

"You will not! I forbid it! You will not throw up! I will not allow you to!"

I fairly snarled at him. The sudden outburst surprised me as much as it did him, but it was the only thing that would have worked. José's eyes widened for the first time and he lay very still staring at me. But he kept those antibiotics in him. A moment later, he put out his hand for the cup and sip by sip swallowed every last drop. That stayed down, too.

The Mother Superior had soaked the bandages with water from the kettle. Now she began to remove them. Her hands were steady and gentle, her face soft with pity. José's mouth widened and turned down in a classic mask of tragedy and he made little grunting moans as she worked. When she pulled off the last long pad of gauze, sticky with greenish pus, the stench grew so strong, the sight was so ugly, that I had trouble keeping my stomach and face steady. I don't think I could have touched those bandages, but the Mother Superior folded them neatly and set them aside. She even managed to smile at José as she said, "Poor boy, it hurts now, but it will be better soon."

The arm itself was truly appalling. One great abscess from the heel of the hand to the elbow, another from just above the elbow all the way to the armpit, and in the armpit a third, all covered by a thick blanket of pus. The nun picked up a large black bottle and started pouring a brown liquid into a basin of water.

"I've been washing the pus off with creosote and water because that's the only disinfectant I could find. Then I put on a fresh, dry bandage after I've got it clean."

I tried not to look shocked. "We won't need that now," I hastened to explain. "The antibiotics will disinfect through the bloodstream. I'm going to give him two grams daily to start with. And I think we'd better just wrap up the arm and not try to scrape the pus off. The more pain he suffers, the more exhausted he gets and he needs all his strength to get well. Anyway, creosote isn't really very good for a case like this. It's awfully hard on tissues. Are you sure you have nothing else?"

"We have a whole room full of medicines, but nobody knows what they're for," she told me sadly. "Except, of course, the castor oil and the boric acid."

"Boric acid would be fine," I said. "We can keep the dressings wet with that and it will be a lot more comfortable for him."

They had pounds of boric acid. We made up a solution with the boiled water which I put into a thoroughly washed plastic squeeze bottle which had contained nasal spray. I thought it would seem more magical applied that way. We drenched the dressing and I gave the spray to José's mother, instructing her to keep the bandages wet day and night.

"Now you will sleep," I told José. "And in another hour, I will return and give you more of the lemon medicine." His eyes closed, the shadows around them and under his jutting cheekbones were frightening. He looked dead! I grabbed his wrist. The pulse was still strong and he opened his eyes to say, *"Gracias, señora."*

We went outside and just stood breathing the clean afternoon air until we stopped smelling the stench of corruption.

"Now let's go look at the medical supplies," I said.

"No," the Mother Superior answered. "First you must have a cup of tea. You look awfully pale."

The idea of swallowing anything was repulsive, but she insisted. Somebody had chosen just the right moment to put a vase of fragrant flowers in my room. After sniffing them and drinking strong tea from a delicate china cup, I revived.

The bishopric had furnished them with enough medical supplies to equip a hospital. The walls of the dispensary next to Father Plácido's office were lined from floor to ceiling with shelves loaded with boxes and bottles, and huge cartons containing the overflow sat on the floor. As we cleared and sorted, I found they had many of the newest drugs . . . everything anyone could wish. A lot of them were for ailments rarely seen in jungles, stomach ulcers and high blood pressure, for instance. There were many I knew nothing at all about and others, cortisone preparations and remedies for various heart diseases, which I would never feel competent to use. They are dangerous in the hands of the unqualified. All those we put in big cartons for storage until someone wiser than I should come along. There still remained hundreds and hundreds of small boxes containing medicines which could safely be used by anyone who could read, for they were accompanied by informative printed discussions of their uses and dosage, the dangers of any side effects which they might occasion, and contraindications for their use.

We started by clearing the shelves and labeling them. This section for skin infection, that for respiratory, these shelves for simple diarrheas, those for diarrheas with fever. . . . When darkness came, I had got three more half pints of liquid into José and he was getting strong chicken broth and vitamins for dinner. But we had scarcely made a beginning on the medical supplies.

That evening the five nuns gathered in the room next to mine, a sort of conference room, where Father Plácido gave nightly lectures on theology. They invited me to join them, but I felt I would be out of place. The Mother Superior said, "The lectures are really most interesting. Padre Plácido, though still very young, has already attained a considerable reputation as a theologian and metaphysician and his publications are widely read in Europe."

I pleaded fatigue and the need to write up my notes. Metaphysics and theology are not my field. But the sounds which came through the open door soon convinced me that the priest was a very good speaker. It didn't sound like preaching. His clear voice had a natural conversational note and I was surprised to notice that the nuns, with no hesitation at all, frequently interrupted to ask questions. Even more surprising were the occasional quiet chuckles and, once or twice, real bursts of laughter. I'd always thought these solemn subjects utterly incompatible with humor.

The Mother Superior had said that they were performing some religious observances which kept one nun at prayer all through the night. So they could easily look in on José at intervals and see that he was given his liquids and the 4 A.M. medication. I wanted to give him his ten o'clock dose and check his condition.

I found him awake, staring at the ceiling, and the light of the single candle exaggerated the craggy cheekbones and the shrunken eyesockets. He was despondent. The medicine had done him no good, he told me, he was going to die. His parents both had been killed by snakes, and his wife's father too. Now his turn had come.

His temperature was still high. When I touched his forehead, I thought it felt faintly moist but I couldn't be sure. Remembering his response when I had forbidden him to vomit, I tried bullying again.

"José," I said sharply, leaning over him, "look here!" I fixed him with a sort of wide-eyed glower that I imagined one of his witch doctors might have used. "You cannot die because I will not permit it even if you want to. I forbid it! Remember this! I will not allow you to die. You are very sick now. Tomorrow you will still be very sick. But the next day you will be much better. Only remember that I will not permit you to die! I will make you well and you will help me make you well. You must think hard about getting well. Now swallow these capsules with all that is in the cup."

I gave him another half gram of antibiotics, another vitamin capsule and another half pint of the sweetened oatmeal water which we were alternating with the lemonade. I thought he looked a little more cheerful when I took back the empty cup. I turned to where his mother and wife sat silent in a corner, their eyes shining wide in the candlelight. "And you too!" I snapped. "See that he remembers what I have said, that I will not permit him to die!" The wife looked frightened, but the old mother quavered, "Yes, señora." I swept from the room.

I hoped that I had not done something blasphemous. But it had impressed José, I knew it had. Maybe it would convince him that he did not have to die of snakebite just because so many of his family had.

Padre Gregorio stepped out of his office as I came from the sickroom. "Tell me, señora, is José going to be all right? Do you think he can live?"

That was the question I had refused to ask myself. Now faced with it, all the inflation fizzled out of my ego. I could feel my shoulders sag.

"Padre," I answered, "I don't know . . . I'm sorry . . . I just don't know."

I walked on to my room feeling miserably inadequate and dismally, achingly tired.

CHAPTER

XVI

W HEN I HURRIED into José's room the next morning, I thought at first that he looked a little better. His skin had lost some of that ugly yellow-gray and I thought he smelled better. Or was that just wishful thinking? Maybe I was just getting used to it. His pulse was still fast. Perhaps a little weaker than yesterday? I wasn't sure. His breathing was so shallow it was hard to count the respirations. When I removed the thermometer from his mouth, I found he had only one degree of temperature. But then, early morning temperatures are apt to be low. It didn't mean his fever was over.

He seemed even weaker, more exhausted than he had the afternoon before. Of course, I was no longer a novelty to him. Maybe that was why it was just too much trouble to turn his head and open his eyes. He answered my questions vaguely. He didn't seem to know whether or not he had perspired during the night. I was finding it difficult to maintain my mask of confidence. I made him take his vitamins and drink the oatmeal gruel I had brought with me. Then I let him go back to sleep. His dose of antibiotics wasn't due until ten.

The Mother Superior and my breakfast were waiting when I returned to my room. Both lifted my spirits. The nuns' bright confidence was contagious and the coffee was hot and strong.

We worked all morning on the medicines. At ten, when I went to give José his medicine, he was awake and his temperature was climbing as I feared it might. "You say I no can die?" he asked again. I resumed my portentous role. "I have said it," I told him firmly.

"But when you go away? When you go away from La Chorrera?"

163

His wife had been doing my laundry. I realized she must have heard of my plans and told him about them.

"I will not go until you are better," I promised. "But even after I have gone, even when I am not here, I still will be somewhere. Not far. And you will not be permitted to die."

But I went back to the dispensary worried and uncertain. The Mother Superior looked at me and forbore to ask questions. Instead she smiled and said, "Look, my daughter, you are doing all you can. We are convinced you are doing all that anyone could. The rest is in God's hands." She paused briefly. "Now these antibiotics have months to go before the expiration date stamped on them. Shall I put them on the shelves with the other good ones?"

Padre Plácido joined us after lunch. He'd been studying the literature that came with the medicines and he wanted to check his interpretation of some of the medical terms. His profound knowledge of Latin and Greek had been very useful. As the day wore on, I became more and more impressed with his keenness.

At four we found José's fever had broken. He'd sweated so copiously, we had to change the bedding, but his temperature was almost normal. "Body no hurt now," he told us. "Only arm hurt. You change cloth today? Arm no smell." I told him we'd let the arm rest until tomorrow.

Back at the dispensary, the Mother Superior joyously told Padre Plácido, "José is going to be all right. His fever is gone and he is getting well!"

"We can't be sure yet," I cautioned them. "We'll know a little more tomorrow. If his temperature doesn't go up again that will show we've got the infection under control. He's going to need a lot of care and it's still too soon to be sure of anything. But the acute stage may be passing and, perhaps, I'll be able to start after my wild Indians in a few days." I felt more optimistic than I dared admit.

"I think I've already found your bearers," the padre reassured me. "Will six be enough? One of my boys paddled down to the natives' houses last night. He came back today and told me that he and five friends would be willing to take you. And if you need more, there shouldn't be any difficulty."

I said six would be plenty. We talked excitedly while the evening drew on. I felt wonderful when I went to dinner. José was going to get well. I really believed it now. The dispensary shelves were filling up with an orderly, well-documented array of medicines. One more day would finish the job. And soon I'd be on my way to real adventure after so many weeks of delays and disappointments.

The blow fell that night. I'd just finished eating when the Mother Superior entered my room. She looked worried. "I am afraid that I have news that will disappoint you."

"José!" I started for the door. "What happened?"

"No, not José. José is fine. We gave him rice and chicken meat in his soup and he ate it all. Then he asked for tea with powdered milk. And his temperature is still normal. He's really getting better."

I drew a breath of relief. "Then what . . . ?"

"It's about your trip to the savages. I'm afraid they aren't there any more. We heard about it from an Indian who lives near here. He went to El Encanto for Holy Week. He came back over the trail and just got here at dinnertime."

"If my savages have moved, I'll track them to where they are," I said with determination.

That could not be, she told me. My Indians had been converted and gone to civilization. I stared in disbelief. Gently, torn between joy for the success of mission she was dedicated to and sorrow because mine was failing, the Mother Superior gave me the details.

Padre Javier who had the mission at El Encanto was a gentle old missionary, so beloved by the Indians that they called him "Papa" instead of "Padre." He had spent decades among primitives and he understood them. When he heard from Padre Luis of the savage tribe which had thrown him out, Padre Javier laid careful, long-range plans. He was determined to convert the tribe, not by shock tactics but by infiltration, keeping himself in the background.

He began by sending Witotos from his mission, a couple at a time, to make friends of the savages. The first few of what I could only consider the subversive elements were chased away. But every few months others would arrive. Finally, the savages began to listen to their stories of the splendid life at El Encanto. By last Christmas, they had warmed up considerably, and two young men of the tribe were emboldened to go with their new friends to watch the Christmas festivities.

Padre Javier saw to it that the two young strangers had the time of their lives. They returned to their people laden with gifts and eager to convince their elders that the whole tribe should move to the mission. Months of discussion and deliberation followed. As

Holy Week drew near, more of Padre Javier's Fifth Column dropped by to tell about the wonders of the Holy Week festivities. The conservative element of the tribe was finally convinced that this white man was not out to enslave them as thousands of their tribe had been enslaved in the days of the rubber boom. The women made themselves little bark dresses under the supervision of those who had seen women who wore dresses and the whole tribe went to El Encanto for the fiesta. Went and were conquered. Now they were putting the past behind them.

"So, if you want, you can still go to their houses," the Mother Superior finished her account of the tribe's conversion. "It's only about seventy-five kilometers of trail and the men are all ready to act as bearers. But I am afraid that you will only find empty houses or, perhaps, one or two Indians who may come back for the last of their possessions."

The Mother Superior looked at me commiseratingly. I was crushed. Too crushed for speech. She started to say something, but hesitated, patted my shoulder and silently left me alone.

It was just as well. My anger exploded, filling me with a red glare. Such damned, wretched luck! It wasn't fair. I had missed those Indians by days, at most two or three weeks. Why couldn't they have waited a little longer to be converted? Without doubt, Padre Javier would have a star in his crown! And the Mother Superior was pleased! But what about my plants? All this dismal journey, the heat, the rain, the riding in an open boat, the fly-bitten weeks at Arica in a hot jail—all for nothing!

Oh, I had collected some good botanicals in the past, but not in the last miserable months. The irony of it! I had come to get the wild Witotos' magic medicine to take back to civilization and instead they had taken civilization to their bosoms. Now they would never acknowledge that they had any tribal remedies. Padre Javier would probably frighten them with damnation. Several Indians along the way had told me that Padre Luis disapproved violently of witch doctors and threatened those who consulted them with eternal fire. Padre Javier would do the same and the frightened Indians would obligingly forget their tribal lore . . .

But, I speculated, maybe a few conservatives would remain in their tribal houses? Perhaps if I went over the trail and found them and was just as subversive as Padre Javier's boys had been, they would avenge the dispersement of the tribe by giving me their magic? But as soon as I thought of that plan I knew it was non-sense. There wouldn't be any uncivilized reactionaries left; that wasn't consistent with tribal behavior. Having conferred and reached a decision to move to the mission, they would all stick together. I could walk all the way to El Encanto. But why? To watch the converts building new houses, planting new fields—and not remembering even a single puny plant that would guard against evil spirits?

There was a trail to Rió Caquetá. Teresa and her brothers had talked about it. But they told me there were missions there, too, and that all the Indians were fairly civilized. They, too, probably used boric acid solution to wash the gnats out of their children's eyes. Even if I heard rumors of interesting tribes at Caquetá, I probably wouldn't have funds enough to reach them. It would be a lengthy trip, two extra months at the very least, probably three. My money wouldn't hold out that long.

"Just a wild Indian chase," I told myself in the darkness. It didn't sound funny.

The next morning my resentment over the fickleness of wild Indians must have been painfully obvious. The Mother Superior treated me with even greater consideration—if that were possible. I tried to hide my bitterness from her but she was too sensitive not to notice it. She made no references to my aborted plans, but immediately plunged into our worries over José. The nuns who had taken his temperature when giving him his round the clock medication had said it remained low. But this morning, even though his arm was still painful, shouldn't we change the dressing?

José moaned despite the Mother Superior's gentleness. When she lifted the last long, thick pad of gauze, she could hardly believe her eyes. "*Ave María Santísima!*" she exclaimed. "This is a miracle!"

There was no smell. Every bit of pus had lifted off with the pad except for a narrow patch about a half an inch in length near the base of the wrist. Even José stopped moaning and said, "Is clean!" What was left was truly as clean as fresh-cut meat. But when I saw it my heart sank. I had had no idea of the extent of the damage. The whole inner arm had been hidden under that horrible blanket of matter. Now from the wrist halfway up the forearm was an area, two inches wide in one place, where there was simply no flesh at all. The infection had eaten it away and the tendons and bones, creamy white and brittle, shone in the morning light. Bordering the open wound were strips of raw, red, skinless flesh which in some places extended over the entire circumference of the forearm. It didn't look particularly revolting because it simply didn't look real. Neat and shiny, it was far more like an anatomy-class model than the arm of a living being. The upper arm had a flayed appearance, too, and there was a two inch square of skin, black and leathery, which was beginning to slough off. But at least no bones showed.

I stood silently, wondering what on earth to do. José settled that for me. "Yes, body no pain. Better. Arm no smell. Better. But arm too much pain! Ooooooh!"

I remembered putting on the dispensary shelves dozens of tubes of procaine and picrate antiseptic jelly for burns. I ran for a tube and smeared it on quickly. José groaned for a minute or two, then stopped, surprised. "Pain little now!"

The Mother Superior looked puzzled. "There's procaine in the salve," I explained. "That's a good local anesthetic. With less pain he ought to rest better and that should help speed his recovery."

We put on new bandages and José reminded us to fill the squeeze bottle with boric solution. He was sure that was the real curative agent. The pills went to his stomach, so they made his body better. But the strange bottle had spat on his arm and the arm began to heal. Wasn't it obvious? After all, his arm had been much sicker than his body.

We found Padre Plácido in the dispensary. "Look, señora!" he said. "Have I got these right?" He showed me dozens of medicines he had sorted while we were with José. He hadn't made a single error, though some of them he had not seen before. And he had used very sound judgment about setting aside for storage the ones which would be dangerous for the unskilled to use.

The Mother Superior was jubilant over what she called José's "miraculous" recovery. "He's practically well!" she said.

"Madrecita!" I protested. "You can't really believe that! There's been no miracle! Didn't you see his arm? Didn't you see how much tissue has been destroyed? We've beaten the infection . . . at least for the present. But I just don't know enough . . . Miracles? He needs the miracle of growing new flesh and skin to make that arm well again. I don't know whether a surgeon would amputate or do some grafting, or what. That would be the miracle, Madrecita, the arrival of a surgeon!" My voice was getting shrill. "You haven't got a miracle yet. You've only got antibiotics. Please, if there is the slightest chance to get him to a hospital, take that chance. Or send runners out to see if you can find someone who knows something to come and care for him. I wouldn't even know what to do if the infection should flare up later. He can't go on taking antibiotics forever!"

Just then we were startled to see Padre Gregorio go flying across the football field outside his classroom, sprinting like a first-rate track man, his white robe billowing behind him in the wind. "It's Monsignor!" he shouted. "Monsignor!" Padre Plácido ran after him. They disappeared on the path to the river.

"It's our monsignor arriving," the Mother Superior told me. We have been expecting him for weeks. Listen. Can you hear the motor?"

I could. From the edge of the bank, we saw a white boat coming up the river. The Mother Superior ran to tell the nuns to change to their white habits and to get the children down to welcome the monsignor. I hurried to my room and put on the only skirt I had with me. Blue jeans seemed too informal for welcoming a prelate.

We met again on the long path leading to the port. The nuns were in flowing white habits with sky-blue panels down the front and sky-blue veils. I was astonished. I didn't know a religious order wore habits so beautiful. They would have looked like something out of a sixteenth-century painting except that, of course, they wore no makeup. I've noticed that most of the feminine saints on the walls of art galleries have such lovely coloring that they might have been turned out by an expert makeup man. But these nuns' sun-browned faces were only a little pinker than usual as they hurried down the steep path.

Halfway down we met the two priests returning. "It isn't our monsignor. It's only a lancha." But that was exciting, too. Padre Gregorio cheered up. "They have gasoline, so we can use the boat and even have electric lights again! And kerosene and sugar and cloth . . ."

"And shoes?" one of the nuns asked.

Yes, shoes, too. We started back up the hill and the Mother Superior told me, "We need everything for our little girls. We'll buy chocolate and dress materials and combs and pretty ribbons for their hair. *Por Dios!* We'll buy the lancha itself!"

She was so excited and pleased to be able to brighten the lives of her charges that she and the other nuns practically ran up the hill to change back into their work habits. When I got back to the dispensary, I felt guilty. I remembered how I had shouted at her about "miracles."

Padre Plácido joined me in our work at the dispensary. In an hour we would be finished. I asked him about the lancha. Where was it bound? To Tarapacá—Tarapacá where the military post was. The corporal at Arica had told me there was a weekly plane service from there to Leticia and from Leticia I could take another airline to Iquitos. Flying with my tail between my legs, maybe, but at least I could get away from the damn defeating river. And I would save a lot of time.

"I must leave with the lancha," I said to Padre Plácido. "Would you ask the owner if he'll take me? He'd be much less apt to refuse you than he would me. What's his name?"

Padre Plácido said, "He has a most peculiar name. Don Anemia."

"It can't be," I laughed.

"That's what I thought, too." The padre joined my laughter. "I even asked a second time. Our Indians know him. They say that's what they call him and he certainly answers to it."

Still chuckling, we went about finishing stocking the medicine shelves.

"Señora," Padre Plácido said hesitantly as he looked down at me while stretching to put a bottle on a high shelf. "Señora . . . about leaving us. Can't you stay until the monsignor arrives? He'll surely be here in the next few days. You have done so much for us, he will want to thank you."

I made a nervous gesture of polite refusal.

"And, señora, we have gasoline now. We can take you to the Indian houses. I do not like to see you so disappointed."

"Oh, I shall get over that. . . ."

"Yes, my daughter," Padre Plácido said softly, "but not through resentment. You resent that the wild Indians have been sent to us and you will not find the botanicals you are searching for. That is why you told the Madrecita that there is no miracle yet. But there are miracles, señora. The wild Indians have been sent to us for their physical and spiritual care. A whole tribe has joined a mission . . . And José is still alive. It is not for us to say these are miracles. But miracles are God's generous answers to our prayers."

Yes, José was still alive. I who knew nothing had helped.

"Stay with us a little longer. The monsignor will take you to Leticia."

"But I cannot, padre. I have obligations to meet. I must send the plants I have already collected to the States as soon as possible. And, perhaps, it will be days before the monsignor arrives. I must seize this opportunity to get on my way."

I had hoped to show that I didn't resent the missionaries taking my wild Indians away from me and all I was doing was being self-important again. Padre Plácido said no more and I, too, remained silent.

By six o'clock, the last shelf was finished and I went down to the boat by flashlight. A man stood on the shore supervising the unloading of mountains of cargo. "Excuse me, señor," I asked, "are you Don Anemia?"

"Yes. At your orders, señora."

"Would you be so kind as to tell me how you spell your name?" I couldn't wait to make the usual polite speeches, I was too curious.

He spelled it out. "O-n-e-m-i-o."

"Oh! I just wanted to be sure that I pronounced it correctly, being a foreigner," I stammered. "It's a beautiful name, but I have never heard it before."

Then we got down to business. This was not a passenger boat . . . it was too small. But the padres had given me a big buildup and Don Onemio was anxious to oblige. "The only trouble, señora, is that I do not know where to put you. There are no cabins for passengers. I bunk down in the little store and the crew pretty well fills up the decks."

"What about the *albarenga*?" I asked. The barge lashed alongside was as big as the boat itself.

"It has no deck where you could lay your bedding. We use it only for cargo. Not much of a place for a lady."

"Couldn't I hang my hammock over the cargo?"

"Oh, a hammock. Of course, if you use a hammock, it can be arranged. We will take off around eleven in the morning, señora. It will be a pleasure."

That evening all the nuns and both priests tried to make me stay until the Monsignor arrived. "And what about José?" the Mother Superior asked. "A few more days of your care would be better for him."

"No, Madrecita, you know now as well as I what to do for him. And Padre Plácido knows an amazing amount about the medicines in the dispensary. He will be able to help."

The Mother Superior was so trusting, so good, I wanted to explain to her my feeling about losing the wild Witotos. But I couldn't exactly explain it properly to myself at that moment. It was only later in bed that I really was able to. Why, I asked myself, was I still smarting? Why did I feel shame about missing them by a few weeks?

I learned something about myself that night. I realized that I have always been proud, even boastful, about good luck and ashamed of bad. Now there's an atavistic trait! No wonder I get along with primitives. If only I could find some to get along with . . .

In the morning, I didn't hurry too much with my packing. Don Onemio had said eleven. Experience with tropical people led me to believe that it would be three or four in the afternoon. The nuns had agreed. They had arranged for the little girls to get into costume and do the *bombacha*, the typical dance of Colombia, which the madrecitas had taught them. They were waiting on the patio now to put on their performance.

Half the little girls wore fancy little blouses and wide skirts of bright colors. The others were disguised as boys in typical Spanish costumes of long black trousers and boleros with white shirts tucked into dashing red sashes. A few had drawn smart black mustaches on childish upper lips. The nuns sang, clapping their hands to the rhythm, while the children danced.

In the middle of the performance, word came that the boat was ready to leave. Don Onemio was not only on time, he was early. I took a few moments to go see José for the last time.

He was really improving rapidly. His temperature remained normal. He was noticeably stronger and brighter than before. I told him the boat was waiting to take me away. The Mother Superior now knew everything I knew. I had taught her. "She will take care of you. I have given her your medicine. And she will make you well."

"You leave little bottle that cure my arm?" he asked.

"I'm leaving it right there on your table," I assured him. "You can see it now."

"Is well," he said. "Good-bye, señora."

"José!" The Mother Superior spoke sternly. "Aren't you going to thank the Señora for saving your life?"

José's eyes were on the little squeeze bottle. "Thank you, señora," he said. "*Muchas gracias.*"

I turned to wave at him from the door, but he wasn't looking my way. Expressions of gratitude don't even exist in most of the Indian tongues I know anything about. It isn't fitting for Indians to express emotions except, perhaps, warlike ones. By the time we got down to the boat, I was wishing uncomfortably that the mission people had caught a little of that from their wards. I wanted to thank them for their hospitality, but they were so busy thanking me that I could scarcely get a word in.

"It would be a miracle," the Mother Superior said with a twinkle in her eye, "if we could keep you permanently with us. You know you are just as welcome as a Protestant as you would be as a Catholic, don't you?"

"It is a miracle that José is alive," I said softly as I kissed her cheek.

As we pulled out into the stream, I heard the Reverenda Madre say, "We thank God for sending you to us."

I wished to God He had sent someone wiser and more humble.

CHAPTER

XVII

T HE LANCHA took off as soon as I was aboard and a stout, smiling Indian woman introduced herself while I was still waving at the receding figures on the shore. She was Victoria, the cook, and she asked if she might give me a cup of coffee. I followed her around the little cabin amidships which housed Don Onemio and the general store. A table stood on the rear deck just behind the railed ladder leading down to the engine room.

"On this table, señora," Victoria told me, "you will always find a thermos full of hot coffee. It is Don Onemio's wish that hot coffee be ready at all hours for anyone who might want it. Please help yourself whenever you wish. My kitchen is there," she pointed to a tiny cabin, aft on the right, "and you must let me know if there is anything I can do for you. And this is the bath." She opened the door of the tiny cabin on the left to show a very clean flush-toilet and shower. Everything worked. I was feeling greatly encouraged until I went to see where the boys had hung my hammock in the albarenga.

Don Onemio had warned me that it would not be fun to travel with the freight. "You must remember that we have to take any kind of cargo that people want to ship. I'm afraid you'll find it unpleasant, and it would distress me if you were displeased with the Boyacá." He had even refused to let me pay for anything more than the cost of the food I'd consume, which he estimated at a modest three and a half pesos daily—less than fifty cents in our money. "I cannot charge for your passage with the accommodations so unsuitable for a lady."

But all Don Onemio's consideration had not prepared me for the shock of finding a large black pig regarding me moodily from under my hammock. Pigs can bite. This one was as big as a pony and wicked yellow fangs protruded from his enormous mouth. I shuddered as I imagined them closing on my leg. I'm vain about my legs. Still, I didn't want to distress Don Onemio, so I squatted on a box well out of reach and surveyed the situation.

That barge was really loaded. It was thirty or forty feet long, with a little deck in its pointed front and a slightly larger one at the back, leaving a deep space in the middle. On and under these decks were piled big cylindrical baskets of *leche caspi*, rubbery sap of a tree, destined eventually for some chewing gum factory. Heavy wooden boxes, more leche caspi baskets and innumerable twenty-gallon drums of diesel oil for the motor were stacked in the body of the albarenga in such a way as to leave a well in the other for the pig. There was no odor at all and even the pig looked scrubbed. Later I learned that Salomón, a deckhand, washed my home and the pig's every couple of hours. Don Onemio kept an immaculately clean boat.

However, the sanitary aspects worried me less than the danger of being bitten by that monster. But try as I might, I could find no other place for my hammock and no other place where the pig could humanely be stowed. So I worked out a route that would keep me safely beyond his reach. Entering from the front, I could climb over the leche caspi, hop to one of the oil drums and from it to my hammock which was high enough for safety. From the hammock I could step onto a stack of wooden boxes and from there a good leap would take me over the pig to an oil drum that gave access to the rear deck. Thanks to ballet and the fact that riverboats do not rock, I had it made.

The *Boyacá* was making fast time. I asked Don Onemio if it had an unusually powerful motor and he laughed. "You just didn't notice what a swift current this river has. If you went upstream with a thirty-five horsepower Johnson, you wouldn't. But paddling . . .! It's quite a river. The *Boyacá's* motor is very good. It's new and it's powerful for a boat this size, but I assure you we made nothing like this speed going upstream. It took us more than a week to get from Arica to La Chorrera. We'll do the return, even with a few stops to take on skins and leche caspi that are being rounded up for us, in about two days."

When I congratulated him on having such a fine boat, he told me that he was not the owner. "It makes me feel good when every time we stop people come running, all happy because we bring things they've been needing so long. We carry a little of everything, medicines, food, clothing, blankets, things for the kitchen, like pots and knives and plates and spoons. Sometimes they pay us in Colombian pesos or Peruvian soles. Sometimes they pay with leche caspi or hides or chickens or meat. Sometimes they can't pay us right away, but we give them the stuff they need and collect on our next trip. They always pay sooner or later . . . or almost always. There are only one or two families who can't be trusted with credit, but I know who they are. Mostly along these rivers you find simple, honest people. I'll never get rich doing this, but it's a good, healthy life in the open air with the forest all around you."

"What a contrast," I remarked, "the slow life along the rivers and the swift flight from Tarapacá to Leticia by plane. Have you made the trip by air? It's once a week, isn't it? Fridays, the corporal said. I hope we don't arrive just after the weekly plane leaves. I'm anxious to get back to Iquitos."

"But, señora, you weren't expecting to fly from Tarapacá? Why, that service was discontinued a year and a half ago. I'm awfully sorry, but I'm afraid that you'll have to wait for another lancha. But there will be plenty of those now that the river is rising."

I stared at him, too dismayed for speech.

The *Boyacá* carried a crew of five, besides the cook, Victoria. There were two *motoristas*, for you aren't an engineer in Latin America unless you have an engineering degree, two steersmen and a deckhand. Most of them showed more Indian than white blood. They seemed a good-natured lot and not afraid of any kind of work.

After lunch Victoria brought the pig a big basin of the same delicious pork and yuca stew that we had enjoyed. Solicitously she set it down. He just looked away.

"I'm worried about him, señora," she said. "He's been with us for two days now and he eats nothing."

"Maybe it's because it's pork," I suggested. "Perhaps he's sensitive and it hurts his feelings."

Looking down at him from the safety of my hammock, I noticed that he had extraordinarily long, curving eyelashes, just the kind I would like to have. He looked awfully sad. It must be pretty dreary for him, I thought, tied by the leg like that in an alien world with no mud in it. I could hardly blame him if he felt like biting people.

I had just drifted into the delicious sleep of the siesta when water pelting in my face woke me. Thunder was booming and the rain whipped through the opening in the side of the albarenga. I scrambled out and tied my rain poncho over the opening, teetering perilously over the pig to secure it. It blew down immediately and I was a nervous wreck before I got back into my hammock. But my arms and legs were still intact and I finally fastened the poncho so that it kept us dry. I hope the pig appreciated it.

After dinner I went to the albarenga and found Victoria emptying the pig's untouched basin of stew over the side. She looked at me, her round face troubled. "I've been thinking about what you said, señora. Maybe the pig doesn't like to eat pork. So now I've boiled up a huge big batch of yuca for him plain. Maybe he'll eat that."

But in the morning, the washbasin of cooked yuca was still full. Propinquity wasn't making me any fonder of that pig, but I was beginning to feel sorry for him. He seldom moved, just lay there quietly on his side, looking so sad that I expected any moment to see tears roll through those enviable lashes. I once had a dog who cried real tears, so why not a pig?

Examining him more closely, I discovered one reason for his unhappiness. The rope around his ankle was tied so tightly that the flesh of the foot was badly swollen. I called Salomón, the deckhand, and persuaded him to undo the rope and knot it around the pig's middle. That looked pretty squeeze-proof. Then we discussed his diet. He wouldn't eat meat, he wouldn't eat cooked yuca. How about raw yuca? Victoria peeled some for us and we tossed him a piece. He sniffed, then gobbled it. We gave him some more. He ate it as fast as Victoria could peel it. He ate and ate, then fell asleep, but he still had that melancholy expression.

At breakfast the next morning, Don Onemio announced that we would be in Arica by nine o'clock. I could have my things put aboard while he completed the brief formalities of registering with the police. I wanted to give farewell gifts to María, who had been so helpful, and to the corporal's wife. In my footlocker there were a couple of pearl necklaces that would be suitable. They were really very pretty, imitation pearls on a delicate, imitation gold chain, and I had bought them to wear myself.

We were in the Putumayo now and the river was very much higher than when I left to go up the Igaraparaná. Suddenly Victoria called to us, "Look, señora! Don Onemio! The dolphins!"

There ahead we saw two great dark bodies arching and wheeling in and out of the water. All the sandbanks, the wide beaches were hidden by many feet of muddy water. And the dolphins were having a wonderful time. They seemed to enjoy showing off. There are two varieties of freshwater dolphins peculiar to the Amazon and its larger tributaries, the white and the larger red ones. These were red, though they looked black in the harsh glare of the sun.

I suppose that the legends which have grown up about the dolphins in the Amazon region are due to the fact that they are mammals with secondary sex characteristics not unlike those of humans. Their playfulness probably has something to do with it, too, and their size is impressive. I am told that they sometimes grow to ten or twelve feet in length. In any case, no native would ever kill one, even to get the teeth which are supposed to be very effective love charms. I once met a man who was said to have given a hundred pesos and his new blue suit for a dolphin tooth, but I didn't like to ask him how he made out with it. I didn't know him that well.

But everybody around the Amazon knows that dolphins are very fond of humans. I've heard that they sometimes save the lives of canoemen who get shipwrecked in storms. But I've heard more often the wiles they use to lure humans to live at the bottom of the rivers. Not to drown them, but rather to keep them as pets. I asked Victoria about it.

"Oh, yes, señora! They do charm people into joining them at the bottom of the river. But they change them by magic so that they can live in the water. Then they never want to return to the dry land of humans. They once almost got a friend of mine, Juan García, who lives down the Putumayo."

García was a fisherman and he had gone with his partner to fish from a temporary camp they made just above the mouth of Río Yaguas. One afternoon Juan had a headache, so he left his partner still fishing and went home alone to their camp. He was astonished to see a woman alone at the tambo. When he got closer, he saw that she was very beautiful and he thought she must be a gringa, for her skin was light and she had long golden hair. She came toward him holding out her hand and greeted him in a very friendly fashion.

But there was something strange about her. Juan didn't want to touch the hand she held out to him, so he just said "Good day" and dodged around her toward the house. When he entered, she followed him. She held her hand out to him again, but he didn't take it.

"*Perdone, señorita,*" he said. "I cannot shake hands with you. My hands are dirty from fishing. Excuse me, I must go wash."

He dodged out again, but she just smiled and followed him. He didn't like the way things were shaping up and decided it might not be such a good idea to go down to the river's edge. Glancing back over his shoulder he saw that now there was a man, equally fair, standing beside the woman. Both of them smiled and held out their hands.

"But first I must make the fire. My partner will be arriving any minute and I have to get our dinner ready." Juan hurried around the corner of the tambo to the little lean-to kitchen at the back. The two strangers followed him now, talking in an extremely friendly fashion. He was silent while he laid the sticks but they kept right on chatting in a most amiable manner. As they drew nearer, he heard the man say to the woman, "Don't take him yet. Wait until he stoops to kindle the flame."

That really terrified Juan. He squatted frozen, the matches in his hand. The smiling strangers slowly approached, each with a hand held out in a gesture of friendliness. At that moment Juan heard his partner paddling to the shore. He let out a yell.

The two fair strangers turned and ran for the river. In they plunged. It was very deep there, and for a few seconds they were lost to view, but a moment later, just beyond the spot where they had dived in, two enormous dolphins broke the water. Leaping and curvetting, they disappeared around the bend.

"Juan was so scared and so mad he wanted to go straight to the police and lay charges against them," Victoria finished. But his partner wouldn't let him. Dolphins can't be arrested. But Juan isn't a fisherman any more. He decided to work leche caspi instead.

The rain that began that afternoon was different in character from that we had had before. This was no temperamental explosion. This was the slow, enduring rain of the wet season. Winter they call it here. It fell from a sky the color of a dirty mop, smearing the jungle along the banks with gray rags of mist and damping the ribald shrieks of the parrots.

It didn't drum energetically on the roof that night as I lay in my hammock; it fell silently, except for a monotonous leaky faucet drip from the roof. By morning it had filmed the decks with a slippery scum of moisture. My hammock felt damp, the clean clothes I got from my rubber bags were clammy to the touch and a smell of mildew pervaded the albarenga. I wouldn't have been surprised to see mushrooms growing on the pig.

It was late afternoon before the rain tired, but even then the sky didn't clear. The sodden air was motionless, the river flat, with a metallic sheen in the distance. The rain hadn't come to its end. It was only resting.

About five we reached the mouth of Río Yaguas. A rectangular clearing had been hacked out of virgin jungle and in it stood a neat line of thatched houses on tall stilts connected by a stilted board-walk. A larger building, bright with strong blue paint, stood in the center of the row behind a tall flagpole where the red-and-white flag of Peru hung limp in the muggy air. As we neared the shore, Don Onemio told me that this was a Peruvian police post. Then I saw the big shield of the Guardia Civil with its motto "Honor" over the door of the big building, the Comandancia.

The two policemen who came aboard wore uniforms of the same greenish-gray cotton as the Colombian police, but they did not wear hoods or towels over their heads, though we were still in the gnat zone. These men had the look of old jungle hands. It is a rather special look. It's not just a matter of being lean and weather-beaten, but rather the relaxed alertness of a man whose sharpened senses keep watch for him, subconsciously noting the meaning of the flick of a wing, a ripple showing where a fish has jumped, a rustle in the brush or one leaf disturbed among a sea of leaves—any one of a thousand sounds or sights which would pass unnoticed by city-bred eyes and ears. And it is a look of muscles in complete repose but ready for instant, effortless movement.

Don Onemio introduced me to the shorter and slighter of the two, Sergeant Ramírez, comandante of Puesto Yaguas, and I presented my passport and the special credential given me by the chief of this police zone. The sergeant had good news for me. The Peruvian lancha *Almirante* was now at a rosewood oil distillery only an hour or so upstream. In a few days, she would be leaving for Iquitos. I could transship here or in Tarapacá. The sergeant thought I'd be wiser to board her here since military personnel were being transferred from the army post and I would be more certain of finding a passage before they crowded aboard.

Meanwhile I could stay at the house of the Tuesta family. Don

Juan Tuesta was a civilian fisherman, and his wife, Doña Luisa, did the post's laundry. She came aboard just then, a fat woman in a crisp pink dress. I liked her dark, friendly face and her air of bustling competence. She said they'd be delighted to put me up, so I went to see to my baggage.

As I untied my hammock, I looked down at the pig. He was eating well now, but he looked just as melancholy as ever. I was still sorry for him, but, I reflected, pity is not akin to love. Not for me anyway. Parting was sweet, without sorrow.

CHAPTER

XVIII

THE PIG was not my only reason for wanting to go ashore at Puesto Yaguas. I had always wanted to spend a few days in a jungle outpost of the Peruvian police. I had once written an article on the Guardia Civil and the more information I assembled on them, the more I found to admire. Their record in the jungle was an impressive story of ingenuity and fortitude. Many city criminals think that if they can just reach the trackless tropical forest, their only problem will be snakes and wild animals. They couldn't be more mistaken. The jungle police invariably track them down. Examining the data, I had thought that the factors behind the extraordinary record of the jungle police must include fancy logistics and elaborate technical equipment. So I had gone to interview a high-ranking officer with my little notebook full of careful questions about how they supplied and equipped their jungle branches. Penetrating questions, I thought.

I began the interview by asking, "How do you transport your men and how do you manage supply and maintenance of technical equipment in remote jungle outposts? Do you have your own planes and helicopters like the Canadian Mounted Police? Or do you charter them?"

The officer took off his glasses and regarded me earnestly. "No, señora," he said gently, "I'm afraid you do not understand. We haven't funds for that sort of thing. Supplies consist of two uniforms per man with underwear, shoes, a raincoat, some bedding and a mess kit. The technical equipment which is kept at the posts consists of a sending and receiving radio, an outboard motor and a carbine for every man. As for transportation, we just tell them where they're to go and they get there by any means available, a riverboat, a canoe or on foot. I'm afraid we just don't have a real supply system. All we have is men. But men, señora!" he said. "Carefully selected, intensively trained, they can do their job without a supply system. If we could only get the funds, it would be wonderful to supply them with all the things they now lack."

I remembered that interview while the sergeant introduced several other guardias who came to buy things from Don Onemios shop. They were a hardy-looking lot. All of them wore uniform shirts, but three or four were clad in trousers of faded khaki bought from some passing river peddler. Two pairs of trousers don't last long if you're patrolling a jungle.

It started to rain again as my baggage reached the Tuesta house at the far end of the clearing. Like the other houses, it was of comfortable size, with a bedroom, a living room and a kitchen. Doña Luisa told me that she and her husband were from San Martín Province. They had come there only four months ago.

It was a house of people with very few possessions. No furniture had to be removed before my hammock could be hung in the living room, for it contained only three benches ranged against the walls. The house had a well- and often-scrubbed look, but the walls separating the rooms gave only token privacy. They were of *pona*, palm slats, reaching about halfway to the soaring thatched roof. They were a little harder to see through than a picket fence.

From the living room I saw that the Tuestas' bed was only a straw-filled mattress lying on the floor under a big mosquito net. The other furniture in the bedroom was a striped hammock and a couple of wooden trunks. The kitchen seemed crowded by comparison. It contained a large adobe table stove, a board table with two benches, a long shelf against one wall where chipped enamel washbasins sat above earthen jars of water, a box holding a dozen bottles of kerosene and a good deal of firewood.

Don Juan Tuesta arrived while we were still hanging the hammock. He was a small, thin, enthusiastic man with a black mustache. When he talked, he gesticulated with his whole body, and a strand of curly black hair flopped over a bright brown eye. "What a pleasure to have a visitor from the great world in our house!" he exclaimed, shaking my hand vigorously.

I told him of my search for jungle medicines. "Magnificent!" he said excitedly. I almost expected him to slap me on the back as a gesture of appreciation for my courage and daring. "This is a noble mission, señora. Our forests have treasures little known. My wife can show you some of them. And is all that your baggage? How splendid you own so much. What can be in them all?

"But we have something wonderful, too!" He darted into the bedroom and returned leading a little girl by the hand. "This is Gloria, our daughter. We have a game. Every day when it is time for her daddy to come home, she hides and he has to look behind the mosquito net to find her." He bent to kiss the child's cheek. "Isn't she lovely?"

She was a pretty child, tall for her three years, with long lashes and black eyes made blacker by the pallor of white children who live in the tropics. She was very shy. When Don Juan released her hand, she ran to her mother in the kitchen.

During dinner I tried to swerve the torrent of conversation to jungle medicines, but I didn't have a chance. Don Juan was too eager to hear about New York. Did everybody really have electric lights and refrigerators? How magnificent! And is it true that people ride to work on trains deep under the earth? Just imagine! And can you look out the window and see streets jammed with fine new automobiles like bright-colored fish crowding up a river to spawn? How beautiful that must be! I had never thought of a traffic jam as a thing of beauty before . . .

After dinner he widened his scope. "Even China you know? And do they sing when they talk, like the men in the Chinese restaurant in Iquitos? In France do even the children drink wine at all meals?"

He was still going strong when Doña Luisa tucked Gloria into the hammock and announced that it was time for bed. But even Doña Luisa couldn't silence Don Juan for long. I'd just blown out the little kerosene lamp and settled in my hammock when his voice drifted through the wall.

"Señora, how long does it take to get from New York to Lima by boat? And by air?"

The quiz program threatened to go on all night. Finally, I asked him to excuse me. I was really very tired. And I'd like to go to sleep. Then he was quiet.

The next morning I observed the amenities by making a formal call on the commanding officer of the post. A guardia told me the sergeant was in the radio room. Would I have the kindness to wait in his office. He placed a chair for me near the shabby desk in a little

Rukas, the Jívaro witch doctor, putting final touches on his makeup before our photo session. He's wearing a ceremonial headdress; the long, beautifully woven ribbons of cotton, ending in tassels of human hair, probably belonged to the head of a vanquished enemy. On Río Corrientes, which runs into the Río Tigre.

Maina warrior—heir apparent to his uncle, chief of their tribe—drinking a ceremonial welcome of *masato*. His stool is reserved for high-ranking visitors. In the Jívaro cultures, it's very important never to sit until you have been invited. Some tribes adhere to rather rigid rules of etiquette. I lucked into a good start with these people by somehow knowing not to sit. Note the blowgun on lap. Río Macusari, Peru 1959.

Maina wearing a feather crown, typical of Jívaroan tribes. The crown is made of thousands of tiny toucan feathers carefully tied in a mesh with fine string made of palm fibers, so the feathers fan out like a gorgeous caterpillar. Río Macusari, Peru.

Maina warrior named Sambeeky in ceremonial dress, sitting on a stool carved from a solid block of wood, wearing his best clothes bartered for work from the local *patrón*. The men of this tribe only wear white bead choker necklaces; his bracelet is cotton woven on a narrow loom, edged with monkey teeth. The gun is treasured and cared for.

Maina working on a blowgun. After the bore is carved with a machete, it will be polished and sanded thoroughly with a long hardwood rod, twirled back and forth until the channel for the dart is absolutely straight and smooth.

Witoto maidens resting between dances at the fiesta. Their outfits consist of feathers, beads, and clay paint. In festival finery, Witoto women are the best dressed naked women I've ever seen. Negro Urco, Río Napo, Peru.

On the trail between the Río Algodón and Putumayo. With Hilario, a Coto, the most inappropriately named person I've ever met, the glummest person in the jungle, carrying my cameras and strobe light. The trail is completely inundated for most of the distance between the Napu and the Putumayo—it is not unusual for parts of the trail to be knee-deep, but this day was worse than usual.

Maina children enthralled by their first radio concert, some Colombian dance music (boleros).

Antimalaria sprayer entering *maloca* (Bora Indian house). Río Igaraparaná, Columbia. A *maloca* of this size houses fifteen to twenty people.

A Ticuna family on the Colombian Amazon. This is a typical house of Indians who have become somewhat acculturated and who no longer live in the communal lodge. The houses have few walls (for coolness) and little furniture. Possessions are hung from the roof to prevent mildew and to keep them away from vermin.

Author with friend Nelida on the trail between the Río Napo and the Río Algodón. The vine, *escalera de makisapa* (large monkey ladder), I learned years later, is used by the Campa tribe of Southern Peru as a lifetime contraceptive.

Maina widow (with hair cut short) helping the author with necklace of white glass beads. Upon the death of her husband—this woman's died of natural causes—a widow crops her hair. She will wail ritually several times a day at stated intervals for two years after her husband's death. On Río Macusari.

In the woods around Yarina Cocha, on Río Ucayali, Peru (1983). *Photo: Ted Long*

room with no other furniture except for some files and a rack of lethal-looking carbines. As I sat staring out of the window at the row of houses, mud-colored in the dreary gray rain, I heard the dit-dat-dit of a radio in the next room. This must be the hour they were in communication with Iquitos. I was swept by a sudden wave of nostalgia for pretty summer dresses and taxis and ice cream and people to laugh with over a cocktail served by a white-coated waiter in the well-polished lounge of the hotel.

Sharply I took myself in hand. These fits of self-pity had to stop. Their real cause lay in the fact that this was the first trip I'd ever made which had brought no moment of real danger, no excitement. Well, then, I'd get my thrills vicariously. This was my chance to hear first hand the stories of men from whom danger was part of the day's work. The sergeant now; he'd had years of jungle service. Surely he'd have a story to tell. He entered and greeted me briskly. He didn't look like a man who cared much for heroics. Better start, I thought, with just routine questions.

There were six other police on the post, he told me. Day and night, there were two men on alert duty here in the building. Anything in line of duty was done by two men, a "pair" in police parlance. "That's an inflexible regulation whether they are on routine business or whether they are sent to solve a crime and bring back dangerous criminals. Two guardias can handle anything. But one man alone? The jungle has too many natural hazards."

"What are the worst hazards here?" I asked eagerly.

"Our gravest problem is lack of transportation facilities. We have only a boat which is not suitable for paddling. The motor which came with it is an old one and has been laid up for months waiting for new parts to arrive. So we cannot do such extensive patrolling as I would like. When we get a complaint, I have to send a pair in a borrowed canoe to take care of it. Fortunately, this is a quiet area. There's almost no theft. You've noticed, señora, how few houses have any doors? People whose possessions cannot be locked up have to respect the property of others."

"What was the last complaint?" I again asked eagerly.

"That was typical," he replied. "A man came to tell us that his son was disobedient and disrespectful. So we told him to send the boy to us and a 'pair' talked to him about how his parents had taken care of him and what he owed them in return. He promised to do better.

"The case before that? Oh, that was a woman who came to

complain of the way her husband was carrying on. We asked her if she was a good wife, if she took care of his children, if she was pleasant to him . . . Treated him like a husband should be treated. She admitted that she nagged him a bit. So we had him come in and gave him a little talk about his responsibilities as a father of a family."

I hadn't come here to listen to stories of marriage counseling. "What other cases come up?"

"Well, they come to us if anybody in the family is sick and our *enfermero* takes care of it. Every jungle post has an enfermero, a guardia who has been given a special medical course, adequate for most of the sickness or injuries people get around here. You see, it's the Guardia Civil's duty to take care of all citizens in any way it can. Of course, the service can't afford to furnish the enfermero with much in the way of medical supplies. He pays from his own pocket for a lot of things he'll need and, if they can, civilians usually pay him back. Trouble is, these are pretty poor people. Sometimes it's expensive to be an enfermero. Of course, the state is supposed to reimburse him for medicines given to personnel. And if a guardia is seriously sick or hurt, we send him back to Iquitos when a lancha comes along. The police surgeon takes care of him free of charge and he even gets reduced rates at the hospital."

"Reduced rates! Doesn't the service take care of the men's hospitalization? What if a guardia gets shot bringing in a criminal? Does he have to pay for an operation to dig out the bullet?"

"He only pays the operating room and hospital, things like that," the sergeant said cheerfully. "Maybe medicines if he needs anything special. But the surgeon is free. And, anyway, we don't get shot very often. Mostly the criminals come quietly."

I had noticed a red scar on the heel of the sergeant's hand. It looked like the sort of wound he might have received disarming a man with a knife. Now I asked about it. Maybe now he'd begin to give me an adventure.

Instead, he looked sheepish. "I was cutting new soles for my shoes from some leather I had brought along here. The knife slipped. But I just stuffed the cut with spider eggs and it's healed up fine. You ought to tell your pharmaceutical company about that. Spider eggs are a great dressing.

"If you want a good story . . . Well, Barbirán did some interesting tracking to bring back two murderers. He's on twenty-four-hour duty now, but I'll send him to you tomorrow with orders to tell you the details. Now I must ask you to excuse me. I have a report to prepare."

The rain had stopped to let an uncertain sun peer through when I returned, and Doña Luisa asked me to give her my laundry. As I pulled the dank, smelly clothes from the rubber bags, Doña Luisa shook her head disapprovingly. "Those bags, señora, they are poor. Commercial quality. You see how the rubber peels where it is scratched? Good bags you cannot buy in Iquitos. These have only three coats and of weak rubber. So they do not keep the clothes dry. Better to have Arévalo put more baths of good rubber on them. He does well."

Arévalo was the other civilian on the post. He worked rubber and leche caspi and provided meat for the guardias who had little time for hunting game.

I asked how long would it take. Doña Luisa squinted her slanting black eyes as she calculated. One, two days to draw the rubber from the trees and prepare it with sulphur and gunpowder. Two more days to apply the baths or a full day of sun, for each coat had to be dry before the next could be applied.

"But there won't be time," I protested. "I must leave for Iquitos when the lancha goes tomorrow."

"Men from the rosewood distillery came this morning," Doña Luisa said. "The lancha will first go to Remanso, nearby, up the Putumayo, for a load of rosewood and take it to the distillery. Only after that will it go to Iquitos. Five, six days, maybe eight, as God wishes."

I didn't even fuss. I was beginning to learn that transportation in the jungle should be regarded as an act of God. At least I knew there was a lancha. It would come when it would come. So I told Doña Luisa that I would like to have the bags done.

Don Juan bounced in that evening accompanied by a good-looking young man with candid, light brown eyes and the kind of curly brown hair that won't stay combed. "My friend, Grimaldo Arévalo," Don Juan said. "Ay, señora, such fish traps as I am building! Tomorrow I will finish and then comes the high water and such an quantity of *gamitana*, such *paiche*, such *súngaro* in my trap! And I will go with my harpoon like this!" He swung an imaginary harpoon with his whole body lithe and taut. "And like this! And I will pick out fine fish for everybody!"

I was regarding Arévalo curiously. He was fishing something from his pocket, a little bottle. "Señora," he said, "Don Juan has told me of your quest for medicines and I thought you might like to have this." He had a slow, diffident smile. "It's jaguar fat. Very good for rheumatism and sprains. You just rub it on and the pain stops. I use it on my whetstone, too, for sharpening knives. It's good for a lot of things."

I thanked him and asked if I might pay for it. He was shocked. "No, señora, that's a gift to welcome you!"

Doña Luisa was bustling around the kitchen. "You eat with us, Grimaldo," she called. "And the Señora wants you to bathe her bags with rubber. Three of them."

This boy was a real woodsman. Eagerly I asked him about jungle remedies. He said his father had always used them. Now there was the bile sac of the *majás*, a large rodent. That's a great cure for snakebite. Everybody knows that the majás shares his burrow with snakes. Then there's the fat of the black crocodile, a spoonful three times daily cures bronchitis, even tuberculosis. "But remember, señora, when you're hunting crocs always to aim behind one eye. They dart backward to escape." The fresh skin of a howler monkey wrapped still warm about the throat cures laryngitis, and a vulture's warm body split and bound to the chest, bloody side in, will cure pneumonia . . . "But you have to keep it there until it stinks real strong, señora."

Nobody seemed to consider this conversation unsuitable for dining. Regretfully, I told him that I was afraid that such prescriptions might be difficult to fill in New York.

The next morning, still eager for the firsthand account of tracking murderers in jungle, I asked Doña Luisa where I could find Barbirán. She told me that he would still be at work. The *turno*, alert duty, lasts from noon to noon, and afterward he would want to sleep. Why not wait until tomorrow? The sky was clearing and this promised to be a fine day. In the afternoon, when she had finished her washing, she would take me into the woods to get some medicinal plants.

"Here, señora, the plants are not all the same as in my province. San Martín is eyebrow of the jungle, with more altitude than the Putumayo, so the soil is different. But there are still some medicines I know here. Not far from the post I have seen the *sangre de grado* tree you spoke of, whose sap stops bleeding in women who have given the light to a child."

"Eyebrow of the jungle" for the tropical foothills, and "giving the light" for giving birth are common terminology in this part of the world.

"But it is well we go today, señora," she went on, "for this is Tuesday. And near the tree I have seen some leaves which you should use for yourself, señora. You need them. And they can be gathered only on Tuesday or Friday."

Eagerly I questioned her, but she would tell me no more. She just smiled mysteriously and said, "They will be good for you."

I fidgeted through lunch, through siesta time, then through the lengthy bathing and dressing of little Gloria. At last we set off under a sky washed to a clean, pale blue, walking slowly because little Gloria's legs were so short. She had to be lifted over fallen trees and carried across the deeper puddles. She was used to me now and she talked a lot, but we didn't seem to speak the same brand of Spanish. After a while, she let me carry her. I felt flattered, but I would never have believed such a small child could weigh so much.

We came to a clump of tall bushes laden with golden fruit. The granadillas are ripe!" Doña Luisa exclaimed. She picked one and ate it, but when I reached up to the branches she warned me, "Better not, señora. They will make you sick."

I told her I'd eaten lots of granadillas and they'd never given me any trouble.

"But these are wild granadillas, señora," she insisted, "granadillas of the jungle are stronger than those of the coast."

I broke open one of the fruit and tasted the pale, juicy pulp with its crisp seeds. It was a little different, smaller, with a sharper sweet-sour taste and more seeds. "But they're delicious!" It was hot and I was thirsty. I reached for more.

Doña Luisa fussed. "Señora, these hurt the stomach that is not accustomed."

"This trip has taught my stomach to be surprised at nothing," I assured her. "It is a very blasé stomach." Happily I gorged on the granadillas. It was a very hot day and it took nearly a dozen to slake my thirst.

The sangre de grado tree was only a few minutes beyond. A tall slender tree, with smooth pale bark, it didn't look at all juicy, but when Doña Luisa slashed it with her machete, sap the color and consistency of blood flowed as from a wound. I was elated as I held a cup to catch the liquid. I'd wanted it for so long! This I knew was a most effective hemostatic agent; it was one of the plants the pharmaceutical company wanted especially, the one I'd used externally to stop the bleeding from a bad cut on my arm. The medicine I had seen given by mouth to stop internal bleeding in a woman hemorrhaging after childbirth. I knew this one could save lots of lives. I tasted it with one finger, just to make sure. It had that same acrid, bitter nastiness I remembered. It was really the right one! When we had filled the bottle I'd brought in my shoulder bag, I cut leaves from the tips of branches and carefully put them in the bag to take home to my press.

"And now, those mystery plants of yours?" I asked.

Doña Luisa pointed to a little hollow. "They are there, señora." She showed me two kinds. One was tall with leaves like canna lilies but less fibrous. The other was a bushy weed growing close to the ground. Doña Luisa crushed some of each in her fingers and a flowery fragrance filled the air.

"These, señora, you need. They will quit you of the bad air," she said, nodding portentously.

"Bad air—you mean I smell bad?" I was so shocked I quavered.

Doña Luisa laughed, "No, no, señora. You smell good. The bad air, that is not to smell. No, the bad air . . ." She thought for a moment, then went on, her wide face very serious. "Bad air, señora, is like since you are on the Putumayo. Everything falls bad for you. You say is bad luck. Look you, señora, the river which has much water always, it dries itself when you come. You pass much hardship to find a certain tribe. Always they are in that place. But you come near and already they are no more. At where you arrive, never is good food to sell, never motorboats to carry you. Plants you seek to heal the sick. That is good. Are many here. But all this time, you find nothing."

She shook her head emphatically. "No, señora, is not regular bad luck. You have too many disappointments, one follows another like footsteps. We of the jungle know things that those of the city do not know. We can see the bad air. Is different from bad luck. Bad air is directed on you. Is an evil wish from someone who envies, some angry one. It is put upon you. Nothing will fall well for you until we wash it off."

"You mean like the evil eye?" I asked.

"No, señora, the eye is more strong. With that you are sick to the death. Or hurt, so never you walk again. Or have bad loss. Like the thief take all your money, all your papers, all your things, so never you can get home. When he steal only little things, but you need them, that is bad air. It brings always disappointment and trouble, but it is not mortal. The eye, only a witch can take that off, but the bad air, anyone can quit you of that."

She stooped and began gathering up great armfuls of both kinds of leaves, explaining their use as she worked. We would need a lot. Even little Gloria would have to help us carry them. Getting rid of such long-standing bad air would take lengthy treatment. First, for three successive nights, I must bathe in water thick with crushed leaves. After bathing I must rub down with a strong infusion of the leaves in alcohol. Three evening baths of the leaf-scented water would be enough, but I must rub down with the alcohol infusion for at least twenty-eight nights.

All the way home the scent hung about us. I could hardly wait to begin treatment. My eau de cologne had given out and I'd been following my baths with a rubdown of plain alcohol bought on the lancha. It had a sickly smell like aguardiente, and I hated it. But long ago I'd learned how important it is in this part of the world to follow a bath by dousing on something antiseptic, so I'd just held my breath and sloshed. But these leaves . . . Their perfume was something between magnolia and honeysuckle with perhaps just a hint of gardenia. Not nasty-sweet like most of the perfumes named for those flowers, but clean and sharp as the fresh blooms themselves. I hoped the alcohol wouldn't change them.

It didn't. The alcohol and the bathwater Doña Luisa brought to the kitchen for me that evening were both as fragrant as the fresh leaves. They were also a deep bottle-green which tinted my skin unattractively. But I didn't mind, because I smelled so delicious.

In the middle of the night I woke with a violent abdominal pain. By morning, I was very sick indeed.

"Ayyyy! It's those granadillas," Doña Luisa exclaimed. "Señora, I told you not to eat them. They fell heavy on the stomach."

Whatever it was hadn't fallen on, but through. Personally I was convinced that no fruit could make me this sick. It was probably amoebae again. I've been hospitalized often enough with them to know the symptoms. It felt more like mice, but then it always does. So I started in on the paregoric and other specifics.

Nothing helped. The enfermero, Vásquez Mendoza, came to see me in the afternoon. We decided that the antibiotics I was taking were more efficient than the sulfaguanidine he had, but I gladly let him give me some of his bismuth.

The next day I was no better. In the afternoon, the enfermero killed one of his four hens and brought it to Doña Luisa. "Make the Señora a good strong broth and then stew some rice in it for a long time. Perhaps that will help," he told her. He wouldn't let me pay him for it and I was so touched that I tried hard to eat. But the food seemed to do more harm than good.

The third day I was only faintly better. Don Juan came back from his fishing early and went to the woods. He returned with a huge macaw, its scarlet and blue feathers stained with blood. "How can you kill anything so beautiful?" I protested.

"But, señora, this will make you well. The macaw is a fine strong bird. He makes strong soup, it is medicine. You eat the soup that Luisa will make and tomorrow you are better. You will see!"

Sinful though it seemed to destroy such loveliness, the soup was delicious, the first thing I'd eaten that tasted good. And the next day, though still shaky, I was well enough to go looking for Guardia Barbirán and persuade him to give me his story.

XIX

I FOUND Barbirán "at exercise," a euphemism meaning that he was off duty but engaged in the endless task of keeping the jungle out of the clearing. All day, whenever it wasn't raining there were two or three guardias busy scything. But instead of long-handled scythes, they used machetes, which is very good for the waistline.

I thought Guardia José Alberto Barbirán probably would have been overweight by now, if he hadn't been in the Guardia Civil. He was a strongly built man nearing his middle years, with sharp Spanish features under flat black hair. He came with me to Doña Luisa's house to talk, and sat on a bench with his elbows on his knees, occasionally gesticulating with thick, square hands.

"Yes, Señora, he said, "I've been in the Guardia Civil ever since 1948, and before that I was seven years in the army. I've served in almost every part of the jungle. Even at Puesto Esperanza."

"Is that where you did that famous tracking job?" I asked.

He looked modest, but once he began to talk he spoke fluently. He wasn't inflicted with the sergeant's professional reticence. "No, señora, Puesto Esperanza's the most distant of all our posts, halfway down the border of Brazil. Not so far, maybe, by plane but the way we get there takes at least a couple of months. We go up the Ucayali to Atalaya on a lancha. That's nothing, maybe ten days, but then the work begins. You have to buy a canoe there and then go up one little river after another. Took us twenty-nine days to paddle to the place you abandon your canoe and take to the trail over a watershed between the two river systems. And at the end of that trail, there's nothing but a little stream, so you have to cut down a suitable tree and axe out another canoe and carve some paddles. After that it's

only seventeen days more, and all downstream, to reach Río Purus
and Puesto Esperanza. But the portages are rough. All those little
rivers are blocked by rapids and fallen trees or rocks. The guy who
was with me swore we carried our canoe farther than we rode in it.
But once you get there, Esperanza's a nice little post."

"The sergeant promised you'd tell me about tracking those two
murderers who abducted the women," I reminded him.

"That was when I was at Moyobamba, and it wasn't two murderers, one was only a thief. But didn't the sergeant tell you about
any of his own captures, señora? Like the time he and another man
had to get two delinquents out of a village of tough Indians who
were hiding them? Or how he got a confession from two Indians
who'd killed a white man?

"That was a real funny one, señora. Nobody would ever have
known there was a crime if Sergeant Ramírez hadn't started wondering how a man could drown in a shallow pool. You see, the
Indians were on their way home with six bottles of aguardiente
they'd bought to cure their little sister's measles. They met up with
a white fisherman who suggested they try it to see if it was good. So
they all got drunk and started fighting, and one of them hit the
white man on the head with an oar. His family found him in the
water and just buried him. When we heard of it, we couldn't dig
him up to look over the corpse for injuries because there were no
civil authorities to issue a disinterment order. The sergeant had to
figure it all out, find the culprits and trick them into confession.
Pretty smart work, that."

"But the sergeant told me your case was the most interesting and
he promised you'd give me all the details," I insisted.

"You mean that abduction and rape? Yes, that was a real queer
one. For days, we didn't even know what we were tracking. All we
knew was that two women had mysteriously disappeared. We had
to follow the only thing we could find that looked like a clue."

The complaint that came into Moyobamba headquarters stated
that Celia Acosta, single, white female, seventeen years of age had
disappeared from the home of her parents Abel and María Acosta in
the hamlet of Soritor. Guardias Barbirán and Julio Chuquiván were
sent to investigate. Barbirán, the senior of the two, was in command.

Soritor is a tiny, isolated community on the watershed between
the Suche and Mayo rivers. As they walked the trail, the two

policemen speculated on the case. Chuquiván was a wiry, eager young man recently graduated from the police school, and his sharp black eyes were bright with the hope of adventure.

"You think it will turn out to be a murder?" he asked. "I never worked on a murder case yet."

"No, I doubt it," Barbirán replied. "They'd have found the body before this if there was one to find. Even if it was hidden in the woods. They looked for her over a week before they came to us. And those people, they know how to track. Born to it. And anyway, the only time you get killings in these parts is when somebody gets fighting drunk. And then of course everyone knows about it. What I think is she just eloped. The guy who brought in the report said she was pretty. And she was old enough to get married."

"Yes, but he said that she didn't have any romantic interests," Chuquiván argued, "and in any place like that, with not much more than a hundred inhabitants, everybody knows everybody else's business. They'd have talked if she had a boy friend."

"Some of these tropical girls are smart," Barbirán said. He stroked his little mustache reminiscently. "Don't forget it isn't like those cold, bare mountains where you come from. Around here, you don't have to go very far into the brush to be out of sight."

"Maybe so," replied Chuquiván, "but if she eloped, why isn't there a man missing, too?"

They were silent for a few minutes while they climbed a steep and slippery hill. At its top, Chuquiván began again. "She couldn't have just got lost. Sergeant says these jungle gals never go wandering off where they can't find their way back. You know what I think? I'll bet you she got abducted!"

"Abducted!" Barbirán snorted. "Didn't you look at any maps or vital statistics before we left? Who the hell is there to do any abducting in those parts? Nothing but jungle and swamp. The only settlers are those in Soritor. Nobody else anywhere around, except maybe a few stray tribes of Aguarunas. And they never go for white women."

They arrived at Soritor in the early afternoon of the next day. It was a community of hunters and small farmers. The two policemen reported to the Gobernador, who invited them to make his house their headquarters. They questioned the girl's family first, then, systematically, all the other residents. Obviously, Celia had really had no boy friends. The elopement theory was out. No strangers had appeared in the district for a long time. They found no hint of motive, no clue, until they reached the most distant house of the community.

In a ramshackle little hut an old woman and three children were smoking fish on a rack over a smoldering fire. The family appeared to have far more Indian than white blood, and the old woman's Spanish was poor. The guardias asked where they could find the man of the family. The crone told them he was out fishing, but it was late now. He'd be back soon. "And the children's mother?" they asked.

"Poor my daughter!" the old woman said mournfully. "Doñatilda no come back much time."

Patient questioning elicited the fact that Doñatilda had gone to the river one morning to wash the family's clothes. She had never returned. Doñatilda's husband, Dionisio Torre, arrived while they were questioning the woman. He was a short, stocky man, very dark, who spoke more Spanish than his mother-in-law, and he confirmed her story. Several months ago, Doñatilda had gone to do her washing. When she did not return by noon, he had gone to search for her. He had searched for days, and her brothers had helped him, but she was never seen again. Her description? She was a very small woman, very dark, thirty-one years old, of Indian blood though she spoke good Spanish.

"Why did you not report her disappearance?" Barbirán demanded.

"Report? Is to go to Moyobamba, tell police? But Señores Guardias, is clear what passes with Doñatilda. She is good wife. Is good mother. Never she go from children. She go only to little creek to wash the clothes. Water is not deep. Donatilda know to swim good. She no drown. But she no come back. She is gone. Many days we look for her, but nothing. Is clear what passes. Comes big snake, he swallow her. Or comes demon from water, he carries her away. Her mother say is water demon *yacuruna*. I say is water boa who eat her."

Barbirán quickly established that when Doñatilda vanished her husband had been off in the jungle felling trees with three other men. He could have had nothing to do with her disappearance. Now, with two women inexplicably missing, the case appeared more sinister. Again the guardias questioned everyone in the community. Again, they sought traces of strangers. Had anyone seen anything, however trivial, that seemed strange or unusual?

One man had. His name was Arturo Chuquisuta, age twenty-eight, and he was a hunter. Two days ago, he had skirted a long swamp and noticed a tree lying across its deepest part.

"A tree should not lie there," he told the guardias. "There is no reason. I ask myself why is it there, unless it is a bridge? But why is a bridge where there is no trail? In all that part there are no trails. No one passes there. Too many swamps. I pass there only because I have followed far the tracks of a deer."

Again the policemen questioned the man of Soritor. No one had gone in that direction for months. No one knew of any bridge. But this was their only lead and they decided to follow it.

A fresh trail is not too difficult for the experienced tracker. True, in the rain forest there is little bare earth to take footprints. Animals perhaps, but never humans, can take many steps without disturbing the thick layer of dead leaves covering the ground. If it is a wet day and the tracker sees one leaf that is drier than the others, he knows a human foot has turned it over. In fine weather the underside of leaves holds moisture. An occasional leaf damp side up is the giveaway. But following an old trail is quite a different matter. It requires intent and tedious circling over a wide radius, with careful scrutiny of every centimeter of ground.

Progress for two searchers alone would be impossibly slow. Barbirán asked the Gobernador to select the two best woodsmen from the many who volunteered. They were the brothers Juan and Aníbal Campos, short, dark, quick-moving men who looked enough alike to be twins. Quickly, they and Arturo Chuquisuta were formally deputized, and told to be ready to leave at five in the morning.

Only one more thing remained to be taken care of before the weary policemen could retire to the beds awaiting them at the Gobernador's. They needed food for the party. Neither of them had brought much money, but they pooled what they had. It was enough to buy fifteen cans of sardines, about all the little village store afforded. To this their host added a generous sack of *farinha*. Farinha, a staple for jungle travel, is one of the few foods I like less than salt fish. Made from yuca, grated and dried, it needs no cooking. Most people eat it dry, but it makes me nervous. It has the flavor and consistency of small pieces of broken teeth, and I'm always afraid that what I'm chewing must contain bits of my expensive porcelain caps. Farinha soaked in water, however, is different. It softens and swells to many times its original bulk, and a few handfuls of farinha will fill an average stomach quite comfortably.

When they assembled the next morning, a little before dawn, the policemen found four instead of the three assistants they had expected. The Campos brothers had brought along an Aguaruna Indian who worked for them. "Chato is better than any white man in the jungle," Juan, the elder brother, explained. "He's got eyes and ears like a wild animal. And he can move through the worst brush quiet as a snake. He's a good boy, Chato is."

It was a beautiful morning with plumes of mist rising through the branches. With nothing to watch out for until they reached Arturo's fallen tree, the men joked and chatted as they walked. After two or thee hours the going got stickier. There were pools instead of puddles and long stretches of bog. The two policemen removed their high-laced shoes and tied them around their necks It was much easier to walk barefoot like their companions.

They came to the "bridge" in the early afternoon. It was a *cetico*, one of the commonest of jungle trees, and its slim trunk lay across the surface of the water in the middle of a long, narrow swamp. Meticulously, they examined the earth around the water's edge, but not even Chato could discover any indication that there had ever been a trail in these parts or that a human foot had ever trod here. When they waded out for a closer look, they discovered that the tree hadn't just fallen. Its trunk showed clearly the marks of the machete which felled it, and the powdery mould on it's smooth, pale bark was bruised in two places, as though by passage of a bare foot. The tree bridged a hollow where the water was waist-deep.

At the far edge of the water, Barbirán beckoned the men to close around him. Softly he said, "Now we know we're following somebody, even if we don't know who or how many. From now on, nobody speaks above a whisper. And nobody smokes. One whiff of tobacco could give us away as good as a shout. Now we'll spread out and start looking. If you find anything, whistle twice like a bird . . . like a *paujil*. There's plenty of them around here."

He didn't have to say more than that. They knew what to look for. There was small chance that they'd find anything so helpful as a footprint, but no woodsman would be fool enough to venture through this jungle without leaving an occasional sign to mark his way back. Heads bent and eyes intent they circled. It was that sign that they must find, and it was slow work. An hour passed, two hours, but they had covered only a few hundred yards when the paujil whistle sounded twice.

Silently the men converged on the spot where Aníbal Campos stood. His whole body, rigid as a bird dog's, pointed to a seedling, pencil-thin and less than two yards long. It had been sharply bent about a foot above the ground. "They go there!" he whispered, flinging his arm in the direction indicated by the slant of the seedling. "There" was almost at right angles to the line given by the bridge.

"This is no hunter," Arturo whispered. "Is somebody does not wish it known where he goes."

"Smart guy, huh?" Chuquiván remarked.

"Is no Aguaruna!" Chato's eyes were scornful under the straight black bang of hair. "My people no have to bend little trees. Aguaruna know where he go."

"Almost like an old con's trick." Barbirán grinned happily. "Could be we're on to something real good. Come on—spread out there. And maximum caution. *Vámonos!*"

Again the men formed in a long line and started circling slowly in the direction pointed by the seedling. But they found nothing more, and soon the light failed. They camped on a patch of higher ground where the earth was fairly dry. They did not dare to make a fire or smoke or speak above a whisper, but they did risk cutting a few palm leaves to make beds. They worked so quietly that any sound which rose above the shrilling of frogs or the sawmill whine of cicadas would seem nothing more than a slight breeze rattling a dead tree. While they ate their cold rations, Barbirán assigned sentinel duty, two men on guard for three-hour shifts throughout the night. Then they slept.

They were back on the job before the morning light was strong but it was after ten o'clock before the paujil whistle sounded again. This time it was Chato who called. They found him far off to their left, standing at the edge of another of those endless swamps and pointing out toward its middle. The men clustering around him stared. Then Barbirán whispered, "What is it? I don't see anything." Nor did the others.

"Bridge," the Indian whispered. He led them into the muck. The tree had fallen into the middle of a deep bog, more mud than water, and had sunk so deep that they distinguished its outlines only when they were almost upon it. But it was there, another cetico, and when they heaved its end above the surface of the mud, it too had been cut, and recently, by a machete. Like the bent seedling, it pointed another change in direction. As they separated again to form a new line, Juan Campos said, "What did I tell you? Ever see anybody with eyesight like that Indian's?"

They had been circling again for a good half hour when Chuquiván, passing by chance near Barbirán, waved violently at him. Barbirán stopped. "What you got on your leg?" Chuquiván hissed.

Barbirán glanced down. There on the back of his bare calf, just below the trouser leg he'd tied up with a piece of vine, was something that looked like a small brown sausage.

"Hold still. I'll get it off," Chuquiván whispered as he tried to dislodge it with his machete. The soft brown sausage split in two and bright blood spurted down Barbirán's leg

Juan Campos ran up. "Jesus!" he whispered. "Don't you know enough not to cut the head off a leech? Now its mouth is still inside, stuck to that big vein, and the blood will keep spilling."

Barbirán sat down, snatched off his belt and began to wind it around his leg above the gush of blood.

"What's that for?" Juan asked.

"Gotta make a tourniquet to stop the hemorrhage," Barbirán answered.

"That's no good, not with the head still inside there. Here, I'll fix it." Juan took a pack of cigarettes from his pocket and began carefully to strip the tobacco into a big leaf. By now the other men were crowding around.

"Tobacco mixed with urine," Arturo said. "Yeah, that will draw the head out and stop the blood."

"You crazy?" Barbirán protested. "Want me to lose my leg?"

All the local men insisted. They were used to leeches. The swamps were full of them. This was the only treatment that would do the trick. They'd all used it.

While they talked in low whispering voices, Chuquiván produced a handkerchief. It wasn't clean, but it was the only one in the crowd. He handed it to Juan as he urged, "Look, chief, we got no medicine anyway. And these guys are used to this sort of thing. They know.

What else is there to do anyway? You can't just keep a tourniquet on it forever."

While Barbirán was still trying to make up his mind, Juan slapped the unsavory mixture on the leg and bound it expertly in place. "O.K. now," he announced, "you can walk."

Frowning, Barbirán got to his feet. He twisted to look down at the bandage. No blood seeped through. "It's time for lunch anyway," he said, sitting down again. "Then I'll see how it feels."

They ate quickly and resumed their circling. Hour after hour they worked and found nothing. Barbirán grew uneasy. Not about the leg. The bandage had got lost in one of the swamps and he could scarcely see, let alone feel, where the leech had been.

But what if their quarry had made another right-angled turn after that last bridge as he had after the first? They'd been working straight on for more than four hours now without a sign of human passage. Maybe they ought to go back to that second bridge and start all over. To follow a trail this far, and then lose it . . . That would be too much!

It was Chato who found the path. The Indian worked faster than the others and he'd got some distance ahead of the line. At his whistle, the others hurried up.

"Look," he whispered, "is trail, much passing."

The faint, continuous depression in the dead leaves lay almost directly across their line of advance.

Barbirán put his lips to Arturo's ear. "Sure you never heard of anybody settling here?" he asked. Arturo shook his head emphatically. "Aguarunas, maybe?" Barbirán turned to ask Chato but the Indian wasn't there. Without a sound, he had drifted down the path and was squatted some distance away at its edge. When the others joined him, he pointed to a spot where the leaves had parted to show two indistinct indentations in the mud.

"Man walk," the Indian breathed, "white man. Going there," he pointed to the left. "Then, after, come back going there." He pointed to the right.

It's easy enough to distinguish between footprints made by a foot which has worn shoes and the splayed toes of Indians who have never been shod. But Barbirán, closely though he looked, could see only a vague, shapeless smear. Yet the Indian spoke with certainty. "Somebody living there." And he pointed down the path to the right.

Tensely, the men started down the trail, but failing light soon made them withdraw some distance into the woods. The unknown habitation might be very close. The men knew that now they must not only speak in whispers, they must also eschew any unnecessary movement. There was always the danger of startling some sleeping bird or animal into sudden flight or a cry that did not belong to evening. And there was the even greater danger of stilling the normal noisy nighttime chorus of frogs and insects. Sudden silence in a jungle night is a more certain betrayal than a sudden cry.

Huddled under a tree, they discussed the situation in whispers. Everyone was sure that if settlers had moved into these inhospitable swamp-girt woods, they would have made their presence known in Soritor. Chances were that this was a new group of Aguarunas. Like so many other tribes, it is their custom to move into an area, plant their chacras and settle down until an insect plague invades their crops or a couple of years' hunting has made the game wary and less plentiful. Then they move to some other district. Only Chato was sure that the path had been worn in the leaves by whites. But pressed to explain, he could give no reason for his belief.

Food was running short. That night two cans of sardines had to be enough for the lot of them. They didn't dare risk cutting leaves for a shelter. Instead, they slept under a big tree, with sentinels posted.

In the middle of the night, a hand shook Barbirán awake. He jumped to his feet, his carbine at the ready.

"Shhhh, listen, chief." It was Arturo who was on guard.

"What is it?" Barbirán hissed. "What's the matter?"

"Hear that frog?" Arturo whispered.

Barbirán listened. "I hear a thousand frogs," he replied. "What is it, somebody signaling?"

"No, the one that goes *hoo, hoo, hoo,*" Arturo replied. "That's the 'winter' frog. Means we're gonna have rain."

Barbirán swore elaborately. It was frustrating to have to swear in a whisper. "And you wake me up just to listen to some castrated frog?" he asked furiously.

"But it's a 'winter' frog," Arturo insisted. "Means a storm."

Barbirán growled softly and went back to sleep. But not for long. Thunder, lightning and a torrent of rain woke the men. Hastily they spread the two guardias' rubber ponchos and crowded under them, drenched and shivering. It was cold and it was wet but they could talk now. They could have shouted without being heard ten feet away in that downpour. But nobody felt like talking. Unhappily they huddled, cramped together until dawn came and the rain stopped.

They set out in the first light without bothering to eat. The path showed clearer as they went along, slowly, silently. At noon, they opened one tin of sardines and shared them carefully. That left only four more tins. For how long, Barbirán wondered. The path seemed endless. All day they crept along it.

Almost three days gone and still we have no idea whether we'll find those missing women or whether we're stalking a harmless lot of semi-civilized Indians, Barbirán reflected uneasily. He looked over his shoulder at the men following. Those he could see were walking with steady caution. Their faces held the same alertness, the same good-humored determination they had shown on leaving Soritor. That was to be expected from Chuquiván. He'd been trained by a year of rigid discipline in the police school, a year of constant reminders, day and night, that to wear the uniform of the Guardia Civil is to wear honor itself. For this demanding honor, any Peruvian is proud to sacrifice comfort, security, self-interest, even his life if need be. But the other men, they had no uniform to live up to. Sure, they were used to hardship, to enforced silence while stalking game. But they were not used to being forbidden day after day to smoke or to talk or to relax their vigilance when the long day's work was over. They were not used to the monotony of a trek like this and they were not used to following orders meekly. They had no uniforms to live up to. But Jesus! Barbirán thought, they're taking it just as if they had!

About five-thirty Arturo, walking at the head of the file, suddenly stopped and beckoned to them, signaling at the same time for caution. Through the trees ahead of him, the men saw a clearing where yuca grew and *plátano* trees made orderly lines. They all stared for a moment, then as one man they withdrew far into the woods to consult.

A plantation meant a house. And this was no new plantation; whoever made it had lived here for some time. Funny no dogs had barked. Even Indians always keep dogs, for hunting and to warn of the approach of marauding jungle beasts. They decided to send Chato to reconnoiter. He could move so silently that even dogs would never hear him, and he would take care to keep downwind.

They sat under a tree to wait, so excited that the rule of silence chafed as never before. Time passed. Darkness fell. Barbirán jumped when a hand touched his shoulder. Nobody had been aware of the Indian's return, though they'd been straining their ears for the slightest sound.

"Celia is there!" Chato whispered. "I see her! Inside house, I hear voices of men, voices of women. Then Celia come out back, go to henhouse. Almost is dark, but I know her. Is Celia!"

Carefully the men questioned him. Then Barbirán summed up the information.

"There's a clearing about seventy yards square and the house stands in the middle. Thank God, it's not one of those Indian houses, open all the way round. This one has only two doors, one in front, one at the rear. It looks as though there might be another room up under the roof, but there are no openings above. There are no dogs. We can handle this easy. Here's what we'll do.

"Chato couldn't find out how many of them there are, but we can be sure they're armed. So we'd better give them a real surprise. We'll wait until the hour of deepest sleep. Say 3 A.M. We'll surround the house a little before that. When we close in, Chuquiván, you and Arturo can cover the back. Juan and I will go in the front door. Anibal, you and Chato will place yourselves one at each side of the house, ready to help Chuquiván, if he needs you, or to grab anybody who gets by your brother and me. Don't any of you shoot unless you have to. But if you hear a shot inside the house, then start shooting fast, all of you. *Jesús!* They'll think it's an army!"

Strategy decided, they opened all four cans of sardines to celebrate the end of their quest.

Around three o'clock when they stole to their appointed places, a thin slice of late-rising moon showed through curdled clouds. Barbirán and Juan Campos paused for a moment at the black rectangle of open doorway listening to the quiet breathing within. It sounded like two people and it came from their left. Barbirán snapped on his flashlight as he leaped toward the sound saying, "Hands up! We're police!" The yellow beam showed a man and a girl lying on a pallet. The girl's mouth opened and her enormous black eyes stared, but she didn't make a sound. Barbirán snapped handcuffs on the man who was struggling to get to his feet, and the man shouted, "*Amigo!* The cops! Run!"

Overhead, they heard the thump of feet, and Juan ran to a ladder in the corner of the room. The girl on the pallet screamed "We're saved! Police! We're saved!" Then she went into hysterics. Before Juan could climb to the top of the ladder they heard a loud crash, then a shot rang out.

Out in back, Chuquiván and Arturo had started toward the back door when a figure smashed through the thatch of the roof, dropped to the ground, stumbled, and started to run.

Chuquiván yelled, "Halt!" But the man kept running, so he raised his gun and fired. When Arturo's head poked through the hole in the roof, Chuquiván was putting handcuffs on the fallen man. "O.K. here!" he called. "One prisoner. Nobody hurt. I just fired into the air and he dropped."

A thin, dark woman slowly sat up on the pallet behind Juan. When his light fell on her, she, too, shrieked and ran for the ladder, almost falling into the room below. The two women embraced, laughing and sobbing together.

Barbirán told me that the most harrowing part of the whole business was trying to calm those hysterical women. Kind words only made them howl louder. It was Arturo who solved the problem by bellowing, "Silence, women, and get us something to eat! We're starving!" That brought them to their senses.

Only then did Barbirán realize how hungry he was. While the women plucked scrawny chickens, he tried to question the manacled men sitting on the dirt floor with their backs against the pona wall. They were giving no answers. They just sat there, staring straight ahead of them.

Except for the straw-filled sacks which served as a bed, the room's only furniture was a crude bench. Barbirán shoved it in front of the two men and sat studying their faces. One was short and stocky and his flat features showed a mixture of white and Indian blood. The other was pure Indian, taller than most, and strikingly handsome. That was the man Barbirán had caught downstairs, and as he had trained his flashlight on him, the face seemed somehow familiar. He moved to one side and scrutinized the bold profile. Then he remembered. He had seen that face on a WANTED circular tacked to the wall of Moyobamba headquarters, seen it daily. Juliano Tantawatai, convicted murderer, escaped years before from Moyobamba jail while awaiting transfer to the penitentiary. The half-breed would be Otóniel Cuevas, thief, who had broken jail with Tantawatai.

Barbirán's heart thumped. Here was a real catch! It took an effort to keep his voice level as he said, "Tell me, Tantawatai, why did you break jail like that? Been living here ever since you escaped from Moyobamba?"

The prisoner spoke for the first time. Vehemently he denied that he had ever been in jail. He had never before heard the name Tantawatai. He had never before been in trouble with the police. His voice grew humble. He was only a poor farmer, honest and hard-working. Hadn't they seen his *chacra*? That should be proof enough. This was the first time he had ever done anything wrong. But his was a lonely life. Man was not meant to live alone. Every man has a right to the comfort of a woman in his house.

Barbirán cut him short. "*Estúpido!* You couldn't fool the police before, and you're no smarter now. Remember we took your picture when you were arrested? We still got it. Remember we took your fingerprints? They'll prove who you are the minute we bring you in. You and your pal, the thief Cuevas. And you'll have a lot pleasanter trip home if you confess before we leave. But if you don't . . ." He grinned fiendishly and rubbed his hands together.

That was all that was needed. The prisoners broke. They poured out the story of how they had tunneled under the walls of the old jail and sought safety in the jungle. They had set up housekeeping with tools stolen along the way . . . a machete here, an axe or shotgun there. But it was years before they had dared to steal a woman.

They hid in the brush near Soritor for days before they had a chance to snatch Doñatilda. Cuevas had gone up to where she squatted, washing her family's clothes, and told her with great politeness that her husband wanted her. He was in the woods and had said she was to come at once. Unquestioning, she followed him to the thicket where Tantawatai hid with a poncho ready to throw over her head. Cuevas slapped his hand over her mouth to stifle screams already muffled by the heavy wool. They carried her for a short distance, then set her down with a shotgun at her back. She was so terrified she could only weep, "Don't kill me, don't kill me!"

"You come along nice and quiet, and you'll be all right," they told her, "but scream or try to get away, and you're dead."

They had no further trouble with her. Doñatilda was timid and submissive by nature. After that first, terrifying day, she did not try to escape. They used her as a communal wife and farmhand. She was accustomed to working in the fields with her husband. But Tantawatai, always the dominant one of the two men, grew bored.

"You can have her," he told Cuevas. "I'm gonna get me a real woman, something younger and prettier, all for myself. And you're gonna help me."

They had made several trips to Soritor, spying on its inhabitants from hiding-places in the surrounding jungle. Celia was just the girl for Tantawatai's exacting tastes. After seeing her he would settle for no one else.

But Celia seemed always to be accompanied by some member of her family. They watched for days before they had a chance to catch her alone. Then they used the same technique. Cuevas told her that her father had sent him to fetch her. And when he led her into the woods, the waiting Tantawatai was ready with his poncho. But Celia was no easy prey. She fought back with surprising strength. Tantawatai had to carry her over his shoulder the whole of the first day, with Cuevas walking alongside, clutching with both hands the poncho over her face. When they stopped to rest they had to tie her up with tough vines. She had no fear of their guns. She dared them to kill her. When they raped her, she fought like a tigress.

Even after they got her home, she remained defiant. Never could they make her work in the chacra. Instead she tried to run for the woods, though she knew she could never find her way home alone. She even succeeded in spurring Doñatilda to rebellion. Since her arrival, the two men had found it necessary to lock both women in the henhouse every time they absented themselves.

"She will not be tamed, that one," Tantawatai said, and there was a wistful respect in his voice. "She has much character. After that first day, I keep her for myself. Cuevas cannot touch her."

They left as soon as the posse had eaten. The return to Soritor took two days of walking, but the whole community turned out to give them a triumphant reception. "Celia's family insisted on throwing a big fiesta that night," Barbirán said to me. "They wouldn't believe us when we said that all we wanted to do was sleep. The next day we had to start back over the trail to Moyobamba at dawn, with those two criminals to guard every step of the way. I can tell you, señora, we sure were glad to get them home and turn them in. I slept for two days straight."

"When you brought them back, weren't your chiefs pleased with you? Did you get a reward?" I asked.

"Well, there wasn't any money reward posted for them. But you know what they did about us, señora, me and Chuquiván? They put our pictures in the monthly magazine of the Guardia Civil!"

The expression on his face would have been appropriate for a scientist modestly announcing that he had been awarded the Nobel Prize.

CHAPTER

XX

I LEFT Puesto Yaguas as abruptly as I had arrived. I had taken advantage of a sunny afternoon to photograph some unusual aspects of police work in the jungle behind the Post. Unaware that the humid atmosphere had finally driven mad the timing device on my German camera, I was clicking away happily, spoiling roll after roll of film, when one of my Guardia models suddenly gestured for silence.

"Listen!" he said. "The lancha!"

We all heard the dull throb of motors and ran for home.

I had little time for farewells. Doña Luisa helped me pack. The rubber duffel bags were sleek amber now instead of peeling white. Arévalo had given them five coats of fresh latex mixed with kerosene, salt and gunpowder to make them resistant to all kinds of damage, and Doña Luisa had examined every inch before pronouncing the work first-rate and allowing me to pay for it.

The *Almirante* was said to be one of the fastest boats plying the river. Passengers and cargo shared the enormous scow pushed by a small tugboat with a powerful Caterpillar motor. When I clambered aboard I found only three or four passengers, and a truly appalling smell emanating from beneath tarpaulins covering a huge rectangular mound in the center of the deck. It left barely room enough to hang hammocks like spokes of a wheel around its edges. I asked what it was.

"Salt fish," answered the rubicund man who had introduced himself as Eustacio Martínez, manager of the *Almirante*. "And we've already got more than three thousand metric tons of it right there in that stack," he added proudly.

Six hundred and sixty thousand pounds of fetid, fuming fish I'd have to live with until we reached some place where I could get a plane to Iquitos! Never would I have believed that I'd look back with longing on traveling with a pig. But I did now. That lovely pig who didn't smell at all.

"Just hang your hammock wherever you like," Don Eustacio said hospitably. "Enchanted to have you with us." He bowed and bustled off.

A husky young man in Guardia Civil uniform gave me a hand with my hammock. He was Wilfredo Vásquez Rengifo and he was returning to Iquitos after having served a couple of years at a post named Corbata up the Putumayo.

"This will be the best corner for you, señora," he told me. "It's the only place the roof doesn't leak."

I asked why he hadn't moved in there himself and he laughed. "On a boat like this it saves trouble to pick a good leaky spot right at the start. There's sure to be ladies coming aboard sooner or later, and then I'd be moving anyway. A little water does no harm to a man, but I hate to see ladies get wet."

A very proper sentiment.

At Tarapacá people swarmed aboard. From there on, the barge teemed with families, infants, children of all sizes, cages full of noisy exotic birds, tiny monkeys tied by cords around their middles, boxes and bags and baskets. Hammocks hung so close they bumped. Low-blooming mosquito nets unfolded over people sleeping on the floor. The young deckhand whose bed had been the bench under the head—salt-fishless end—of my hammock gave his place to a mother and child and curled up on two suitcases under my middle. He was really better off there. Like the envied few who had rolled their blankets under the dining tables, he was now protected from water dripping through the roof. A boy with a steaming bucket of leche caspi was daily sent topside to patch the leaks, but every time it rained, water flowed through in a new place.

At each stop, the block of salt fish grew higher. It was all *paiche*, a giant fish often attaining a weight of more than two hundred pounds, which is found only in the Amazon River system. The folded slabs carried aboard were as big as blankets, wet blankets oozing malodorous streams as their salt drew moisture from the humid air.

Unfortunately, the smell did nothing to spoil my appetite, and as the days passed I grew hungrier and hungrier. The principal meal of the day, noontime dinner, usually consisted of chicken soup, chicken, rice, beans, yuca and boiled plantains. But the chicken soup was the palest I've ever seen through, and the size of the portions made the rest of the meal, despite its high carbohydrate content, a first-rate reducing diet. I had bribed the cook to supply me with boiled drinking water. One day, having received a single wing tip as my share of the chicken, I asked him how many fowl he killed for each meal.

"Usually two, señora," he replied. "Unless they are very small. Then I am allowed three."

"And how many people does that feed?"

"Oh, thirty-five perhaps, perhaps forty." He shrugged.

At every stop, all passengers surged ashore in search of food, but the little villages seldom had anything to sell except bananas. I couldn't face another banana even when somebody else was eating it.

We left Peru behind and both banks of the river were Colombia. "Colombia the gem of frustration," I muttered, scowling at the rain-veiled shadow of jungle. We left it behind and entered Brazil, where the Putumayo changes its name to Içá. People dark as good Brazilian coffee poured aboard with swarms of the sweetest-tempered children I've ever seen, and soft Negroid voices filled the air with Portuguese.

There is something extraordinarily right about Portuguese as the national language of Brazil. Portuguese has the rippling swishing sound of great slow rivers. It is very like Spanish, but Spanish softened, half melted by the warm, damp tropical air.

We left the Içá and turned up the Amazon, which in this part of Brazil they call the Solimães. Being on the Amazon again made me realize that I was really heading for home. That only made me feel worse. Homeward-bound without having completed the mission I had set for myself.

I was on the front of the barge one evening glowering at a medium spectacular sunset when Guardia Vásquez Rengifo sat down beside me. "*Caráy!*" he exclaimed, slapping vigorously. "These Amazon mosquitoes are so big that I bet they got bones in them. Still they're better than the gnats on the Putumayo, no, señora?"

My bitterness boiled over. I told him what I thought of the Río

Putumayo! It took restraint to avoid using language not fit for the ears of a nice young man who couldn't bear to see ladies get rained on. Then I told him why . . . my wild Indian chase . . . the plants I hadn't got . . . the witch doctors I hadn't met . . .

"But, señora," he said earnestly, "you must not go home feeling like that. Our jungle has disappointed you and, señora, it pains me. Give us another chance. Peru has many more rivers, little rivers that lead into places that are still wild. Like the river my wife's brother, Wenceslaos, lives on. The Indians there are barbarians. No missions, no lanchas . . . even the boats of the little traders never go up Wenceslaos' river. I have been trying to remember what he told me about the witch doctors there. They have some real special medicine that Wenceslaos told me about . . . something to do with having babies, I think. But it was a long time ago and I don't rightly remember. My wife might know."

I said that I remembered the photograph he had showed me. She looked charming.

"Oh, she is!" he exclaimed. "Luz is wonderful. Look, señora, I know what you ought to do. You're leaving the lancha at Leticia day after tomorrow, no? From there you will fly to Iquitos and you ought to get in a few days ahead of us. *Bueno*. When you arrive, you go to see my wife. Here's the address. The house is very poor—but you won't mind that, will you? You see, I get a decent salary, but we're putting my wife's other brother through law school in Lima. He's brilliant. Anybody with a mind like his deserves a chance. We even sold my encyclopedia to help him with the tuition. But though we are poor, we would be honored to have you in our house.

"What I was thinking is, Wenceslaos just might be in Iquitos now. He comes to town two or three time a year. Then he could take you up his river and it wouldn't cost you a cent. He and his wife don't often get a chance to have visitors. But if he's not there, Luz will tell you about the Indians, and if you think it sounds interesting, she'll do all she can to get you there. She loves to help people. And, of course, when I arrive, I'll do anything I can."

It was too dark to see his face now, but his voice was enthusiastic as he went on. "You do that, señora. Don't give up and go home until you've got everything you came for. We'll make a witch doctor out of you yet." He laughed. "But don't go home disappointed in my country."

I assured him nothing could make me think ill of Peru. And I'd love to meet his wife. But as to the trip . . . well, I didn't see just how I could manage it. Privately I admitted that it was out of the question. My money was almost gone. Even if I got free transportation, how could I afford the supplies and trade goods I'd need?

But when we parted, I was fighting a sudden attack of optimism.

Leticia is a town that sits high on the Colombian bank of the Amazon, with Brazil in the haze across the river. It hasn't much in the way of paving, but it does have airlines, radio communication with the world, a Peruvian consulate, a bank, a hotel. And it does not smell of salt fish.

We arrived at sundown. It was wonderful to sit in the hotel dining room and eat several portions of beef. It was pure joy to retire to a room that was all mine, out of sight and hearing of anyone else; a room where I could wander around undressed before climbing into a real bed with a mattress and sheets and a soft pillow.

The Iquitos plane wouldn't leave for several days. That would allow me time to go to the local bank and have them get cable advice on a check. I'd used up almost all the cash I'd had with me when I left Iquitos. Also I had to get a Peruvian visa before they'd sell me a plane ticket. Mrs. Castro, the amiable woman of the hotel, told me the consulate was close by. It opened at eight in the morning, so I went there first.

The consul was charming. After he had filled out the papers and stamped my passport, I asked him where the bank was and when it opened. He answered me, then added, "But, señora, if you want to change dollars, you will have to do it through some of the local merchants. The bank here in Leticia is forbidden to make any transactions in foreign currency."

I had risen to say good-bye, but the blow folded my knees and sat me down again. "No transactions in foreign currency!" I stammered. "You mean they can't cash a check on New York?"

Now I was stranded in a foreign country where I knew no one. I'd counted my remaining cash that morning. I had about ten dollars' worth of Colombian pesos and Peruvian soles. Not even enough to pay the hotel. I hadn't worried. I had been so sure the bank could arrange matters. But now . . . I fought down rising panic and shut my eyes to concentrate. What to do? I knew nobody in Colombia who would send me pesos. Cable my agent to buy some in New York and wire them to me? But you can't send foreign cables collect. I'd need more than ten dollars' worth of words to

make it clear. Sell a camera? That would be smuggling or something
. . . The idea of breaking laws frightens me even in my own
country. Merely to contemplate such a thing abroad gives me the
horrors.

The consul was speaking so I opened my eyes. "Señora, you
mustn't be so upset! If it's money you need, there's nothing to
worry about. Mike will take care of everything. Let me give you
some coffee." He clapped his hands and a maid in a white apron
popped in with a tray that she must have had ready.

The consul filled a cup and handed it to me. "This will make you
feel better. You have no reason for worry, señora, I assure you.
Mike will cash your check if you wish. Or if you prefer, he will
simply give you whatever you need and tell you to repay him after
you get home. This he always does. And he will be here any
moment, for he always stops for a cup of coffee with me on the way
to his office next door."

"Mike?" I asked. "But who is Mike? And why should he give me
money?"

"Because that is the way he is. His name is Mike Tsalikis and he is
what you call the 'big business,' no? He is the biggest exporter of
jungle animals from South America, and he has also many other
interests all over Colombia, and in the United States and other
countries. He is your compatriot. You have noticed that the people
of Leticia show a special friendliness to Americans? That is because
of Mike. He helps everyone."

While the consul talked, a picture of this kindly big-businessman
was forming in my mind. A cross between Ex-President Hoover
and the Rockefeller Institute was what I expected, but the figure
who ambled through the door for his cup of coffee wasn't like that
at all. He was a narrow, bony young man in blue jeans and sneakers
and he sprawled angularly in an armchair while the consul explained
my predicament. Mike Tsalikis was thirty-one years old, about five
feet ten inches tall and looked as though he had never weighed over
a hundred and thirty-five pounds in his life. His face, with deep-set
dark eyes and jutting nose and chin, was as angular as his body. His
black hair tried to stand at right angles to his head and even his
gestures were angular.

"That bank ruling's an awful nuisance." He grinned when the
consul had finished. "Sure, I'll be glad to cash a check for you . . .
anything you want. Only I think it'd be better if you just let me give

you whatever pesos you need. You can give me a check for that amount when you leave or just send it to me sometime later if that's more convenient. That way you won't be stuck with any leftover Colombian money when you get to Peru. The exchange is sort of shaky just now." He rose to his feet. "Why don't we go and get you organized right away?"

Dazed, I followed him into the street. As we walked along, everyone stopped to shake hands with Mike and I noticed that they all, laborers, children, even ceremonious old ladies, greeted him warmly as "Mike." Nobody called him Señor Tsalikis or even Don Mike. It isn't at all common to see a foreigner universally addressed with such warm familiarity.

"It's so far away down here," he said. "It's such an awful long way from home. When I see somebody in trouble, with no friends or family anywhere around, it makes me feel terrible." Then his head snapped toward me and his chin jutted. "But don't get me wrong. I'm a businessman. I'm an American businessman, and it doesn't do me any good to have American prestige lowered by Americans going broke here . . ."

I have lived a long time in South America and I've often wondered just what percentage of my country's perennial troubles there are due to our national policies and how much to people. Latin-Americans are the most personal people I have ever known. You cannot deal with them exclusively on a country-to-country or a business-to-business basis. You've got to be person-to-person. I've seen a big project fall through because the representative from the States was a man who never thought to ask, "How are your wife and children?" or to let those he dealt with into his life in any way.

Mike knows how. He feels the need deep within himself. What a pity the State Department cannot make his attitude a prerequisite in engaging people! Yet at the airport before I climbed into the plane, I felt inadequate to tell Mike how grateful I was for the many things he was doing.

CHAPTER

XXI

THE FLIGHT from Leticia to Iquitos takes three and one half hours. As I fastened my seat belt, I told myself that in only two or three days I would be on my way back to New York. Of course I would. It was the only sensible thing to do. There was just enough money left in my bank account to get me home comfortably if I didn't run up any extra hotel bills before leaving.

Even though I hadn't found my wild Indians, I had done my share. I had spent four months out of touch with civilization and I'd got almost all the medicinal plants I had gone after. There was only one category missing. It was a pretty important category, but it was the one type of botanical secret nobody had ever been able to persuade the Indians to disclose. I really shouldn't be feeling so glum about it.

I remembered the day I had lunched with the pharmaceutical gentlemen in New York. I had taken a strongly negative position on two of the medical secrets they wanted investigated. My scientific bent, I told them, just wasn't bent far enough. I flatly refused to go up and down jungle rivers asking, "Anybody know any good aphrodisiacs?" That, I told them, was no job for a woman. They finally agreed and withdrew their request.

But on the second subject, contraceptive plants, they had some forceful arguments: the lives of women too frail for surgery and the tragedy of the unwanted children of the poor.

It wasn't statistics that changed my mind. You can examine newspaper graphs of soaring birthrates and inadequate food production in crowded, poverty-ridden countries and you may shake your head. But when you remember what it was like in cities where at night you must pick your way carefully along the curb to avoid disturbing the homeless asleep on bare pavements, when you have seen a little boy found dead from cold and hunger on the stone steps where he spent all his nights, it isn't your head that shakes. It's your heart.

I promised the pharmaceutical company that I would try to learn the contraceptive secrets of the jungle Indians. But, I warned the eager gentlemen, the chances were against my getting anything. No one ever has, though many scientists have tried. Anthropologists have known for decades that certain tribes have children precisely when they want them and at no other time. It is even known that they achieve this through plant medicines taken by mouth. But the secret has been jealously guarded, for such things belong to the most sacred type of magic, the magic of giving or withholding life. And these tribes have a profound conviction that to reveal their knowledge to an outsider will rob the magic of its potency.

I had made a number of jungle trips before I even suspected the existence of such medicines. I remember how puzzled I was by the obviously low birth rates in some tribes. I kept trying to dream up a reasonable explanation. Finally I decided it must be due to their custom of sleeping in hammocks . . . and all those rainy nights. That hypothesis lasted only a couple of weeks. It was discredited by a local wolf who tried to climb into my hammock when I was taking a siesta. A white man, of course (I've never had that kind of trouble with Indians), and he was drunk enough not to be put off by my insect repellent and muddy blue jeans. Obviously an old hammock habitué, he made it quite clear that he was not just looking for a quiet spot to take a nap. I dumped him on the floor—hammocks are handy for dumping drunks—and stalked away with my theory and disposition in ruins.

A medical missionary who had worked with a remote group of savages gave me the first really solid information on Indian plant contraceptives. He and his wife hadn't been with the tribe long when he had to deliver a baby by Caesarean section. The mother had a pelvic malformation which made normal birth impossible, and the missionary was very worried about what might happen if she had another pregnancy. He and his wife knew that it would be impossible to convince the husband that he must, for all time, give up his marital prerogatives. Even to suggest such a thing might alienate the primitives they were working so hard to win. After long prayers for guidance, they decided to tell the woman that if she had another child she might die.

The woman was far less upset than they had expected. She said it was too bad; she had hoped to have more children, but if she couldn't, well, she couldn't. They asked if she planned to leave her husband. She said oh, no, why should she do that? He was a good man. She would merely get the witch doctor to give her a medicine so that she would not conceive again. And in the eight years the missionary was with her people, she never did. Nor did several other women who had perilously difficult pregnancies. In each case, the witch doctor had given them medicine. One dose had been enough.

When I left Iquitos for the Napo, I had great hopes of getting a specimen from my Witoto friends. They do use one contraceptive plant, at least the old Witotos did, although I suspect it has rather toxic side effects. Old Ema admitted to knowing the remedy. But even old Ema, the matriarch of Negro Urco and truly my friend, was reluctant to talk about it. Magic, she said. I didn't give up, but concentrated on winning her confidence.

Ema loved listening to my little transistor radio. Often we sat on the porch until very late, talking and listening to the tangos and boleros from Bogotá. The music was underlined by the shrilling of cicadas, often punctuated by the hooting of tree frogs announcing the coming of rain. Usually we sat in the dark because the light drew so many flying things. I am as afraid of big, dark, dusty moths as some people are of snakes. At home, I have to conceal this reaction and have learned enough self-control to sit rigidly quiet unless the winged horrors fly at me too suddenly. But in jungle nobody thinks it's silly. I was delighted to learn that there are big moths everybody's afraid of. The natives say that on their wings they have "poison dust" which causes a nasty inflammation wherever it touches the skin. Some allergenic substance, I suppose. True, these are very rare, I have never seen one, but it's nice not to have to be brave.

Ema, sitting there in the dark, loved to talk about the past. She told me about the intertribal wars of her childhood, how the enemy would attack from ambush, how the women would snatch their children and flee. Any woman who was caught was carried off. All boy children were slaughtered. She told me of witches and their spells.

Ema herself had been struck by lightning as a result of some magic that had sort of slopped over. She had gone to visit a woman who had offended a very powerful witch living some distance away. Ema figured that the witch did not know she was there when he sent lightning to strike the house. The other woman was killed, but Ema, the innocent bystander, was "dead, too, for many hours," she said. The mourners, Ema's mourners, had gathered around her bier, wailing ritually, when she sudddenly terrified everyone by moving. Hastily, they carried her to the house of her uncle, who like her father was a witch doctor of some note.

With his therapeutic magic, Ema's uncle brought her back to life. But her well-being thenceforth, he told her, would depend on strict observance of certain taboos. Forbidden to her were the meat of the red deer, the white deer, the big wild pig, the armadillo and many other kinds of game. "If ever I eat one of those," Ema explained, her voice matter-of-fact, "I die."

Ema talked freely of many tribal matters, but it was a long time before she knew me well enough to admit that there were certain leaves women took to avoid having babies. These are given to most Witoto girls when they reach puberty, she told me. The effects of a single dose last from six to eight years and it is considered a wise precaution against the girls' becoming pregnant before they are mature enough to be mothers. One night, when we sat late in the dark talking of many things, she promised that in the morning she would bring me a sample of the leaves.

When morning came, I had a hard time controlling my eagerness. Ema knew how much I wanted those plants. I had been bringing up the subject for days and when at last she offered to get them for me I had not hidden my delight. But Ema is not the sort of person whose sleeve you can twitch every few minutes. I waited until midmorning before going to the large, shadowy kitchen house which was her realm.

She was sitting in her hammock, her small sitting-hammock, not the long one she uses for siestas, and I knew something had gone wrong the minute I saw her hands. They were not peeling some sort of vegetable into a bowl on her lap, they were not mending shorts or trousers, they were not even twisting palm fiber against her knee to make cord for the weaving of hammocks. They were folded in her lap.

I said good morning and she said good morning, but she didn't look at me. "Ema," I asked, "the leaves that women take so they won't have children, did you get them for me?"

Ema said, "No, señora."

I waited. After a while, she said, "Without their icaro, their magic, they will not work. You can never learn the song that makes the icaro. It is Witoto song."

Her face was as quiet as ever, but her hands were so tight that I changed the subject and told her how much I had enjoyed the armadillo she had given us for breakfast. Ema is the oldest living member of a reigning Witoto family. Her people still obey her and her responsibility to them is heavy.

That evening Ema brought me a gift, a bunch of exquisite egret plumes, carefully wrapped in a piece of fine white cloth. She had treasured them for years. Neither of us ever mentioned contraceptive plants again.

On the Tamboryacu, the Algodón, the Putumayo, it was always the same. Few Indians could be persuaded to admit that such things existed, and if they did, their eyes would slide away from mine and they would add, "But that is witchcraft." And then the curtain would come down and I'd be left outside. That curtain is something you must respect. Sometimes they lower it by going into spasms of giggles; sometimes they almost convince you that they really don't know what you are talking about; sometimes they just turn stony. But when they shut you out, it is useless to try to force an entrance. Bribery, cajolery, any kind of insistence will arouse only suspicion and hostility. And then you're in trouble.

I thought of all that while the plane droned over the monotonous tapestry of treetops. And I thought of my conversation with Guardia Vásquez Rengifo that last night on the lancha. Ideas about brother-in-law Wenceslaos' river had nagged me steadily ever since. "Some very special medicines—something about having babies." Ethnographic maps showed that area to be inhabited by Aguarunas, Jívaros, Muratos, and Mainas if my memory was correct. Weren't some of those the very tribes reputed to know the secret of plant contraceptives?

When we left the plane in the muggy twilight of Iquitos, I was still telling myself that there was nothing I could do but go home. Nevertheless, it would do no harm to call on Vásquez Rengifo's wife the next morning. Merely a matter of courtesy, of course. After all, her husband had been very kind, and she would probably be happy to hear that he'd be arriving in two days. Maybe her brother Wenceslaos would be there.

Vasquez Rengifo's wife, Luz, was a slender young woman with a gentle voice and enormous black eyes which widened with delight when I told her how soon her husband would arrive. Her brother Wenceslaos? She looked rather puzzled when I asked whether he were by any chance in town. She did not expect him to come to Iquitos for several months. When I explained my reason for asking, she insisted that I should not let his absence deter me from visiting his river. He lives on the Corrientes, she told me. That was one of the tributaries of the Río Tigre. Many interesting tribes live on the headwaters of the streams which run into the Corrientes.

"There are only two white families on the river," Luz told me. "My brother, who went there a few years ago, and the Guimets, who have been there for a long time. One of the Guimet boys, Ernesto, is living in Iquitos now. He could tell you all about the Indians. Perhaps he could take you up there in his boat. He loves the river and it would not be a long trip, not much over a month to go there and return. We can go to see Señor Guimet now if you wish, señora. His house isn't far from here."

Don Ernesto Guimet wasn't home, but his wife, Doña Conchita, said she thought he might like to make the trip with me. He had taken her up there once and she had been greatly amused by the Indians. I gathered they lived very much as they had in ancient days. I managed to bring the conversation around to their medicines.

Doña Conchita said they had one which made it impossible for a woman to conceive. Some sort of root, she thought. An Indian woman who worked in the kitchen of her father-in-law's house had been given some by the witch doctor. No, she didn't know what kind of root. The woman said they'd mashed it thoroughly before bringing it to her in a gourd. She had taken just one teaspoonful and after that she had never had another child.

"And they have another root that will take away the effect of the first one," Doña Conchita continued. "They say any woman who takes it can have a child whether she has had the not-to-have-babies medicine or not. They know a lot of things, those Indians. My husband could tell you more about them. Why don't you come back later, about five this afternoon? Ernesto will be here then."

I returned to the hotel in great excitement. A reversible contraceptive! Tensely I went over the bank statements in the sack of mail which had arrived during my absence. No matter how I figured, I had only enough money to get back to New York. But to learn of a reversible contraceptive and a potent medicine to promote fertility—I couldn't just walk away from that!

Don Ernesto was a short, active man with a quick smile. He confirmed what his wife had told me about the powerful medicine of the Indians and he said he would be willing to take me there and introduce me to the tribe. But when he named a *per diem* price, my heart sank. Thirty days' travel would cost me more than I had, even without considering what I would need for supplies and trade goods. I tried to bargain with him, but it was useless. He made a profitable business of renting his motorboat to people right here in Iquitos. To absent himself from his affairs at this time would not be easy. It simply wouldn't be practical for him to make the trip for less.

"If it's their medicine that interests you, señora, I have already told you as much about it as you'd be able to learn by going up there. This is the most guarded of all their secrets. Magic they call it. I've tried to find out what plants they use. *Por Dios*! Such drugs would be worth a fortune! But they won't discuss it even with me and I've been their friend since I was little. You, señora, are a foreigner. You couldn't get a thing out of them."

Privately I disagreed. I was a woman and this was magic treatment for women. Then, too, I am not convinced that being a foreigner is such a disadvantage as people think. Local whites make no attempt to hide their feelings of superiority. They are the bosses. But I go to the Indians to learn their wisdom. How can I feel superior to people who know so much more than I? The Indians sense this essential difference between the native whites and myself. I'm sure they do.

But, of course, I couldn't say that. To suggest that I might succeed where Don Ernesto had failed would have been extremely bad manners, so I said that although I was curious about their medicines, I was principally interested in seeing and photographing Indians who had not had too much contact with whites. I told Don Ernesto that I would be most grateful if he could find someone who would take me at a price I could afford.

I lay awake for a long time that night, trying to figure out some way to make the trip. It would hardly do to write to the pharmaceutical company for more money because I knew of a tribe that had the medicines and I thought I could persuade them to give me some. If they asked why I thought so, I could give only the most unconvincing answer: I had a feeling I could. But I did feel it strongly. If I could just get to those Indians, I could break the secret. I knew it.

The next morning when I came downstairs, the desk clerk said a man named Paco García was waiting to see me. He was a strongly built, dark-jowled man in his forties who had heard from Don Ernesto of my wish to go up the Corrientes and some of its tributaries.

"Ernesto told me the price he asked you, señora, and I think it very high," he said. "Of course, he has a big boat with a powerful motor which uses much gasoline, and he earns well with it here in town. My boat is smaller. It uses much less gas. The motor is good. For twelve years, I have used it with no trouble. Now it is out of commission, but it needs only a single new part to be as good as ever. If you like, my wife and I will take you for half of what Ernesto asked. Ana was born on the Río Tigre and we both know all that region."

We went to talk it over with his wife. I liked Doña Ana at sight. She was a small, quiet woman with long curling eyelashes and long curling hair, and she seemed competent and sweet-tempered. She said she would enjoy the trip. She liked to travel on rivers and it would give her a chance to see her brother who lived near the mouth of the Corrientes.

García didn't know how soon he would be able to get away. He had some business to attend to before he could leave, but he would call at the hotel that evening to discuss the matter further.

On my way back to the hotel, I consulted Luz. She did not know the Garcías, but she knew of Doña Ana's family. They were good, respectable people, she told me. As for García, Ernesto wouldn't have sent him unless he considered him reliable. The price, Luz assured me, was really very reasonable.

That evening I advanced García the money to buy the new part for the motor. It would take several days' work to get the boat in good running order and he would need a few days to finish up some business. Say, ten days in all. I said that would suit me very well. I could use the intervening time gathering information, laying in supplies and trade goods, and sending that balky camera to Lima to be repaired. We shook hands and he left. But half an hour later, he was back again.

He looked worried. "Señora, we have calculated wrong. Ten days from now will be Tuesday!"

"Tuesday?" I was puzzled.

"But surely you know, señora, that to leave on a Tuesday would be most unlucky. So we must make it eleven days more."

I remembered, then, the old Spanish superstition which makes both Tuesday and Friday days of ill omen. I do not argue with people's beliefs, so I said, "Oh, of course! Wednesday will be fine."

We shook hands again. It was done! I was going!

The next morning I happily cashed a check big enough to take care of all expenses for the trip. There went my going-home money, but I couldn't worry about that now. After all, it's getting to things, not getting back from them, that is important. If my ancestors had insisted on a round-trip ticket, would they have made it as early American colonists or later as pioneers in the West? Certainly not!

XXII

W E LEFT on a morning of sunlight and cloud puffs. Our route would be up the Amazon, then the Marañón to the mouth of Río Tigre; up the Tigre, turning off into Río Corrientes; then far up the Corrientes to its tributary, the little Río Macusari. We should find Mainas Indians somewhere up the Macusari. I knew that this time I was really heading into adventure and I loved it. I was delighted with the security of having my own boat instead of being at the mercy of chance transportation.

I was pleased, too, with the boat itself. It was a roomy dugout, twenty-odd feet long with the usual built-up sides. The midsection flooring was of planks set solidly together. Most boats are floored either with cane or with boards loosely spaced and I'm forever fishing in the bilge under them for cigarette holders, pens and other narrow objects which I've lost through the cracks. I also approved of the pamacari. Stoutly braced, well woven and almost high enough to stand under, it covered the entire boat, except for the tip of the prow. I wouldn't have to move around on my hands and knees. Don Paco García, in his seat at the tiller, and I, sprawled on a blanket amidships with the cargo for a backrest, were as comfortable as we could be.

Doña Ana was less fortunate, though she didn't seem to mind. She was the crew, the laundress and the cook. Whenever she wasn't crouched on the unshaded bow watching for snags or submerged obstructions that might foul the propeller of our outboard motor, she was perched amid a clutter of pots and pans in the unfloored front of the boat. About the only time she had a comfortable seat was when she took over the tiller every day after lunch while her husband enjoyed his siesta.

But worst of all, she had to spend hours daily battling with the decrepit and explosive primus stove on which she prepared our meals. That stove was possessed of evil spirits. Whenever she went to work on it, I pulled in my legs and cowered at the greatest possible distance. Nothing ever happened with the first match she lit, but the fifth, or perhaps the fifteenth, would trigger a whoosh of flame which threatened to set the pamacari afire. Then it would go out and she'd patiently start anew.

Smoked wild pig from the Iquitos market was the principal feature of our diet and it had to boil a long time before it softened up. Sometimes when lunch was almost ready, one of the three wobbly legs of the stove would suddenly collapse and stew like molten lava would stream across the bottom of the boat. On these occasions, Doña Ana might sigh, "Ayyy! This primus!" But that was as near as she would come to losing her temper. For such a pretty woman, she was extraordinarily patient. And she was one of the quietest women I've ever met. Even after dinner, when her chores were over for the day, she would sit smiling through the smoke of her cigarette and let her husband do the talking. He had spent most of his life in the jungle, but jungle lore and adventure didn't seem to interest him. Instead he liked to talk about what he called his philosophy of life.

"Now me, señora, I am a man who must have freedom. Steady jobs are all right for a lackey who likes being ordered around." His finely shaped mouth curved in disdain. "That is not my way of being. I will work for only one boss: myself. Sometimes I get people's crops to the markets for them. Sometimes I pick up commissions here and there. Ana works, too. She has her little table where she sells fruit at the market. But there's no money in it, so we are poor.

"It is not that we have to be poor. I have been offered many good jobs. Even in a bank. It is my cousin's bank and he wanted me to work for him at a fine salary. But I told him, 'No!' A man like me to go to work every day as a subordinate, taking orders from some insignificant official? Being bossed around? I may be poor, but I have my *amor propio*!"

He had his "pride" all right, but looking at Doña Ana's shabby, mended clothes, I remembered that the literal translation of amor propio might be given as "self-love." Yet Ana's eyes, fixed on her husband's handsome, heavy features, expressed only dazzled admiration.

The little five-horsepower motor chugged steadily upstream. The fine weather lasted only for the first day or two. After that, the rain began again, turning itself off and on like a sprinkler system under too much pressure. We passed the mouth of the Ucayali and were in the Marañón. The river was swollen and treacherous with debris, and the settlements along the banks grew gradually farther apart. But this was still well-inhabited territory and there was always a house nearby when darkness fell and our day's travel was over.

The Garcías spent their nights in the boat. Their mosquito net fitted neatly under the pamacari and the flooring of the mid-section was wide enough to be used as a bed for a couple legally married and fond of each other. I preferred to sleep ashore. It gave me a chance to get acquainted with river dwellers and sometimes to pick up useful bits of information. They were pleasant, friendly people who took it for granted that anyone who came along at nightfall would bring his bedding and doss down on their veranda. Being a foreigner and a woman made me a novelty, and often they would sit talking until quite late for jungle people.

Most of them were totally incurious about the world beyond their river, but occasionally I would be embarrassed by a question such as, "Did the Shah Mohammed Reza Pahlevi ever get the Iranian Majli to pass that law limiting the voting franchise to those who could read and write?" A copy of the Spanish edition of *Life* magazine or the *Reader's Digest*, vintage, perhaps, of 1949, had come their way to be read, reread and practically committed to memory. They were eager to hear about the next installment of the lives of world leaders they had read about. I never knew the answers, but they were too kind to show their wonder that a person lucky enough to live in the great world, with so much information available, should not have an encyclopedic knowledge of international affairs.

The first Sunday it didn't rain at all. In the early morning we turned into Río Tigre. Wide where it entered the Marañón, it narrowed rapidly, and the stretches of virgin jungle grew longer and more beautiful. May on the Tigre must be a month of flowering. Flamboyants stretched vermilion fingers to the sky, bushes were hung with big blooms like lilacs and there were shrubs with clumsy, shiny red blossoms that looked like wax flowers made by a beginner. Some trees were hazy with pink or white or yellow blossoms, others were enmeshed in nets of pale pink morning glories. Birds swooping low over the water streaked the air with more color, small, darting birds of yellow and brown, shiny birds of black and scarlet, breasts of Chinese red set off by iridescent slaty wings and backs. Loveliest of all, the pure white egret sailed slowly from the river to perch in trees, watching us as we passed.

As the day wore on, Doña Ana grew positively garrulous with excitement. She told me about her brother, Abelardo Echavarría, whom she would soon see for the first time in three years. Abelardo's wife, Clarita, was the daughter of his neighbors, the Toledos, who lived only two hundred yards away. Abelardo had two children, the youngest born since Doña Ana had last visited the river. "Imagine, señora, a niece two years old and I have never seen her! Would it bother you if I fixed dinner early, just today? Then I can get my work out of the way and change clothes before we arrive. We will get there exactly at nightfall."

Why bother with dinner at all? We could just open some cans. "Oh, no, señora!" Her voice was shocked. "You need a hot supper and so does my husband. Besides, it will help me pass the time."

She had gauged our arrival to the minute. The light faded and still we pushed upstream. The river became an achromatic gleam against blackish foliage along the banks. All strong colors of the day had left the earth to hang in the sky, trailing after the sunken sun like vivid, diaphanous scarves.

Doña Ana, in her best white blouse and flowered skirt, crouched on the prow. We rounded a bend and she shouted, "There! There it is!" On a bluff high over the river I saw a very large house with a glimmer of dim light inside. A gaggle of canoes was tied before us in the port.

Nobody noticed the sound of our motor and no waving figures awaited us on the bank. Halfway up the steep path, I understood why. A hum of voices and a noisy wailing, like a nurseryful of infants, drifted down through the soft night air. We climbed the stairs to an immense veranda in whose shadows at least twenty adults sat around on boxes or benches and innumerable children played on the floor. Small kerosene lamps made islands of brightness. Many of the people looked more Indian than white. Almost every woman had a child at her breast. Everybody, babies and all, rushed to embrace the Garcías. They received me cordially but with a shyness that showed how seldom they met a foreigner.

When the flurry of our arrival had abated, I said to Doña Ana, "I didn't realize you had such a big family."

She laughed. "Oh, all these people are not relatives. I have only my brother and his children. We are not at his house, but in the house of Don Dionisio Toledo. My brother's is the next house. All these people . . . they aren't even relatives of the Toledos. They are from along the river and have dropped in for a visit."

On the Tigre a social call means hours of paddling, and Sunday is the day for visits. Don Dionisio's house was the largest and it had become a general rendezvous. Settlers for miles around put their families, their cooking pots and their bedding into their canoes and started out at dawn for the Toledos'. Most of them lived too far away to return on the same day. They would start home in the morning. Everyone had an air of being dressed up. The women wore fresh printed cottons, the men had new-looking whites or khakis and the children's clothes were miniature copies of the adults'. Yet I was the only person in the place wearing shoes.

I was impressed, as I always am, by the affection with which older brothers take care of the younger members of their families in this part of the world. Quite as many boys as girls sat cradling sleepy babies in their arms or cuddling younger brothers or sisters on their laps. Several boys brought their charges to me to be admired, as proud as though they were new parents. It is not considered sissy for a South American adolescent to show tenderness for small fry. They are natural, warm and charming, and they rarely grow up to be neurotics.

Mothers were putting their children to bed, two or three at a time, on sheets spread on the floor under mosquito nets. In a little while, we made our adieus and with Don Dionisio, brother Abelardo and Clarita picked our way by flashlight across a wide field to Abelardo's house. It was a smaller edition of the Toledos'. Doña Clarita got her children out of bed and she and Doña Ana sat in a corner admiring them. The men started slapping each other on the back all over again and I drew García aside to suggest that he get a bottle of aguardiente from the boat. I had bought an enormous demijohn of the liquor before leaving Iquitos; it is better than money for buying food from the people of the river. Now I thought it would be nice for García to offer a toast to the family—but I had

not foreseen the enthusiasm with which they would insist on recip-
rocating. Don Abelardo brought out his demijohn. Don Dionisio
ran home and returned with a load of pisco, a rare treat on these
rivers. A few of the guests returned with him, and soon it was
evident that a binge was shaping up.

I had been having trouble with my throat and although I'd been
taking antibiotics for three days it was no better. Now it was so sore
that it hurt me to talk, but it gave me an excuse to hang my
hammock and go to bed. The soft voices reminiscing and relating
news lulled me to sleep quickly. When I woke a few hours later, the
voices were no longer soft. The volume increased as the clarity of
their speech diminished. Doña Ana and her sister-in-law were in the
same corner talking quietly, but the men, around a table covered
with bottles, were laughing, gesticulating, swapping boisterous
stories. At two in the morning, I crept from under my net and went
down to sleep in the boat. Nobody saw me go.

I awakened late when Doña Ana leaned over me with a steaming
cup of coffee. She looked as clear-skinned and as clear-eyed as ever,
but her face was anxious. She asked me about my throat. It was
better. She told me that nobody had gone to sleep until after
daybreak. "Clarita and I had so much to talk about, we didn't go to
bed at all. But we drank only that first toast—nothing more. I am
afraid, señora, that my husband has gone to sleep now and I can't
wake him up. I have tried but he just goes on sleeping. My brother
had gone to sleep, too, but he was able to wake up."

"Let them sleep it off," I suggested. "We can leave later or even
tomorrow."

But at eleven o'clock, Doña Clarita took matters in hand. She had
spent the morning cooking a splendid brunch for us, soup, venison
steaks with fried eggs, yuca and plantain cooked in half a dozen
ways, and it was not going to go to waste. Somehow she got the
men to the table. Abelardo was sober but shaky. García looked sick.
His bloodshot eyes were surrounded by dark circles, and lines that
hadn't been visible the day before cut shadows in his face. When
Clarita set a heaped-up plate before him, his mouth tightened
spasmodically as he tried to look as though he were eating.

I felt sorry for him and asked whether he felt up to going on
today. He scowled. "Does the Señora think I am too drunk to
manage my own boat?" he demanded, his voice thick and fuzzy.

"Of course we will go on. We will leave as soon as the Señora has finished her lunch."

I started to protest, but he cut me short and turned to the embarrassed Abelardo. "Now you see the position of your brother-in-law. He is a *peón*. The peón of the Señora. A peón with his day's work still to be done. Tell my *patrona* that her peón is at her orders. He will do his day's work."

We all laughed uncomfortably. *Patrona* means boss. A *peón* is a laborer, the lowest rung in the caste system. As Don Paco had used it, it meant almost a serf.

"But, Don Paco," I tried to speak lightly, "you are the captain of the boat. Surely it is for the captain to decide whether the boat he commands is to sail or stay in port."

Doña Ana shot me a grateful look from under her eyelashes, but her husband was not appeased. A spoon clattered to the floor as he lurched to his feet. He bowed unsteadily. "At *your* orders, Patrona, we will leave at once. There is no time even for the siesta." He started for the path to the river.

"It is his stomach hurting," Abelardo said apologetically. "Always when Paco drinks it gives him a pain afterward."

It gave me a pain, too, I thought, but nothing like what he was probably suffering. I couldn't help feeling sorry for him.

"But he is right about your starting now, señora," Abelardo continued. "You have just time to reach Don Audáz's house in Río Corrientes by nightfall. After Don Audáz's there is no other house for several days of travel. Nobody lives on the lower Corrientes, not even Indians. It is completely wild. So it is well that you pass this night under a roof."

Hurriedly, we gathered our gear. As I climbed into the boat, Abelardo said, "Señora, here is a little gift for you. My sister says you like such things." He fished from his trouser pocket a jaguar's claw and a bit of brownish fur.

"My sister will tell you how to use it," he shouted as we moved out into the stream. "May it work well for you."

"Keep it always with you, señora, and it will bring you money." Doña Ana smiled.

I was delighted. I collect native amulets and superstitions. I hoped this one was in good working order. Then, surely, after I gave the pharmaceutical company all these wonderful plants, they would be grateful enough to contribute something toward the expenses of this second venture. I was going to be in a spot if they didn't.

All the plants I'd collected on the Putumayo trip were still in my plant press. I had dithered a lot about what to do with them before we left Iquitos. I was afraid to ship them ahead. Even air express in this part of the world is subject to inexplicable losses and delays. These specimens were irreplaceable. Careless handling in customs or at the New York plant-quarantine station might cause irreparable damage.

I considered leaving them in Iquitos. But whom could I trust to sun them every bright day, to guard them vigilantly against moisture and to check them every day or two for signs of invasion by insects or other pests? They were too precious to let out of my sight until I delivered them. They had cost me dear in time and money, especially the ones I hadn't collected yet. I needed that jaguar's claw!

I told Doña Ana how much I appreciated her brother's gift. "I'll have the claw set in gold and hang it on my bracelet. But what about the fur? Won't it look rather queer on a charm bracelet?"

Doña Ana laughed. "Oh, you won't need the fur. My brother gave you that, I suppose, because here on the river we are used to having them together. But the fur is not for money. It is for something quite different."

Her voice was calmly informative as she explained. The woods around here are full of jaguars—that's how the river got its name. Her brother often shoots them, for the skins bring a very good price. But there is an extra danger for any father who kills a jaguar. If he doesn't take the proper precaution, one of his children will sicken and die.

"When my brother has shot a *tigre*, he hurries home and grinds part of a claw to powder. This powder he mixes with the ashes of a bit of tigre fur which he has burned in a dish. Then he doses his children with the mixture. He will also make a little scratch on each child's arm with a tigre claw. If he does all this, he can be sure that his children will not die. Instead, they will be well and strong. My brother must do all this even if he shoots a tigre and it gets away. For if it has been hurt, it may die later—and that, too, would be fatal for one of his children. That is why people along the river always keep in their houses a few tigre claws and pieces of fur.

"It is supposed to be good for anything else?" I asked. "Like crocodile teeth? Somebody gave me one to protect me against the attack of any reptile."

Doña Ana shook her head. She had never heard of any other use for tigre claws. But in view of my narrow escape from being eaten or, at least mauled by a jaguar a few nights later, I think I can furnish grounds for a new superstition. After all, the claw was in my pocket when I got into my hammock that evening.

That was the only time I really should have had a gun. But I don't suppose I would have used it had I had one. Real danger, the actual peril-of-your-life kind, is something I never quite believe while it is going on. Such disbelief has nothing to do with courage. Courage is doing something you're afraid of, like asking people for money. I can be badly frightened by an income-tax form; I can be terrified by a flying insect. But jaguars . . . they're so improbable.

On the long, uninhabited stretch of the river we had kept to our usual sleeping habits, the Garcías staying in the boat while I hung my hammock and mosquito net in the brush. I love sleeping out in the jungle at night; it makes me feel adventurous. The jungle comes most busily alive when the day shift has retired and the night shift wakes up and goes to work.

Dusk isn't like that. Dusk begins loudly. The howler monkeys resume their concert with the first coolness of late afternoon. By sunset they have worked themselves into a frenzied crescendo that drowns out everything but the screeching flocks of parakeets. Cicadas whine like a distant sawmill. Thousands of birds squabble raucously over the best spots to roost, but soon they grow sleepy and their fussing gentles to muted chirps and coos. In the first moment of the night there is almost silence but not quite. For now all the little nocturnal creatures that have slept through the long, hot day wake up and go bustling about their business. And the dark is filled with tiny rustlings and buzzings and scurryings no more hostile, no more menacing, than the distant clatter of typewriters in a busy office.

I had slept uneasily the night before. Pushing upstream in the last wisps of light that day, we strained our eyes looking for a place to tie up. But the net of jungle along the banks was impenetrable. Finally we came to a narrow sandspit jutting into the water almost parallel to the shore. There were no trees on it, so I could not hang my hammock. On the highest spot, I spread out a plastic sheet to keep out the damp and laid a blanket over it. García cut poles from the edge of the woods to make supports for my mosquito net. My bed lay not more than five feet above the water. I worried. I had seen a flash flood on a small river like this snatch up a heavy canoe and set it atop a fifteen-foot bank in no time at all. So far it had been raining only in the daytime, never at night, but jungle weather is temperamentally unstable. And flash floods are usually caused by rain falling far upstream.

Tired though I was, I was even more reluctant to fall asleep when, sweeping my flashlight beam idly across the water, I picked up a crocodile's eye. It reflected the light, red as a tiny campfire, and I pointed it out to García.

"It's only a white croc," he said. "White crocs never bother anybody. It's the black crocs that eat people."

Maybe so, but I was not pleased, lying there listening to his squeaky "mmmp . . . mmmp" in the night. His mating call, I wondered? It wouldn't attract me. I don't like crocs.

I slept fitfully. Each time I woke up I would flash my light to see if the river was rising. It was a relief each time to see the same set of footprints in the sand with no water encroaching on them. At dawn a downpour sent me scurrying for the boat and started the river rising. It kept on rising even after the sun came out and by midday the leaves of low-growing bushes were whipped by the current. It was only a little past four when I noticed what looked like a tunnel breaking through the matted foliage along the bank.

I suggested to García that this might be a good time to stop for the night. "It's early, but we may not find another place where we can get through the brush. Tonight I'd like to sleep on dry land. I want to be sure I will not be under water by morning if the river continues to rise."

García agreed. "Your tunnel, señora is a game trail made by animals coming down to drink. Ought to be good hunting here. I'll see if I can shoot a deer for dinner." He took his shotgun and disappeared in the brush while Doña Ana and I started looking for a place to hang my hammock. Near the water's edge the trees were too close together, but a few hundred yards inland we came to a tiny, natural clearing where a great tree had fallen. Tree ferns and clumps of those feathery palms you see in pots in the lobbies of elegant, old-fashioned hotels bordered the clearing. In the center, two tall, slender trees stood the right distance apart for my hammock. I began hanging the hammock at once, but Doña Ana noticed I didn't have my mosquito net and started back to the boat for it.

"Don't bother," I told her. "We didn't have any mosquitos last night and there may not be any here either." They are often scarce in uninhabited country.

"But, señora," she asked, "what about bats? There are many vampires all through this region. You should always use a net to keep them out."

I knew all about vampire bats, of course. You hear a lot of speculation about how they manage to suck so much blood from a sleeping person without awakening him. For them, toes are the choicest morsels. Before attacking, native folklore has it, a bat fans his victim with his wings, inducing a mysterious hypnotic sleep. Another theory argues that their saliva contains some fast-working anesthetic as yet unknown to science. However they manage it, vampires can extract enough blood, sucking, regurgitating, and sucking again, to cause a marked anemia, but their unfortunate victim will know nothing about it until he wakes in the morning with a punctured toe and a feeling of utter exhaustion.

Doña Ana brought me a bucket of water when she returned with my mosquito net. While she prepared dinner, I took a slow, cool, dip-and-splash bath and a luxurious rubdown with eau de cologne. Then I sat on a log and thought how enormously lucky I was to be in this enchanted place at this enchanted moment. A little breeze, full of the fresh, loamy scent of evening, rattled softly in the palms. Leafy branches stretched black lace against a sky that was darkening to a thin, transparent blue, still luminous with the afterglow of day. While I watched, the first stars pierced it, faint pinpricks of light that grew in intensity and number until they crowded the sky with brilliance. Beyond my little clearing, in shadows spread by the trees, other points of light darted, hovered and disappeared. I thought they were stars, too, until I saw them moving. Fireflies.

Doña Ana called me to dinner—smoked meat again because Don Paco hadn't shot anything. I ate fast and hurried back to my log. But the magic blue hour had passed and it was night.

Getting ready for bed is a simple matter when you're sleeping out. In any emergency, I'd feel much more vulnerable undressed, so

I prefer to sleep in my clothes. This night I just brushed my teeth and cleaned my face. Then I kicked off my boots and climbed into the hammock.

I have a habit of reading until I am sleepy, but I couldn't now because my flashlight was too dim. I'd forgotten to put in new batteries. I was tired anyway, so I snapped off the meager beam and was wriggling the blanket over my shoulder when I was startled by a peculiar noise. Some animal was going "umppf . . . umppf" in the darkness beyond my mosquito net. I lay still, wondering what it could be. I remembered the time I had hung my hammock near the edge of somebody's property and had been bothered all night by cows who came and breathed on me. But there couldn't be any cows here. This was uninhabited country. The sound, too, was different.

It came again and I listened hard. I'd heard that noise some where. But where? Then I thought of Yori. Yori and his ghost tigre. That's what it had sounded like when he imitated the ghost tigre's sniffing around his house at night. Well, I didn't believe in ghost tigres and as for a real tigre . . . preposterous!

It had to be the deer that Garcia had failed to shoot. I didn't intend to be breathed on by deer all night, so I shouted "Scat! Go away! Scram!" It occurred to me that I had shouted in English and I wondered curiously whether South American jungle deer were bilingual.

Evidently not. Seconds later I heard the snuffling grunt again. It was closer now . . . just outside my net. This could be a nuisance. Irritated, I jumped from the hammock, grabbed the mosquito net with both hands and shook it violently, bellowing, *"Vete! Lárgate! Fuera de aquí!"*

That did it! I stood listening for a moment. Nothing. I hadn't heard it go away. Maybe it was still there, but if it would be quiet and not bother me, I wouldn't mind. I got back into my hammock. Only the usual night noises now. Sleepily I thought, At least the deer understand Spanish . . . I yawned. I slept.

It wasn't noise that woke me hours later, it was water, a lot of cold water running down my neck. Groggily, I reached for my flashlight. By its feeble glow I could see a heavy sag in the mosquito net overhead and from the sag a jet of water spouting down. Outside, the jungle roared under whips of rain. I had slept heavily; the blanket was drenched, I was drenched—and furious. During dinner I had asked García to cut some palm leaves and make a shelter over my hammock, but he had insisted that there was no need. Hadn't it been raining only in the daytime? Weren't the stars out? When I argued, he said it was too late. I'd be all right if I just draped my nylon poncho over the mosquito net. I had done just that and look how much good it did!

I crawled from beneath the sopping net and started for the boat. With the rain and the failing batteries in my flash, I couldn't see much and what I could see looked strangely different. But I knew that downhill led to the river. The descent became steep and slippery. My feet flew out from under me and the flash went out and wouldn't light again. Painfully, I slithered along on my bottom, afraid to risk a fall if I walked. Finally I hit a root, a big root. I hoped it was the one I had stumbled over coming back from dinner, for that one had been very close to the river. I sat still and yelled, "García! Hooooo! García!" Nothing. I tried again. Finally I heard Doña Ana call, "Señora? What's the matter?" In a few minutes García appeared, appropriately clad in swimming shorts. I was too mad to speak as he lit me back to the canoe.

Doña Ana cleared their bedding away and got out the thermos of hot water and the instant coffee. I said, insincerely, that I was sorry to disturb them so early—it was four-thirty—but I was cold. Doña Ana heated more water on the primus and got out cheese and crackers. By the time García got back with my dripping gear, I was in warm, dry clothes and it was all beginning to seem funny.

"What kind of animal goes 'umppf . . . umppf' in the night?" I asked.

Doña Ana frowned. "Where did you hear that, señora?"

"Tonight something was going like that around my hammock."

Doña Ana carefully set down the cup she was refilling. García dropped the blanket he was folding and stared at me. "What happened?" he asked in an odd voice. "What did you do?"

"I shooed it away. May I, please, have my coffee, Doña Ana?"

She just sat there, her mouth partly opened. García leaned forward, his arms akimbo, staring at me from under his heavy brows. "You . . . you *shooed* it away?" he stuttered.

I explained about shaking the net and bellowing first in English and then in Spanish. "Whatever it was understood Spanish all right," I laughed. But they didn't see the humor. "What's the matter with you two? I just asked what kind of animal goes 'umppf.'"

Suddenly García threw back his head and roared with laughter. "A tigre! The *otorongo*, the big tigre! He comes for the Señora and she shoos him away. *Jesús María!* Like shooing a pig she shoos him away. Great is the United States of America! *Jesús,* these gringas! 'Scat, you *tigre!*' she says. And it goes away!"

Doña Ana came out of her trance and she started laughing too. I was getting cross. "Nonsense!" I said when they quieted enough to hear me. "You're pulling my leg! No, I mean, you're pulling my hair!" I was mixing up my idioms in the two languages. "It couldn't have been a tigre. They're big and heavy. I would have heard it moving away and I heard nothing. It must have been a deer."

They started laughing all over again. Then García grew serious.

"The deer, no, señora. The deer is timid. He does not come to sniff people. And if he runs, you can hear him go through the bush. But the tigre, he is bold. He is curious and when he is curious he goes 'umppf!' No other animal makes that noise. And when the tigre moves, big as he is, you can hear nothing. Even on dry leaves, the tigre walks with silence. No, señora, that was a big tigre you shooed away."

I still wasn't convinced. Finally he said, "Come, we will search for his tracks. Then you will believe me!"

I pulled on a waterproof and we sloughed up the bank through the heavy rain. It was getting light but García kept creeping about with his flashlight held close to the ground while I huddled under a tree, watching. "Here, señora," he called finally, "come and see the track made by your deer." He was about eight feet beyond where my hammock had hung. Under one of the clumps of old-fashioned hotel palms, he showed me a footprint in the wet earth. Overhanging palm leaves had kept the rain from obliterating it. "Your tigre crouched here for awhile. See the mark of his pads? Look close as I shine the light from the side. You can see even the marks of his claws."

I looked. It was a good, clear print and terrifyingly large. García straightened up and started laughing again. "He was a big one, the deer you shooed away!"

I tried to laugh, too, but I wasn't awfully good at it. I had suddenly begun to feel sick. I explained to García that it was the cold that made me shiver when we headed back for the boat.

XXIII

ALL DAY it kept raining hard and unremittingly. It was the rain of the new moon, Doña Ana explained. Rain like that stops being a bore and becomes fascinating. There was no wind and the rain poured straight down. Big heavy drops bounced back from the flat brown water like millions of marbles dropped on a tile floor, and with almost the same sound. The river rose fast. The current midstream was stronger than our motor and we had to scrape along the edge of the drowning forest. Vine-matted branches clawed rents in our pamacari and the water that dripped through on us was stained brown by the thatch.

In the early afternoon, Doña Ana suddenly said, "I think I hear a motor." I listened, and sensed through the roar of rain a throbbing rhythm different from that of our own outboard. Then round the bend came a boat, low, fast and as gray as the falling water. Two men in black, shiny-wet rubber coats stood in the prow. We waved. They waved back but kept going like men in a hurry.

"It's the police," Doña Ana said. "The police who went up to investigate Baúl's murder."

I hadn't heard of any murder. Excitedly I asked her about it. She looked uncomfortable. "That's what Audáz was telling us about when you came back from your bath and everybody stopped talking. Remember?" I shook my head. "At that house we stopped at the mouth of the river?" Doña Ana asked again. "The last time we stopped in a house. Only Paco didn't want them to tell you about it. He was afraid that it might make you nervous. This is why Don Audáz kept telling you not to ask these Indians about magic or medicine, and not to show them those glass eyes that look so real.

Baúl was a white man . . . but the Indians killed him for being a witch."

"Baúl or Raúl?" I asked. Raúl is a common enough name, but Baúl is the Spanish for box or trunk. I had never heard it used as a name.

"He was called Baúl de Brujerias . . . trunkful of witchcraft," Doña Ana explained. "He liked to be called that because he wanted the Indians to fear him. Whenever anyone died he would always boast, 'He made me angry so I killed him with my magic.' It worked very well. The Indians were so terrified they sold him animal skins, or leche caspi, or one of their women at any price he chose to pay. You see, they were afraid that he would send a demon to make them sick or even to kill them."

"That sounds more dangerous than smart," I remarked.

"Oh, it was," Doña Ana replied. "But he got by with it for a long time. You see, he also knew how to cure sickness with roots or leaves or the sap of trees. He knew how to make icaro, good magic, with the medicines of the jungle. But mostly he made trouble."

I was beginning to wish they had left him alive until I'd had a nice long talk with him.

Doña Ana told me that Baúl—nobody remembered his right name—had taken a fancy to a little Indian girl and told the tribe to send her to his house, much as you would tell the butcher to deliver a pound of lamb chops. But, unlike most Indian women, this girl wasn't submissive. When she said she didn't want to go, her uncle, who was the chief and very fond of her, wouldn't let her be sent by force.

Baúl was deeply affronted. He said he would show those dirty barbarians what happened to anyone who defied the Baúl! He would make the girl suffer. But months passed and nothing happened. The Indians grew less punctual with their tribute of skins and Baúl kept blustering. He said that he was delaying his vengeance to give the girl time to reconsider. After all, she was a pretty little thing and very young. There wasn't any great hurry. But she had better not try his patience too far, he said, or he would turn his magic against her.

Another month passed. One morning the girl was bitten by a snake. She died that afternoon. For three days the drums sounded a heavy, monotonous throbbing in the forest. Then five men of the tribe came to Baúl's house. They were quiet and polite. They accepted cigarettes and matches. They drank the masato that Baúl's daughter-in-law poured for them. Then they told him of the girl's death.

Baúl spat on the floor. "Yes, I know," he said. "I gave her plenty of time. Then I got angry. Who angers Baúl does not live long. I sent my snake demon to finish her."

He fished a package of cigarettes from his pocket. When he bent his head over a lighted match, an Indian swung his machete. It fell with such force that it split the bald head all the way to the jawbone. Then the Indians went home.

"Poor Indians," I said. "That man deserved to be killed. But I suppose the police have caught his executioners and are taking them in that boat down to Iquitos for trial. It seems a shame." For once I was sorry that the police were so efficient. Jungle Indians do not stand imprisonment well. Sometimes they sicken and die just, apparently, from being locked up.

Doña Ana said the wonder was that Baúl had lived so long. But she didn't think the police would have caught his killers. "The Ecuadorian border is not far away," she said, "and there are more of that tribe just across the line. The murderers will surely have gone to join them, and, of course, the police can't follow them beyond the border."

I was relieved. I had been so interested in Baúl's fate that I'd even forgotten the rain. Now I noticed the river was more swollen. Our progress against the current was painfully slow, and sometimes we scraped branches hidden under water. Twice they fouled the propeller and Garcia had to stop the motor and, muttering angrily to himself, put in a new pin. Big trees, their roots loose in the sodden earth, leaned perilously, ready to fall. They were too tightly webbed with vines to fall fast, but now and then we would hear a long tearing crash in the distance.

Rain had poured down steadily for more than twelve hours. The sky of the jungle seems bigger than any other sky, but even so, I wondered how it could hold such a weight of water. Then, just before dark, the rain stopped. It didn't slacken or slow to a drizzle. It simply stopped and the clouds were gone. Around the next bend, under a sky like an empty pearl shell, we saw houses.

The first house, small under its heavy thatch, appeared deserted, but across the river and about a hundred yards upstream we saw another, larger and more imposing, on high stilts under a tremendous peak of thatch. A dozen or more canoes were tethered in its port and the sound of our motor brought men running down the bank. As we pulled up, a boy of about seventeen jumped on our prow and said, "Good evening, señoras. I am called Diego and I speak Spanish very well. Much pleasure to know you. Good evening, my señoras, have you cigarettes?"

I gave him a pack and he thanked me politely. He wore bright yellow trousers and a vivid turquoise shirt. His face was painted red with horizontal black stripes.

I said good evening and much pleasure, too. "Ah," he said, "that is boots you put on. Is well, my señora. I know boots. Very good, boots. You wear all time?"

I said no, only in the evenings to keep off the mosquitoes.

He said, "It is very well, my señora, thank you. How much you pay for boots?"

I said I'd paid a hundred pesos.

"Is very well, my señora. A hundred pesos each boot?"

I said no, one hundred for both.

"It is very well, my señora. Thank you, my señora. Do me the favor of to come to house. Is house of my aunt. Many people come. Now is fiesta."

Helping me gallantly from the boat he continued, "I am only one here can talk Spanish. I talk very good, very fast." Indeed he did. "I learn from capitán of army. He take me to serve in his house when I am little. Many years I stay with him."

We climbed up the bank, Doña Ana and García behind us. They were accompanied by some of the older men with whom they were chatting in a language I didn't understand, but which both of them seemed to speak fluently. We clambered up the notched log serving as a ladder to a pona platform under a big thatched roof, and I reflected that we didn't make a very good argument for white supremacy. My shirt was damp and wrinkled, my muddy blue jeans so baggy at the knees that I looked as though I were getting ready to jump. García was if anything less presentable. His shirt, patched in half a dozen places, was streaked with oil from the motor. His ten-day beard was as shaggy as the brush of parasites on a jungle log.

But Doña Ana still looked pretty. The rain had made her hair even curlier and her blue plastic raincoat neatly covered the shabby clothes she wore for work in the boat. I thought we looked like tramps beside her and was puzzled that the Indians clustered even more about me than about her until I remembered my boots. The Garcías were barefoot. I wore boots, proof positive that I was a big shot.

There must have been forty or more Indians there, and they gathered round us examining our clothes and accepting cigarettes. Clothes were evidently of great importance that day. If it hadn't been for the red and black designs painted on the faces of our hosts, I might not have realized they were Indians. They had dark skins and slanting eyes, but so do many of the civilized folk living along these rivers. The bright, rather shapeless cotton dresses of the women and the new-looking shirts and trousers of the men would have pleased the most exigent of missionaries. Even the children wore clothes like the adults. I was startled to see that one man actually had on a pair of shiny yellow shoes. He must have carried them in his hand until he got inside the house, for there was not a speck of mud on their gleaming surface. The rest were barefoot, but compared with García and me, they looked chic, sleek and civilized. The guest list for this party must have been made up of the best-dressed people in the jungle. I was disappointed. They looked far too elegant to be a good source of plant magic. Yet this was one of the two tribes I had been most hopeful about.

They were Jívaros, but not at all like the savages I had met in Ecuador on the upper Santiago River. These, I learned later, had migrated to this part of the jungle a generation earlier. It was obviously a tribe which had already given up many of its ancient ways of living. The classic Jívaro house is an enormous dirt-floored oval with an outer wall of strong closely set staves firmly planted in the earth. This house was just a thatch roof over a platform on rather high stilts. Like many of the houses along the river, it had no walls at all.

Their pots and other artifacts, I noticed, were different. too, showing influences of various other tribes. And the language the Garcías spoke with them was Quechua, not Jívaro. Jungle Quechua, but still stemming from the great empire of the Incas. But the two or three words of Jívaro I still remembered were greeted with wide smiles.

They served masato, however, in the old ceremonial way. Three women in turn offered bowls of creamy, saliva-fermented liquid first to Don Paco, then to Doña Ana and me. The Garcías were used to masato and downed it willingly. I had to drink it, too. Refusal would be tantamount to spurning my hosts' friendship. Even limiting myself to a squeamish sip would be an affront. The constant spate of Diego's Spanish made it easier for me. I had to concentrate so hard to understand his swift, slurring speech that before I realized what I was doing I'd drained the bowl. That delighted the interested circle surrounding us like the crowd around any visiting lion at any cocktail party. This was Diego's chance to impress the boys with his *savoir faire* and he was making the most of it.

He said, as I handed back the bowl, "You like masato much, my señora, it is good. Thank you, my señora. Good to drink more."

I said thank you, too, and I told him he was very polite, as polite as any gentleman I knew.

He beamed, translated the compliment into Jívaro for his admiring audience, and turned to me again.

"It is very well, my señora. Yes, Diego very polite. Capitán all times say, 'Diego, you son of chief, your uncle big witch doctor. Your people chiefs. Diego have to learn to be polite like gentleman.' With your permission, where you come from, señora? Where is your house?"

"In the United States of America."

"Is very well, my señora. Thank you, my señora. This place, where is your house, is big city? Big like Iquitos?"

"It is a big country with many big cities. Very big cities, bigger than Iquitos."

"Is very well, my señora. Thank you, my señora. Is far from here? Many days travel? Like Iquitos?"

I answered, "Beyond . . . beyond," making the pointing gesture used in this part of the world to indicate very great distance. "It is many weeks' travel."

"Is very well, my señora. Thank you, my señora." Diego's eyes had begun to wander. The intellectual effort was telling on him, and, even worse, he was losing his audience. Half-a-dozen men had broken away from the circle around us to join the group around García, just as at any cocktail party with several guests of honor. I could see that Diego was searching for a tactful way to extricate himself from a fatiguing social situation. Rather desperately he said again, "It is very well, my señora. Yes, very well, thank you." Then his face brightened as he found a graceful out. "Thank you, my señora. Much pleasure, my señora, to talk with you. But now, with your permission, my señora, now I must go urinate."

And he left me.

By now more women had joined the masato delivery service, trotting steadily between thirsty Indians and the huge masato pots which stood at the far end of the house. Voices were much louder, more excited, and I realized that although our arrival had startled them into momentary sobriety, an all-night binge of heroic proportions was under way. Alcohol peels the civilization from an Indian faster than it can strip the varnish off a cheap coffee table. Quickly I told Doña Ana that I was tired and hungry. Couldn't we go somewhere else to spend the night? Doña Ana thought a moment. It's just as difficult to leave a jungle cocktail party early. But she too wanted to get away. She beckoned to the Indian woman I'd seen her chatting with.

"This is Tesa. She has a house across the river and she's ready to go home. We can prepare dinner there and you can spend the night with her. It would be better to go right now. I'll get Paco."

The Indian woman went ahead of us to the boat. She was followed by a half-grown girl carrying a little boy. As we started out of the house, my swain Diego leapt toward us protesting. This was no time to leave! It was a good party. He was going to play his flute and somebody would play the drum and everybody would get very drunk. Beautiful. Very drunk. I wondered how much more inebriated Diego could get, but I said we would come back soon. We were just going to take Tesa to her house.

Diego slid down the bank with us. He didn't want us to go. Much pleasure. Would I give him another pack of cigarettes? Would I sell him my shirt, my boots? He crowded into the boat with us, almost tipping it over as he teetered perilously on its edge. He'd go with us to make sure we would come back to the party soon. I was a good señora, very good. Would I marry him? Would I take him to my country? He would like to marry me. He would like to go to my country.

"You are very polite," I said. "But they will expect you to play your flute at the party. It would be impolite to disappoint them. Besides, there is no masato at Tesa's house. She brought it all over to the fiesta." Tesa added a few quiet words in her own language and Diego clambered ashore just as Garcia came aboard.

Tesa didn't look much like the other Indians. They had round faces with short noses; her head was longer, her features aquiline and finely carved. Like the other women, she wore her long, black hair loose over her shoulders and her dress was the neat, brightly printed calico, its loose waistline too short, its length uneven. If any Indian woman's dress fits her anywhere it is merely by coincidence.

Tesa didn't speak Spanish, so García interpreted while Doña Ana cooked the smoked wild pig one of the men had given us in return for my cigarettes. Tesa had been born far away on the Marañón River, but her father had died when she was a baby. Her mother had become the wife of Diego's uncle, Rukas, the witch doctor, who brought her and Tesa here to live. Tesa's husband was a wheel, too, I gathered, although I never learned his official position in the tribe. He was the man with the shoes.

Their house was the biggest in the community. It had a platform floor on stilts, two rooms with walls of pona off to one side and an elegant railing enclosing the large veranda. Even whites seldom have railings. It was an uncommonly fine dwelling for such a small family. There were only Tesa and her husband, their year-old son and ten-year-old Norama, Tesa's daughter by a previous husband. No aunts and uncles, no in-laws. Since housebuilding is a communal job participated in by all the men of the tribe, Tesa's husband must indeed be a VIP.

While we sat on the floor eating by the light of my kerosene lamp, the little evening breeze brought sounds of revelry from the party. Now and then we would hear a snatch of strange, monotonous melody from Diego's flute and the rhythmic booming of a deep-voiced drum. Occasionally we heard a shout of laughter. Dinner over, Garcia hurried back to the party.

Tesa was less shy when Doña Ana served as interpreter. She sent Norama to bed with her little brother, then asked if it was true we were going to visit the Mainas on Río Macusari. We said we were. Tesa sat quiet for a moment, her eyes fixed on the narrow hands in her lap. Without looking up she said, "I fear them. Much fear. There is talk of war. Each time my husband, Alejo, goes hunting, each time my stepfather, Rukas, goes in his canoe to visit a sick person, I feel fear. If a dog barks in the night, I feel fear."

"Why should there be war?" I asked. "What's happened?"

Tesa explained. The witch doctor of the Mainas had died. They believed that Rukas had killed him.

"But was he murdered?" I asked.

"No," Tesa replied. "He was old, old. Only two days sick and he died. But now they think Rukas did it with witchcraft. The shaman's son took *ayawasca*, and when he was in the trance, he said he saw Rukas making magic to kill the old man. So their honor demands revenge. If they make war, there will be many dead.

"They are terrible in war, the Mainas. I have heard. They come in silence at night, kill the men and the boys and carry off the women. The mother of my husband, she is very old, and she told me how this happened. She saw it when she was young. Sometimes they do not come to the houses at night, not if they have enough women. Sometimes they wait in the forest until a hunting party goes to kill meat, and then they attack from ambush. If they kill one of us, our men must fight to avenge that death. And there will be long trouble. Many will die."

Doña Ana looked worried as she translated Tesa's words. When she had finished, Tesa lifted her head and looked at me. "Perhaps the señora could tell us something. I do not understand. But my husband's mother says that when they killed our men, the corpses her people found had no arms or legs. The Mainas cut them off and carried them away. Why would they do this? Do you know?"

Doña Ana shook her head, perplexed. I said that I had heard of tribes who took the arm and leg bones of slaughtered enemies to make flutes. Such flutes were supposed to hold much magic. "But you don't have to let them kill you," I added. "That happened in the old days, but now there is a Peruvian army post on Río Tígre. They would protect you."

Doña Ana was interpreting. When she got to the part about the army, Tesa's face grew stiff and empty, with the closed look I've learned to watch out for.

"This is of my people," she said. "Is not of Peruvian army. Is of Jívaros."

I hastened to correct my blunder. "Of course it is of your people. I know that. But Diego has told me much of the capitán whose house he lived in. The capitán who is his friend, his ally. And Diego is son of your chief. Do Jívaros not fight by the side of any tribe whose chief is their true friend? Would they not aid the capitán if the Mainas tried to kill him? I have known Jívaros in Ecuador. They were brave warriors. They did not hesitate to risk their lives for their friends."

Tesa was silent for a moment, then her face softened. The primitive look was gone. She was just a woman who was afraid.

"Capitán, yes, he is friend of my people," she said. "But he is gone, long time gone. We do not know where."

"You must have other friends." I knew it was a risk, but I liked her. I had to help if I could. Privately I thought all this talk of war was nothing but camp-fire dramatics, but her fear was real.

"Who gives the women their dresses?" I asked. "Who gives the men their clothes, their machetes?"

"That is Don Mauro," Tesa answered. "He gives us things when we take him animal hides or leche caspi. He gives Mainas things also. He is our friend. But also he is their friend." Her face brightened for a moment. "To my husband, Arejo, he gave shoes. To nobody else did he give shoes."

"Then if he is your friend, and also friend of the Mainas, can he not know of this?" I spoke slowly, letting Doña Ana translate a phrase at a time, while I watched Tesa intently, ready to change direction at the first flicker of hostility. "Must people die because some young Maina, not properly trained as a witch doctor, failed to understand what the ayawasca showed him?" Her face wasn't turning stony, it was growing more alive. I thought she knew what I was going to say next. "It is clear your husband is the valued friend of Don Mauro. Why cannot he tell Don Mauro of this? Why cannot Don Mauro show the Mainas that they would be fools to start a war because of an unlearned witch doctor's mistake?"

Tesa only replied, "I will ask my husband." But she smiled brilliantly. She no longer looked frightened.

We heard the motor approaching, then Don Paco's voice calling Doña Ana. She said good night quickly and hurried away. She seemed pleased that her husband hadn't stayed at the fiesta tanking up on masato.

My interpreter gone, I thought all communication with Tesa must end. So I rose from my cramped position on the floor, stretched luxuriously and turned toward my hammock, expecting her to retire to the little room where her children slept. Instead she spoke. I whirled to stare at her and she repeated it. Tesa had spoken to me in Spanish. Very bad Spanish, very slow and groping, but still intelligible. She had said, "Where your husband?"

"You know Spanish?" I gasped. She giggled and asked her question once more.

I sat down on the floor again. I explained that I no longer had a husband. No, he was not dead. But now he had another wife instead of me. No use trying to explain divorce to an Indian, I thought.

Tesa leaned forward, regarding me earnestly.

"Abandoned?" she asked, shaping the word carefully and correctly. Such a fancy word! I was so astonished I could only nod. She seemed to take that for emotion too deep for words and she tapped herself on the chest, nodding sympathetically. "Me too." Then she pointed to me. "You have sons?"

I said I had no children. We settled down to exchange confidences like any two women who have recently become friends.

Tesa's Spanish was queerly pronounced and her vocabulary extremely limited. When she couldn't find a Spanish word, she would drop back into her own language, but her gestures and expressions were so eloquent that sooner or later she would get her meaning across. Many words and phrases I used brought only an intent look of inquiry. But with gestures and pantomime we managed to understand each other surprisingly well.

I learned that Tesa, like many women of her tribe, had been given in marriage when she was still a child. Her husband was cruel and brutish. She grew up hating him. She had one child by him, her daughter Norama, and then made up her mind never to give him any more children. She confided in her stepfather, Rukas, who was very fond of her. He gave her the root of a plant. This, he told her solemnly, would prevent her from ever conceiving again. This one dose would do it. But if ever things got better and she changed her mind, he wanted her to let him know. He would give her a second root that would reverse the effect of the first.

Tesa took the medicine and, though she lived as usual with her husband for two years more, she had no more children. Then, to her considerable relief, her husband deserted her and went to live with another group of Indians. It was a year before she was willing to consider matrimony again, but then she went to live with Arejo as his wife. Arejo was good. Arejo was kind, not only to her but also to her daughter, Norama. But it was not until she had spent six happy years with him that she was quite sure that this was a good marriage and that she was willing to bear his children.

Again she consulted Rukas. He was very pleased. He liked Arejo. And he gave her another root which she chopped up and swallowed under his directions. This medicine would make any woman fertile, he assured her. Less than a year later she had given birth to the fine, strong boy who was now asleep in the next room. Tesa smiled radiantly. "Now all good. All happy."

Tesa leaned forward, stretched out a swift hand and tapped me on the knee. "Señora do also like me," she said, her voice warm with sympathy. "Then happy."

I was afraid to speak. This woman knew the plants I'd sought so desperately for months. They were that near! I almost asked her then for them. But I remembered old Ema. Ema was my friend, my good friend, but this magic was too big for her to give me. The friendship between Tesa and me was a new one, delicate, tenuous. I didn't dare ask such a gift. I didn't know what to say, so I just sat there, not even trying to keep the anxiety out of my face.

Tesa gazed at me earnestly for a moment, then she went on, "Señora have bad man. Is good no sons. Now bad man gone. Is good. Now Señora find good man. Stay with him. Much time Señora, no sons before much time." She shook her head slowly in emphasis. "Then Señora know is good man, then Señora have sons. Like me. Señora happy like me."

Was this the time to ask? I clasped my hands tightly, they were shaking. "Tesa," I said, "I feel fear. If I take man, and man is bad, and I have sons . . . or if man is good, and I have no sons . . ."

Tesa shrugged and turned up the palm of one hand in a small, impatient gesture. "Take medicine like me. First medicine for no have sons; then medicine for have sons."

This was it. Now I had to risk it. "But Tesa." I took a deep breath. "I cannot. That is why I am afraid. These medicines do not grow in my country."

Tesa was shocked. "Here all grows. Good medicine, all women take. Plant for have baby," she pointed out into the darkness, "by my house grows. Rukas give me. I plant. Morning I give you roots."

"Oh!" I let my breath out. "Tesa, with my heart I thank you." I longed to drag her down that ladder right now to get them in my press before I slept. But that wouldn't do at all, so I just said again, "I thank you. Tesa, you are good."

At that moment a dog barked sharply and fell silent. We heard a squelching in the mud, and a man's voice muttering. Tesa's face lit up. "Is Arejo," she said. "Arejo, drunk, drunk, drunk!" Laughing, she sprang to her feet and flew out of the house. There was only one thing on her mind now and that wasn't my future progeny.

I heard someone retching painfully while Tesa made little soothing noises. Then she helped her muddy, spattered spouse up the notched stick and into the house. She was beaming as she sat him on a bench and said, "Fall in earth, fall in river. Dirty. Come home, make clean."

Tenderly she sponged his face, neck and chest with water from an earthen bowl. She got fresh clothes from a wooden box and helped him into them. Then she combed his hair, guided him down to his canoe and sent him back to the party. She giggled as she came back into the house. "Arejo go fiesta."

In her absence, I had opened my plant press. Now I got out a dried specimen that Teresa, the Ocaina girl, had given me. "You know this plant?" I asked. She studied it, then said yes. She had seen some of it growing in a swampy spot some distance from the river. Indians remember the location of plants and herbs just as we remember the locations of grocery stores and drugstores. Tesa had seen this plant and remembered. But what was it for? she wanted to know.

I repeated what Teresa had told me. "You take a bit of this leaf and eat it before you go to a fiesta. Then you can get very drunk, but you will never get sick and the next day you feel fine." I had packed the plant carefully. Considering the awful stuff they drank on the Putumayo, it must be a terrific detoxifying agent.

Tesa was delighted. Her people did not know about it. I gave her one of the leaves so that she would be sure to get the right plant. She thought it would be a godsend to her tribe. Little did she know that the plant she was going to give me would be a godsend to my tribe, too. A plant to combat sterility in women . . . And the other, the contraceptive?

I was afraid to refer to plants again. I waited anxiously for her to return to the subject. We talked very late. With practice, our pantomime improved. With enough arm-waving, we could put across some pretty subtle meanings. I would love to have a silent movie of that conversation. I have an idea it might prove quite intelligible. Tesa told me of her tribe and of the tribe her mother had belonged to, the mother who had known a little Spanish and had taught her daughter how to speak. Incas, she called them. I grew more tense as time wore on and still she said nothing more about my plants.

Such tension is accumulative. I was beginning to wonder how

much longer I could go on without blowing a fuse when a howl came from the baby's room. Tesa sprang to her feet. "Is my son. My son from plant like I give you, morning. Now I sleep. You sleep."

Smiling, she left me without another word. Jívaros don't go in for the little ceremonies of our speech. But she couldn't have bade me a sweeter goodnight. I fell into my hammock exhausted and listened briefly to the drunken music across the river. They were really making a night of it.

It was very early when I woke, but Tesa was already kindling the breakfast fire. Across the river everything was hushed. The celebration was over, the tribe was sleeping it off. I asked Tesa about Arejo. She laughed and waved a hand at the predawn mists over the river. "Sleep. All sleep now." I gathered he'd passed out before he got around to coming home.

When the fire was blazing under the black earthenware pots and the mists were growing thin, Tesa said, "Now I get plant."

I didn't really know why I'd said that. But seeing Tesa's face, I knew it was the right thing to say. She looked very pleased, and I was glad I hadn't tried to rush her, now or the night before. You must never snatch at anything offered by an Indian. Primitives have a way of life and thought that is alien to us, a different sense of what is fitting. It's perfectly true that when some Indians offer to get a plant, it is essential to follow up without delay, without giving them time to change their minds. But that is so when dealing with anyone you do not trust. Trust . . . It dawned on me then why Tesa looked so pleased. She had given me her friendship. This had proved mine for her. I'd shown I trusted her, that I knew she would fulfill any promise she made.

The Garcías came up from the boat and Tesa abruptly stopped speaking or understanding Spanish. Even when Doña Ana said to me that she was glad I'd had such a good place to spend the night, that she thought Tesa a very nice woman, and Don Paco shrugged, "Nice, well maybe for an Indian. The house looks clean enough," there was not a flicker of comprehension on Tesa's face.

The Garcías had to interpret my farewells. I thanked Tesa for her hospitality, but made no reference to plants. Now two secrets bound our friendship—her knowledge of Spanish and the medicines.

XXIV

DON PACO informed me that though the moon was still "unripe," it had grown enough for the worst of the new-moon rains to be over. The river was a little lower, but beige puffs of foam still floated downstream, mocha meringue on café-au-lait, marking the course of currents as clearly as lines on a maritime chart. Freshly washed, the foliage massing the banks gleamed and glistened and little birds colored like Christmas-tree ornaments flashed in the morning sunlight. I nearly fell out of the boat trying to net one of the enormous, iridescent blue butterflies that occasionally sailed out over the water. We had only one brief shower in the afternoon.

We stopped at another Indian house that night. Like the three or four other dwellings we had noticed during the day, this also belonged to members of Tesa's tribe. None of the men of the family were at home except one shriveled ancient who was said to be well over a hundred years old. The women looked just like the ones we had seen at the home of Diego's aunt, only far less dressy. They all wore faded, raggedy dresses, but the old man was clad in an *itipi*, a sort of knee-length sarong wound about his stringy loins. It fitted him far better than his skin, which was much too big for him and hung in loose, crinkled folds around his shrunken arms and middle. The absent head of the house, we learned, was named Shari.

Nobody objected to my hanging my hammock there, though my being dressed in trousers like a man was the cause of considerable tittering. Nobody spoke Spanish; they knew Quechua, but they were far from communicative. They did tell us, however, that we were only a half day's journey from the house of Don Wenceslaos Rengifo. At last I would meet Luz Vasquez's brother. If he were anything like his sister, he would be fun to know and, even more important, tremendously helpful. I was counting on him to take me to the Mainas.

We reached his house in a fine, misty rain after lunch the next day, a long house large enough to look low even though it stood on stilts. Doña Elena, his wife, received us at the top of the stairs. She was shy and flustered at meeting a stranger. She knew the Garcías and invited us to come in, sending an Indian woman for a refresco, a punch made of jungle fruits. I produced the letter Luz had given me for her brother. What a shame, Doña Elena exclaimed. He was off working in the jungle with a crew of Indians. They wouldn't be back for days, perhaps a week.

She placed the unopened letter carefully on the table around which we sat. I was wishing she would open it, for I knew it contained a request to do everything possible to make my trip a success. If she read it, she might find someone who could go with us to interpret. But I didn't like to ask her to read her husband's mail. And her shyness was contagious. I didn't have the nerve to tell her of its contents. I did, however, hint a little.

I explained why I wanted especially to see Don Wenceslaos. Then I asked if it were true that the Mainas spoke no language but their own. She said it was and added that they didn't like strangers very well. No, they wouldn't be likely to attack us. Nothing like that. They would probably simply refuse to have any dealings with us. "If only my husband were here." She looked worried. "He would know what to do. He would probably send one of his boys with you, but they are all away in the woods with him now."

"Perhaps we can find an interpreter at Don Mauro's house," I said. "That's only a few minutes upstream, I understand."

She shook her head, looking even more upset. "But Don Mauro is not at home either. There's only his youngest son, Eduardo. Don Mauro left for Iquitos some time ago to see a doctor. His stomach was bad. He thought it was an ulcer. He must have arrived there just about the time you left."

Oh, no! Not another wild Indian chase! Well, I still had Tesa's promise. At least I would get those plants.

We left and went up to Don Mauro's house. García said he had brought a gift for him, anyway. The whole family were old friends and we would stop to see if something couldn't be arranged. When we tied up to the Guimet port, García got from the prow of the boat a large rock that had sat there all through the voyage. I'd assumed it was brought along for an anchor, but now he started for the house with the rock under his arm. I asked why.

"This is a present I have for Don Mauro," he said.

"But a rock? A rock for a gift?"

Both Garcías laughed at my shocked expression. "But, señora," Doña Ana explained, "up here a stone is a most acceptable present. You can't sharpen knives or machetes without stone and there's not a bit of rock anywhere along these rivers. For miles and miles, there's nothing but clay and silt."

Don Mauro Guimet's house was named Valencia, and for this part of the world it was palatial. It was not built of pona, but of real lumber, large thick planks. But it was the paint that made it really imposing. You almost never see a painted house on these rivers. The main body of the house was a solid, brilliant blue, the same strong blue used for the Bay of Naples in mural paintings on the walls of small Italian restaurants. In contrast, the intricate wooden grilles of the high railings that bordered the vast veranda were painted a shining red and white. The whole effect was as gaudy as a macaw. The Indians probably found it simply gorgeous and were quite as impressed as Don Mauro intended them to be.

A good-looking young man was running down the path to welcome us. Don Paco introduced him. Eduardo Guimet, Don Mauro's son. He was a slender, quick-moving boy of seventeen, and he had the diffident good manners of a well-brought-up Peruvian.

In rocking chairs on the shady veranda, I explained my mission while Indian women served us with soda pop imported from Iquitos. Eduardo didn't know much about native remedies; his family preferred more conventional treatment. He thought the Mainas must know a good deal of jungle medicine, but did I realize how difficult I might find them to deal with?

I rather thought I did. I had read of their history. They had once been one of the greatest nations of the region. One of Peru's largest provinces, Maynas, was named for them. The Spanish first penetrated their territory toward the end of the sixteenth century. The Indians fought bravely, but wooden spears were ineffectual against Spanish armor. The seventeenth century saw the Mainas subdued and enslaved and the Spaniards moved them about, several thousands at a time, with considerably less care than they showed when transporting cattle. Chronicles of this era report the death rate of

Maina slaves to have run as high as 90 per cent in some areas. During the next century or two, revolt and punishment, suicide, infanticide, smallpox and other diseases of European origin just about wiped out the tribe. Many ethnological studies list them as extinct. The handful of Mainas living on the Macusari probably owed their survival to flight and to their steady refusal to have any traffic with the whites they had every reason to distrust.

Don Mauro had settled here decades ago. He had gradually won a certain degree of confidence from the tribe, though I gathered that the basis of their relationship was mainly commercial. The Indians brought their animal hides and leche caspi to his store to exchange for merchandise. Sometimes they performed specific communal jobs for him. But I gathered that he never interfered with their way of life.

"If you came with us," García suggested to Eduardo, "they'd let us stay in their houses, wouldn't they? And you could interpret for us."

Eduardo grinned. "Sure! They've been my friends since I was a baby. My father used to take me up there when I was knee-high. It would be great fun! I have had to stick around here all the time. I haven't been up the Macusari for months." His smile vanished. "But what will my father say when he gets back? He told me I'd catch it if I went off anywhere and left the place all alone with nobody to look after things. I'm supposed to be in charge here until he gets back. But it seems a shame. They'll hear your motor and they'll know it isn't one of us. And then you won't even see them. They'll take off and visit relatives upstream, where a boat can't go, until you're gone."

"I'm so sorry you can't come," I said. "It would be such a help . . . and so much pleasure to have you with us."

Eduardo's mobile face suddenly brightened. "You know, señora, maybe my father would want me to go. He feels very strongly about hospitality . . . and you're a foreigner and a lady. It wouldn't be very hospitable of me to refuse to help you, would it? *Vaya!* My father would consider it a disgrace to refuse to help a foreign lady who had come so far."

By then it was already three o'clock. Eduardo said it would be dark long before we could reach the only place on the Macusari where we could spend the night ashore. In any case there were a few things that he must attend to before he could leave. It would be better for us to stay at Valencia tonight and make an early departure in the morning.

The Macusari is a swift, knotted little stream that empties into the Corrientes a short distance above Valencia. We'd chug across an almost circular stretch that you might call a pool if the water weren't so swift and then the banks would almost close in on us; later we'd scrape around a bobby-pin curve through a passage so narrow that branches on both sides would snatch at the laundry draping our pamacari. Doña Ana had spent the late afternoon at the Guimets' washing our load of soiled clothes. Heavy cotton slacks, even thin shirts, won't dry overnight in that climate, so in the morning she always spread them on the pamacari to catch what sun the shaded rivers afforded.

Little rivers like the Macusari are manic-depressives. After a few days of rain, they get into the manic phase. They become raging torrents, unsafe for boats because of the danger of being rammed and either stove in or upset by uprooted trees hurtling downstream. These trees frequently tumble along below the rushing surface of the water, for much of the wood which grows in these forests is too heavy to float.

But a few days of dry weather sends these rivers into such a depression that instead of being dangerous they become impossible to navigate. The listless water wandering from pool to pool is too low to cover logs and debris lodged in narrow channels by the last freshet. If you travel at all when this happens, it is only by interminable chopping through and portaging around obstructions. And when you get to the far side of one, you may not find enough water to float your boat.

We were lucky now. The river was neither too high nor too low; it neither threw things at us nor refused us passage. The jungle along the banks so close to us was utterly unspoiled, exquisitely abloom. This time the wild—or, at least, reasonably uncivilized—Indians were in no danger of being spirited away by priests. I was happy.

That night, we camped on a little sandy bank above the river where Eduardo's family had built a shelter. I didn't worry about being sniffed at in the night because the tambo was very close to the water and Eduardo slept there, too. But before we fell asleep, he told me a strange story about a family who had camped there a few months before.

There were four of them, father, mother, grown son and three-year-old daughter. They were awakened from a sound sleep by the screams of the little girl. The father snatched his flashlight. Its beam spotted a big jaguar near the edge of the clearing. He was running for the forest with the little girl in his mouth. The two men chased it, shouting and shooting in the air. Only a few yards into the brush, they were lucky enough to find the child, still shrieking, but quite unhurt. Not a scratch on her anywhere, for the tigre's teeth had fastened only in the blanket in which she had been wrapped. I felt sure it must have been my tigre. The poor thing obviously suffered from nerves. My "shooing" him had probably caused a relapse. I could visualize him now, a shaking jungle neurotic, afraid of howling people, shunned by his enterprising normal kin.

We reached the first Maina's home the next evening, a big, dirt-floored rectangle with the usual high thatched roof. I noticed nothing unusual until I saw the family beds. They were little platform stalls, a foot or two above the floor, with sides and backs of split palm and about the size of a double bed.

Cushicooey, the stocky, baggy-eyed head of the family, was an inept ambassador for his tribe. If the other Mainas bargained to their own advantage as he did, I could understand Tesa's fear of a war with them. Their peace treaties would make a civilized dictator look like a two-bit gangster.

Cushicooey immediately demanded cigarettes. I gave him a pack and he asked for more. Then he demanded matches and again asked for more. When I refused, his nagging was endless. His curiosity was not fettered by any ideas of dignity and he regarded the rest of my possessions as possible loot. He opened my zippered overnight bag and examined its contents. I had to snatch my lipstick from him as he was about to paint his face with it, using my mirror. He wanted me to give him my sweater, my pajamas, my eau de cologne.

Cushicooey, fortunately, had not had enough contact with our culture to steal what I refused to give. Jungle Indians, at least among all the tribes I have known, never steal unless they have been intimately exposed to civilization. It just isn't done. There is nothing important enough to be worth acquiring at the expense of their self-respect and the respect of their fellows. No one is willing to exchange these intangibles for something portable and perishable. In the humid, vermin-infested forest, everything that is not living matter sooner or later is ruined by insects or humidity. It's far more important to *be* something valuable than to *have* something of value. Status does not depend on the quality of one's possessions, but on the quality of one's self.

Cushicooey, although he didn't steal, had nevertheless become infected with minor civilized viruses. He had learned a little Spanish and along with it a keen appreciation of the white man's commercialism. Most Indians given a gift will make some return merely as a matter of dignity. Not Cushicooey.

I noticed a lot of thriving, busy hens scratching in the earth behind the house and I was tired of our diet of salt fish and smoked game. "May I have some eggs for my dinner?" I asked Cushicooey. Yes, all I wanted. Then he named a price that would have been exorbitant in New York. I reminded him that I had given him a half-dozen packages of cigarettes, a lot of matches, some highly scented pomade for his hair, a mirror and a comb. "Is gift," he said indifferently. "Then whatever I give you is a gift, but what you give me I must pay for?" I asked. He said, quite simply, "Yes." Highly indignant, I ate salt fish again for dinner.

I got even with him the next morning. We were leaving early, but Cushicooey was hanging around looking for more presents. I was in a hurry to get out of there before I lost my dignity. Climbing into the boat, I knocked over one of the big tins of trade goods and a glittering, tinkling stream poured out . . . necklaces of bright beads and little silver bells. They were so gaudy, it was obvious even to García that they were the most expensive costume jewelry I had brought with me. Cushicooey's eyes grew beadier than ever, and his breath came out in a long "Ahhhh!" before he could even say, "Give me!"

"No!" I said. "These are valuable. I have them to give to people who give me presents and to trade for things of value that I want. Cushicooey gives no gifts. He gives nothing in return for gifts. Cushicooey only wants to take, not to give. These are not for him. I must save them to present to people who are not like Cushicooey."

I settled under the pamacari as regally as I could in messy blue jeans and told García to shove off. Cushicooey ran along the bank excitedly yelling, "I will buy! I will trade! I will give fine things!" I got a nasty satisfaction in pretending I didn't hear him, looking straight through him, through the matted brush on shore, straight into the heart of the forest.

The house of Saucali, the chief of the Mainas, was a long way upstream. We reached it about four in the afternoon after plodding over a long jungle path, for it was set about a quarter of a mile back from the river. The house, perhaps thirty yards square under the usual soaring roof shaped like an open book, was dirt-floored and, like Cushicooey's, had no walls. For beds, instead of stalls, it had platforms, six- or seven-foot rectangles of split palm, standing a few feet above the floor. Half a dozen masato pots large enough for Ali Baba stood in a central clump. Three of the platforms were occupied by women dressed only in pampanillas, knee-length sarongs of home-woven cotton dyed a dark color, their sagging breasts bare. Two of the women had the usual long hair falling over their shoulders, but the other's hair was cropped in a modified crew cut. I guessed that her husband had recently died, for in many tribes a woman's head is shaved when she becomes a widow.

Another house, much narrower, had been added to the back of Saucali's. It contained two lines of platform beds separated by an aisle down the middle. Eduardo explained that Saucali's grandsons and nephews lived there with their families. Only guests and Saucali's nearest kin slept in the main house. I learned that Saucali had many male relatives, and again I thought of Tesa's fear of war.

Saucali received us seated on his throne with his two youngest grandsons, boys of ten or eleven, standing just behind him. The throne was not very grand, just a stool crudely cut out of a block of hardwood set against an enormous hand-hewn plank which was braced against one of the uprights supporting the roof. Thus placed, the plank served as a backrest for the throne. Each Maina house has a throne, the traditional seat of authority, and only the head of the household may use it. No one else sits in it, ever. I wondered what would happen if I sat down in one . . . But I would no more think of doing so than of usurping my host's chair at a formal dinner.

Saucali was old and frail. His bobbed hair—I have never seen an Indian bald at any age—was limp and lusterless and his skin above the worn trousers that were his only garment sagged away from his bones. His eyes focused uncertainly and his gestures were nervously feeble. He seemed to totter even when he was sitting perfectly still. But for all this, he somehow had the presence of a sovereign.

Eduardo said the woman with the shaven head was Saucali's brother's number-two widow. The other two women, one old and one young, were the old chief's wives. "The very young woman with the infant at her breast," I asked amazed, "is that Saucali's child?" Eduardo said it was. I wondered if this tribe had the geriatric medicinal plants which are used in another part of the Amazon Basin. Some of them are reported to extend virility into extreme old age. But it's hard to gauge the accuracy of such reports because in so many tribes it's considered perfectly proper for a husband's male relatives to help out with the begetting.

Nobody spoke Spanish, so Eduardo interpreted. He told Saucali that I had come a great distance to know him and his people and the old gentleman looked pleased. I gave him a package of cigarettes and matches. He said something to his wives, who ran outside and returned in a few minutes with a big stem of green cooking bananas and a pile of yuca which they laid on the ground in front of me. I gave Saucali a mirror and a comb. They brought me a heap of wild pig. I asked Eduardo how much I should pay. He explained that the old man wanted to thank me for my presents, the food was his gift to me. Not to be outdone, I presented the older wife with a blue and orange necklace with bells and a similar one of red and yellow to the younger wife. Then we sat and beamed, all very pleased with ourselves and each other. Cushicooey receded into a distant part of my mind. He was a peasant; Saucali was an aristocrat.

A wailing chant sounded from the other house, a woman's voice rising and falling, then rising again with a banshee sobbing effect. Eduardo explained that this was Saucali's late brother's number-one wife. She had to perform this ritual several times a day until her husband had been dead for two years. She keened for all of ten minutes before she came out to greet us, smiling, with the tears still wet on her cheeks. Though no longer young, she was the most attractive of the women. She had not lost her front teeth as all the others had, even the youngest ones, and her face expressed an intelligent curiosity. When she came forward, she placed her hand on my shoulder in a friendly gesture of welcome. Within seconds, we were communicating by pantomime.

As with Tesa, I enjoyed conversing in voiceless language. Saucali's sister-in-law made a gesture of admiration for the necklaces on one of the platforms and then pointing to the open neck of my shirt quite obviously asked why, if I owned so many lovely things, I didn't wear them myself. I smiled, grimaced and shrugged to say, "Really, dear, nothing could help me in these clothes!"

Quickly she chose three of the gaudiest necklaces and, chuckling softly, tied them around my throat. Then she stepped back to admire the effect and I struck a pose and revolved slowly like a mannequin in a house of *haute couture*. Next, I selected one for her. When I presented it, she pantomimed a surprised "Oh you-really-shouldn't! It's-too-much!" I had to quiver with insistence before she would accept it. She pantomimed delighted thanks. We both laughed and I hoped I was winning a friend.

The afternoon sun was low enough to reach in under the eaves of the great open-book roof. Women were beginning to kindle little cookfires, four or five of them scattered on the floor of the vast room. A young Maina warrior clad only in dark blue trunks appeared at the edge of the clearing. He strode with the gait of a panther, a proud, free panther, to a little stool just inside the eaves and seated himself with his long blowgun resting across his knees. He sat straight-backed, impassive in an attitude of perfect repose, neither speaking nor looking at anyone. His hair, blue-black and shining, was cut in a thick bang across his brow, but in back it fell thickly to his waist, where it was cut straight and even. He didn't look much like other Amazonian Indians I had seen. His skin, gilded by the slanting sunlight, was a trifle lighter and the lines of his face and body recalled a picture I'd seen in some archaeological book. I thought a moment . . . the Bull Dancers of Minos, that was it. His shoulders were almost too broad for his slender waist and hips. His straight nose was finely chiseled, his beautifully shaped lips showed perfect teeth and his eyes were striking. Large, long, and thick-lashed, they showed almost no mongoloid fold.

Sitting motionless in a pose of immobilized swagger, he didn't look real and I stared at him as I would stare at a splendid piece of sculpture in a museum. Two women with correct expressionless faces served him the ritual masato in earthenware bowls. He drank from each without a glance at its bearer, still superbly impervious even to our outlandish presence. Only after the women had trotted away did he unbend and become just a strikingly handsome Indian.

Eduardo told me this was Yambiki who lived about a half mile downstream. He had sat on the honored-guest seat, a stool crudely carved from a massive block of wood, because he was of the highest rank. He would become chief when Saucali died. Every Maina house has a similar stool for the use of the highest-ranking guest, a male, of course. In Amazonia women don't rank.

Four other *chobones*, as the long-haired Maina men are called, arrived soon. They didn't make entrances or sit on the stool, because they lived here. They were Saucali's nephews. Two of them were almost as handsome as Yambiki. Altogether, they were the most beautiful male animals I had ever seen, and it seemed a shame that all the beauty of this tribe had been endowed on the men. The women were far less decorative, very small—although the men were tall for Indians—with nondescript features and unfortunate figures.

Yambiki and the other men, after a few words with García and Eduardo, came to crowd around me. Yambiki, as befitted his rank, spoke first. Eduardo interpreted. "What is your father's name?" I told him. "Is he now alive?" No. "Where was his house?" San Francisco, California. "What is your mother's name?" "Is she alive?" "Where did she come from?" As soon as I had finished answering Yambiki, the man standing next to him went through the same list of questions, then the third man, the fourth, the fifth. All of them I answered gravely. I was beginning to catch on: here was some more Maina etiquette. So when they had all finished questioning me, I returned the compliment, solemnly asking the same set of questions of each of them in the order in which they had addressed me. Eduardo looked pleased with me, for I was showing good manners.

When the ritual quiz was over, they drifted off to their respective family fires for dinner. Some wives had prepared wild birds, brought by the hunters I supposed, which they had plucked and then roasted whole without bothering first to remove the entrails. Others ate smoked wild pig. All had yuca or plantains boiled or roasted in the coals. They ate everything with their fingers. When the men had finished, the women ate. I have never in any tribe seen an Indian woman eat with her husband.

Doña Ana had our dinner ready by then. Don Paco, she and I ate together. Uncomfortably I wondered how many other local customs we had already violated. The Mainas were awfully strong on protocol. If they conserved their tribal customs this tenaciously, I thought, would they also cling to other ancient formalities, such as avenging the death of their witch doctor? But of course that was nonsense. This was Peru and they were such beautiful people. . . .

After dinner I got out the radio and set it on the platform that had been assigned to us as living quarters. The Garcías would sleep there; I had hung my hammock at the far end of the house. Other Indians were still arriving. Eduardo told me that they lived in houses up and down the river and the news of strangers had brought them. They were fascinated by our clothes, our possessions, but dignity restrained them from Cushicooey's lack of inhibitions. They merely stared, remaining shy and distant until I turned on the radio. It was exciting to them. Their eyes shone wide as the music came from Bogotá, but they sat quietly, not crowding or pushing, close to it. Only the children created a problem. They had to be watched constantly. Whenever one of them thought himself unobserved, a small brown arm would reach out furtively and we'd hear a sudden, stern warning from one of the adults. The children were longing to open the box to have a look at the people inside who were making the talk and the music. It was Saucali who finally called a halt. At least I think he did. The tired old man lay down to sleep and then the others did the same.

No big Indian house is restful at night. For one thing, as is to be expected in a polygamous society, it's like an overcrowded nursery. All night babies cried, mothers shushed and overexcited children whispered and giggled. The adults, too, were eternally coughing, spitting, or just getting up and walking about.

But it wasn't the noise that kept me awake. It was the fire. Not the cookfires, they were banked for the night, but a big, bright blaze under a room-sized rack where yuca was being smoked. I couldn't figure out why they worked at it all night. Smoking is the commonest way of preserving foods in the jungle, but smoked yuca is far from palatable and rarely prepared unless a large party is going on some expedition where food will be difficult to come by. As for example, when a whole community is moving to some distant place . . . Or was it to be used for a war party?

The Mainas had already filled a number of baskets large enough for a grown man to sit in and still the work went on. When I'd asked why, they had blandly told me the men were going hunting for meat to be smoked and sent to Iquitos for sale. Could be, I thought, but I had seen tribes on long hunting parties. They subsisted on masato, the fermented mash without added water, and fresh meat from the animals they killed, the parts not suitable for smoking. This preparation on such a scale seemed, like the Mainas' manners, too elaborate.

I thought about worried Tesa and Rukas and my pal, Diego. It was a long time before I could fall asleep.

CHAPTER

XXV

An INDIAN HOUSE awakes long before dawn, and wakes even more noisily than it sleeps. I rolled out of my hammock and brushed my teeth for a fascinated audience. More sightseers had arrived, disappointingly dressed in their best civilized clothes, except for a few women who clung to the ancient habit of the pampanilla and the bared breast. Women are always more conservative than men. Some of the women wore short blouses as a protection against the chill of early morning. The costume did nothing for figures already ruined by childbearing, past or imminent. Again I noticed the women's lack of front teeth. The men's teeth were invariably magnificent, but some of them showed black traces from chewing yanamuco, the tooth-preserving leaves I had been given at Negro Urco. I wondered whether the leaves were taboo for women.

The morning started out on a pious note. Two women brought infants to Don Paco to be christened. I do not think the Mainas consider themselves Christians, but the word had got around that white people believe it most important to use this kind of magic for the protection of their babies. I have an idea that the Mainas went in for christenings the way some people take vitamin pills: they do not think them necessary, but they might possibly do some good. They knew about godparents, too, and I was invited to be godmother to one of the children, but Don Paco said I couldn't because I was not a Catholic. So Doña Ana and Eduardo held the children while García, solemn and sonorous, intoned the impressive ceremony. But I didn't think it was right for him to receive a chicken for each christening. After all, he was only an amateur priest.

Even Yambiki this morning had concealed his classic lines under immaculate white trousers and shirt. I asked Eduardo, who stayed close by to interpret, if the men no longer used feather headdresses and itipis. Of course they did, he told me, but only among themselves; to meet whites they dressed as white men do. "Out of courtesy?" I asked. Eduardo laughed. It was rather because they thought that our kind of clothes demanded more respect. I gathered his father had done nothing to discourage the idea. "Clothing is a very satisfactory commercial item," he explained.

At my urging, Eduardo tried to persuade Saucali to stage a fiesta in native full dress, but the old man would not cooperate. There was too much work to be done, he said. But he was very vague as to what the work was and Eduardo could learn of no communal project about to be undertaken. Again I felt a twinge of uneasiness. I know that many tribes eschew frivolous types of diversion before setting off for any excursion of a bellicose nature. But Saucali finally agreed to send a small group of men home to dress in formal attire provided that I would promise necklaces to those who did.

As news of our arrival spread, tribal families from farther and farther away kept arriving. I spent hours taking curious visitors down to the boat for conducted tours through my possessions. They crowded aboard, their strong sense of personal dignity not quite defeated by the curiosity consuming them. When I opened the bags and turned their contents out for their inspection, they could not resist smelling, feeling, examining everything minutely. They obviously thought this the shopping opportunity of a lifetime. Unfortunately, I could use only a limited number of bananas, smoked game, chickens, eggs, tame jungle birds, blowguns and darts. And I could not spare my flashlights, clothing, cooking equipment or bedding.

I was delighted, though, to trade Yambiki a shirt for his blowgun. It was a fine blowgun, about nine feet long, with a bone from a jaguar's leg for a mouthpiece. But then, too, it was a very fine shirt, one I had bought in New York to trade for something special. It was of a superior quality of cotton in the reddest possible red with two five-inch stripes of silver lame—guaranteed tarnishproof—down the front. Ever since I had bought it, I had wondered just what type of male the manufacturers had had in mind. But if Yambiki must wear clothes, this was the right thing for him and I was happy that he was the one to get it.

I didn't want to go into competition with the Guimets, so I firmly refused to be traded out of the less gorgeous shirts I habitually wore. The Mainas coveted everything I had except my cameras, my toothbrush and my forks. Jungle Indians use spoons whittled from wood, but forks are of no value to them. Forks are rarely seen along the rivers. On trips into the wild, the Garcías, like the Malaria Control men and even Don Alfonso Cárdenas, merely augment their fingers with a spoon. But I don't like getting my fingers into food, and I stubbornly clung to the convenience of a knife and fork. With Indians that always puts me in the spotlight. When I eat, they gather around as though I were a performing juggler. They seem to regard my eating as a wonderful parlor trick.

That morning, between conducted tours to the boat, I, as usual, took photographs. I had brought along a few copies of *Life* magazine with the idea of demonstrating the purpose of all this camera-pointing and also because I thought it would be fun to show them how we live at home. Now I tried it.

First I turned to city scenes. I showed photographs of tall buildings, explaining that many people where I came from lived in houses like these. The Mainas looked at them with complete incomprehension, occasionally revolving the magazine to see if the pictures made more sense upside down or from the side or from the rear. Quickly I abandoned the idea of trying to explain the bright-colored advertisements for automobiles and turned to some magnificent color plates of jungle animals. That was different. Enthusiastically they pored over the pages, shouting the Maina names for animals they recognized. They grew so excited I half expected them to start shooting at the pictures.

I tried to explain that cameras, I held my Nikon out to them, made this, pointing to the pictures. They looked at me with scorn. Animals like these made by that little thing? They knew where animals came from and it wasn't from a leather-covered box you could hang around your neck. I explained further. Not living animals, but pictures of them. I pointed again to the page. It was this that was made by a thing like my Nikon. They knew better than to believe that a picture that big could come out of such a small box. Why, the page hadn't even been folded. Señora was making a joke. I gave up and laughed with them. Better to let them think I was clowning if that would allay the distrust I feared was gathering behind their bland, beautiful faces.

To get back into their good graces, I got out some bright red nail enamel and started to refresh my manicure. That aroused the usual admiration, but unlike other primitives the Mainas did not immediately clamor for me to paint their nails, too. When, however, I offered to do so, they accepted graciously with evident pleasure. Next I drew some designs on my forearms with a ball point pen, then held out the pen to them. They liked that, too, although the blue color was a bit daring for Indians accustomed to painting their faces only with red and black.

By noon many more Maina families had arrived and the big house was alive with color and movement. We had just finished lunch when Eduardo introduced an Indian in his late thirties, not so handsome but taller than most, with the usual long hair streaming down his back. "This is Anguesha. He is the only Maina who knows Spanish, but he speaks it well. His father was the first of the tribe to become my father's friend, and Anguesha lived in our house when he was a boy."

Anguesha greeted me pleasantly and thanked me for the pack of cigarettes I gave him. He had forgotten most of his Spanish, he said modestly, but, though his grammar was vague and his vocabulary limited, he wasn't hard to understand. I felt more at ease with him than I did with the others. Even when these beautiful creatures smiled, it was with a watchful reserve that reminded me of a State Department official dealing with a Trade Commission from the Communist bloc. But when Anguesha's eyes crinkled, he seemed genuinely, even sympathetically, amused.

I had noticed a number of blowguns in all stages of manufacture leaning against the back eaves of Saucali's nephews' house and I asked Anguesha whether it would be all right to take pictures of them. I know that for the Jívaros a woman's presence is taboo when they are preparing poison for their darts. For all I knew, the Mainas might have blowgun taboos. Anguesha offered to go through the various steps of blowgun manufacture while I took pictures. I was delighted. I had always wondered how they were made to have such uncanny accuracy. I have seen Indians bring down a flying bird at a distance of thirty yards or more. Of course, it isn't the dart that kills, but the poison, usually curare, on its tip.

Blowguns are made of two tapering, channeled pieces of wood cemented together. Anguesha first showed me how these two sections are whittled into shape, rounded on their outer surface, perfectly flat on the inner. It takes a lot of patient whittling and shaving to get them so straight and smooth with no tools but a machete.

The next step was to groove the inner surface. To accomplish this, Anguesha wedged the shaped piece of wood firmly into a pair of vises standing at an appropriate distance apart. The vises were made of posts driven solidly into the ground, their upper ends slit to hold the blowgun. Stretching a cord down the length of the wood, Anguesha marked a straight line down its middle with his machete, then started to carve a groove down its length.

While he was painstakingly doing this, Sengali, one of Saucali's nephews, without a glance in our direction, briskly set a blowgun section into another pair of vises and went to work on the groove already indented along its middle. His machete was braced in a small, sturdy forked branch in such a way that he could maneuver its tip accurately without cutting his fingers.

Anguesha's eyes crinkled with amusement. "See, señora," he said. "Like Sengali do now. He open canal in blowgun. Señora make picture." Sengali kept on pretending we weren't there, but he was obviously not displeased when I leveled the camera at him.

After the groove is made as even as it can be made with a machete, it must be given a finer and more accurate finish by sanding. Anguesha showed me how this is done with a long rod of some sort of wood that was as smooth and as hard as iron. I never could find out how the rod was made. I asked Anguesha if it wasn't terribly difficult to get it perfectly straight and symmetrical, but he just said, "With sand." Then he gathered a handful of wet sand from a clay bowl nearby and smoothed it meticulously along the machete-carved groove. He placed the rod in this, then found the matching section of the blowgun and fitted its groove carefully over the rod. Squinting through the smoke of a cigarette stuck to his lower lip, he made sure it fitted perfectly and that the juncture along the sides was unflawed by any irregularity. Then he took it off and showed me how they sand the groove by twirling the rod tirelessly.

The blowgun sections, he told me, must be sanded for a long time separately. Then the two sections are bound together with the rod still inside and the sanding is continued until the bore is flawlessly straight and smooth. Only then is the sand washed out, the rod removed and the two sections cemented together with a strong, sticky resin. They are then bound tightly with tough vines and left undisturbed until the "glue" has dried.

A Maina's blowgun looks as though it had many coats of the finest Japanese black lacquer. The thick, glossy finish is applied by rubbing the exterior hour after hour with a block of resin from a tree that grows in the jungle. Sengali had a chunk of it. It looked like a piece of anthracite coal, but it smelled like the incense burned at high mass. I wanted to buy some, but they weren't interested in selling. The first lacquering is done before the hollow bone mouthpiece is set in the larger end, but the final lacquering and polishing take days. And after each day's hunting, the Mainas rub their blowguns again with the same care with which we might oil a favorite shotgun.

When I had enough pictures for a do-it-yourself course on blowgun-making, I asked, "Anguesha, but what about *cargajos?*" A *cargajo* is a quiver for carrying darts. It is made of a hollow section of bamboo in which the hunter places his foot-long slivers of wood with dark poison on their pointed tips. A gourd like a hollow globe is lashed to one side of the bamboo tube to carry the white, cottony kapok which must be twisted around the blunt end of the dart in sufficient bulk to fill the bore of the blowgun so that the hunter's breath can send it flying.

Anguesha explained that the Mainas do not make cargajos because there is no bamboo growing anywhere in the surrounding jungle. "Cargajo come from other tribe. Poison for darts from other tribe." He gestured vaguely in the direction of Ecuador. I understood then why Yambiki had been willing to trade me the blowgun he had made, but boggled at selling me a cargajo until I produced a length of calico in addition to the magnificent shirt.

Back at the house, I found that García had been showing the Mainas that he could drink as much masato as anyone. He wasn't drunk, but his voice and gestures were bigger than usual. I told him Anguesha had shown me how blowguns were made.

"Anguesha!" he sneered. "Look at him. Don Mauro treated that Indian like a white boy. Even taught him to read and write. Gave him a chance to amount to something and what does he do? Go back to his dirty tribe. Look at him now. Degenerated, I call it! Long hair, blowguns, nothing but a stupid barbarian. Shows you can't train one of these animals to be anything but an animal!"

I was outraged and embarrassed. Anguesha was about four feet away. He must have heard every word, but he just stood there looking as relaxed and pleasant as though he had heard nothing. I started to lash out at García—then stopped before I uttered a comparison between his manners and those of the Mainas. He had a lot of masato aboard and was in a nasty mood. If he answered me rudely, we would both lose face. So I just said loudly and clearly, "I think Anguesha is a most admirable man who knows what he wants from life," and stalked priggishly away.

I was unhappy. These people surely knew many jungle medicines, but my every attempt to introduce the subject met with evasive tactics. My winning ways had got me nowhere. My presents had been received with dignity and reciprocation but no confidences. Even Anguesha had backed away from every question about their medicine. I had hope, even so, that sooner or later he would grow less cagey. García's boorishness had knocked that hope on the head and there was nothing I could do about it. In the minds of these people I was of the same tribe as García. Before his outburst, I had seen the beautiful faces more and more often become masks to hide their thoughts and the secrets I sought. But now even the widow who had liked me yesterday avoided me. I was progressing backward. The Mainas would share no magic with me.

The group of men whom Saucali had sent to dress in Maina finery returned almost too late for pictures. Their crowns, made of a profusion of small red and yellow feathers attached to a mesh of woven palm fibers, were worn low across the brow, wrapping the head like gigantic, fluffy caterpillars of brilliant color. Crossed over their shoulders, like cartridge belts, long necklaces of tiny beads with a pendant fringe of hollow seeds rattled when they moved. But under these adornments they wore shirts and trousers and not even bribes of whole bottles of nail polish would persuade most of them to divest themselves of Don Mauro's civilizing influence. I was glad that I had persuaded Yameo to pose in full dress earlier in the day. He was one of Saucali's nephews, and he had dressed up in feather crown and itipi for me after I had shown the pictures in *Life*. I think he really believed the camera made pictures and he hadn't been reluctant to be immortalized in all his finery

That night the radio concert was brief. Everyone seemed surprisingly willing to go to bed early. I lay in my hammock trying to work out some way to overcome the growing antipathy I sensed. I wasn't sure of its cause. Had I been precipitate and pushing by my questions about medicines? I didn't think so. I'd been awfully careful about it. Was García's attitude the cause? That seemed more likely. If his assumption of superiority annoyed me so severely, what had it done to the Mainas?

Did they resent the fact that we were friends of Rukas' tribe? Did they think we had come to spy on them for the Jívaros? That didn't make sense. The more I thought about it, the more confused I grew. I hated to admit that I was simply up against the Indian's devotion to his icaro and a firmly rooted determination to share nothing with the white race which had treated his race so cruelly. For if that was it, I was licked. I hadn't a chance.

Oh, well, I consoled myself, I'm not always a failure. I had plants from other tribes. And I had Tesa's plants to look forward to. It would do no good to lie awake all night.

I was just slipping over the edge of sleep when a soft sound startled me back to wakefulness. I listened. Against the usual obbligato of jungle nights, the house was strangely silent. Not like last night. No whimpering babies, no whispering children, no one moving about to tend the fire under the yuca-smoking rack. The sound came again, a rhythmic swish . . . swish . . . swish. Cautiously, I lifted the net and peered out. It was black dark. All fires had been extinguished and the early scrap of moon had set, leaving only dim starlight outside. The swishing paused, then came again. I tried to think what it sounded like. It reminded me of the noise native women make when they sweep the earthen floors with the little bundle of fresh leaves they use for brooms. Leaf brooms . . . but nobody would be sweeping in the dark. Leaves . . . the rhythm grew faster. Suddenly I knew. Witch doctors' leaf fans . . . the *ayawasca* ritual!

Ayawasca is a vine whose sap contains a narcotic alkaloid inducing hallucinations and delirium. A number of laboratories have studied it. It wasn't a plant I wanted, but I had heard how the Indians use it in magic rituals. Sometimes the witch doctor drinks it himself to divine the future, to look into the past, to see who is responsible for a misdeed or what ails a sick man. Sometimes the witch doctor gives it to the patient. When the patient is groggy, the shaman waves fans made of fresh leaves. Their rhythm is supposed to direct the movement of the soul of the unconscious man into the

future or the past, or to observe something taking place at a
distance.

I lay there listening. Then I heard a man's voice muttering in
Spanish. It was García! I wondered what he was up to. Someone
else spoke in Maina-accented Spanish. It could only be Anguesha.
"You dizzy, too, now? You like very drunk?" The fans subsided to
the slow rhythm again as García asked in a muzzy voice, "What am
I doing here?" "You bring white woman," Anguesha answered.
"Remember?" Then someone began to whistle softly a tune as
monotonous as the sound of the fans.

Cautiously, I crept from under the mosquito net. This was something I did not intend to miss. I had read about the ayawasca
ceremonies, but I never had had a chance before to spy on one.

It was fortunate that I had on the red pajamas which I had
brought in case of a shortage of trade goods; they looked black in
the darkness. I crept toward the sounds, crouching low in order not
to be silhouetted against the paler night outside. The dirt floor was
uneven, but at least it didn't creak. I passed the sleeping widow and
her children, blacker humps in the dark, slipped by other anony-
mous humps, my every motion so slow that there wasn't even the
faintest whisper of cloth against cloth. I was pleased with myself.
Outscouting the Indians! I inched closer and closer. I was soon near
enough to distinguish the separate figures of the group. García, in a
white shirt, was stretched out on the ground. Around him, four
squatting shapes were profiled against the lesser darkness outside.
The shadow at García's feet held the fans. I could see them waving.

Suddenly, two small boys nearby shouted something in Maina. I
understood only one word, "Señora!" Everywhere, dark forms
seemed to rise straight up from the floor. In a moment I was
surrounded. I straightened up, and with faltering dignity, I said, "I
just had to go outside for a moment!"

Nobody answered, but one of the dark shapes took my wrist
and led me out behind a bush. Others followed. I had no need to
"go outside." It was extremely embarrassing. When we went back
into the house, I walked in the center of a small, compact group.
It wasn't light enough for me to be sure whether they were men
or women, but they were considerably shorter than I. They edged
me toward my hammock like tugs nudging a liner into her berth.
One stooped and lifted up the mosquito net while hands pushed

down on my shoulders. Ignominiously, I crawled back into my hammock.

I was seething. I was humiliated. I was angry because I had been rather frightened. I had been treated like a little child and I had lost face. And there wasn't a damn thing I could do about it! I wished I knew more about Maina beliefs. If I made a fuss and insisted on joining the party, they probably would do nothing more drastic than simply call it off. On the other hand, ayawasca magic might be considered a tribal secret. Perhaps no one outside the tribe—except an unconscious patient like García—could be included. Particularly not a gringa. If I got caught spying on the party again—as I was tempted to do—and later someone got sick or had an accident, they might blame it on me, or, even worse, on Eduardo, who had brought me to disturb their pet demons. I didn't dare do anything except lie there and fume.

The whistling and swishing began again. I waited what seemed a long time, then peeked from under the net. Four dark figures guarded me. Would they leave if they thought I had gone to sleep? I began to snore, softly, rhythmically. Forced snoring is a surprisingly unpleasant job. Your mouth gets dry, your throat gets scratchy, then both get downright painful. I kept at it as long as I could, then sighed as though I were changing my position and peeked out again. It had worked. My guards had disappeared. Just as I was snaking under the net, a voice sounded the alarm. Once more I retreated, frustrated and furious.

All this time García had been mumbling, but I caught only a phrase here and there. "Stupid Indians . . . Witches can't make you sick . . . Witches are nonsense. . . ." Unconsciousness hadn't made him any more tactful. A few minutes later, I heard him begin to retch. Ayawasca acts as an emetic when the hallucinatory effect is wearing off. The unlovely sounds meant that the show was over. I gave up and went to sleep.

XXVI

I was still in a nasty mood when I awoke the next morning. I rehearsed several cutting speeches which I intended to make to García, but after one look at him I abandoned them. His eyes were sunk so far back in his head that they would have been invisible if they hadn't been such a bright red. His mouth sagged, even his beard looked limp. He had a hangover big enough for six people, and I was too sorry for him to do more than ask why on earth he had let them give him ayawasca.

He said for his stomach. He was almost certain he had an ulcer. Several of his friends had them. So he had asked the Indians if ayawasca would help. They said it certainly would. Why didn't he try it? The "stupid animals," I thought, saw their chance to get even. And if by any chance they suspected our party of ulterior motives, ayawasca might help them find the truth. I cannot imagine anything less apt to soothe an ulcer, if that is what García really had, than a violent emetic. No doubt about it, the Mainas were crafty.

The river was going down. The good weather looked as if it were going to hold, and if it did, the little river might be unnavigable in another day or two. I told the Garcías to take our gear aboard.

I made my farewells as brief as possible. I wanted to get García away before the Mainas decided to try something stronger than ayawasca on him. Anguesha asked if we would give him, his youngest wife and children a lift in our boat to their house a half hour or so downstream. The boat would be crowded, but Maina etiquette—and I had had my fill of it—forbade a refusal. It wasn't long before I was happy that they were with us. The river had fallen startlingly during the night. We hadn't gone far before a fallen tree completely blocked a narrow spot in the river. On the way up, enough water had swirled over it to make it possible to rock and shove the boat over it. Now the tree was above water level.

García said his stomach hurt too much for heavy work. His head hurt, too, when he bent down. Anguesha gave him a look of pity and promptly persuaded Eduardo to help him move it. They struggled valiantly, but the tree wouldn't budge. Finally Eduardo and both the Garcías held the boat while Anguesha hacked away at the tree with an axe. It took time to chop through the hardwood, but he finally made it and we scraped through. By the time we arrived at Anguesha's house, I was feeling sheepish about my hasty departure from the Mainas. It had been dignified, but it had also been full of resentment.

I presented Anguesha my atonement in the guise of a length of calico and a necklace for each of his wives. "I want to thank you for all of your help, Anguesha," I said. "You translated for me yesterday. You are a good man and my friend." Carried away by my own graciousness, I added a bottle of red nail polish and a ball-point pen.

"Señora not angry because no see ayawasca magic?" Anguesha looked confused.

"But no!" I said. "Of course not! You don't think I would have gone back to bed if I had cared to watch, do you? I was sleepy." Let him tell that to the tribe! It was a bit late for face-saving, but I felt a lot better.

Going downstream is about three times as fast as going upstream, but my thoughts dragged. The trip to the Mainas had been fruitless. I had collected nary a medicinal plant. I didn't even get to see a magic ritual. The men wouldn't wear their ceremonial costumes correctly. The people were suspicious of me. . . .

But I had been suspicious, too. Just because they were smoking yuca in huge quantities, I thought they were going to war. But that is the sort of thing you can believe lying awake at night, listening to alien sounds. Daylight fades such fears.

Actually, they had more reason to be wary of me than I of them. A snooping gringa trying to get their icaro. A gringa who had just been visiting a tribe who may have killed their witch doctor. A spy, perhaps. Yet with innate graciousness, they had treated me with respect . . . even when García had drunkenly spouted the doctrine of white supremacy. I wondered how much I could have relied on my own graciousness if they had been visiting me. I didn't care to think of that. I preferred to think about the plant growing outside Tesa's house.

Before midday, we passed Cushicooey's house. I was thankful we weren't forced to stop. I had a headache that should have belonged to García. By sunset, we were at the little tambo where we had spent the night, which now seemed so long ago. As we went ashore, I thought I heard music. We all listened. Then a boat came around the bend, an open boat with four young men in it. One was playing a guitar, the others sang. García and Eduardo both knew them; they were river people prospecting for rosewood trees. They came ashore to join us. To them everything was fun. They sang as they helped Doña Ana hang my hammock and chattered while they stretched their blankets on the floor of the tambo. They were so pleasant that I suggested to García that he offer them a drink of aguardiente.

That was a mistake. García gave them a drink, but he poured one for himself, too. The men then said it was their turn. They brought out a demijohn—demi? It was too huge to be demianything—and insisted they were the hosts at this party. We were only visitors to the region. García was delighted. When Doña Ana had dinner ready, he refused to join us. "My stomach," he said. "Can't eat." But he could and would drink.

Doña Ana and I sat in the boat until she was obviously quite sleepy. My headache was worse. I felt as though I had a sprained skull. I kept waiting for the laughter and songs to die down, but instead they got louder and less melodious. Finally, I went up to my hammock and asked very politely if it weren't time to go to bed. A man who was sitting on the edge of my mosquito net got up with equal, if unsteady, courtesy, and said, "It is as the distinguished Señora wishes. Now we will all wish you a very good night." Then he sat down on the mosquito net again.

I managed to get him off it so that the hammock would hang straight, but that was all I managed. They stopped singing every few minutes to pass the aguardiente, and each time it passed, the jokes got more bawdy, the laughter louder. Ten o'clock came. Eleven o'clock. Every few minutes, someone would lean on the hammock ropes and nearly toss me to the floor. By now they were shouting at each other as though the aguardiente had made them deaf. I thought enviously of the deaf.

By eleven-thirty, I had run out of patience. Every time I stuck my
head out to suggest that they call it a night, they offered me a drink.
Each time, I said I didn't want a drink, I wanted sleep. And each
time, this was greeted as an excruciating witticism. The din beat
painfully against the headache that now reached halfway down my
shoulders. I had had enough. I gathered up my blanket, jerked the
mosquito net aside and stalked out.

A few feet from the tambo, a low shelter of palm leaves had been
built to make it possible to cook outside when it rained. I crawled in
among the ashes. Nobody noticed. Nobody took the hint. So I
stomped back and got my flashlight. This time, as I turned the light
on and grunted while squirming back under the shelter, one of the
men said, "The Señora, what's she doing there?" It was Eduardo.
He came running over and asked, "But, señora, what happened?"
Eduardo was the only one who was sober.

"I just want to get some sleep because my head aches and the
noise is terrible," I said plaintively.

"Oh, señora," Eduardo begged. "Please, señora." He ran back
and spoke at length to García. It sounded like an argument.

García staggered down. "What do you think you're doing? Get
back to your hammock. I'm going to give the orders from now on.
You'll do as I say quick or I'll go away with the boat and leave you
stranded."

I squirmed around and stuck my neck out like a turtle. A snapping turtle. "You may go!" I said with as much dignity as possible
under the circumstances and pulled my neck in again.

"I swear it!" García shouted. "Unless you return instantly to your
hammock, I will leave you and your baggage here alone in the
morning. Return instantly! And remember that from now on it is I,
García, who am the boss! García takes orders from no one!"

I said nothing and stayed out of sight. Soon I heard the other
men close by. They sounded worried, almost sober. "You must not
talk like that to a lady. You're crazy!" "You wouldn't dare leave her
stranded!" "She might starve!" "A tigre might get her!"

García's bass rumbled like thunder. "I swear I will. I'll leave her
here! García takes orders from no one!"

I stuck my neck out again. "Please don't worry," I told the men.
"The man is drunk and insolent. Last night he took ayawasca. I
think he's still showing the effects. If in the morning he wishes to

leave me here, there is nothing I can do about it. But I assure you that I am not afraid of him—and I am not afraid to be left alone. I will be quite all right. I can manage . . . please don't stop the party. I am perfectly comfortable here. I have enoyed the music and I thank you." I pulled my neck in again. That would show them a gringa could be a lady.

The mention of ayawasca had a sobering effect on the men. I thought it would, for the river people know and respect its poisonous potency. Immediately they protested that I must not stay under the palm shelter. They wanted to go to bed. They had to be up at dawn. They would be uncomfortable if I didn't go back to my hammock.

I peeked out. García was staggering down to the boat, calling over his shoulder, "You'll see. I'll leave her here! I'll leave her here stranded in the middle of the wilderness! To starve!"

"He's gone now, señora," Eduardo said. "Wouldn't you be better in your hammock?"

"If the party is over," I said.

"All," said Eduardo reassuringly, "are about to pass out."

I went back to my hammock.

The next morning my head still hurt, severely, but the rivermen were all up, lively and bustling, before dawn. It seemed most unfair. They were so hearty that I began to wonder whether aguardiente might have some health-giving factor until García stumbled ashore. That was no overdose of vitamins he was suffering from.

The men were reluctant to leave after I had served them coffee, a luxury item for jungle people. They were uneasy. They were afraid that García might follow through with his threats of last night. I was reassuring them when Doña Ana, looking embarrassed, came to collect my gear. They went off then with friendly farewells.

Back in the boat, I called to Don Paco that we were all aboard and he could start the motor. Nothing happened. Eduardo, crouching on the prow with a paddle ready to shove the boat into the stream, looked anxious. Doña Ana was staring unhappily at her folded hands. I crawled over the baggage amidships to where García sat hunched by the tiller. "What's the matter?" I asked. "Can't you get started?"

Don Paco's lower lip stuck out so far a pigeon could have roosted on it. "Of course I can . . . if I want," he mumbled. "I can handle the boat. Been handling it for years and I could get it going now if I felt like it. But I won't. I'm through taking orders. Especially from women!"

Clearly it was time to face him down before he ordered me ashore again. I might have shown uneasiness if my head hadn't ached so. But it hurt so badly I didn't much care what happened . . . I spoke very quietly. "Señor García, you will now do me the favor of starting the motor and heading downstream. Immediately!" I made the last word snap.

Rather to my surprise, he obeyed. But I remained there looking slit-eyed at him until we were in midstream and on our way. Then I climbed back and relaxed on the blanket Doña Ana had spread for me. I get headaches occasionally in cities, but this was the first time I had ever had such a bad one, or such a long one, in jungle. Maybe the Mainas had disliked me, too.

The river was so low that Eduardo remained squatted on the prow to shout warnings of obstructions and to point out the more navigable channels to Don Paco at the tiller. All during the trip, he had taken over all Doña Ana's duties except the cooking. It distressed him to see a woman handling the heavy paddle or carrying all our gear as Doña Ana habitually did whenever we stopped for the night.

Even with such shallow water the current was so swift that we arrived at Valencia about eleven in the morning. I was sorry to say good-bye to Eduardo. He had been a joy to have with us, always quietly good-natured, always eager to help in every way he could. Even the Mainas had shown a certain warmth for him. Without him, I would have had no blowguns, no pictures. I wouldn't even have seen those beautiful, irritating people.

The Corrientes was even swifter. We were at the Rengifo house before I had had time to settle my aching head on the blanket. A large, bright blue boat was in the port. As we pulled into the shore, a man in immaculate khaki ran down to meet us. Don Wenceslaos Rengifo had a lean, broad-shouldered body that moved swiftly. Such a pleasure that I was here at last. He had read his sister Luz's letter, for which he thanked me, and his distress at missing us on our way upstream pained him much. But not, I thought, as much as it pained me. We must let him make up for it now. But first to the house. He had heard a motor when we were still on the Macusari and he had been so certain that it was our boat that his wife now had lunch ready for us.

His absence had been due to a long hunting trip, shooting and smoking meat for the Iquitos market. We had a wonderful lunch of venison, the meat of some small, delicious jungle animal and heart of palm, as well as the usual dishes of yuca and plantain. While we ate, Wenceslaos talked. He was completely at the disposal of his sister's friend. We could all stay there, for a long time he hoped, and he would take me to meet tribes on many of the small tributaries. I'd find some of them most interesting.

I yearned to accept his hospitality, but that meant many more days of paying García's fee. Our agreement was that he should receive the same sum whether the boat was in motion or not. And I simply didn't have enough money. Perhaps it was all for the best. I shouldn't leave Tesa hanging fire too long. She might think I had gone over to the Mainas! So I told Don Wenceslaos how sorry I was. But I had to get back to Iquitos as soon as possible. I was already overdue in New York. That was true enough.

Don Wenceslaos was grieved. He pulled a magnificent jaguar fang from his pocket. "You must take this, señora, as a slight memento. I have carried it a long time. They're supposed to bring good luck."

He spoke in a strange native tongue to the Indian woman serving us. A moment later, I saw three men go down to the boat with baskets of smoked meat which they put aboard. Behind them came women laden with a stem of bananas, a stem of plantains, a huge basket of yuca.

"But, Don Wenceslaos," I exclaimed, "that's far too much! Why, we couldn't eat all that in a month!"

"*Vaya!* señora. It is nothing. What you can't use, you can give away when you get to Iquitos. Perhaps Doña Ana knows people who might like it. Now I have a gift for you . . ."

Before I could protest, he hurried into the house. The jaguar fang was a talisman, I gathered, and a memento is not a gift. He emerged with a magnificent boa-constrictor skin. "This I killed a few months ago," he said. "Perhaps you could use it to make a suitcase or a handbag or shoes and a belt." It looked big enough for all of those. Next he produced a magnificent red-and-yellow feather crown like those the Mainas had worn. "This is a souvenir of the Indians around the Río Macusari."

I just looked at him. For once in my life, I was really speechless. I had coveted one of those crowns, but nothing I had, no lavish combination of trade goods would get one for me. It takes a long time to make one. The feathers are from the small red-and-yellow spot, like a taillight, on the great-billed toucan. They are so fine, so delicate that each crown has at least four of them tied together in every knot of the mesh. When you consider how many birds must be killed to provide feathers for a single crown with its hundreds, perhaps thousands, of knots, you realize why the Indians won't easily part with it.

"This is really too much!" I said inanely when I caught my breath. But my face must have shown how I felt, for Don Wenceslaos looked enormously pleased.

We took a long time over lunch, what with my reports on my host's family, the Garcías' news of mutual friends and our laughter over Don Wenceslaos' many anecdotes of life on the Corrientes. He was so amusing that Don Paco seemed to have forgotten his hangover, though he didn't eat much, and I had forgotten how anxious I was to get on to Tesa and the plants. Suddenly I remembered that it was getting late. What's more, I was growing increasingly apprehensive about six large *makisapo* monkeys doing acrobatics on the porch railings to which they were chained. It occurred to me that we had better get away before it occurred to my lavish host to present me with them. But I made my farewells with regret. These people were fun—in her husband's presence even the shy, silent wife had blossomed into a gay and confident hostess. I would love to know them better—and not for acquisitive motives. Every time I looked at my precious loot I felt embarrassed.

We couldn't make Tesa's house by dark, but we did get to Shari's, the Indian house we'd stopped at on the way upstream. The men of the family, we were told by the women brought to the bank by the sound of our motor, were away again on another mysterious jungle excursion. When Doña Ana was nudging the boat ashore with her paddle, I made a sudden decision. I couldn't face another night in an Indian house. After all, I was paying for this boat and I'd put up with enough nonsense from Don Paco. Tonight he and Doña Ana would sleep ashore and I would stay in the boat. It was more than a bad-tempered whim. I was terribly tired, and traces of the headache lingered. We would get to Tesas tomorrow and I would need a clear and painless head. I was determined to get not only the fertility plant but the contraceptive roots as well.

So I said that I would like to sleep in the boat that night, that I was sure they wouldn't mind, since I had left the boat to them every night since we had left Iquitos. Don Paco started to growl something, then looked at me and fell silent. Doña Ana said, "But, of course, señora. It's certainly your turn."

I thought we'd never finish dinner, which Doña Ana had prepared in the boat. I was longing to be alone. It had been a muggy, sticky day and there was a fine big raft tied in the port alongside our boat. I could get out on that and dip and splash gallons and gallons of water without worrying about anyone's carrying it up to the house. There weren't even any mosquitoes. I could hardly wait.

Finally the Garcías jumped ashore. Don Paco walked a few steps up the path, then turned to shout at Doña Ana, who was making sure the stake to which the boat's chain was attached was firmly planted in the earth. "Hurry up!" he called. "Get that bedding up to the house. You don't think that I am going to carry all that stuff, do you?"

She laughed as though he had said something tremendously witty. But at last she followed him through the dusk and I lay back, stretching every muscle in sheer pleasure. I was alone, really alone for the first time since the night of the jaguar.

For me, lack of privacy is the number-one hardship of jungle travel. You are always in sight or hearing of interested observers day and night, when you're eating or sleeping, changing clothes or bathing. Even in the shelter of an opaque mosquito net, there are always the sounds of people around you, the sound of talk or murmurs. Someone is always snoring or coughing or spitting, soothing children or moving about. It's like being breathed on all the time. It isn't the noise I mind so much—I've trained myself to sleep through any number of decibels—it's the unremitting pressure of personalities, the pressure of being always a stranger in the midst of a tight-packed group. You don't feel like a stranger when you're by yourself.

The early moon sparkled on the river. I gloated as I pawed through bags for soap, towels and eau de cologne, as I got out fresh pajamas and a sheet to lay over the blanket on the floor. Then as I turned back, ready to strip off my sticky clothes, I saw six or eight small, naked boys perched silently on the edge of the boat. In the light of my kerosene lamp their eyes shone like black olives. They had somehow managed to climb aboard without a sound.

I said, "Good evening. Please go away. I want to take a bath." They stared silently.

I made polite gestures urging their departure, then shooing, then menacing gestures. They didn't even giggle. I tried ignoring them, sure that they would tire of watching nothing happen. But these kids were not easily bored. After fifteen minutes of that silent, steady observation, it occurred to me to blow out the lamp. Under the pamacari the darkness was impenetrable. In a few minutes, they decided the show was over and, suddenly noisy as a flight of parakeets, splashed ashore.

I gave them plenty of time to get to the house and then lit the lamp. By the time I had unbuttoned my shirt, they were back again, silent as moths. Wearily, I again blew out the lamp. This time I waited, sitting in the dark of the pamacari, listening to the soft ripple of the river and the background sounds of the night, long enough for them to be gone for good when at last I relit the lamp. I bathed long and lavishly. In heavenly solitude, I slept.

We arrived at Tésa's house just before noon in a sudden rainstorm only to find the place deserted. An old woman in the next house downstream told us that everybody was at the house two river bends below. It was pouring when we tied up amid the tethered canoes. García was still sulky. He said he wasn't feeling well, so he stayed in the boat while Doña Ana and I ran through the rain to the house.

The whole tribe was there and welcomed us as old friends with a spate of questions which Doña Ana had a hard time answering, though she was even more fluent in the tribe's language than her husband. My prestige had grown. I learned that the night of their party, García had given them an exaggerated account of how I shooed the jaguar away.

"Was this another fiesta?" I asked. No, they had gathered here to harvest a large crop of yuca, but the rain had driven them indoors. Festivity seemed to be their fate and they accepted it graciously. The women trotted back and forth with masato. My beau, Diego, had practically thrown himself around my neck when we arrived. "It is very well, señora. Thank you, señora," he said ceremoniously. "Now we have music for the señora." He produced his flute, someone else got a drum and away they were with their same monotonous melody. I handed out cigarettes and matches with a lavish hand. It seemed a good time to be lavish. I had a hunch.

When we had drunk the ceremonial masato, Tesa led me off to a corner. In Spanish, she whispered, "The plant. You want?"

Yes, much," I answered. She smiled. "Now go my house, you me, boat." I thanked her. "It is good. But a little later? Now I talk to your stepfather, Rukas, the witch doctor. Which man is Rukas?"

Tesa pointed out a middle-aged Indian sitting with two others on the only bench in the house. Except for some fancy tattooing he didn't look much like a witch doctor. He had a broad, cheerful face and was dressed in patched and faded khaki.

I hurried down to the boat and got out three plastic artificial eyes, one dark brown and artfully bloodshot, one clear dark brown and one the same blue-gray shade as mine. Doña Ana came to interpret as I went over to the old man. "Rukas," I said, "Rukas, the witch doctor, I have something to show you. Something from my country many, many weeks travel from here."

He looked at the eyes I held in my outstretched palm and rose slowly to his feet. Others crowded around peering over my shoulders. "Eyes," I said. "Not real eyes from my people, but eyes that have been made and painted." I explained that in my country, if a man loses an eye we make him one of these to put in its place.

Rukas hesitated a moment, then bravely put out a finger and touched one. Somebody breathed in sharply. "Eye can see?" he asked.

"No," I told him. "In my country, our witch doctors cannot make such eyes see. They have not learned this. Men wear them only so they will not be ugly when one eye is gone."

Rukas grinned knowingly. "Too ugly cannot get woman."

I agreed. I told him that I knew he was a very great witch doctor. So great that he might know the magic to make the eye see. Therefore, I wanted him to have one. He must choose the one he liked best.

Doña Ana had to repeat that several times. Rukas tore his gaze from the prostheses to look at me again. Then he touched me lightly on the chest, pointed to the eyes and tapped his own chest in one swift, swooping motion of inquiry. I nodded and held up one finger to show that he must take just one. A wide smile passed over

Rukas' face. He bent over the eyes again and with a frowning dignity examined them once more. He chose the clear brown.

One of the men at Rukas' shoulder demanded, "Give me one, too."

"No," I answered. "These are gifts only for witch doctors. They cannot even be given to chiefs, and they can be given only to one witch doctor on any river. Tell Rukas no one else has one, only he."

With great dignity, Rukas sat down again, but he couldn't keep his grin smothered all the time. It kept breaking through. The other men clustered around him. They wanted to see the eye and touch it, but Rukas wrapped it carefully in a rag, then in an empty cigarette package and thrust it deep into a little pouch which was tied to the tough vine which served as a belt to hold up his trousers. He'd got the idea all right. The eye was something too valuable, too potent for vulgar examination and exhibition.

Though he little knew, Rukas was going to do me a very great favor in exchange, and I thought I would like some pictures of him. I asked Doña Ana to tell him that I knew he was a very great man and had wondered why he didn't wear the feather crown and other elegant trappings of the great. She laughed and said, "I will tell him, señora. I will do it so that he will want to show you how fine he can look." She moved to his side. They talked earnestly for a while and then Rukas rose and called one of the young men, giving him rapid orders.

Doña Ana returned and whispered, "He said he would surprise you. When we return from Tesa's, he will be most elegant. He is sending that boy to fetch a box from his house across the river." Then she called Tesa and we went down to the boat.

Tesa was careful not to speak Spanish in front of Doña Ana, but she was looking enormously pleased. She was even happier when I got out some of the necklaces and told her to take her choice. When we drew up at her clearing, she was still trying to decide between two of them. I told her to take them both and she threw up her hands in delight. She hung the necklaces around her neck, beamed at me and jumped ashore. We went to the house together, leaving the others in the boat.

In a few minutes, she had filled a basket with two kinds of plants growing in their native soil. The one like marshgrass leaves, she explained, in Spanish now, was the one which makes it possible for any woman to have babies. She looked at me earnestly. Now I must find a good man like her Arejo and marry again and have a baby. Then I would be as happy as she was.

The other, a bulb the size of an onion, was for the baby. When it was born, I must wash the bulb carefully, mash it to a pulp and make the baby swallow it. Then he would always be healthy like Tesa's children.

I thanked her fervently. I said maybe I'd find a man I could marry. But I would have to live with him for some time before I could be sure that he would make a good husband and father, wouldn't I? What a pity I couldn't get the plant that kept women from conceiving.

Tesa looked surprised. Of course. She should have thought of that. There was none near her house, but her aunt, Rukas' sister, had some. It was her house we had just come from. "We go back. Ask. She give," Tesa told me.

Back downstream we went. Arriving, I left the plants in the boat, but I gathered up quantities of cigarettes and many more necklaces which I slung around my neck. Rukas was just putting the final touches—black lines on a red background—to his makeup. He was splendid in a bright yellow shirt and vivid turquoise trousers. Then he tied a curious headdress around his brow. I had never seen anything quite like it before. It consisted of a headband of the narrow cotton belting with elaborate designs in color which they weave in Ecuador. From it at intervals hung more of the belting, each strip ending in a little tail of human hair tied with bright wool at the top. Over this he adjusted a feather crown like the Mainas' and similar to the one Don Wenceslaos had given me.

He was gorgeous. There was nothing fake about my admiration. Everyone watched solemnly while I took pictures of him, although I am sure they didn't know what the Nikon was doing, and I'd given up forever the idea of using magazine pictures to demonstrate. Besides, I couldn't bear to wait much longer for those plants. I must not seem too eager. But surely I had let enough time elapse, taking pictures and handing out cigarettes, to avoid any appearance of unseemly haste. So I carefully kept the secret of our private language by asking Doña Ana to ask Tesa to ask her aunt.

I watched while she took Auntie aside and spoke earnestly to her. A few minutes later, Auntie went down the steps and headed purposefully across the clearing and into the jungle with a basket in her hand. She soon returned with the basket filled with earth,

scraggly greens trailing down the sides. She led Doña Ana and me
to a distant corner of the veranda.

"This root you see?" she asked. "You take little piece. Wash well.
Chop. When you know you are to have baby, eat one spoonful
morning, one spoonful night. You are cured. It come out."

Doña Ana was translating fast. She suddenly turned scarlet and
paused to look around her. The men, clustered at the far end of the
house, were talking. Every few minutes they would stop to laugh. I
would have sworn they were swapping stories.

I looked at Auntie. "Oh . . . oh . . . no!" I stuttered. "That wasn't
what I wanted."

Auntie looked puzzled. "Is good," she insisted. "We use. All
women use. Good medicine."

I explained that I wanted the leaves women took so that they
would not conceive. Her face cleared. Yes, she had that, too. She'd
run and get me some. In a little while, she climbed back into the
house with another basket of weeds in earth. This one, she explained, you take a teaspoonful just once of the root. She showed
me the little bulbs. This was a sedge. Never get child again. Only
get child if eat Tesa's plant.

I was aware of a sudden silence in the men's corner. A chilling
silence. Slowly, they walked over to where we squatted on the floor
and looked at the plants. Then Rukas and two elders retired and sat
on the bench like judges while the other men grouped around
them. The oldest man on the bench spoke at length. Everyone
listened. Looking grave, they turned to Rukas who had an air of
slight embarrassment as he made a long statement.

Then everybody talked at once. I was trying not to show how
worried I was, and so was Tesa. I had been afraid something like
this might happen. I knew I must not speak. Finally, Rukas mo-
tioned and everyone was silent. Then he addressed me directly.
Diego, frowning anxiously, translated. "Rukas say you know plants
already before you come here, no?"

"Of course I knew them," I said. "Did I not ask the women for
them? Did I not even say their names when I asked for them? Can I
say their names and say how they are if I do not know them?" That
was going a little far, but I had been thinking this out for days. I
knew Tesa would back me up as well as she could. And I had
planned a way of answering any specific challenge.

Blandly, Tesa spoke at some length, lightly but earnestly, and the tension eased as she talked. When she finished, she smiled reassuringly at me. But her smile vanished when the old chief spoke up, his voice stern. Diego translated. "Please, my señora, my uncle say if it is true that you know the names of plants then you say them now that he can hear."

"Diego," I said earnestly. "You know that I do not speak your language. That is why you who speak Spanish so well must tell your uncle my words. I do not know the Jívaro names of these plants as I do not know the names of any things in your language. But I do know their names in my own language and will say them now."

He translated at breakneck speed and turned anxiously to me again. I assumed an air of triumphant assurance. I pointed to each plant in turn and said in English, "This is an elliptical logarithm! This is a rhomboid hypotenuse! This is a trigonometrical perimeter! And this last is a nonparalleleloid isosceles!" I intoned each syllable majestically, for mathematics is to me the most mysterious of magic.

And it worked! Rukas had been watching with the judicious air of a professor listening to the recitation of a student. When I finished, he nodded as though I had every answer right!

He addressed the others at some length, his voice smug. When he finished, his eyes met mine for just a fraction of a second, then we both looked away. We understood each other perfectly. Magic for magic, we said mutely, an eye for an eye.

I told Auntie to take a necklace or two. Her husband helped her choose them. I gave everybody more cigarettes and waited nervously for somebody to make a move to go. I didn't think I ought to be in a hurry to leave. But I was burning to get the plants into the boat. Finally, one of the men said they must get going, now that the rain had stopped, or they wouldn't have time to dig enough yuca to make masato. That broke up the party.

They all helped to carry the baskets to the boat. Auntie told me how to care for them, which needed more water, which might suffer from too much sun. I had no chance to tell Tesa how grateful I was, but I think she knew. Her face, the last I saw as our boat swept around the bend, looked awfully pleased. She had kept her promise, and done it with the approval of her people.

For the rest of the day I stared wonderingly at the plants. The scraggly, grasslike leaves certainly didn't look much like the most sacred magic of the jungle, but they must be, mustn't they? What else would explain that sudden chilling hostility, the flare-up of tribal distrust when the elders noticed what was going on? Now that I'd come through it successfully, I was glad that it had happened. For it seemed to me that this was the clincher, solid evidence that I had obtained the real icaro; that I'd got the plants so often sought in vain ever since Franz Boas, the father of American anthropology, first revealed that these tribes knew botanicals which could control the fertility of women.

I could hardly believe my luck.

CHAPTER

XXVII

IN A WEEK I was in Iquitos. A few days later my return to New York was all arranged. A friend in Lima had lent me the money. I felt hesitant about borrowing it, but I was positive I would be able to pay it back immediately after I delivered my plants.

When the pharmaceutical gentlemen in New York gave me the check for a thousand dollars, they hadn't asked me to sign anything at all. They hadn't even asked me to promise anything except that I would give them whatever plants I had collected. They trusted me.

In Iquitos, I was certain they had not expected me to be able to produce so much for so little. When they had all my plants and read my report, surely they would be delighted. Then I would simply tell them about my on-the-spot decision to take a second trip for the contraceptive plants they had been so eager to get. When they knew, of course they would compensate me. It didn't turn out that way at all. Apparently I understand primitives better than businessmen.

But even if I had known about those complications in advance, nothing could have kept me from going up to the Macusari. That trip had given me something much more valuable than money. I thought about that the night before I left Iquitos for home, sitting in my hotel room surrounded by trunks and bags and suitcases. I had had adventure, the acquaintance with a beautiful, "extinct" tribe, a chance to observe their way of life and the friendship of the members of another tribe whom I'd never forget.

But far more important was the conviction that this trip had made it possible for me to be the first to break through the centuries-old secrecy surrounding the tribal magic of transmitting and withholding life. I would have to wait years, perhaps, to know the real usefulness of the plants, for proper clinical evaluation of such material is a slow and arduous job.

Tests on small animals (monkeys, probably, because there is great variation in the function of reproductive systems of other species) might prove the plants' effectiveness in a relatively short time. But even if testing on primates might show quick and positive results, that would be only the beginning. There must be meticulous chemical analysis to identify the active principle of each root. There would be the separate problem of determining just how each biologically active agent accomplished its miracle. For the contraceptive plant, for example, this would mean learning whether it worked by inhibiting ovulation, or by somehow making the ovum unsusceptible to fertilization, or whether its action was rather by preventing secretion of one of the many hormones which condition the uterus to hold and nourish the ovum. Besides all this, there must be long investigation of possible side effects harmful to the reproductive system or other organs of the body.

I was glad that work would be done by others. My job was done. I had brought back the plants and they were sitting right there, between two footlockers and a duffel bag, packed and ready to go.

The job of packing all that I had collected in addition to my usual equipment was raw material for a nervous breakdown. But I was not in the mood to break down; I was too happy. I had obtained everything I had come for—except a visit with the wild Witotos. But I had a feather crown!

I tried it on as soon as I could get to a mirror more than two inches in diameter and I found it shockingly becoming. Just the hat for cocktail parties. Later, in New York, it moved even the haughty proprietor of one of the town's haughtier restaurants to enthusiastic cries of admiration. I also had some extraordinary ceremonial masks and costumes of the Ticuna Indians near Leticia. Mike had given them to me, but not to wear in New York. Two other masks, old ones of the Bora tribe which had been given to me on the Putumayo, were superb. The abstract designs some primitive artist had drawn on those flat, curving face shields of pale wood strongly recall the paintings of Miró.

None of those things had been too hard to pack. What worried me were the nine-foot blowguns—I had two of them—and the plants from Tesa and Auntie still thriving in their native soil. Silva, my room boy, solved those problems. He bound the bone mouth-pieces of the blowguns with thick wads of cotton, then bandaged the long tubes with strips of heavy muslin. The plants he transferred from their fragile baskets to big, square biscuit tins with holes punched in the bottoms. Then he set them in wooden crates and they were ready to travel.

The one remaining task was to write a detailed report on each plant. I had a hard time keeping it cold and businesslike. They were much more than just plants to me . . . more, even, than medicines which might someday ease or save the lives of thousands. For to me, each plant represented the person who had given it.

I opened the plant press. I was proud of the way the plants looked. No one would ever have guessed that they had been dragged through months of rough and humid travel. All my anx-ious care, the frequent dusting with powdered naphthalene, the tiresome sunning on every possible occasion, had kept them free from mildew, insects, every imaginable kind of damage. Fastened with cellophane tape to large, stiff sheets of white paper, each plant bore a number to identify it in my plant notebook. But my instruc-tions had said that the report must give not only the place of origin, general description, type of native soil and climate, but also the name of the plant. That was my difficulty, for many of the names were given to me in some outlandish tongue.

Two of the plants had been scientifically identified for me by a Peruvian botanist who spent a day or two at the hotel. They were among the more important plant medicines, I thought. The *Incira*, which Hilario considered the only decent, civilized way to remove an aching tooth, had been identified as a *Moraceo, Chlorophora tinctoria L. Gaud.* And the *sangre de grado*, which taken by mouth stops internal hemorrhages and applied externally disinfects and stops the bleeding of a wound, was a *Euphorbiacea, Croton salutaris; C. planostigma Klotzch.* I still had the paper the botanist had written the names on before he hurried out to keep an appointment. Unfortunately, I hadn't seen him again. As I copied the careful printing, I wondered if Hilario was as glum as ever and whether he still thought North Americans were barbarians.

I had only Indian names for most of the rest and those varied from tribe to tribe. Some were not difficult. *Yanamuco*, for exam-ple, the leaves that turn the teeth black and preserve them from caries, had to be spelled the way it sounded. So did *aysifera*, the red-stemmed weed with the green leaves which Ema had told me the Witotos eat to prevent obesity. I thought of the way Ema had looked that morning when she said she could not give me the Witoto contraceptive plant. It had hurt her to go back on the promise which she had made too impulsively. I had been disappointed, badly, but I could not resent her refusal. Her first loyalty had to be to the tribe that respected and obeyed her. Otherwise how could they respect the last remnants of nobility left to them?

But some of those Indian names? How do you spell something between a whinny and a grunt, something which sounds different every time you hear it? There was the weed Antonio had given me. Its rather large, pale green leaves unfurled from a thick central stalk in a way that was far too pretty for what Antonio had called it. Up there, on the wide, shady veranda at Negro Urco, I had written it first in my notebook as *Mweeg*. Then he pronounced it again for me. I scratched out the first interpretation and wrote *Ameéwuh*. The third time it came out as *Uhmweebuh*. Then at the Colombian police post on the Putumayo, Teresa identified it as the plant whose leaves had so miraculously healed without scarring the terrible burns on her legs and she had called it *Hooweéyo*. That, she said, was its Ocaina name.

There were others, like the plant Yori had given me for gallstones, that I had been unable to obtain names for. Yori hadn't known. Poor Yori, I still felt sorry for him. I hoped he had followed my advice to move his family upstream beyond reach of the evil witch doctor and his ghost tigres. Until he found a wife who loved the children, the Canadian mission would be a haven for them.

I struggled with Indian plant names until I realized that no ordinary typewriter symbols could ever represent the weird sounds Indians can make. I gave up and simply applied numbers to the more difficult ones. I hated to do it. It seemed almost as bad as calling Ema and Antonio or Tesa and Rukas "the natives." They are not just Indians. They are people of warmth and integrity, dignity and courage. They are my friends.

I finished the list late on a warm, moonlit night. The Amaaon glinted past just across from the hotel. But I could not hear its whisper or the thousand tiny noises of a tropical night. They are missing in cities.

I strapped the plant press tightly. These plants would make the full circle from the witch doctors with feathered crowns and painted faces to the witch doctors with scrubbed hands and white coats who would assess their value in big, shiny laboratories. It would take a year or two to pile up statistical proof of the plants' medical effectiveness. I wondered what Rukas would think of our witch doctors. Probably about the same things that they would think of him.

CHAPTER

XXVIII

IT TAKES time to get back to the comfortable insensitivities of the worldly world when you've been so long away. In the jungle your senses grow keener. You hear a boat approaching or the distant rolling vibrations of thunder long before they're near enough to make a real sound. The skin of your bare arms, your face, learns to feel the faint cool touch of changing atmospheric pressure that warns of an approaching rainstorm. You see more acutely. With Indians I must be able to catch the most minimal change of expression, to see almost through the skin a tiny tightening of muscle, a momentary immobility or the flick of an eye which signals that I'm pressing too hard for some bit of information and only instant retreat will save me from arousing hostility. This heightened sensory awareness is the first thing lost, and that is fortunate. Keeping it, the noise and glare of cities, the impact of so many people, would be unbearable.

But there are other things I try to make last as long as possible, things like the delight of not having to fuss with a smoky kerosene lamp but merely flipping a switch and being instantly surrounded by enough light to show even the corners of the room. Or turning on a faucet and getting a clean, clear stream of water, even hot water. And no mud on the way to the bathtub! Even when I was in Lima, waiting for the ship that would take me to New York, I would look at an ice cube and wonder what Rukas would make of it. I'd imagine myself telling him to hold it between his hands and show the tribe how his magic turned it to water.

It wasn't until I was on the boat that I realized how tired I was. In Lima I'd been too busy to notice. There were friends to see and parties and press conferences. The company's agent had been more than kind. He'd told me that the scientists in the States were enthusiastic about the *sangre de grado* hemostatic he had forwarded. He thought the contraceptives would cause a sensation and cautioned me against being too explicit when describing any plants to reporters. He used influence to get me a cabin to myself on the next Chilean Line boat to New York. And he paid my hotel bill.

September is a lovely month at sea. I spent almost the entire twelve days aboard eating and sleeping and caring for the contraceptive plants in their tins of earth. Every day I carried them up to sun on the top deck and every night I gazed fondly at them and dreamed of fame and fortune. The boat ride agreed with both of us. They put up new shoots and I must have gained a few pounds; the sharp corners on my cheekbones disappeared and my clothes stopped looking as though I'd borrowed them from somebody a size or two larger.

The arrival in New York was a bit deflating. I had not expected cheering crowds or roses scattered on the gangplank, but the company representatives who met the boat, though courteous, seemed totally unimpressed, even blasé. They were helpful enough in shepherding me through customs but not at all helpful about where the plants would go and who would research them. The company, they said, was at present in the midst of moving its laboratories from one city to another, and everything was in a state of upheaval. When I asked how soon I might hope to hear some results from the preliminary screenings, I thought they looked at me oddly.

I was swept by a sudden feeling of bereavement when finally they disappeared, pushing the cart laden with herbarium specimens and living plants. I hated to be separated from those herbarium specimens I had fussed over so constantly, setting them to sun (to prevent mildew) at every possible chance and having to stand guard to save them from curious children and dogs, puffs of wind, or sudden rain showers. It was even sadder to lose the plants I had cared for with the anxious tenderness of a new mother handling her first child. I've never considered myself psychic; but could this have been a premonition?

During the next week I tried to reach the assistant director of medical research to whom I had been sending reports, but he and the rest of the company scientists were as elusive as blue morphos, the huge, iridescent blue butterflies that are among the loveliest and most irritating of all the inhabitants of Amazonia. Actually the scientists were more elusive, for the morpho hovers tantalizingly low over your boat until the second you make a swipe at him with a net. Then, with the merest lazy shift of those gorgeous wings, he wafts just far enough to one side to make you overbalance and fall in the muddy stream, unless you are very good at instant recoil. I'm sure they get a lot of fun out of it.

The research men did no hovering at all. I saw them just once; we lunched at the old Overseas Press Club. I was a member, but I did not get stuck with the bill. From the moment we met, they kept up a steady barrage of questions: how long could this plant be stored without losing its potency; could that one be cultivated, given the right soil and climate? Their teamwork and timing were superior. I had no chance to start in on my questions until our coffee came. As soon as I began, they suddenly remembered appointments elsewhere, and dashed away. I never saw them again, nor could I ever reach them by phone. They were always away moving those laboratories, apparently in much the same way as 'one little ant carried away one grain of rice, and another little ant carried off another grain of rice and. . . .'

I was beginning to wonder. But if the Research Department was evasive, the Publicity Department was pervasive, indeed. Their offices were here in town and they phoned constantly. I must be at such-and-such a place for a press interview at such-and-such a time, or for a radio interview, television show, or to meet the science editor of some magazine. More than once, they asked me not to reveal the amount they had paid me to get them the plants. I hoped that might be because they had not yet decided how much they would reimburse me for the second voyage, on which I got them the contraceptives.

I rather enjoyed the interviews. During my years as a reporter, I had always liked interviewing, but there's no denying that to be the person answering, instead of asking the questions, gives a cozy feeling of importance. That made a welcome challenge. Only one interview turned out to be a traumatic experience. That was my first television appearance.

I have never been photogenic; my best camera angle has always been through a screen door at twilight. Knowing that, I approached the matter with a certain nervousness, but not without some pleasure, too. I had never been on television and that made it

new and exciting. It was "The Today Show," run at that time by
Dave Garroway, and everybody said he was kind to his guests.
What's more, I wouldn't have to get to the studio in the cold gray
dawn; at that time they were taping the show in the afternoon and
running it the next morning.

Arriving at the studio, I was turned over to a makeup man who
set earnestly to work, applying layer after layer of some kind of
waterbased makeup. After a surprisingly long period of plastering,
and some delicate artistry with brushes and pencils he said, "You're
going to like this," and turned me toward the mirror. I was astonished. All haggard shadows and hollows had disappeared. My face
felt strangely stiff, but I was ravishing. "I never would have believed
anybody could make me look so lovely," I told him. A little hair-
spray, and it was time for me to hurry before the cameras.

The first part of the interview went beautifully. Mr. Garroway
asked all the right questions and I wasn't a bit nervous. Then he
asked if the tribes had any contraceptive plants taken to make men
infertile. I answered that I had never known of any. I thought their
effectiveness might be hard to judge because in some tribes it was
considered perfectly proper for a husband's brothers to help out
with the begetting.

Mr. Garroway burst out laughing. I started to laugh, and felt
disaster strike. My face began to crack; then it crumbled; bit by bit I
could feel it falling off, all that exquisite facade. The friend who
watched the show with me the next morning said it looked like scar
tissue. She was trying to be kind. It was much more like a mud road
that had been heavily rained on, then dried into cracks and flakes by
the mid-summer sun. That evening, on arriving at a welcome-home
party, I warned all friends, "Just one remark about losing face
before millions, and you'll need a witch doctor."

Weeks passed. My literary agent and dear friend, Ruth Aley, took
over the matter of finding out whether the pharmaceutical company
intended to assume any of the extra expense I had gone to. She said
that they ought to help out also with taxis I had had to take to get
to all those interviews, and even that the time I spent on them
should be counted in on a regular hourly basis, since it was all at
their request. That had never occurred to me.

She got a definite answer, at least: I must expect nothing more
from them. They had promised and paid me one thousand dollars.
With that payment they had fulfilled their bargain, and they saw no

reason to reimburse me for any further expenses I had chosen to incur, including taxi fares to New York broadcasts.

Ruth was furious. She said that if I'd permit it, she would like to picket their New York offices. I actually believe she would have done it! I was distressed for that nice man who represented them in Lima. I hoped he hadn't had to pay that hotel bill out of his own pocket. Thank goodness, I'd gone to the least expensive place I knew of.

Friends kept asking me about the research on the plants I had brought, especially the contraceptives. They needed to be taken only at considerable intervals, didn't they? The plants sounded much more convenient than the Pill, which had just recently come on the market. How long would it take for the plant substances to be readied for public us?

I felt rather silly having to answer that I had no faintest idea of what was going on or where, nor did I expect to be told anything. Of course, if this company eventually came out with a long-term contraceptive, I would suspect my plants had something to do with it. But I'd never know for sure.

Letters from people who had read press interviews or heard broadcasts asked the same questions. There were even inquiries from Europe, especially Germany. A number of people in that country seemed to have been given the impression that I was on the permanent staff of the company and was sent frequently on lavishly supplied expeditions to wrest from wild tribes their lifesaving secrets. Some wrote to ask me to get jobs for them. Others sought to be employed as field botanists or biochemists on my next expedition for the company. All the foreign letters had been addressed at the company's New York office, and then forwarded to my apartment—with a snide snicker, I'll bet. They did nothing to improve my disposition.

Most of the letters from this country asked me to send them one of the plant medicines I had discussed. Most numerous were the requests for *aysifera*, the Witoto antiobesity herb. I have never really believed in that one; too many other factors could easily be involved. First, there's the nearly fat-free diet; jungle animals, even wild pigs, are leaner than any seen in the United States. Then, too, in these wheelless societies where no one is exempt from doing his share of hard physical work, the average Indian gets as much exercise as an athlete in training. Body structure, too, could be important. The Witoto is somewhere between an ectomorph and an endomorph, and that means there is not much genetic tendency to get fat.

Many others asked for some of the incira sap. "I got a terrible toothache, right now. Please send me some of that stuff for getting rid of teeth right now, airmail."

But there was one which really grieved me. It was from the mother of a hemophiliac child, asking for some of the *sangre de grado* and any other hemostats I might know. It hurt to have to refuse her. It was necessary, of course, even though I did have one bottle I'd saved for my own use. For one thing, we know that hemophilia results from the absence of a certain substance found in normal blood. Not nearly enough is known of *sangre de grado* to assume that it would correct this particular deficiency. Second, it might have some unknown side effects that could be fatal to such a delicate child. And third, even though no one offered any pay for things requested, the Food and Drug Administration just might send me to jail for practicing medicine without a license. I never, repeat never, give jungle medicines to anyone. Trying them on myself is all right; I have no organic defects and have enough medical training to be alert for most of the bad reactions they might provoke. But if I gave any untested drug to someone with unrecognized hypertension, kidney malfunction, a cardiac problem, or indeed any weakness at all and it caused damage, it could only be my fault, morally and legally. I cannot, will not, take that responsibility.

New York is a wonderful place to find out almost anything you would like to know; you meet so many people with connections in so many places. Around the first of the year I met a woman who had a nephew working in the company's laboratories. She had contributed to her nephew's education, and they were close friends. She set herself the task of finding out just what was being done with my plants. It took the nephew longer than we had expected, because auntie refused to accept his first answer and told him to investigate more thoroughly. It still came out the same: what they were doing about the plants was exactly nothing! Nephew could find no trace of either plants or herbarium specimens. No research project that concerned them was under way or even being discussed. It was exactly as though they never existed. Nephew, rather a solemn young man I gathered, said his mention of contraceptive plants had brought the suggestion that maybe the stenographic pool had got

to them before the scientists could, but he thought that was supposed to be a joke. He had an idea that both plants and specimens
might be among the things that got lost or mistakenly thrown out
in the confusion of moving the laboratory. He had found just one
definite bit of information: at least half of the thousand dollars I
received had been put up by the Publicity Department, which was
now congratulating itself on getting a million dollars worth of
publicity for peanuts.

It was Ruth that broke this news to me. I was stunned by its
implications, then furious.

Me! They'd used me for a publicity stunt? Me, spending every
cent I owned and going into debt just to get them a lot of lousy
publicity? Me, nearly getting eaten by a jaguar, living for twenty-
five days on nothing but salt fish (I was striding up and down
Ruth's big living room now, making gestures). Me, going through
months of hardship and danger to get healing plants of inestimable
value to the entire world, only to see those plants treated like
garbage?

"I thought you said you had a pretty good time on that trip,"
Ruth said, mildly.

I had to admit that.

"Then why don't you get busy with all those notebooks and write
a book about it," Ruth suggested.

"I've told you a thousand times, I won't write books. It takes too
long. I write magazine articles."

"Well why don't you write a magazine article about the trip?
Make it a long one. Let yourself go. Put in everything in your note
books." Ruth is a very wily woman.

I started the article. Before the first chapter was half done I knew
that what I wanted to tell could never be squeezed into a magazine
article.

CHAPTER

XXIX

T HE BOOK took all of 1960 and a snip of 1961. I thought it would go faster, because I had kept such complete notes. On jungle trips of any length, it is impossible to carry enough reading matter to last through all those long days of river travel. And anyway, sooner or later, I want to do some of the talking. The interests of people like boatmen and their wives are extremely limited. If all the words that move through my head came out my mouth they would be bored to mutiny. Or shipwreck. So I talked on paper, sprawled on a blanket, my back against the gunwale (can you call the side of a canoe a gunwale?) with a school-supply blankbook propped on my knees. They are ideal for jungle writing, those blankbooks, with backs as solid as wood and the pages so sturdily sewn in that they don't disintegrate even when you drop them in the water. And I wrote what I saw and heard, what this person or that one said, and how he looked when he said it and what I thought about it. It is the ultimate freedom of speech; when annoyed, I can be snide in a way that would be dangerously impolitic in speech. And I can do it in the comfortable certainty that there's no one for miles around who can read English. It is most therapeutic.

As I worked on the book in New York, the urge to go back grew steadily stronger. It was not only homesickness, though that was bad enough. Jungle can be habit-forming; writing about the sounds, the scents, reflections in the water and the magnificent vitality of the rain forest made me realize how thoroughly hooked I am. But that was only part of it. Even more insistent was the feeling of frustration: I had set out for the purpose of making some very valuable medicines available to people who need them. And as time passed, I realized that I had actually accomplished nothing of the kind.

Return? Get more of the same plants and try to convince some-one else that they must be investigated? I did a good deal of ethical dithering before I reached the conclusion that it was not through absentmindedness that the company had omitted any request for exclusive rights to any plants I brought them. It was sheer lack of interest, and I might as well face it. There was no dog in that manger. Even if there had been, they could not have expected one thousand dollars to tie me up for life.

My publisher's advance got me through the year of writing and enabled me to repay the money I'd borrowed in Peru. I also received an inheritance, a very small one, but enough to manage another jungle venture. This time, since I was using only my own money, I could keep whatever I got, at least until I interested somebody in researching it. And if I accomplished nothing else, once I had more herbarium specimens I could start getting proper botanical identification of what I had.

As soon as I had delivered the complete manuscript to the publishers, I took off. First, I'd decided, I would visit Tesa.

This trip I had to travel by air to Iquitos. My time was limited by having to get back for publication day, sometime in October they thought, and I did not get away from New York until the end of May.

In Iquitos, I set about hiring a boatman. García was away, somewhere, so there was no need to dream up a reason for getting somebody else. I had dreaded hurting Doña Ana's feelings, but one trip with her ill-tempered husband was enough. This time I hired a good-natured young man in his late twenties and his financée, Marina. Felipe charged a little more, but he had a better boat with a faster motor. You pay for such travel by the day, so the total price should be about the same. Neither Felipe nor Marina had ever been on the Tigre and Corrientes, but I assured them that I could show them the way. That made me feel most professional: Nicole the jungle guide.

After we turned into Río Tigre we began to hear ominous news. There had been an epidemic among the Jívaros and many had died. Measles, they said. That was frightening. The tribes have not devel-oped the immunity that centuries of exposure have given us. They are as vulnerable to our common "childhood diseases" as we would be to an outbreak of bubonic plague if we had neither vaccines nor modern medical help available. Illnesses native to their homeland they handle efficiently, but they have nothing to protect them against these new and alien products of our civilization.

As we pushed steadily upstream, I became more worried. All the reports we got were contradictory. One night we'd stop in a place where they told us there were almost no Jívaros left alive, the next night our hosts would say that reports of the epidemic were greatly exaggerated. "You know how these river people are; they blow up any story until it's ready to burst," I was told by a young officer in the military post at the mouth of the Corrientes.

When, late on a sunny afternoon, we rounded a bend and saw the first two Jívaro houses, my heart sank. There were no canoes in the port of the big house where the party had been going on the first time I'd seen it. Its roof was beginning to fall in, and the floor was covered with dead leaves. The house across the way was in similar condition. Around the next curve of the river, when we came to Tesa's house I was almost afraid to look. Then I jumped on the prow and started shouting and waving. The house was in its usual perfect order; a canoe was tied in the port and at the far edge of the little clearing I could see a woman and a small child watching us.

"Tesa," I shouted. "Tesa, you're not dead! You're all right! You're here!"

Felipe had cut the motor. As we grounded, Tesa came slowly toward the water, staring unbelievingly.

"It's me, Nicole," I said. "Tell me quickly, is Arejo all right? Is Norama all right?"

They were, though it took her a little while to get sufficiently over her surprise to be able to speak Spanish. She didn't seem to mind speaking it in the presence of Felipe and Marina—apparently the reserve had been for García and his wife. Arejo and Norama had gone to see what was in his fish trap. They would be back soon.

That night I discovered that Arejo spoke quite good Spanish, much better than Tesa. So could several others of the tribe, he told me; they simply did not choose to let people like the Garcías know it. I asked why, but a shrug was all the answer I got. Once more it was brought home to me that the minds of these people, after all these years, are still unpredictable to me. I made a mental note to be very careful about what I said in the future when I was among Indians who seemed not to understand Spanish. In fact, I would do about the same thing when speaking English in their presence. Sometimes they show an uncanny ability to catch meanings.

Sadly they told me of the epidemic. Some loggers had come up the river in search of rosewood and some of the tribesmen had been glad to earn a little money working with them. Then one of the lumbermen fell sick. The disease spread fast. Rukas had been one of the first to die, my friend Rukas the witch doctor. That was a blow. And Auntie? She was all right. Tesa and Arejo named the ones who had died; they were about fifteen, mostly the oldest or the youngest members of the tribe, but my swain Diego, the very polite young man who had interpreted for me, was among them. Tesa's family all had had very light cases, except the baby. He had been dangerously ill, but he was fine, now, nursed back to health with the aid of the tribe's special pediatric plant medicines and the piripiri for fattening children.

Then why were all those houses empty, I asked.

I should have known, Tesa's look implied. After such a tragedy, after a death in almost every house, they had abandoned their homes and moved away, some distance upstream. Their houses, now, belonged to the dead. Tesa and Arejo were moving, too, but they had decided to go down to the Marañón, where Tesa's mother came from. That was how I had happened to catch them, why they hadn't already departed. Such a long move would require a lot of food. They had stayed to prepare quantities of smoked meat, dried fish, and farinha for the voyage.

Why were they leaving the tribe and going off on their own? Because there would be schools on the Marañón. They wanted their children to be able to read and write and count and do sums.

We talked very late. When Marina and Felipe left for the night, I was astonished to see Tesa move to the bench where Arejo sat and cuddle next to him, with her head on his shoulder and his arm around her. Never before, in all my years of tribehopping, have I seen the slightest caress, the most minimal gesture of affection between Indians of opposite sexes. Love, to them, is a very private matter, and I cringe when I think how they would react if ever they came to New York and saw boys and girls locked in embrace on the streets. I realized that Tesa and Arejo were treating me as practically a member of the family. I have seldom felt so flattered.

But in the morning, when I told Tesa that I needed some of the piripiri and suggested that we look for it in Auntie's abandoned *chacra,* she was as shocked as though I had proposed a burglary. Come to think of it, that is probably just what it seemed like to her. That was not Tesa's *chacra,* she told me sternly, it belonged to Auntie. Anything Auntie had planted belonged forever only to Auntie. It made no difference that Auntie had abandoned it, never to return. It could never be touched by anyone else, except with Auntie's permission.

And anyway, she added, there would probably be no more piripiri there. Auntie had moved away well before the last rainy season. That had been a very wet one, and without careful tending, the water would have stagnated in pools on the *chacra* and the piripiri would have rotted.

I decided I must go to visit Auntie; it was still early morning and Tesa thought that with such a good motor we could get there before nightfall.

It was almost dark when we reached the first of the new houses on the bank. Many old friends were there, but I thought I noticed a lack of warmth in their greeting. I had a feeling that they were edgy, nervous. I had brought valuable presents: shotgun shells, knives, necklaces, even a bright red shirt for Auntie's husband, and that is a gift of distinction in these parts. They expressed pleasure in the presents, but they didn't seem so happy about them as they had on the previous trip, and their uneasiness remained unabated. They didn't follow me to Auntie's house where I would spend the night. They scattered, to their homes I suppose. Auntie went to bed early.

In the morning I asked her if she had brought any of the piripiri she gave me before to plant in her new *chacra.* No. A very flat no, though I cannot believe that any tribeswoman would fail to transplant any medicinals that were portable. When I asked permission to look around her old *chacra* and take any plants I might find, she laughed. It did not seem a friendly laugh. She said I could take anything I could find, but I'd find nothing but useless weeds. She was very sure of that. Any piripiri would have rotted.

And she was right. Back downriver, Tesa immediately took me there. My saying that I had Auntie's permission was enough. But the little clearing had nothing at all of interest to me.

All the way back to Iquitos, I worried. Tesa and her family had shown genuine delight at my visit. But what was wrong with the others? Surely they couldn't believe that giving me the forbidden plants, breaking the taboo, had anything to do with the misfortune that had befallen them. The epidemic had come more than a year after I had been there; how could they connect me with that? I think they just weren't sure. That's why they were uneasy but not downright hostile. If they had been certain I was the cause, then they would have had nothing at all to do with me. They would have accepted no gifts, I would not even have seen them. They would have melted away into the brush, even if it meant hiding all night. Or they would have found some ruse to make me go away. I felt very sad about it, much sadder about them than about having to return to Iquitos empty-handed.

I still had time; it was only the end of June. I would find those contraceptive plants somewhere. I was quite certain of that. I'd heard vague reports of their being known by several other tribes. And I wasn't really returning empty-handed. I did have the plants which Tesa had used to bring her little boy back to health, though I didn't think they were very exciting. And I had one other that grew more interesting the more I learned about it. Oddly enough, I had not got it from an Indian, but from Felipe, who, when I engaged him, had said he knew nothing at all about medicinal plants.

On our way up Río Tigre, not more than an hour or two above its confluence with the Marañón, we had stopped at a place where a lone settler was clearing land. We found the poor man in very bad shape. He had been scything sawgrass when a blade of it whipped his eyes, cutting both corneas. One was beginning to heal, now, but the other looked horrible. It oozed pus, the lid was swollen and fiery red, and he said the pain was almost more than he could bear. As always, I was carrying several tubes of ophthalmic ointment; I had some based on antibiotics and the old standard yellow oxide of mercury. When I offered them to him, he said he had already tried both kinds. He'd bought them from a river peddler. The antibiotic was responsible for the improvement in the eye that was healing, but nothing had done any good for the bad one.

"I know what you need for that, señor," Felipe said. "You got it growing right here in front of your house, plenty of it." He showed us a kind of tall grass. "You just pick a good big stalk like this, and then you pull it apart at the joint, like this, and then squeeze it like this, see . . . you sort of milk it. And look there, that drop of sap coming out, that's what'll cure most any eye trouble, if you just put in one drop every morning and another every night. Two drops every day." He put a drop in the man's bad eye.

"*Vaya*, that didn't hurt, did it?"

The man said he couldn't tell. The eye hurt so much all the time that nothing could make it feel worse. But he was very grateful. At least he had something new to try.

About a fortnight later, when we reached the little homestead on our way home, the man recognized the boat and hailed us, excitedly. He threw his arms around Felipe in a big *abrazo*. "Look at my eye," he said, "look how much better!"

The change was remarkable. The less damaged eye was now in perfect condition, and the other, though not entirely healed, had improved amazingly. It was still bloodshot, but there was no pus; it looked clean, and most of the swelling was gone from the eyelid. He insisted on presenting Felipe with a chicken, which rode all the way to Iquitos with us, looking most unhappy in the pointed front of the boat.

When I asked Felipe how he learned about the marvelous grass, he said, "It was an old lady who cured me, when I was working in Brazil. I had *carnosidad* and it was getting bad. And that's how she cured me. Took a long time, maybe a few months, but it cured it. And I figured if it'll cure *carnosidad*, it'll cure anything."

I was impressed. Carnosidad is pterygium. Our doctors do not know its cause, nor do they know any cure but surgery, and that is pretty tricky and not always completely successful. You see comparatively few cases in the United States, but in Amazonia (and other equatorial areas) there's a lot of it. Pterygium is a peculiar growth of tissue that starts in the inner corner of the eye and slowly spreads to cover the cornea. The result is disturbed vision, and sometimes blindness. I examined Felipe's eyes carefully. They were perfectly clear, normal. He said it had been more than two years now, and no sign of the growth had returned.

Thanks to Felipe's faster motor we were in Iquitos just four weeks after our departure. One of the first things I did when I got back was to go across the street to the steep bank that leads down to the Amazon. I thought I had seen that grass growing there, and my room boy, Ríos, had carnosidad. He had been very worried about eventually growing blind. I had, on my last trip in 1959, given him all kinds of ophthalmic ointment, none of which had done the slightest good. Now I gathered some of the grass and showed him how to use it, telling him that he could not expect a rapid cure, but must continue the treatment for a considerable time. He promised that he would use it faithfully.

An old friend, Don Guillermo Godoy, came to see me the day after my return. He is a small, slim man, soft-spoken like almost all jungle habitués but far better educated and traveled than most. He had often told me of the land he had taken way up near the Ecuadorian border. The Indians there were very primitive—the tribe's existence had not even been known until 1945, when they killed some Peruvian soldiers sent into the area to determine the new boundary line after the 1941 war between Ecuador and Peru. They were not a truly hostile tribe, Don Guillermo explained; they were just timid, and the soldiers had frightened them. Soldiers are not always nice to Indians—the understatement of the year.

Earlier, just before I had taken off for Tesa's, Don Guillermo had told me that in a month or so he was going up to see how the Arabelas were getting along. The tribe was named for the little river they lived on, which flows into the Curaray, a tributary of the Napo. If I got back in time, he would be glad to take me along. Now I learned that he would be leaving in about a fortnight, so I arranged to go with him. He knew a great deal about the medicinal plants of the region, but he had never heard of any contraceptives. Nevertheless, I could learn a lot from him, and this trip would make it possible to replace the herbarium specimens I had given the pharmacologists.

Meanwhile, I would spend a little time with some Yaguas who lived near the Amazon, only a few hours by speedboat from town. I had originally been introduced to them by a man they loved dearly, Antonio Wong, whose death a few years ago was mourned by the whole region. I had always wondered if it was not his Chinese origin that first made the Indians feel so at ease with him—his eyes were very like theirs. But then too he had known them since he was a little boy and visited them on fishing trips with his Canton-born father.

When Antonio heard of my failure to get the contraceptive sedges from the Jívaros, he told me that he had an idea that the Yaguas used them, too. The old witch doctor had told him that any time he wanted to be sure his wife would have no more children, he had only to ask the old man's help.

A few days after our return, Antonio took me downriver in his speedboat. The old shaman was off on some business of his own and not to be found; but Antonio made a great point of telling the Yagua chief and the young witch doctor, Primo, that I was a dear friend, almost a sister to him. They must treat me with the same confidence they had for him. Even so, it wasn't until a week later, when I was about to go back to Iquitos, that Primo could be persuaded to give me one of their contraceptive plants. It was a sedge, like those I'd gotten from Tesa, but Primo brought me only one tiny root. He seemed very nervous about it and warned me that the other Indians must never know that he had given it to me. I was jubilant when I got back to Iquitos, but Antonio was annoyed.

"Only one miserable little bit of root!" he exclaimed. As though he felt he must compensate *me* for his own disappointment, he promised that when I returned from the Arabela trip, he would have many more waiting for me, "and everything else they've got in that line . . . to make babies or to get rid of them. They would be ashamed to give me one sorry little root like that. I'll see to it next time I go down there."

CHAPTER

XXX

THE PROMISED trip with Don Guillermo took us first up the Napo. We didn't make very good time the first few days because Don Guillermo had thrown himself into the plant-collecting project with such enthusiasm that we seemed to spend more time stopping than going. The boat was a big one, over thirty-five feet long, and Don Guillermo had brought along five peones, all jungle men. Every few minutes, those first days, somebody would spot a plant I really had to learn about. We'd pull over to the edge and they would jump ashore, to return with an armful of something new to me. It was wonderful to have so many willing helpers to do the splashing through the mud and getting stung by ants. I have long suspected ants of being hypochondriacs . . . medicinal plants are always crawling with them.

We also stopped at just about every dwelling we came to. Don Guillermo knew everybody and seemed to be enormously popular. He would introduce me to Don So-and-so and tell of my mission. Then Don So-and-so would tell us about any plants he knew that grew within a reasonable distance of his place. If the interesting material happened to grow nearby, we would be taken to it at once. But if it happened to grow at some distance, or if the active substance should be the sap of some tree, we would arrange for our host to collect it at his leisure and have it ready when we returned on our way home. Everybody seemed delighted to help. Of course, people in this remote area are always glad to see a new face, but I also think that it pleased them to find some foreigner who did not consider their knowledge utter nonsense.

As we neared Negro Urco, I suggested we stop there for the

night. I had seen Juanita in Iquitos, and she had told me that although Don Alfonso would be away on the Algodon, tending to his rosewood oil distillery, Ema was there and would be glad to see us. To my surprise Don Guillermo was balky. Finally he told me that he did not wish to accept any hospitality from a man who so mistreated his Indians. He'd heard all about it. Don Alfonso worked his Witotos to death and didn't even give them decent food.

I was indignant. Utterly untrue, I told him. I'd stayed there more than once. And I knew that Don Alfonso was positively indulgent to his people.

Don Guillermo said I had been fooled. They had put on a show to impress me. Being a gringa, I'd be quite unable to see through the pretenses.

At that I insisted we stop. I had brought presents for Ema, including photographs I'd taken before, and I must have a chance to deliver them.

Ema was delighted to see us. We must stay the night. She cooked a splendid dinner of venison.

"Venison," Don Guillermo exclaimed. "How do you have venison when Don Alfonso is away?"

Ema explained that Don Alfonso always left a few men behind, so they could have a little rest with their families after they had a couple of months at the distillery. He left them guns and ammunition, with orders to keep up a good supply of food. Meat was no problem, Ema explained. "The hunting is good here."

When we started out again the next morning, Don Guillermo said, "Just wait until I get back to Iquitos! I'll tell those no-good gossipers a thing or two. I apologize. You know, even when Ema was talking I couldn't quite believe it. Then those three men came out, after dinner, to say hello to you. I know Indians. I can tell at a glance the kind of patron they work for. These men were in great shape, straight bones, good muscles, healthy eyes. And no timidity; they walked in as though they owned the place. Happy-looking guys. You don't see that very often in these parts. When I see Alfonso, I'm going to apologize."

Even with all the stopping it took only a couple of weeks to reach our objective. Of course, after we got upstream a few hours we stopped less often. The area nearest the mouth of the river is always more populated; even before we reached Negro Urco the dwellings were quite far apart, and we had collected most of the plants that Don Guillermo and the crew knew about.

The Arabela was another of those twisting, knotted little rivers with a wide pool here and a passage almost too narrow to squeeze through there. One bright, sunny midday, we reached our destination, a cluster of thatched huts atop a steep hill. Don Guillermo had told me a lot about the young American couple living there; in fact, he was responsible for their presence.

All his life Don Guillermo had hated the exploitation of Indians by whites and mestizos, but he had never been able to do much about it; that made it even more frustrating. He met the Arabelas not long after the tribe was discovered. Since nobody knew they were there, no *patrón* had moved in to force them into servitude, and he decided that this was one time nobody was going to. He hastened to establish his claim to the land on which they lived. That made him their *patrón*, but a *patrón* of a very different kind. Interests elsewhere made it impossible for him to stay around to look after them, and he could not see himself as a schoolteacher. Besides, he did not know their language. Nobody did. Yet he was convinced that only education could give them any defense against those who would try to take advantage of them. Adequate medical care, he felt, was almost as important as education. He could not manage all that, but he knew who could.

Don Guillermo had seen the work of missionaries of the Summer Institute of Linguistics (Wyckliffe Bible Translators) in other parts of Peru, and that was exactly what he wanted for the Arabelas. He applied to the institute to send someone to the Arabelas. When they got over the shock—other *patrones* were busily trying to drive this subversive element out of the country—they sent Ferne and Roll-and Rich, a young couple "of the most *simpático*," as Don Guillermo told me.

Before SIL translators can be sent to a tribe, they must have thorough training in the science of linguistics. It takes a first-rate intellect to be able to learn how to go into a group which speaks only a language unrelated to any known tongue, break it down, create an alphabet for it, sort out its grammar and then teach those who speak nothing else to read, write and do arithmetic, first in their own language and then in the official language of the country to which they are native. SIL translators must also be trained in ethnology, a certain amount of medicine, and assorted mechanical skills—for example, how to keep in working order the two-way radio by which they talk daily with their home base, and which they can use to discuss with the base doctor proper treatment for any sickness of the Indians or their own families. When they have completed all this, they are sent to jungle survival school before being sent to the tribe with whom they will live permanently. This is usually in one of the more remote and inhospitable parts of the world.

Don Guillermo had not exaggerated; "most *simpático*" was a barely adequate description of the Rich family, Ferne and Rolland and their two (now there are three) children. There was a sort of clarity about them, not limited only to their strikingly clear eyes and skins, but to their way of thinking. They were the first missionaries I had ever met with whom I felt perfectly at ease from the moment they came tearing down the hill shouting, "You speak English" in response to my "Good morning." They were also an enormous lot of fun. I suppose you have to have a quick sense of humor to live that kind of life and enjoy it as they do. Their enthusiasm is as keen today as it was then. I know; they are still among my most cherished friends.

The Arabelas, as it happened, did not know any contraceptive plants, but they did not lack for other jungle medicines. One old woman was particularly wise in this subject. Day after day she trotted into the jungle, returning hours later with great bundles of medicinals. And night after night, she, Ferne, and I sat under a hissing gasoline lantern, surrounded by an interested crowd of Arabelas, while the old lady explained how the plants should be used. Ferne interpreted and I took notes.

Although the trip downriver was uneventful, when I got back to Iquitos, I found I had over a hundred new specimens, not counting the three kinds of piripiri that Antonio, true as always to his word, had got for me from the Yaguas. He had them growing in big tins, each lot very carefully labeled; this one for inducing fertility, that one to provoke abortion, and that one to prevent conception. Antonio had painted the labels on the cans and warned me not to mix them up. They looked so much alike that he didn't see how the Indians could tell them apart. But they could. I recall a conversation some years earlier with an American botanist, who had shown me two plants that to my eyes looked not a bit alike. Yet tribesmen had told him that the one with the narrow leaves was the male of the

species and the one with the wide leaves was the female. He had
needed to study them closely to determine that they were, indeed,
very closely related.

Later, at the Lima airport, as they weighed my baggage, the
expression on the face of the airline clerk reminded me of my
grandmother, a woman with a strong sense of propriety who found
my casual way of traveling hard to bear . . . a bundle of tribal
masks, a nine-foot blowgun, the basket of pottery, the rolled-up
pelt of a nutria and an enormous dried snakeskin. Well, at least I
didn't look like the usual tourist.

The airline I was on flew only to Miami; I had to change to
another plane. That meant I had to go through customs in Miami.
All went well enough until we got to the plants. Then a State
Department of Agriculture official insisted that to be allowed in the
country, they must first be fumigated.

But my New York plane would leave in an hour and a quarter.
Could it be done by then? I think that shocked him; they were very
busy—it might take them a couple of days. Then could it be done
when we reached New York? Kennedy Airport has the same facilities. No. He unbent sufficiently to explain that anything coming
from the Amazon area might easily be infested with microscopic
beasties which would get along fine in the warm Florida climate
and which could endanger the horticulture and agriculture of the
state. But he promised that they would be sent on to me by air at
the first possible moment. "We do it all the time," he said. "Valuable plants, orchids, all kinds of delicate things. Our people are
experts; we haven't had a complaint in months. Your plants will
arrive in great shape; they always do."

I couldn't see how any malignant organism could sneak out of
those sealed plastic bags, just going from one plane to another; nor
how, if clever enough to manage that, it could get out of the
antiseptic looking airport and get on with destroying the agriculture of Florida. But law is law and I could see that this was one I
could not win. So I gave up.

That official had been right about one thing: the plants eventually arrived in vigorous health. I was the one to wilt when I saw
them. My carefully numbered bags had vanished. All the plants had
been shuffled into one tangled mess, then dumped into a single big
package. I had no slightest hope of separating the fertility inducers
from the contraceptives or abortifacients. I stared at them for days,

trying to detect some dissimilarity. Finally I gave up and presented them to a very pleasant Englishwoman at the Brooklyn Botanical Garden.

At any other time such a fiasco would have sent me into a decline. Getting extremely angry always makes me sick. Instead of sleeping, I lie there, my mind clenched like a fist on sharp and hurtful thoughts, broken bits of injustice, indignity and burning fury.

But, as if sent to take the edge off my frustration, just then my book came out. It was wonderful and exciting: parties, letters, interviews by all the media. This time, on TV shows, I made sure that all makeup men used only creamy stuff so my face wouldn't fall off again. That gave me such confidence that on the *Tonight Show* I made a bullseye with a blowgun. Never before had I been able to hit even a thatched roof. Then, best of all, the book reviews started coming out, and they were kind beyond my dreams. With all that going on, how could I get upset about the loss of some plants that I knew I could replace as soon as I got around to it.

But even after the book had had plenty of time to get around, nobody cared to research any of my plants. I still don't understand why. Some things, like the tooth extractor, the hemostatic and wound-healing materials (I had several now, in addition to the *sangre de grado*), and some for skin infections which resisted all known treatment, could be investigated without requiring costly or complicated techniques, at least for the part of the testing which would establish their efficiency. Again and again I talked with companies, and with foundations which were supposedly searching for cures for specific diseases. Always I collided with members of the raised eyebrow school, the I-never-heard-of-it-therefore-it-cannot-exist brotherhood.

After some months of this, I woke up to the fact that nothing at all was going to develop. So why was I staying here and wishing I were there? I am completely free. No one is dependent on me for anything. I haven't even a single living relative, except the widow of an uncle in California. I like her very much, but we had met only on the single occasion when their theater-going trip coincided with one of my periods in New York.

Pingponging back and forth to South America was ruinously expensive, but there was nothing to keep me from living wherever I chose. So I chose Iquitos, sublet my apartment, and went.

CHAPTER

XXXI

IQUITOS IN those days had no apartment buildings. I had hoped to find a house overlooking the river, but there was nothing like that for rent. Finally I settled for a little house only a half block away. At least I had only to step out the door to gaze at that splendid stretch of shining water, reflecting every changing mood of weather, catching and holding the vivid sky at sunset. And dimly, across the sweeping curve it made just here, crouched the low, dark outline of the rain forest, my jungle.

The house was very small and, like so many of the older one-story houses, rather lacking in cross ventilation; but it was charming and its rent was low. In the front there were two *salas*, with floors of very fancy multicolored Portuguese tiles, which, kept highly waxed, looked like printed satin pretty enough to use for a dress. The location was convenient, just halfway between the Hotel Turista and the great native market of Belén. I loved going to market. There was always smoked game from the jungle, crisp heart of palm a thousand times more delicious than those limp slices sold in cans. There was always a bewildering variety of unfamiliar fruits and usually a great quantity of fish, sometimes queer-looking, but all caught only a few hours before being put on sale. Now and then I'd had fresh game from the forest: armadillo (which is delicious), venison, and crocodile meat, another of my favorites, though to be zoologically correct I should call it cayman.

I lived happily in that house nearly four years. Sufficient municipal modernization had recently taken place to provide conveniences like safe drinking water, many paved streets, and daily plane service which brought fresh vegetables from the coast—many vegetables like cabbage, tomatoes, root vegetables and potatoes don't do well in the damp, warm, clay soil of the region. A few travelers came, but only a trickle of tourists. In my vocabulary, tourists are people who travel to have been somewhere; real travelers come to be there, to see and taste and smell and feel and absorb. And many residents, rich or poor, upper class or peon, still clung to the old gracious way of treating strangers; on meeting a foreigner their first thought was "What can I do for him?" not "What can I get from him?"

There were only a half-dozen residents whose native tongue was English, and I was the one the staff at the Hotel Turista knew best. I had stayed there so long and so often in the past that a sort of old family retainer atmosphere had developed. Once, when some money had disappeared from a guest's room, a delegation of room boys came to ask my help in trapping the thief. "Please, señorita, leave fifty-five soles in the drawer of your nighttable. If it is lost, between us we will pay you back. But we think we know who is the thief, and we will watch. You understand, señorita, we cannot let such things happen in our hotel. It puts shame on all of us." The thief was duly caught, and he didn't get away with my fifty-five soles, either.

After I moved into a house of my own, they seemed to class me with the local tourist attractions, and people they approved of were often sent along to visit. When the doorbell rang, I never knew whether it might be a visiting ambassador, an old witch doctor friend who had come to see the city, a traveling writer (John Gunther was one they sent), or some local character trying to sell me orchids or live jungle animals like an outsize snake he wanted me to tell the New York zoo director to buy from him. I suppose it was only natural for him to expect me to know everybody in New York; he knew everybody in Iquitos, didn't he?

One of the people they sent to my house was an American botanist collecting for an American pharmaceutical firm. I thought he had a strange way of working, but he assured me that it was the only proper one. "You're all wrong to expect anything of value from Indians," he told me. "My advice to you, as a friend who has been in tropical botany for years, a friend who knows, is 'Give it up!' You'll get nowhere fooling around with Indians. How can they know anything about medicine? They're illiterate!

"These big companies are out to make money. Do you think they'd hire some ignorant savage as a consultant? No, they hire me, and at a damn good price, too."

He agreed emphatically that the jungle was full of undiscovered medicinals of tremendous value. "But you've got to keep this ethnic stuff out of it; that's nothing but superstition. Me, I'm a scientist and I work scientifically."

His method was to wander through the woods gathering everything he saw that belonged to any plant family that included some species which had physiological activity. If field tests showed one to have any alkaloids or other interesting compounds, it was gathered in quantity and shipped to the laboratories in the States. And there, the pharmacologists would make analyses of the components and then try to find out what they might be good for.

"Don't you get a certain number of false positives on the field tests?" I asked, having learned that the alkaloid test, for one, is not always reliable.

"Oh sure, now and then. But they can catch that in the States and toss out the batch."

It seemed to me a curiously roundabout and extravagant way to work. I was not surprised to hear, a few years later, that little of value had been found and the project had been abandoned. It must have cost plenty, though, while it lasted. I doubted that it had enhanced the value of jungle medicine in the minds of the pharmaceutical industry's chiefs. Oh dear!

Sooner or later on this stay I met every *norteamericano* who came to Iquitos for any length of time. I also found useful friends among market vendors and the relatives of the hotel staff and my cook's parents. Many members of the fine old families, too, were extraordinarily knowledgeable, and everyone was glad to help.

River travel was much cheaper and I went on *lanchas* or *colectivos* or *pequipequis*. *Colectivos* are big canoes with outboard motors, while pequipequis (pronounced pecky-pecky for the noise they make) are boats with inboard motors. In a region where there are no roads of any sort, these craft serve as country buses; they stop wherever and whenever they're hailed. They are not comfortable, but they are great fun because the people who use them, almost always of the poorest class, are friendly, laughing, and kind. And they are full of fascinating stories, for talking is one of the few entertainments that they can afford.

I made occasional visits to the Summer Institute of Linguistics base and learned that the Riches were not the only missionaries with whom one could have an easy and relaxed friendship. They all seemed to have a warm affection for the whole human race. And in those years, I made the first of many visits to Shipibo communities along the Ucayali River.

The Shipibos still worship the Inca Emperor, whom they believe to be alive, somewhere, waiting for the proper time to return and take charge. I have not met any who had a *patrón*; they are gracefully independent and form their own communities, working for the white man only when and as they choose. I have never heard of a Shipibo woman being made a concubine or even wife by a white man. And, importantly, they know and use two species of the contraceptive piripiri and several others of considerable interest. I was particularly impressed by the one they use to ease childbirth, having the good fortune to have a firsthand chance to see how valuable that one can be.

I first got to know the Shipibo through Graciela, a schoolteacher. President Belaunde was in power at the time, and his government was placing primary schools in as many jungle communities as possible, with teachers native to the region. On my first visit, with Graciela's help, I was able to form some close friendships with some of the tribal women. My success was, 1 think, due to my tape recorder. The people here sang beautifully; they were proud to have their music recorded, and enchanted when I played it back to them . . . over and over and over. It is a strange music, hauntingly melodic, with tunes that turn in unexpected but lovely directions. Their voices are true and sweet and some have extraordinary range.

On my second visit to Graciela and the tribe, I chanced to arrive only two days after Graciela had given birth to her fourth child. I remarked that she was looking a little peaked. Little did I know, she answered. If the Indians hadn't come to her aid she would have died.

Her previous pregnancies and deliveries had been easy, and she had expected this one to be the same. Because they had miscalculated the date the baby was due, her husband left on a week's voyage just the day before she went into labor. "Then the baby got stuck," was the way she put it. She had been forty-eight agonized hours in labor when the Indian women came to her with something ground up in a cup of water, and told her to drink it.

"I was so sure I was going to die that I didn't care any more," she told me. "But I swallowed it. Almost that same minute, anyway not more than two minutes more, I felt all my insides relax. And then the baby was born and they were holding him up to show me, and barely ten minutes had passed."

At the end of this stay, I took with me plants of many kinds of piripiri: the contraceptive, an abortifacient, a fertility inducer and the one to ease labor, which was also the base of a rudimentary prenatal care program. That was the one they had given Graciela, but, they told me, if she had taken it as a Shipibo woman does, she would not have had all that trouble. Shipibo women begin taking this at the last month of pregnancy. It is given to the mother-to-be three times a week, and each time she drinks the root ground up in water, she also massages her abdomen with some of the ground plant. The final and largest dose is given just as she begins labor.

They also gave me a number of other piripiris: one to make me fat, one for rheumatism, several for making children strong and one to protect them from witchcraft. Then there was one used as a love charm and another which they said must never be revealed to any man. If a husband's pants are washed with it, it will make him impotent with any women except his wife—or wives, since most Shipibo men have two.

CHAPTER

XXXII

O NE AFTERNOON in 1965 a very correct, even courtly elderly gentleman called on me at my little house in Iquitos. He had wanted to meet me ever since he read my book, he said, and he had been given my address by a mutual friend in New York. I will call him Arthur Jones.

Mr. Jones, until his recent retirement, had headed the South American division of a very big pharmaceutical company. He knew a good deal about jungle; during World War II he had served with the Rubber Production Board, a government agency set up to get wild rubber from the Amazon region in an attempt to replace Asian supplies cut off by the Japanese. What he had learned then convinced him that there was more than superstition to the belief that the tribes cultivate medicinal plants having properties unknown to our scientists, and capable of working miracles if properly developed.

Now that he was free of other duties, he thought it might be both interesting and profitable to investigate some of the plants I had learned about. Would I be interested in such a venture, if he could set up a company to go into it on a solid scientific and financial basis?

Would I!

When he returned to the States, he said, he would find partners to join in the financing; he knew a number of people who might be interested in such an investment for what he called "risk capital." I gathered it had to do with tax brackets and deductions. It took about a year for him to organize everything. Meanwhile, I discovered I had friends in New York who knew him. A very important man, they told me, an industrialist of some standing. Finally the financing was arranged, the company incorporated, licenses for working in Peru attended to, and I received a letter with a check for travel expenses. I was to come to the States immediately and to bring with me as much *sangre de grado* as I could.

Mr. Jones took me from the airport to his home, a large but not ostentatious stone house in acres and acres of private woodlands, and I was instantly and permanently charmed by Mrs. Jones (Ellie) and the three children. One of their dogs, an elderly Labrador of great dignity, had recently cut his foot, and it would not heal. We immediately treated it with *sangre de grado* and the swift improvement astonished the family. But that was nothing compared to what happened in the laboratory Mr. Jones had organized, where the first tests of the material were run.

That work was begun the morning after my arrival. The initial experiments employed rabbits on whose backs superficial but extensive cuts were made. Five days later, Mr. Jones came out from New York in a state of excitement I would never have believed possible in such a cool, rather poker-faced individual. He positively leapt up the stairs.

"It's absolutely incredible!" he exclaimed before he even took off his topcoat. "Unbelievable! They've never seen anything like it. Nothing like it described in the medical journals, either! Ellie, we need a bottle of champagne for a toast. My research director suspects we may have discovered a healing principle hitherto unknown to medical science." He looked at me. "What's the matter, Nicole? How can you take it so calmly? Aren't you excited?"

I said, "Of course, I'm thrilled. But it's not exactly new to me, you know. I've used it so often. Remember my telling you about that dog who had been gored by a wild pig? Or the big cut on my arm? These results are more of the same, so I can't pretend I'm surprised."

Mr. Jones laughed. "You know, I told them before about your arm, and how fast it healed and that there's almost no scar. And they said, maybe you had exaggerated, maybe it wasn't all that bad. Or maybe it was some sort of faith healing, because you believed so strongly in the stuff. So today, I reminded them about that. And I asked them how much faith they thought those rabbits had. You should have seen their faces.

After we drank our toast, Mr. Jones told me that they were

starting chemical analyses at once. "Going at it hammer and tongs. Very complex chemically, that sap.

"The first project is, of course, to try to separate from the raw material some of the more obvious components . . . like tanin, for example. But a larger supply of raw material should be made available without delay. The five bottles you brought should be adequate for the next three weeks or so of work, but once a line of investigation has been entered upon, any interruption, such as would result if supplies were exhausted, could cause serious prejudice. In fact, it is conceivable that under some circumstances the entire procedure would have to be repeated from the beginning."

I agreed that I should get back to Iquitos as soon as possible. In addition to getting an immediate supply of the sap, there were a thousand other things to be done. It had already been decided that I should find and install myself in a house large enough to accommodate offices, storage rooms and a small laboratory for initial testing. Further research would be done in the United States. The house must have a garden spacious enough to allow for construction of an animal house, drying and grinding sheds, and anything else that might be needed.

Having had a year to think over such matters, I had a house already in mind, one perfect for our purposes, and had learned that it could be rented for a reasonable sum.

My salary had already begun. It was not lavish, but Mr. Jones explained that the lawyers were now working on a contract specifying that I would be paid a thousand dollar bonus on each plant found to be of value, and more important, a small royalty from every product sold, once commercial production began. That was where the real money would be. But before that contract could be ready, there were details still to be approved by other partners and a number of legal technicalities to be ironed out. It would all take a bit of time. Then and there, Mr. Jones presented me with a thousand dollar check, my first bonus, for the *sangre de grado*. Since it was urgently necessary for me to get things started in Iquitos, I could facilitate matters by signing a brief and very simple contract authorizing me to make purchases, hire personnel, disburse company funds and generally act as their agent in South America for the specified salary. The contract would remain in force for the next sixteen months. I was starry-eyed as I signed. I didn't even take time to consult a lawyer. The company, I was certain, would take care of my interests, and eagerly I set off for Iquitos, to start, after a decade of delay and frustration, my real life's work.

It had been decided that I should move into the big house, paying the company the same rent I had paid for my pretty little one. It was essential for someone to be on the place day and night: days, to supervise the construction and nights, if a collecting crew had been out after plants, to check over what they brought and see that everything got into presses or drying rooms as soon as possible. I had long known just the people I wanted to employ. They had all done work of one kind or another for me in the past, and I knew I could depend on them. I had no acquaintances in the construction business, but I had good friends who could help. They found me architects and contractors, but they warned me that getting such work done in Iquitos was not like getting it done in any other place in the world. Workmen here, they said, had a cheerfully informal attitude toward their work. They were not at all lazy, but they had a very carefree feeling about time, which they regarded as being of unlimited elasticity. Also they came from very large families; that meant they had an inordinate number of uncles and aunts, brothers and sisters, cousins and godparents, all of whom have weddings and funerals, christenings, birthdays and anniversaries which must be taken seriously.

I am, on the other hand, compulsively ruled by the all-or-nothing law. I have always worked very hard or not at all, but this job required a greater output of energy than anything I had ever attempted. I didn't mind; I was glad I could do it.

The people of Iquitos thought I was mad. "Imagine! She's made an air-conditioned hotel for rats and rabbits, when she hasn't even started to air-condition the house." The rabbits had been sent to test the contraceptive sedges I had planted and which were growing nicely in the garden. First, of course, we had to prove their fertility, so after they'd had time to get acclimated, we put the girl rabbits and boy rabbits together. Instead of the glad little cries I had expected, they merely looked suspiciously at each other and moved as far apart as the cages permitted. And there they stayed, forevermore, in sullen celibacy. I tried different room temperatures, warmer, cooler, I even turned the air conditioners off completely for a brief period. They didn't seem to notice. I tried putting different bucks with different does. They didn't even bother to sneer at each other. I found it terribly disillusioning, after all I'd heard about rabbits.

As soon as the animal house was ready, we went on to build the plant-drying and grinding rooms, concrete storerooms and a building for the big, noisy new generator. New wiring had to be installed throughout. That meant electricians clumping and hammering overhead in the space between the ceilings and roof, sometimes far into the night, since to get enough experienced men it was necessary to employ some who worked elsewhere in the daytime. And the plumbing! For months, muddy trenches crossed floors, terraces and garden as we installed water lines to rooms that had none before and laid pipe for what was, I believe, the first hot water system in Iquitos. If anything more was needed to persuade the local people that I was insane, that did it. The entire population takes several cold baths a day to cool off; nobody in his right mind would want hot.

Andrea was my greatest stroke of luck in all that year. She was an old friend; when I had to find a secretary I persuaded her to give up her job in Lima, where she found the cold winters hard to endure, and come to work for me. She was the perfect person for our work: bright, serious, even-tempered and hard-working, she had been born on her father's big jungle property and had learned Witoto as a child. She also spoke English. Having been a court reporter, she knew more about Peru's complex labor laws than most lawyers and years with the Department of Health had given her a pretty good scientific vocabulary. And, of course, she knew everybody.

At intervals Mr. Jones came down from the States to see how things were going. Often he brought with him some botanist or pharmacologist, always people who turned out to be good company. Each time he came there was a big party—thirty or forty guests to dinner, and occasionally a several-day river "expedition." I should have enjoyed them more, but they meant so many extra details to be attended to that I was growing more and more tired.

As time wore on, I began to worry about that contract. Mr. Jones was going to bring it down on his first trip, but the lawyers didn't get it ready. He didn't want to send it by mail; there were a few points we should discuss before I signed it. Then the next trip, one of the partners hadn't come back from Europe yet, and it had to have his OK, though that, Mr. Jones said, was only a formality.

Still, every time he came, I was disappointed; and it was so important to me. That contract was the reason I had given the company
all my plant notes . . . the result of years of intense, costly, and
sometimes hazardous work. All these delays made me increasingly
uneasy.

Yet Mr. Jones had always been so kind. Generous, even, when
the fire occurred. Fortunately he was in Iquitos at the time—he and
some other people were having a predinner drink on the terrace
when we saw the smoke. Faulty wiring in my clothes closet had
caused it. It was quickly extinguished, but not before most of my
wardrobe was ruined. Mr. Jones had been wonderful; said I would
just have to have a trip to the States to get something new. I didn't
appear to be in very good shape physically, he remarked. (I suppose
that must have been obvious. I had lost too many pounds from
increasingly severe bouts of dysentery, which I had preferred to
ignore.) So he officially ordered me to come to the States for
medical treatment. And the company paid the doctor.

Also he sent me books. For a reading addict like me, living in a
town whose bookshops offer little but school texts and Spanish
translations of Jules Verne or Superman, gifts of books arouse
overwhelming gratitude.

A man like that, with such a lovely family, a man of such wealth
and position—it was absurd to suspect him of being unbusinesslike.
When again, on his next visit, he brought no contract and I began
trying to push a bit for it, I felt like a harpy.

More time passed. The first thing I had done was set up a fairly
regular supply system for the *sangre de grado*, which was the first
plant to be investigated. We knew that one to be a winner, so,
except for some preliminary testing of a number of others, that was
the plant they were concentrating on.

In Iquitos the plumbing and electrical work finally was finished,
and most of the construction. And the people I had hired were
proving even better than I had hoped. They not only knew their
jobs, they knew each other's work, too, and in emergencies could
take over very handily. For example Marcial, the "chief of
expeditions"—that meant boatman, but titles are important—was a
famous ex-navy cook. He took over from Majordomo Humberto
(cook and butler) when there were guests so Humberto could
devote himself to serving. The chief plant man, Fernando, son of a
Cocama witch doctor, knew medicinal plants I had never heard of.

He also knew where to find everything that grew, and he and Marcial took care of all drying, grinding and packing. He was also a very good carpenter and general handyman, but he loved best to work in the garden. Juan, nominally the gardener, could often be found in the kitchen making mayonnaise, which he did very well, and the animal man, Mauricio, turned out to be extremely good at keeping the laboratory equipment shining. Changing around like that kept them all contented. These people are hard and willing workers, but routine bores them.

The first of the year rolled around and soon the rainy season started. It was the approach of the rains that had made finishing the construction work so urgent. Building is impossible when the rains are at their height, but by that time the external work was completed. And we had been able to keep up with the increasing demands of the biochemists at the laboratory in the States. They were finding in the *sangre de grado* new compounds which promised to be valuable in treating more ailments than even I had imagined. But shipments of the sap were now going out with what, for Iquitos, might be considered reasonable regularity. I had time to go to bed with a bad case of flu. Unfortunately, although I have a couple of excellent native remedies for cough, I do not know of any for flu; it seems to be an illness the tribes did not know about until they got mixed up with whites. Having time to think meant having time to worry about that royalty contract. I decided that ten months was a sufficient gestation period for any legal document and composed a long, clear letter quoting the promises that had been made to me and saying that I must know without further delay the exact status of that agreement.

Mr. Jones replied by return mail. This letter had none of the courtly little phrases so typical of his usual style. In fact, I thought I could hear the crack of a distant whip. Mr. Jones said it might be all of five years before all avenues of research were completed. He had not as yet decided even the methods to be used for marketing the different products. That, he said, was for the "nebulous future." Marketing? Marketing had nothing to do with the contract he had described, which had been concerned exclusively with royalties on whatever sales were made. He went on to say that he found it "distressing" that I should be "worrying about anything so remote and undefined." Remote? When it had always been promised for his next trip to Iquitos? Undefined?

I stopped reading for a moment and took a few deep breaths. Because there was no use trying to stay hopeful any longer. I knew what it all meant: it meant my chances for ever receiving any royalties agreement had receded to the more remote parts of never-never land. Grimly I read on. He reminded me that I was most fortunate to be there to see what he called "the realization of your dreams of many years."

That did it! At least it snapped me out of the sick feeling and into a good healthy fury.

That "interim" contract I'd signed still had a few months to run. I sent an immediate reply saying that the state of my health would not permit me to complete the specified sixteen months in the company's service. And that was no lie. Even before that case of flu, I'd been in such dilapidated condition that I'd had to learn to rise very slowly if I'd been sitting for a while. Standing up suddenly would bring on the blind staggers, or even black me out completely for a moment.

The doctor Mr. Jones flew down with said I needed hospitalization as soon as possible. He had warned me the last time I was in the States that overwork in such tropical climate was dangerous and he'd ordered me to return in six months for a fortnight's break. Over eight months had passed, and I had not obeyed. But with all those builders and plumbers and electricians all over the place, how could I leave?

I was put in a pleasant little hospital in Maryland where they found I had picked up, among other things, a parasite named "Providence." Not inappropriate, I thought, since it had helped me to get out of there. But where had it been when I had trustingly handed over my plant notes? At least the contraceptive sedges had been kept from the company: the man who took over when I left had, against everybody's advice, bought a pet *majás*. *Majás* is the local name for paca, a rotund, dog-sized jungle rodent, a cute little animal that lives on roots. The first night it was in the compound, it ate every sedge in my garden. The next night, my replacement ate the *majás*. Its meat is a great delicacy.

To be fair, I must say that the company paid my hospital expenses and the doctor's bill. They also paid for the trip I later made to Iquitos to fetch my belongings, gave me a decent price for the furniture I'd moved from the pretty little house to the company's installation, and gave me some separation pay. Also they returned to me all of the money I had unwittingly advanced them by paying from my personal account expenses that should properly have been paid from company funds. Their auditor was a very nice woman. She was so surprised that, after I had returned to New York, she telephoned me long distance to tell me she was quite accustomed to finding shortages, but this was the first time in years of experience that she had ever found what she called an "overage" in the accounts of anybody entrusted with company funds.

CHAPTER

XXXIII

I FOUND another apartment in New York. How lucky is the snail! Such a beautifully designed house, so complete, and he always has it with him. I retrieved some furniture from the houses of friends and bought replacements for the rest. I sold part of my collection of Amazonian art and artifacts to the Museum of the American Indian; there simply was no room for those hundred and ninety pieces in a small apartment.

I did some editing, some translating, and a little writing. I put my plant catalogs in most beautiful cross-indexed order. Most of my herbarium specimens, unfortunately, were gone. I needed them. Many had not yet been identified, and it is essential to know the Latin names, since tribal nomenclature varies from group to group.

For three years I resisted the urge to return to the jungle. Then I gave in. I had a couple of diamonds left. They brought enough for a few months of travel. This time I went to my friends of the Summer Institute of Linguistics. Their Peruvian base, on a beautiful jungle lake called Yarinacocha, looks exactly like the Twenty-third Psalm, only busier. No lying down in those green fields. This is the place where their school-age children are educated, and it is here that the translators living with tribes return in February and March of each year to discuss new linguistic theories and compare Bible translation methods. These are the months of the worst rains. Fishing is poor and work on the flooded plantations is impossible, so Indians can travel without endangering their food supplies. That is why these months have been chosen for bringing the more advanced tribal students to the base. At Yarinacocha they are given training in teaching. When they have learned enough, they are sent out to more remote communities of their own people to make them literate and thus better able to cope with the relentlessly advancing current of what we call civilization.

Indians who really want to study need place no limits on their aspirations. The institute sees to it that they have the chance to get as much education as they wish. I know one ex-headhunter about to graduate from a university, and I get charming letters in excellent English from a girl of the Piro tribe who is in medical school. I hope she will escape contamination with the white man's contempt for tribal knowledge. If she remains under the influence of the Linguists she should; they show firm respect for all valuable elements of the cultures with which they work.

Friends in Yarinacocha arranged for me to spend hours with the tribesmen they had brought in, but I did not learn much. Most of them were too young to have learned much about plants that heal. But I did find one friend of enormous value. That was Guillermo, a middle-aged and widely respected Shipibo who had spent many years with one of the Linguists as informant on the language and customs of his people.

Guillermo took me to a group of Conibos (a related tribe) on the Upper Ucayali. There I was able to fill my plant presses and obtain all the piripiri I wanted. But the big prize I brought home was a beautiful recording of the entire performance of an old-style Conibo witch doctor, from calling the spirits to healing patients. Later Guillermo translated every word of it for me.

Back on the base, I became friendly with a Campa woman, and she gave me the two contraceptive vines which I had heard about for years but had never been able to find.

In New York, before I had even started planning this trip, I had had a strange but very heartening experience. I received a sum of money from a man I still have never met, and about whom I know very little except that he had a Brooklyn address. He said the money was to be put toward my next expedition, and he claimed that he sent it because he wanted me to locate a plant called *maricahua* which he had seen mentioned in an account of Inca life. Privately I believe that most of all he just wanted to help. I have an impression that he does that sort of thing, but always as anonymously as possible. He helped more than he will ever know. I was feeling extremely neglected when I first heard from him, and the idea that anybody thought what I wanted to do was worth helping—and to the tune of several hundred dollars—gave me a tremendous lift. But I had never heard of anything called maricahua.

Neither had anybody else in Iquitos, around Yarinacocha, or in the foothill jungle of Lamas, where I went to ask some old-timers. But I finally tracked it down only to find that it was a plant I'd known all the time under the local name of *toé*. It is the pink flowered *Datura arborea*.

For some time I had been coming to the conclusion that just learning and field work were not enough. I must try to make some dent in the scientific community. So I wrote a paper entitled "The Attitudes of Four Peruvian Jungle Tribes toward Plants Employed as Oral Contraceptives," and presented it that August at the XXXIX International Congress of Americanists, in Lima.

That was noticed. The Peruvian press loved it; I especially enjoyed the account in one of the more lurid journals which had me held captive by a savage tribe.

The international wire services picked it up. Back in the States again, I was somewhat surprised to learn that the news of "primitive" tribes who had for centuries been practicing family planning, using methods we had discovered only in the last couple of decades, got me mentioned in periodicals ranging from *The Wall Street Journal* to *Playboy*.

Surely, I thought, some company would want to investigate these contraceptives now that our own products were arousing so much criticism. The intrauterine device was having its problems; some women found it uncomfortable, even painful, and there were reports of cases of intrauterine bleeding. The Pill, for obvious reasons, was not well suited to the needs of impoverished masses. But it was drawing fire even among the well-heeled and educated as accounts of unfortunate side effects multiplied. It was blamed for blood clots in the circulatory system; some rumors hinted that it might even cause cancer. Many women complained of headaches and nausea. I knew two women still in their twenties who told me that it had given them varicose veins, and a couple of physicians among my friends refused to let their wives take it.

It seems natural enough to fear a slow buildup of potentially harmful chemicals in body tissues from any medicament which must be taken day after day, year after year. I believe the Indian plants to be a lot safer. How are you going to build up a slow accumulation of toxic substances from anything you take only once every several years? The shortest-acting tribal contraceptive plant I know protects a woman for twelve months when one dose is taken; others work for varying numbers of years. One of the most easily found (and easily grown) is a weed which not only prevents conception but also stops menstruation for exactly three years. But when the effect wears off, women who have taken it become extremely fertile (not however to the extent of having multiple births).

This time, I had not been long back in New York when I began to hear from pharmaceutical companies. Now *they* were calling *me*, and my hopes soared. I refused to be discouraged even by Angus Brooks, a consulting chemist I've known for years. His dour Scottish nature always inclined him to pessimism, so I argued when he said, "These big pharmaceutical firms are out for only one thing: money. You'll find no half-baked do-gooders in that crowd. So what if a few women complain of side effects from the Pill? So what if it could be doing things we don't even know about yet? Everybody has learned, these days, that some carcinogens have to keep on accumulating in the body for maybe ten or twenty years before cancer symptoms show up. But what counts is that women are buying that pill by the millions. So what if our plants are safer? Listen, Nicole. You just try to figure out what kind of dough they make from a pill that a woman has to take twenty times a month, every month of every year. Then you compare that with the earnings from something that same women has to buy only once every several years. Multiply both figures by millions and you'll see if it would make sense for these businessmen to lay out a fortune to investigate your stuff and put it in production."

He was equally cynical about most of the other plants. I was trying to arouse interest in the one that had arrested my arthritis in four days. Painkillers, Angus informed me, are a leading profit maker on every annual balance sheet. Arthritics are perhaps the biggest users of analgesics. He would not back down, even when I phoned to tell him that I had received lunch invitations from the medical directors of his "profit-oriented" pharmaceutical firms. I remember one of them particularly.

This medical director was a very pleasant fellow, but what made a lasting impression was his telling me that he knew for certain that the Indians of the Amazon region had no medicinal plants at all. He knew, because he had gone on an expedition to find out, and they

had told him so themselves. When he told me where he had gone, I
nearly choked on my vermouth-on-the-rocks. It was Andrea's family's place. I knew both it and the Witotos there well. The doctor
chugged up the river to the big old house where Andrea's sister and
her husband still live. The Indians were hastily summoned. He told
them that if they would hurry into the jungle and get quantities of
every medicinal plant they knew, he would pay lavishly for each
plant.

The Indians looked blank. What plants were those? Where did
they grow? They had never heard of anything like plants that cured
sickness. (That! from the Witotos who are such wizards!) So the
doctor went away, convinced they knew nothing of these matters.

Still I have to admire him for trying, especially when you consider what awful things people must have warned him against in the
dark mysterious jungle. I know by experience. People still tell me I
must look out for savages, cannibals, clouds of disease-carrying
mosquitos, predatory beasts, and venomous snakes including one, a
New Yorker told me, that has fangs at both ends, enabling it to
sting with head or tail. (He read about it in a book.) And of course
he must have been warned about rivers teeming with voracious
piranhas, electric eels and crocodiles, and told that water, foliage,
air, and earth are loaded with microbes causing mysterious diseases
lethal to all whites. Any scientist who will leave his clean and
cloistered laboratory and venture into such peril is, in my opinion, a
game guy and one to be admired.

Some companies, on the other hand, said they would like to help
me. If I would just deliver to them a couple of hundred pounds of
those sedges, with proper botanical identification and full instructions on how to get more, they would investigate them. It was
always the sedges they wanted; I don't know why. But two hundred
pounds! That would be the entire production of how many communities? I always had to explain that I could not afford to do this
on my own; would they underwrite the expenses involved? The
mere suggestion ended all communication, except with one company: Merck & Co., Inc. Its vice president for basic research, Dr.
David Jacobus, took the matter under serious consideration after
carefully explaining many of the problems involved, logistics being,
perhaps, the most serious. While it was under discussion, he had the
courtesy to keep in touch. When they finally decided against it, he
was candid in explaining why: a Brazilian expedition, already fi-

nanced and at work in the field, had offered to supply them with what seemed to be quite similar material, which they were already in a position to supply in quantity. This was so obviously economically superior to what I could offer that I understood perfectly. I was naturally disappointed, but it was such a pleasant change to be treated as an intelligent adult that I almost didn't mind.

CHAPTER

XXXIV

Even though nothing came of it, that experience with Merck was encouraging. It convinced me that perhaps it might yet be possible to persuade the pharmaceutical experts that quinine and curare were not the only plants of medicinal value to be found in the Amazon rainforest. And it gave me some idea of how to procede.

I am convinced that safe methods of contraception will eventually be recognized as essential to the continuance of human life on this planet. Even though we aren't anywhere near the final "Standing Room Only," the damage that's being done to the environment should make us feel at least embarrassed. But the environment, the problem of worldwide population control—those are matters far too big for me. I just want to make people stop hurting, to show how they can get rid of a lot of troubling physical conditions without needing treatments too costly, sometimes too dangerous for the financially or physically fragile. That's why I want so much to arouse interest in things like botanicals that prevent hideous scarring from burns—a whole lot more than just the outside of a person can be mutilated by ugly scars. And what about all those people with eyes filmed by pterygium? I've seen them groping through life in the Philippines, in southern Asia, in the South Pacific, and in many, many places in South America. No chance of surgery for any who are poor or living in remote areas. Yet they could be cured by any one of a number of plants that various tribes use to do away with the slowly advancing tissue that blinds. The grass that healed the pterygium of the boatman Nati and the slashed corneas of the settle on Río Tigre is only one of half a dozen I've since learned about.

There are so many plants that I've seen cure such a wide range of problems. But it seemed that contraceptives were the only thing that sparked interest, so it was high time I got on with doing a better job in that area. I hadn't even got proper identification for most of those I'd learned about. The logistical problems connected with suitable supplies of piripiri—the sedges Tesa got me on Río Macusari—looked pretty daunting, but there was another problem connected with them that had long troubled me.

While I was still organizing the operations of the company I built the laboratories for, a famous Japanese botanist came to visit Iquitos. Dr. Tetsue Koyama was known especially for his work on sedges and had come to Iquitos on a survey of the six hundred or so species native to the Amazon region. I had a lot of them growing in the garden, twenty-two in all, according to the Shipibo women friends who had given them to me. The Shipibo names assigned to these *piripiri* most often indicated their specific use, and the ones that I had in the garden included a lot that would raise eyebrows in pharmaceutical circles. I enjoyed imagining the expression on the face of some gent in a white coat if I offered him a sedge used to shut up a woman who talked too much or one to keep a husband from straying.

All the sedges were in bloom when Dr. Koyama came by, which made identification much easier, but I was dismayed by the results of his examination. He said that I had, in all, only four species. A lot of those carefully separated and numbered plants were not merely of the same family and genus, they belonged to the same species, i.e., *Cyperus corymbosis*, of the family *Cyperaceae*. And that single species included the abortifacient, the fertility enhancer, the contraceptive, and the one that eases childbirth.

I didn't sleep much that night. I had to believe Dr. Koyama; he was world famous as an expert on this family. But I couldn't disbelieve the Indians, either, for several good reasons. First of all, though they might make a mistake through carelessness, this wasn't the sort of thing they ever got careless about. In village after village I had seen that one woman would have a neat little bed of, say, the contraceptives while another would have a yard-wide circle planted with the abortifacients. I had established that at least a half-dozen tribes used these same plants for the same purposes, and used them successfully. My notebooks contained pages of information to this effect from sources all over the Peruvian Amazon. Missionaries

Catholic and Protestant, *patrones*, river traders, and anthropologists had told me that Yaguas or Jívaros or Shipibos or Campas, to name only a few, had children only when they wanted them. And always my informant added that it was known that this was achieved by the women's using some kind of plant, but they'd never tell anybody what it was. That was secret, a taboo, and they believed that breaking this taboo could bring deadly misfortune.

I had another reason, too, to believe the Indians. I have never known any Indian to give me a phony. Once or twice only, an Indian had made an honest mistake, but he has invariably said, I *think* this is it. They have all too often claimed to know nothing or simply refused to talk, but none have ever cheated by giving me a plant that was not what it was said to be. I think that may have something to do with their animistic beliefs; it would demean the "mother" (spirit) of the plant. Everything, to the rain-forest people, has an individual spirit which possesses its own consciousness, intelligence, and powers, whether it's an animal or a mountain, a river or a tree. And you'd better keep on good terms with it. I have seen many small acts of politeness to propitiate the spirit of an animal killed in the hunt or a plant destroyed, though they are usually little gestures performed in private or in such an inconspicuous manner as to pass unnoticed.

So I was in a quandary. Dr. Koyama could not be mistaken; his reputation convinced me of that. But the various friends who had given me all these plants unquestionably knew what they were about, and I could not believe that they would deceive me. I talked it over with the young Peruvian graduate student who was working with us while he prepared his dissertation for his degree in phytochemistry, the chemistry of plants. It was decided that he should do some analyses to look into the chemical makeup of the four sedges that by now had me twittering to myself like a demented marmoset. Results of the tests were even more bewildering: each of the four, the contraceptives, the fertility plants, the abortifacients and the ones that eased childbirth, showed different chemical structures, different alkaloids. My friends had not betrayed me, but something had. I didn't know what, but I suspected it was my own ignorance of botany, which was pretty close to total.

A lot of years had to pass before I found what seems to me the most likely explanation. The head of a little local hospital told me he'd given some of the contraceptive sedges to a retired American gynecologist who was making a tour of tropical hospitals and who had offered to investigate. After some months of spare-time research he wrote suggesting the possibility that some kind of fungus infecting the sedge might have something to do with its properties. The piripiri's rhizome, an underground stem that looks like a root or tuber, is the medicinal part of the plant. A batch of it that had been fumigated was inactive, whereas unfumigated rhizomes seemed to have some effect, at least in the laboratory. But the work was still in a very early stage. And that was the last the local doctor heard. His letters to the States remained unanswered, and he was unable to find out whether anything more had been done. That is awfully unsubstantial information from an unverifiable source, but it does sound reasonable in the light of the evidence of chemical differences in the four sedges we had tested years before. A fungus might very well be involved, according to botanists I consulted. I kept asking different authorities and learned that fungi they nonchalantly refer to as "endotrophic mycorrhizae" could live in a plant without causing any detectable effect on its appearance and still produce significant changes in the chemical constitution.

I'm still novice enough to be somewhat cowed by arcane botanical terms, especially anything so grandiloquent as "endotrophic mycorrhizae." Botany is full of equally impressive terms which I pettishly resent because they are so hard to spell, or even remember.

The fungus explanation is still the most reasonable that I've been able to find, but I didn't learn of it until years later. In the meantime I just remained baffled, sure only that if the four groups of piripiri were chemically dissimilar they must be worth investigating, on the premise that the end result of such differences, for all practical purposes, could be considered the equivalent of differences in species.

Now that the public had been shocked by the news that a lot of illiterate barbarians had for centuries been using the oral birth control methods we'd only recently discovered, it seemed high time to get on with learning more about the other contraceptives informants had told about. That gave me an excuse for a financially loony second trip in the same year.

I'd been corresponding with Ferne and Rolland Rich. Now I asked them to arrange for me to stay at the Linquists' guest house at Yarinacocha. They wrote back urging me to come back Christmas, and I did.

XXXV

There was once a time when the news that U.S. missionaries were about would give me a hunted feeling and start me furtively looking for an exit. I cringe with embarrassment when I think of it. How could I ever have believed that weirdo in Bolivia to be typical? Even though he was, for a long time, the only one I had met.

He was a large man with a large voice who represented some strange sect that nobody I know ever heard of. I had just arrived in Bolivia and went to his house to check the references of the cook who worked for him and whom I was about to hire. When he opened the door, I explained and asked if Juanita was honest and kept a clean kitchen. His big green eyes glared at me, and his only reply was, "What do you think of Jesus?" Before I could answer, he boomed, "Do you know what you are? I know. You are a sinner, and you are going to burn in hell unless you're saved." He kept advancing while he went on booming dire predictions, like a very bad imitation of Dante's *Inferno*, and I kept backing up until I bumped against the garden gate. Then I fled.

Later, I met a medical missionary couple who were briefly in Iquitos. They were nice people, but I thought of them as doctors, not as missionaries.

Of course, the Arabela trip and meeting the Riches showed me how imbecilic I'd been. But only a few months before that, some Jívaros I visited on a remote river asked me if I could get them a linguist.

I thought my interpreter must have made a mistake. "Surely you don't mean a missionary?" I asked.

Even though the rest was unintelligible, I could hear the word "ringuista" slowly and carefully enunciated in their reply (Jívaros have no letter L), and I asked why on earth they wanted one.

"The Candoshi on the next river had one," the spokesman answered.

But it wasn't only a status symbol he had in mind. He went on to explain that now river traders could not tell the Candoshis the rubber they were selling weighed only thirty kilos when it weighed fifty; the Candoshis could read the scales. Also the "ringuistas" told them the current prices for each kilo and taught them how to calculate the amount of money they should get.

And they had medicines. Candoshis no longer die in epidemics of measles and whooping cough, and more babies live. And during the last rainy season, when a man was crushed by a falling tree, a plane came and took him away. When he came back, two moons later, they had made him well again.

I said I would try, and I sent a letter to the Linguists' head office in Lima. They thanked me. But they said that they were working with so many tribes, now, that they were already stretched much too thin. If it ever became possible, they would send somebody, but they didn't offer much hope.

So where did all that leave the smug assumption that these busybodies were forcing their culture on the hapless natives? I heard plenty of that from scientists, especially anthropologists, as well as the media of North and South America, and I had blithely endorsed it. Should I, perhaps, be feeling a little silly? The visit to the Riches finished any doubts I might have on that score. Not just a little silly; the only appropriate posture would be a good thorough grovel.

I remembered all that as I unpacked my suitcases in the Linguists' guest house. I still feel embarrassed.

It was December, when the rainy season is supposed to start and sometimes actually does, though like everything else in this part of the world it is often late. This was a good time to seek the kind of information I was after because this is the season when whole families leave their drenched, often flooded little clearings and come to Yarinacocha for the Linguists' schools. Here they can learn everything from pedagogy or paramedical studies to outboard motor repair and how to organize cooperatives and country stores. That makes this the best time to meet older tribesmen who still know and take pride in the traditional medicines. Yarinacocha is one place they can be proud of it. Years of experience have taught linguists how useful it can be.

Rebeca, my Campa friend, was one of my best sources. She was with the Seventh Day Adventists who had their center just down the lake, a short distance beyond the airstrip bordering the Linguists' property. The Seventh Day Adventists were the missionaries with Rebeca's clan . . . I've never been sure which of the Campa groups it was, but they lived in a different part of the jungle, at a slightly higher altitude. I first met her on the path by the lake where I was trying to untangle a climbing vine I wanted a specimen of, and she came over to help me. We were friends from the moment I said I was interested in medicinal plants, and she offered to teach me some of the Campa pharmacopeia. A quietly handsome woman in her thirties, she was exceptionally intelligent, even for a Campa, and the ones I've met have been unusually bright people. Rebeca had been rather a pet of the pastor and his wife. They taught her English, which she wrote well (I had letters from her when I returned to New York), but she was shy about speaking it.

It was Rebeca who got me specimens of the Campa's lifetime contraceptive, the one the medical missionaries had told me about years before news of the "pill" was made public. It is a big, strikingly unusual–looking woody vine, rather like a thick, six-inch wide, ribbed ribbon, and can be seen undulating and spiraling upward around the place where Nelida and I are sitting in the photograph made of the Putumayo trail. Its local name in Peru is *escalera de makisapo* "monkey's staircase," but botanists call it *Bauhinia microstachya* (Raddi.) Macbr., Caesalpiniaceae (Leguminosae).

To prepare the contraceptive, Campa women chop up about a meter of the vine and pound it with a stone, then add the grated seed of one avocado and boil the mixture in enough water to cover it throughout the cooking. I'm not sure how long that takes; it's hard to get Amazonian people to be precise about time or volume, but I'd imagine it would be for about half an hour, perhaps a little longer. The decoction must still be boiling when a cupful is strained off and two tablespoonfuls of wood ashes are stirred in. Beginning on the first day of her menstrual period, and on every day of her period, a woman takes one half cupful of the strained liquid very early each morning and another late at night, and this procedure must be repeated during the next menstruation. "But," Rebeca cautioned, "you must never let anybody know when you're taking it, and you must not just throw away what's left after you take the medicine. You must burn every bit of what's left over."

Rebeca told me that in the early days of her marriage, she had gone through two very severe miscarriages. "The second time, they thought I would die," she said. The doctor told her then that she must give up all idea of having children. She'd never be able to bring a baby to term and the next miscarriage would almost certainly prove fatal. So she had taken the treatment she told me about, and like several other women in the tribe, she never got pregnant again.

The Campa have another contraceptive which, if it's as good as they say, is my idea of a liberator of women. It's local name is *Amor seco*. *Amor*, of course means "love" and *seco* means "dry," but I'm told by people who don't know its secret use that it is so called because its seeds are encased in small flat burrs, which stick determinedly to just about anything they touch. Botanists call its "*Desmodium canum, D. ascendens,* (Sw) DC, *D. axillare* (Sw) DC Papillionaceae (Leguminosae). These look almost exactly alike, the only noticeable difference being in the color of their little flowers. At Yarinacocha everybody who knew about its properties said that the three kinds are equally useful. They all seemed to know about it, but none of them seemed to be able to describe a specific case of its use . . . which may not be so strange, after all, since nearly all of those informants were men and most Indian women believe that the use of any contraceptive must be kept secret.

It wasn't Rebeca who first told me about this one; it was the wife of the manager of a very large, modern, and productive hacienda on the Napo River.

Doña Petronila had been very young when she married and went with her husband to his family's enormous jungle property. This was in Campa country. Her first child was born there before she was sixteen years old, and it was a terribly difficult birth. The Campa midwife who took care of her told her that she must wait three years, at least, before having another child or she might die. No, the midwife told her, there was no reason for her to leave her husband; there was a plant, a little weed, which she could take. That would assure her not becoming pregnant again for three years. Many of the Campa women had taken it, not only to have enough time between children but also for convenience, especially when traveling with their husbands, because it stops menstruation for exactly three years. During that time it is, of course, impossible for a woman to conceive, but after that the menstruation returns, and the woman who has taken it is more fertile than ever.

Doña Petronila was delighted. The next morning, before breakfast, the midwife pulled up just one weed, an herb about eighteen inches tall, and carefully washed the whole plant—roots, stem, leaves, tiny flowers, and seeds. Then she dropped it into a small pot of boiling water, which she immediately withdrew from the fire, covered with a cloth, and set aside to steep. When it was cool, she gave Doña Petronila one ounce of the "tea" to drink, and told her that, in an hour, she could eat breakfast. This dosage was repeated daily for eight days, always in the morning before eating.

The midwife warned Doña Petronila that there were some things she must remember about the medicine. After the three years of sterility, she would be extremely fertile when her periods started again. It was said that some of the women who could not conceive children took this medicine and after the three years of artificial menopause succeeded in having children. Other, older women, sometimes took it to do away with the unpleasant symptoms of a natural menopause. But two things she had to remember; if she should take the treatment again, it always had to be taken in the morning before she ate anything, and never, never should it be taken while menstruating . . . only between periods.

Doña Petronila, active, plump and solid-looking, was obviously in vigorous health—and always had been, she said. Just as the midwife predicted, she got pregnant immediately after she started menstruating again, and went on having children, regular as clockwork, every ten months. The pregnancies were easy and the babies healthy. When they numbered a boisterous even dozen, Doña Petronila decided that was enough and started taking *amor seco* again on a regular three-year schedule, until menopause made it unnecessary. She was fifty-three now, and all twelve children were healthy adults with children of their own.

"And believe me," she said, "each time one of the kids got married, I told the bride about *amor seco*. One of my daughters-in-law says it was the best wedding present she got."

Many tribes know this plant. Yaguas, Shipibos, Conibos, Cocamas, Piros, and Orejones say it's good, but Doña Petronila is the only person I've found who has told me of using it herself.

Another plant Rebeca gave me has saved me a lot of pain. One morning she brought me a big, beautiful pineapple. South American pineapples are the best you'll find anywhere, golden in color and every slice bursting with sweet, superbly favored juice. I told her I was awfully sorry, but I couldn't eat it; I had *patco.* that is the local word for canker sores in the mouth. The mucous membrane under my tongue was blazing with pain from a mass of small white blisters. I'd been getting them every few weeks, and of late so badly that it was hard even to talk.

Rebeca looked surprised. "But that's easy to cure," she said. She stepped out the screendoor of the little *sala* to the shady walk around the guest house and picked a handful of little branches from a small herbaceous border that ran beside the cement walk.

"We call this *pinitza,* she said. "Wash them well, then wrap them in a handkerchief and squeeze the juice on the sores. They will stop hurting, and tomorrow you'll be better."

The little golden green leaves didn't have enough juice to come through the handkerchief very liberally, so I just chewed them and applied them that way. The relief was astonishing; in very few minutes the pain eased, then stopped. That night, when I repeated the treatment, the little ulcers seemed already to be drying up, and the next morning, they were almost gone. Four or five weeks later, the sores returned, but they seemed rather discouraged, feebler, and the little herb did away with them almost at once. They returned only one more time, and then it was a feeble comeback, quickly dealt with, and I was free from them for a long time. When they finally did return years later, I fortunately was in Iquitos, so I could get rid of them in the same way. This is one of the plants most commonly used as an ornamental border all through warmer South American countries and you'll see it in front gardens of half the houses in Iquitos. Strangely enough, its medicinal powers are not known there. My usual plant hunters didn't even know the local name for it but finally decided that it was "Corvina taya." Botanically, it is *Justicia pectoralis* Jacq. *Acanthaceae.* I have since learned that the dried leaves are powdered for use as a hallucinogenic snuff by some tribes in Columbia, but nobody ever got any mind-altering effect from using it as Rebeca taught me to do.

That was a particularly fruitful visit. There were all the Campa plants that Rebeca taught me, and others from a trip to Conibo villages on the Upper Ucayali River. Guillermo Ramírez and his fifteen year-old-son, Lorenzo took me in their outboard-motored canoe, occasionally stopping for a day or two in Canibo settlements along the shore.

Guillermo is an elderly Shipibo who is not a shaman, but has such profound knowledge of (and faith in) the ancient beliefs of his people that he is held in esteem that is close to reverence by both Shipibo and Canibo. The two tribes are almost identical in language, customs, and beliefs; intermarriage has blurred any noticeable difference between them, except for one small distinction in their art. The beautiful, intricate geometrical designs with which they decorate cloth and pottery, if Shipibo in origin, will have only straight lines, whereas Conibo designs show an occasional curve.

The rains had really begun, and it was very soggy trip. There was never enough sun for drying the pressed specimens. Most of the time I smelled like a small-time undertaker's workroom from the formaldehyde I washed plants with before pressing them. I'd started using it on this trip because I heard that was what the Harvard botanists did to prevent mildew. It not only smelled revolting, it peeled the skin off my hands, and despite such sacrifices, a few specimens mildewed anyway. Ever since then, I have stayed with my old system: powdering everything with naphthalene flakes. It's more convenient, solids being more portable than liquids, and the smell, however awful, can be confined in plastic bags. Thanks to Guillermo's sponsorship, I was given a wide variety of specimens used by the Conibo for a wide variety of problems.

I found new friends in Tushmo and San José, villages only a short walk from the Linguists' Center. They are tiny communities with, I'd guess, no more than two or three hundred inhabitants. Many family names are of tribal origin, and like their ancestors, these people depend on the forest around them to take care of most health problems and seldom consult modern MDs. Most of them, I noticed, seem to live well into an active old age.

Don Frederico Panduro, Don José Awanari, and Don Gilberto Icawati were in their middle years when first I met them, and like most of their generation were skillful in all phases of jungle life, including its medicines. They have taught me a lot. Don José and Don Gilberto are fishermen by profession, but they know where to find practically any of the surrounding jungle's botanicals, just as a drugstore owner knows the location of a product in his stockroom.

I don't think it is only for the money that they are always ready to pull their canoes ashore and go off into the woods to get specimens. These are chatty and gregarious people; solitary days of casting their big circular nets into remote *cochas* and rivers must get a little dull. I last was there in January 1989, and they still brought me surprises, things I had known nothing about, in addition to the things I asked for. They obviously enjoy explaining the uses of unfamiliar plants, and sometimes tell me how to find a neighbor who recently used one, so that I can get a first-hand account of its effect.

I wish I could remember which of them it was who told me about *capinuri*. That must have been some twenty years ago. Capinuri was credited with curing so many dissimilar ailments that I privately raised a lofty eyebrow and put it in the "Oh, yeah?" section of my files. I've learned not to ignore accounts of a plant just because wildly unlikely powers are attributed to it; I file everything. But I don't have to believe everything.

Botanists know capinuri as *Clarisia nitida* (Allen) Macbr. (Moraceae). Jungle people say that purely by external application, just smearing it on the skin and leaving it there, it will cure arthritis, heal the most rebellious boils, speed the mending of broken bones, cure sprains or dislocated shoulders; and they claim it will even heal hernias. And that's not all: it is also credited with bloodless, painless tooth removal, exactly like the *incira* that the Coto Indian, Hilario, gave me so many years ago.

I could believe the tooth extraction bit. I had talked with a very good dentist from Atlanta who made an extensive river trip visiting small communities and examining their inhabitants. Many of them, he told me, had successfully removed carious teeth with incira. So why couldn't some other treesap do the same thing? And I could accept the idea of its temporarily easing the pain of strains or sprains, like a liniment. But the rest was just too much. I gave it little attention until some years later, when I was again living in Iquitos.

As the decades have passed, Iquitos has become infested with motorcycles the way some dogs get fleas. They swarm in the streets and swoop around corners with such ferocity that a visitor asked me, "How come you see so many people walking around who still have all their arms and legs?"

One of the swoopers caught me one morning. I wasn't badly hurt, just needed a couple of stitches and a bit of bandaging. *Sangre de grado* repairs cuts and scrapes very fast. But although my knees were soon scab-free, they seemed even more swollen than the week before. They hurt, too, but I've learned how to divert my attention from symptoms by a sort of process of procrastination. I've always been a talented procrastinator. I kept telling myself, "Okay, so it hurts. But I'm too busy to bother with that just now. I'll give it my attention a little later." For me, that sometimes works surprisingly well at raising the pain threshold.

The knees didn't improve; they slowly got worse. I didn't know any orthopedic doctors in Peru, so I just kept on heeding them as little as possible.

In a few months it was time to keep a long-scheduled date to attend a graduation ceremony in Yarinacocha. Only a couple of days before I left, I stepped off a curb and found myself suddenly sitting in the street. The left knee, which by now was even more swollen than the other, had simply folded. And it kept on trying to fold whenever I stepped on an uneven surface, giving me the unexpected lurch and stagger of a comic drunk in a B movie. Most embarrassing; as soon as I got to the Linguists' Center, I asked to see the doctor.

He was a well-known general practitioner from Georgia who had volunteered to spend a year caring for the people around Yarinacocha. His very small fees went toward upkeep of the Linguists' little medical station, which took care of anybody who asked for attention.

The doctor's examination was thorough, the results far from cheering. There was a large accumulation of fluid in both knees, but the serious problem was the tendons. Especially in the left knee, they'd suffered considerable damage, which had been made worse by four months of neglect. I would have to undergo surgery. If I couldn't go to the States right away, the doctor would give me the name of an orthopedic surgeon in Lima he'd heard was pretty good. (I thought I heard a slight note of "God-help-us" there.) But I should not delay much longer.

That idea didn't appeal to me. Back in Iquitos, I went through my files and talked with a few knowledgable residents, many of whom knew and praised *capinuri*. A most reliable friend told of snatching an infant niece from the hospital where the baby's parents had taken her for umbilical hernia surgery. Juanita, a forceful character, took the little one and applied capinuri sap. The hernia very quickly disappeared, and the child, now in her teens, had suffered no subsequent problems.

I got a bottle of capinuri. I was told that the proper way to use it was to smear a thick layer of the sticky sap on the skin over the damaged knee, and let it dry to form a lacquerlike coating. This, everyone said, had to be kept dry until it peeled off all by itself. When that happened, the healing was complete.

Bathtubs are practically unknown in Iquitos; everyone takes showers. This was two-bath weather even on the coolest days, and how do you shower without getting your knees wet? I decided to try something easier. After each bath I again coated each knee with capinuri sap and covered the mess with a gauze pad held in place by a couple of strips of adhesive tape. The pain eased almost immediately. In no more than a couple of weeks, everything had returned to normal; no swelling, no pain, no sudden weaknesses. And that is the way it's been ever since. For me at least, capinuri produced a complete and permanent cure. I wonder what it could do for athletes who have similar injuries.

T HIS TIME I had come to Peru via Colombia. The New York-Bogota-Leticia-Iquitos route is a good one, if you aren't in a hurry. It cuts out changing planes in Miami and the risk of having your baggage remain behind. That is not an experience I undergo with grace and kindly understanding. You can also arrange stopovers between flights for visiting and shopping along the way instead of getting passenger's cramp from long hours of sitting.

I left for home with two big boxes of specimens and plenty of information about who uses them and how, but very few proper botanical names. It is essential to know the correct scientific nomenclature for any plant. Local names are generally so very local that in the next province or on the next river they will be unknown, or possibly mean something quite different. For example, if you ask for *mata pasto* in Iquitos or Yarinacocha, you will get a small herb not more than fifteen inches high. This is known by botanists as *Elephantopus spiralis* (Compositae), and it is one of the jungle's more valuable medicinals. I have not heard of any case of kidney infection, however severe, which failed to be cured in a few days if treated by three daily doses of either a "tea" of the whole plant, or a couple of ounces of cold water in which one whole little plant, root included, has been crushed. If, however, you ask for *mata pasto* in some other part of Peru, you will be given leaves or flowers of that fifteen-foot shrub, the first botanical specimen I got back in 1958 when I started serious collecting. That's the one Iquitos calls *retama*, whose flowers were credited with curing the dilated heart of the Iquitos engineer's mother. In many countries, though they may speak different languages, this plant is still *Cassia reticulata*.

I'd heard that the Universidad Nacional in Bogotá had a good herbarium. Its curator, Dr. J. M. Idrobo, is an internationally known specialist on the plants of Colombia, and his expertise includes their medicinal properties. His botanical exploration of remote and hostile parts of the country have made him the man visiting savants ask for when planning a Colombian expedition.

I found him in his herbarium at the university's Institute of Natural Sciences, a smallish, enthusiastic man who speaks perfect English. When I told him about my boxes of specimens, he said that we must go get them right away. He was supposed to be preparing an expedition to La Macarena, a mountainous jungle area that is an immense reservoir of strange botanicals, and whose commercial exploitation he is in an unending fight to prevent. His departure was to take place in little more than a fortnight, but when he saw my collection, he said we must get to work immediately on identifications. I had nearly two hundred items with their uses, Peruvian and tribal names, and habitats all carefully noted.

We started on them that same afternoon and, for more than a fortnight, kept at it all day every day. Some of the specimens required microscopic examination, and one was so little known that Idrobo insisted on checking his identification with another botanist called Calí. All this took up so much time that he must have left for La Macarena with very little in the way of equipment. But then, I imagine he would be used to that. He's the type to travel light.

I was taken home to meet Mrs. Idrobo, a serene and friendly lady with a sly sense of humor. She is also a superb cook. She and the doctor will always have their place among the friends who have been most unfailingly kind and helpful, and I am grateful to them for many kinds of help.

Colombians are an extraordinary people, the most dynamic I have known anywhere. Their energy is extreme, and so is practically everything else about them. They are like the little girl in the old nursery rhyme who, "when she was good, was very, very good, when she was bad she was horrid." Colombians, when they are good, are the best, the most active, intelligent, and helpful of friends. And when they are bad, they are dangerous, not to say lethal. Fortunately, I've had no personal experience with the bad guys; my information about them comes from the news media, whose accounts of their villainy don't seem to lose the power to shock. I was lucky enough to know a few of the kind I admire and enjoy even before I went there, and they passed me along to others.

I have often wondered what causes the high level of energy that makes Colombians so extreme. Can diet have anything to do with it? Theirs would make the American Heart Association feel faint with horror. Breakfast, for example: In hotel restaurants, I've watched, awed, as a lively family at the next table devours a quick early morning meal. They start with a lot of fruit—all Colombians are very big on fruit and on milk—then go on through fried potatoes heaped beside a good-sized steak on which sit a few fried eggs. This is always accompanied by quantities of bread and a quart or so of coffee that is more than half milk. A couple of hours later they will be refreshing themselves at a "milk bar"—in every downtown block there are at least five of these selling milk-with-fruit-juice drinks. And so it goes on throughout their long, high protein, high calorie day. Maybe it takes a lot of activity to let off the steam such a lot of fuel would generate. Steam, improperly stored or conducted, can make bad trouble. Written, that theory looks very silly. But I do like Columbians, so I keep trying to explain all the horrors.

By the time I left for New York, almost all the specimens were labeled with melodious Latin names. The few uncertainties were partly due to damaged or incomplete specimens, partly to arguments among authorities. I had long realized that botanists are not the sweet little old ladies with big hats and gardening gloves I once imagined. They are more apt to be rugged, tough-fibered explorers. But now I was learning how often they maintain conflicting opinions, especially about the identities of species, genera and even families. I now had the concurrence of enough authorities to feel safe in giving the identities of the specimens I had with me and I fervently hoped this would make it possible to arouse enough interest to spur some pharmaceutical house into investigating them.

It did spark some interest, but only enough for a couple of companies to say that maybe we could work something out, provided that I would give them everything I knew and would sign what they called "the usual secrecy agreement." I read two of those. They were practically identical and I needed only to read them carefully to see what they meant. They would truss me up in a commitment to deliver a considerable (and expensive) amount of material and they would make it illegal for me to reveal anything about jungle medicinals to anyone else for a specific number of years. With the exception of the actual freight costs from Peru to the States, it committed them to no payment whatever, except the amount they might in the future, if they felt like it, decide would be appropriate compensation for my services and the materials I had delivered. There was no provision for reimbursement to cover expenses I would incur in getting the plants, nor was even a consultant's fee anywhere mentioned.

Obviously there was no point in continuing along this line, at least, not for the present. But it is infuriating to know that people are hurting, or suffering terrible disfigurement by burns, or going blind because they can't get surgery, when I feel certain I know some things that could eliminate a lot of such distress, things freely found in the rain forest. Of the hundreds of plants in my notes, only a small percentage, of course, can be expected ever to have significant value. Many will prove to be less efficient analogues of products already being manufactured and some others will be found irremediably toxic. Then, of course, there are a certain number which, after raising hopes, will prove to be no more useful than the sensitive plant some people near the mouth of the Napo River think is a contraceptive because it leaves quite magically fold together when it is touched. I love their name for it: "*Cierra tu puerta, ahí viene tu marido*"—"Shut your door, here comes your husband!"

But what about the others, the small percentage that get results our present-day science would never think possible, cures that nothing in our present pharmacopeia can achieve without surgery. The *amuebe* of the Witotos, whose leaves cured the big, infected burns of María, the Ocaina girl, without leaving any scar, is not the only one with such ability. I saw a healing just as remarkable when I was taking some visiting scientists up to Don Alfonso Cárdenas's place on the Napo. We stopped to pick up Guillermo Godoy, who had taken me to the Arabelas some years before. I invited him to join us because the doctors I was showing around the jungle would be interested in his knowledge of medicinals.

When we arrived at his house, Guillermo was putting fresh dressings on the arms of his six-month-old son. The baby had fallen into a cook-fire and the inner surfaces of both little arms, from wrist to elbow, were like raw meat; the burns had destroyed every bit of

skin. The two MDs in our group wanted to get their emergency
kits, but Guillermo wouldn't have it. He pointed out that the baby
was showing no sign of being in pain. He was laughing delightedly
as he raised both pitiful little arms to grab for the bushy red beard
of a phytochemist who had picked him up.

Guillermo showed us the treatment, which he said would make
the burns heal swiftly and safely, with no scarring. He took a freshly
dug young tuber of yuca, *Manihot esculenta*, Euphorbiaceae, the
commonest food crop of the warm countries of South America. It is
important to note that this was the "yuca dulce" commonly used in
Peru. This same species includes "yuca brava," which until cooked
contains considerable cyanide and is never used raw. Between the
brown outer skin of the tuber and the starchy part used for food, is
a white substance (botanists call it the "phloem") that has a gela-
tinous inner surface. Guillermo peeled this off and carefully placed
it, jelly side down, on the skinless surfaces of both arms. The baby
looked amiably interested, but didn't cry even when Guillermo
bound the stripes in place with gauze. His wife would continue the
treatments while he went up the river with us.

We returned some ten days later and hurried ashore to see how
the baby was. All of us, especially the MDs, goggled, speechless,
when Mrs. Godoy brought the baby from a back room. His left arm
showed no sign of any injury; the smooth, soft skin had all grown
back with no wrinkles, no difference in color or texture, to show
where the injury had been. The right arm was in the same perfect
condition except for a small area, one by two square centimeters at
the base of the wrist, where the skin had not yet grown back. That
was still raw-looking, but the rest was perfect.

I have always wondered why none of the scientists who were
there that day ever did anything to promote investigation of a
healing plant so extraordinarily successful and so easy to find in
abundant supply. I did hear a talk-show radio program a couple of
years later in New York, on which one of the two pharmacognosists
who had been present accurately described the healing, but he did
not tell the name, either common or scientific, of the plant which
achieved it.

I stayed in New York for three years and tried sporadically to get
some foundation or university interested in starting a research
project. I wrote proposals. I outlined the evidence I had gathered.
Always they asked for some more concrete scientific information,

some sort of formal documentation. I got very tired of being told, "But you have only anecdotal evidence." Couldn't they grasp the idea that I had not been searching for things on which scientific documentation existed? That was what I was asking them to undertake. Since I had been searching for things totally new to the scientific community, things known only to small groups of people who had had no contact with laboratories, then all that existed was anecdotal evidence. Studies to determine the degree of safety and efficiency of these botanical medicines must be made before they can be used by people outside the small native groups who have known them for centuries. But the analytical work is up to the people in the white lab coats. Me, I'm just a retriever.

And always there is the stress of knowing that such work must get under way soon, while the forest is still there, before the advancing floods of our civilization turn knowledge into mythology or tales of "once upon a time." It all must be worked on before it ceases to exist, not only the knowledge, but the rain forest itself. The things to be studied are part of its living body. You have only to fly over it to see the great open wounds, old, or fresh-made by lumber men, cattle ranchers, road builders, and settlers.

There didn't seem much I could do about it for the moment, but I began to have hopes for later. I noticed that health food stores were broadening stocks of herbal teas and remedies. More books about the lives and uses of plants were on sale every month, and books on alternative therapies were crowding library shelves. The public was beginning to show interest, and that's where the ultimate power lies. If the general public would only get pushy, then things would begin to happen.

XXXVII

Wʜᴇɴ I am too long away from the jungle, nostalgia becomes need. On insomniac nights I keep remembering the clean, green scent of the mornings, with plumes of vapor mounting in the early sun and what it's like to wash in dew, cool and pure and glistening in the cup of a giant leaf. I remember reflected sunsets burning on the surface of the river and the black lace of silhouetted jungle edging the darkening sky. It is so much easier to sleep in a hammock, cosy as a spider in her web, hearing no shrieks of ambulances or police cars, but instead being lulled by the swish of the river and sound of little nocturnal things rustling about their business in the carpet of fallen leaves.

I have never had any addiction except the rain forest. But that one is quite enough.

My rent was being raised every two years; I was out of the country almost half of the time, and the landlord would not alter my lease to permit subletting. For anyone whose income did not inflate with the price index, this made very little sense. Obviously it was time for me to get out of here. This time I would make it permanent by selling the possessions that, now that I thought of it, had been more or less holding me hostage.

I know I have a tendency to burn my bridges before I get to them. I hoped I wasn't doing that again. I didn't think I was. Being over seventy, why should I worry very much about the future? How much more of it could there be? I'd never expected to live this long: it's not customary in my family. My cousins, with cosy, suburban lives, had barely made it to sixty. I no longer had any relatives, no need to feel dutiful about leaving heirlooms. And I needed the money.

I decided to sell everything, furniture and things like the Blakelocks, glum and lowering paintings I'd hung from a sense of duty. Of art objects I'd keep only a few Peruvian things and some Asiatic: the stone head of Kwan Yin, and Hotei, the Japanese god of laughter. I'd never give him up. Rubbing his fat, bronze belly for only a moment is guaranteed to provide something to laugh at before the day's over. Who doesn't need that?

Well-meaning friends offered sympathy for my "giving up all that." What's the use of going to the trouble of packing and storing things, just so that you can know you own them? If you can't enjoy looking at them or touching them, what's the point?

And there were some who seemed shocked that I was planning to move permanently out of New York, the kind who asked, "Why must you keep on running away from everything?" I do wish people could learn the difference between *from* and *to*. Running *from* is sad and frightening; running *to* is wonderful, full of purpose and enthusiasm. I'd never run *from* New York. Where else would I find friends who feel at home in Katmandu and New Guinea, who design beautiful books or beautiful clothes, who singlehandedly sail small boats across big oceans or teach superb cooking or theatre, people who work at all sorts of things, from metaphysics to taming lions and other big cats? I love New York.

But finding the treasure of the rain forest, secrets of healing known to only a few remote tribes, and trying to make them available to my people, that's what I am *for*. That's what I was running *to*.

I knew I'd done the right thing as soon as I got off the plane. Even in the Iquitos airport I could scent the fresh, loamy breath of the jungle.

Lillice and Ted Long at the Linguist's Center took me in and pampered me. I happened to arrive just in time for another graduation ceremony—this time the annual closing of the schools for Indians. I'd attended one of them before and was looking forward to the extraordinary show the students put on. With faces and bodies painted, and dressed in their most magnificent feather crowns, their finest woven or painted *cushmas* or *itipis*, they had proudly performed ancient rituals of song and dance, some solemn, some fierce, all fascinating.

The Aguarunas, being a Jívaroan tribe, are especially known for their valor in warfare and their custom of shrinking the heads of slain enemies. They usually put on the most exciting show, but this time it was different. We were all disappointed when a tribesman (Aguarunas don't have chiefs) who had been a famous warrior until the Linguists made a convert of him, stepped alone onto the little stage. He wasn't even wearing native dress, just very new cream-colored trousers and a pink shirt. And he made a speech.

It began with pious statements and quotes, then went on to what a good Christian he had become. Looking smug, he described the sacrifices he'd made: Jesus didn't like drinking, so he gave up aguardiente. "Is not hard. I tell Jesus, he help me." Jesus disapproved of adultery, so he gave that up. He was pretty pompous as he said. "I do it for Jesus, so is not hard." Then he grew very solemn: "But one thing more I have to do, and that is hard. Yes. Is very hard," he went on. "Much time I think, to stop this is too hard. I love Lord. I tell him, please, Señor, other things I do for you. This one is too hard. Preacher pray with me, and I pray. Very much. Then I can say, 'Bueno, Señor, now I do it. Now I tell You; no more I kill nobody!"

For just a moment, the pomposity disappeared, and he looked like a little boy who's lost the scoop of ice cream off his cone. "Is very hard for me I tell Him, 'You know, Señor, I kill good, very good.' Everybody know me. All say how good I kill. And I like to kill people. *Mucho me gusta!* But for Jesus, I stop! I tell Him, 'For you, I do this. No more I kill.' And is so."

I don't think I had ever realized before that for many tribes, killing was the most important of all sports, the greatest source of prestige.

The Longs had alerted all my old helpers, and they started bringing in new botanicals. I learned even more from the Cashibos and Sharahuas and most of all from the Piro. Their translator, Joyce Nies, spent hours patiently interpreting while we collected information on tribal medical practices from an aged and respected tribesman whose name meant "Antlers." We called him that because in his own language it is totally unpronounceable for anyone not a highly trained linguist like Joyce. She has been fluent in Piro for years, and that's no small achievement. It is a language full of words like "Phnewnapiri, which is *Scleria pterota* (Cyperaceae). That's *cortadera blanca* to the local Peruvians, and it is a cure for pterygium. It has saved several villages from blindness.

The Piro are great jungle doctors. I saw what they call *mgenoklumasne* (*Aya uma* to the local people and *Couropita subsessilis* [Lecythidaceae] to botanists) cure a hideous skin condition overnight. That was on my second Utucuru trip with Guillermo Ramírez and only a week or so after I heard about the effectiveness of *aya uma*.

The Linguists' doctor, who had years of tropical experience, endorsed the value of this one for every kind of skin infection he had seen here, viral, bacterial, or fungoid. A Conibo woman I met on that trip gave me the chance to see what it could do.

The poor woman's brown Indian face was disfigured by a lumpy, swollen stretch of bright red flesh more than two inches wide that lay across her nose from the middle of one wide cheek to the middle of the other. Its surface was so puffy that it looked rather like a patch cut from a piece of worn scarlet quilting and laid across her nose. Never had I seen anything resembling it, except perhaps on the skin of a turkey gobbler's neck, and that resemblance was only in color and texture.

The woman's name was Marina. With Guillermo Ramírez translating, she told me the lesion itched and burned terribly and had been making her miserable for about a year and a half. Some months ago, she went to the hospital in Pucallpa, near Yarinacocha. Pucallpa is a busy, modern little city, the eastern terminal for the only highway reaching from the Pacific coast over the Andes and into the jungle. It has the only general hospital in the region. The doctors were fascinated by Marina's case, but though she stayed several weeks, nothing they tried did any good. So she went home again.

I asked her if she knew where to find any aya uma. It is a very big tree, known to gringos as the cannonball tree because its fruit, which hangs from the trunk on a sort of bark-covered cable, looks exactly like a slightly rusty cannonball. Cut open, it is seen to contain a seed-filled pulp that turns from pale green to salmon pink when ripe. The tree is fairly common, and Marina said she knew where to find one.

I told her to get a half-ripe fruit, one still green inside but not so unripe that it is hard and juiceless. She must scoop out the pulp and smear it on the lesion. I thought that might help her. Without another word she grabbed her machete and hurried off into the woods.

I didn't see her again until the next afternoon. We were loading the boat to continue our trip upstream when Marina hurried down to water's edge. When I looked up at her, I was astounded. All that solid-looking swelling had disappeared; where there had been lumpy inflammation, the skin was perfectly smooth and flat. The scarlet color was gone completely, but she still looked very peculiar because where that patch of scarlet had been, the skin was now white, a clear pale patch sharply delineated against the brown Indian skin that covered the rest of her. Apparently the disease had destroyed the melanins which provided her natural brown skin coloring.

But Marina was happy. She said she didn't care what it looked like; for the first time in nearly two years, it did not burn; it did not itch; there was no irritation of inflammation, no discomfort at all.

CHAPTER

XXXVIII

IQUITOS HAS always been a boom-and-bust town. When I moved back this time, the oil boom was just coming to an end. Petroleum finds in the jungle had failed to live up to expectations, and tourism was the only business that seemed to be growing. Tourist shops selling tribal artifacts were opening everywhere, and many of the better bars were beginning to serve some jungle drinks, especially *chuchuwasi*. That is probably the best known of all jungle remedies, in Colombia as well as Peru. It is also a favorite drink, second only to aguardiente in popularity among men living along the rivers.

Chuchuwasi is prepared by chopping the root bark of a very large tree, *Maytenus ebenifolia* (Celastraceae), and letting it steep for a week in aguardiente or white rum. The resulting infusion is one of numerous jungle potions known as "aphrodisiacs." These are reputed to cure male impotence, whether due to age or illness, and to enhance the virility of the healthy. But more important are the claims made for its ability to cure all types of rheumatism, and to act as a general tonic for women as well as men. I have seen it restore to good health two women who had each, for some months, been in a very debilitated state of health from some undiagnosed illness. And I know many people who insist that it is the best of all antirheumatic medicines. I have also heard reports of its curing cancer and, after several months' dosage, restoring to normal activity an arm paralyzed by long contact with a toxic insecticide. But in my opinion, the evidence supporting these claims has not been sufficiently well established.

I can, however, vouch for its efficiency as an insect repellent—

363

applied externally, of course. And that can be a most useful bit of information for anybody who travels in the Peruvian jungle. Once you've left the city, you can't hope to buy such luxuries as commercial insect repellents, but in almost any settlement there's a good chance you'll be able to find somebody who has a bottle of *chuchuwasi*.

I learned about this valuable attribute at a most unusual wedding. It took place in the village of Picuru Yacu at the house of José Pineapple, a Witoto.

Picuru Yacu is a small village just across the Nanay River from the outskirts of Iquitos and about a half-mile inland. This is a village of mestizos, but in it lives a very small, tight-knit and aloof group of Indians, perhaps a half-dozen families of the Bora and Witoto tribes, who cling to much of their traditional culture and have very little to do with the mestizos surrounding them.

I was first taken to meet them by a friend who thought they might be a useful source of information. The group got together on Sundays at José Pineapple's house. They were friendly but at first not awfully forthcoming.

That all changed after the day that Venancio, a thin, elderly, Witoto who had been blind since youth, came through a heavy rainstorm to my house in Iquitos. He was led by a small nephew, and he was in a state of extreme agitation.

"Save me, señorita," he said as I showed him into the *sala*. "Police take me for kill man, take me prison."

Startled, I said, "Who you kill?"

"No kill nobody," and he poured out a flood of language that may have been either Spanish or Witoto—I found it totally unintelligible. Fortunately, the little boy spoke quite good Spanish, and he explained.

Belisario was dead. He was on a trip up the Tamshiyacu River when he suddenly got sick and died there.

Belisario was one of the three Boras at Picuru Yacu. Now, for the first time, I learned that he and Venancio were both witch doctors and to some extent business rivals. His death started rumors that Venancio had used his occult powers to send a spirit dart to kill Belisario. They were all quite sure the police would believe this and arrest Venancio for murder.

I tried to convince them that the police would do no such thing. They didn't believe in spirit darts. Venancio had been a full day's journey from where Belisario died. Surely, the police would see he couldn't be responsible.

Venancio at first didn't listen; he kept saying, "Save me, Señorita! You know police general. You tell him I no kill." Then I could see him beginning to wonder if my arguments weren't a putdown. Did I think he could not manage a murder by his command of spirits and their darts? Didn't I believe he had the power?

The little boy intervened: "You tell general, Venancio no kill, like you tell him Ríos no steal and they let him go."

How did they know about that, I wondered. That had happened over a year ago. For years Ríos had been my room-boy whenever I stayed at the Hotel Turista, and his wife had worked for me when I took a house. I knew them well and had persuaded the general that they'd arrested the wrong man. And just a few hours after Ríos was released, they caught the real thief with a houseful of stolen goods.

With the Picuru Yacu faction knowing I'd got Río freed, and being unwilling to insult Venancio's professional pride, I could think of no other way out. So I said I would speak to the general. And I promised them that Venancio would not be arrested for Belisario's murder. Then, after some soda pop, they left, vastly relieved. But me, I felt like a shameful phony. And I could imagine that rather elegant, U.S.-educated general's expression if I asked him not to arrest a witch doctor for sending a magic dart to kill a rival some hundred or more miles away.

From then on at Picuru Yacu I was less an outsider and more a friend. Sundays at José's with the people who had first taken me there became productive. When I had a cough, they taught me to chew a juicy stalk of *caña agria* a beautiful big canelike plant which is member of the ginger family, *Costus guanalensis* Rusby (Zingiberaceae). The next day the cough was gone. When I twisted an ankle, Venancio sent his nephew with a bucket of fresh leaves of *sapo huasca, Cissus erosus* (Vitaceae), with instructions to bandage the ankle with a poultice of crushed leaves. Two days of that, and the swelling and pain were no more.

One Sunday morning I met at José's a very young Spanish priest just out of a Barcelona Seminary and only a fortnight in Peru. Father Antonio was a very ingenuous, very friendly, very gentle young man and we were all charmed by him. He loved the Picuru Yacu Indians, and they loved him. But one thing worried him gravely: he wanted to help these people; he felt it his mission to save them from the eternal damnation which he was sure awaited them because they were all living in sin. None of them had been married by the Church.

He pleaded with them until finally Horacio, a middle-aged Bora, was so sorry for the poor youngster that he offered to let himself be properly married.

The next Sunday we took to Picuru Yacu a wedding feast of roast chicken, beans and rice, and a lot of sticky sweets. We had just arrived when Horacio, in bright yellow pants and a turquoise shirt, made an entrance followed by two plump middle-aged Bora women wearing shiny flowered dresses.

Padre Antonio asked which of the ladies was to be his wife.

Horacio beamed. "Both of them," he answered. "They my women!"

The poor young priest was horrified. He stammered as he told Horacio that he must choose only one. He could not marry them both. The Church never permitted a man to have two women; he must choose one of them.

Horacio's face began to show that stony look I've learned to watch out for. These were good women, sisters, he said. They had been good wives, very good, for many, maybe thirty years. He would not put one above the other. Never! He would marry both, or none. When the priest tried to make him understand, he turned and stalked out of the house, the women following meekly behind him.

A few days later the priest, overjoyed, phoned to tell me that Horacio had seen the light. He had sent word he would marry one of the women. The wedding would be next Sunday.

So we all went back to Picuru Yacu with another feast and watched Horacio and one of the women take their vows while the other beamed from the sidelines. Then we drank the health of the bride and groom in *chuchuwasi* and settled down to a convivial lunch.

It was a very hot day. Stinging gnats and mosquitos came in avid clouds and I had forgotten to bring the insect repellent I try never to be without. I was slapping busily when the unmarried sister sidled up and shyly rubbed some of her drink on my arm.

"Mosquito no like *chuchuwasi*," she said. "Now no sting." And she was right. The tormentors immediately moved on to better meat.

I thanked her, and we were friends. After some conversation I asked her why Horacio had changed his mind about marrying.

Giggling happily she explained. She and her sister liked the young priest, much. Very good boy. It gave them much pain to see him so disappointed. And it was very silly, Horacio's refusing just to stand with one of them and say words. So they went to work on him. For two days they steadily harrassed him: he was bad, a bad man. He made that nice boy so *triste*. He hurt him, and for what? Words. Only silly words, Spanish words.

They kept at it until Horacio, thoroughly beaten down, asked, "But which one?"

"Who cares? Take the oldest," they said.

"So Horacio say words. Marry with sister," she told me happily. "Now padre no more *triste*."

And when the party was over, the three of them went home to live happily as before.

I learned a lot in the years I spent in Iquitos, though the inflated economy prevented my making such long trips to remote areas as I had done before. Hiring boats and buying trade goods and presents for informants simply could not be fitted into a stunted income. The *petroleros*, big spenders when they could get away from their isolated jungle digs and rigs for a blast in town, had encouraged river boatman to demand prices that they were very surprised to get. I was a gringa, therefore I must be rich and crazy like them.

I found that there was a lot more information to be had right in Iquitos, especially if one had friends among the local *curanderos*, medicine men. The woods within an hour or so by taxi were rich in interest, and some of my old plant collectors were still working for Adriana Andrea de Loayza, the same Adriana Andrea who had been with me years before, when I first organized the company's collecting system for Arthur Jones.

She was now running the Institute for Botanical Exploration, which in 1975 had bought all the facilities and taken over the lease and personnel of Arthur Jones's company after Jones had fallen ill with the Parkinson's disease which eventually killed him. By that time Adriana had become the director. If they'd put her in charge when I left, the company might still be in existence, but Jones thought he had to have an American running it. His two successive choices were so disastrous that some locals who knew I'd been badly treated held dark suspicions of some sort of occult vengeance.

The first man he sent down had previously been our accountant. He'd come to Iquitos more than once while I was still there. He was a pleasant sort, but he had one fatal defect: he could not accept advice. He always knew better.

The real tragedy came when he was sure he knew better than the plant men who worked there. He'd heard about the mind-blowing effect of *toé, Datura arborea*, a big beautiful flowering shrub growing in the garden. He decided to try its effect. The plant men warned him that it was extremely dangerous, but he tried it, liked it, and despite urgent warnings, got hooked on it.

His memory began to fail. An hour after eating, he couldn't remember that he'd had lunch. The local merchants caught on fast; they presented the same bills several times, and each time he paid them.

When Mr. Jones found out about his condition, the company sent him to the best neurological hospitals in the States, but nothing could be done. The cortical brain cells killed by the plant's poison do not regenerate.

The next director sent down from the States was a very convivial type and entertained lavishly. Popular at first, the rumors began spreading. He was a "sex maniac," in local terms; his parties were said to fit into the classical Roman-orgy tradition.

Mr. Jones, always a conservative, correct old gentleman, paid a surprise visit. His plane got in early in the morning. When his taxi reached the house, he could hear loud music, then the door was opened by an inebriated but affectionate young woman wearing very little clothing.

How I would have loved to be present at that scene.

Adriana Andrea was finally made director, and from then on things ran smoothly, except for Mr. Jones's deteriorating health. In 1975 he became too ill to carry on, and Dr. Sidney McDaniel, professor of botany at Mississippi State University bought the premises and made them South American headquarters for the Institute of Botanical Exploration, which he had recently organized. Adriana had remained in charge, and that arrangement has been very satisfactory to both of them.

Dr. McDaniel knew the region. He had spent a full sabbatical year collecting and identifying the flora of the Peruvian Amazon, in addition to making many shorter trips.

Adriana invited me to stay there; Dr. McDaniel would not be

coming down until the university's summer vacation. I protested that I had never met Dr. McDaniel, but Adriana insisted that he had told her to invite me. I would be much better off there than in a crowded hotel.

I certainly was. Not only was there a cool patio where friends could visit, but I made good use of the efficient new driers for pressing herbarium specimens and of the shelves of the big dehumidifying room. Some of my old plant finders could always be counted on to go into the jungle for materials I wanted and for the new things I learned about. I took my time finding permanent quarters.

XXXIX

Several months passed before I moved to Juanita Schaper's. She and her German husband, Gunther, are old friends who live in a huge garden filled with the trees, vines, and bushes of the rain forest. It is like an unobtrusively landscaped jungle, though since Gunther's stroke and the retirement of their old gardner, it looks rather less landscaped than it did.

At the far end of the property are a few small, sparsely furnished bungalows, which they rent. I waited for one to become available, then took it, though it was so tiny it didn't even have a kitchen, just a hot plate in the bathroom. Most of the time I ate in restaurants, and when friends dropped in, we sat in one of the little pavillions in the garden. It was particularly lovely at sunset and on moonlit nights.

People liked coming there, and friends often brought interesting visitors. Occasionally a scientist who had heard of my work looked me up. I sometimes wondered how many of them would have found me worth knowing if I had lived in an ordinary hotel and didn't serve Amazonia libres, the *chuchuwasi*–Coca-Cola drink invented by a Spanish anthropologist.

Terence and Dennis McKenna were among the first friends I saw when I got back to Iquitos. I had met them while I was still with the Linguists. They were brothers busy with a big research program on mind-altering botanicals and their place in the cultures of Amazonian peoples. They had been collecting the plants and data on beliefs and uses associated with them in several jungle areas for their study of the ethnobotany, microphysics, molecular biology, and pharmacology of psychoactive plants. They were especially interested by those used by shamans of the Amazon regions. They also collected the numerous and varied plants which different *ayahuas-queros* add to their brews. Every one of them has his own prescription.

The two brothers take care not to show their truly impressive erudition. Of course, it was obvious that they were uncommonly bright—nobody who wasn't could be that much fun—but fortunately I had no idea that I was spending my evenings with such extraordinary intellects, so I wasn't frostbitten with awe. I only found out months later, after they'd gone home and sent me their book *The Invisible Landscape: Mind, Hallucinogens and the I Ching*. But by then we were such warm and comfortable friends that I couldn't find them intimidating.

There have always been *ayahuasqueros* practicing in Iquitos, but only in secret. Shamanism or anything to do with the supernatural was forbidden by the law, until recently. Now all that has changed, and many *ayahuasqueros* welcome strangers who are presented as serious people not just looking for kicks. But those within the town limits are a mixed lot; some are serious and well prepared, and some are charlatans. The good ones are dedicated and highly trained men. To perfect their studies they had gone through years of rigidly disciplined deprivation; success requires, they believe, a long period of drastic trial by ordeal.

The sessions must be held after dark and in a somewhat isolated place, and the best practitioners live outside of the city limits. But a growing number of good professionals as well as charlatans have installed themselves within easy reach of the tourist trade.

One I already knew, but I didn't like him. He had a skimpy little mustache above a mouth like a torn pocket. After we paid his fee, he wanted money for a lot of things I had never known others to demand, like perfume we should wear to please the spirits. No serious shaman, the kind who has passed rigorous years of deprivation, would do anything so commercial.

The *ayahuasqueros* the McKennas were studying were highly qualified. The best one is Don Emilio, but like many others he lives an inconvenient distance from town. The one time I visited him, he was generous with information on plants.

One of the people who looked me up was a Dr. Wolfram Wiemann, who came to Iquitos to buy medicinal plant materials for his store in Nuremberg, Germany. That country, always noted for scientific excellence, is far in advance of the United States in the matter of herbal medicines. There is no FDA to deter people from experimenting with healing agents that have not been produced by pharmaceutical companies, and Dr. Wiemann has been very successful. The chief purpose of his trip was to replenish his stock of *chanca piedra* (*Phyllanthus niruri*), which he considered a most important cure for gallstones and kidney stones.

The plant loses none of its effectiveness when dried, so it can be shipped anywhere. Dr. Weimann kept careful records of all his sales, and he told me that he had over a hundred case histories of this one. In ninety-four percent of these, chanca piedra had completely eliminated the calculi within a week or two; the other six percent were people who did not keep the required promise to report results or those he had been unable to locate after they failed to show up. According to his records, not only was the herb infallibly successful in healing, but the only evidence of any side effect was an occasional case of cramps during the expulsion of stones. This can sometimes cause acute pain in patients who have been long-time sufferers from the calculi, but the discomfort always ends in a few hours. Dr. Weimann believed the healing to be permanent. His description of the effects of *chanca piedra* duplicated first-hand accounts I had received from acquaintances who had used it, and also the information given me long ago by my own Iquitos physician, Dr. Gil Villacorta. He told me that he had been prescribing it for years and had never known it to fail or to cause any unpleasant side effects.

I didn't get a chance to go on any trips until Peter Jenson invited me to a tourist camp he had almost finished building. Pete is the owner of Explorama, the oldest and best of the companies that operate jungle camps for tourists. The new place was on the Napo River, a short distance below Negro Urco. Don Alfonso had died years ago, and the military dictatorship that ruled the country from 1968 to 1980 had expropriated all the large properties in Peru. The Witotos at Negro Urco now owned the place. Peter said they were giving him a bad time.

"They object to your moving in and bringing a lot of foreigners close to their property," I said, out of my long experience.

"No, just the reverse!" Pete replied. "They are furious because I didn't build on their land or right next to it. They see tourists as easy pickings."

Things had certainly changed since I had last been in this part of the jungle.

Pete said the Witotos still talked about me, still spoke of me as a close friend. Peter wanted me to explain that where their houses were, the riverbanks were too steep to allow his floatplane to land without danger of knocking off a wing. That was true enough, but privately he told me that he was afraid they would be a nuisance, irritating tourists with insistent begging for cigarettes, candy, money, or trinkets and possibly a bit of petty theft.

That didn't sound like the people I had known fifteen years ago, but I should have remembered that Peter knew a lot about Indians. He had arranged a big fiesta to celebrate my return, and the whole tribe came. They were very glad to see me, and the first hour or two, spent chiefly in energetic dancing and then a big dinner, was pleasant enough. But soon the aguardiente took over and everything changed. In a surprisingly short time some of the men were aggressive enough that both tact and strategically applied force were necessary to persuade them to leave before the impending fights started.

But they still liked dressing up and putting on a show, stamping back and forth in their primitive dances and singing the ancient, rhythmic songs, the sort of thing that tourists find great fun. If the aguardiente could be watered a bit and the more respectable minority could convince the pests that rowdiness was counterproductive, if they learned that the first signs of misbehavior would make all food and liquor vanish, perhaps it would all work out.

I hoped so. The site of the new camp, on a secluded little inlet, was so very beautiful, even for jungle. I have seen few spots as serenely lovely as this little hollow, with its quiet water reflecting masses of flowering trees and its air full of birdsong from the nearby game preserve.

It was depressing to see such deterioration in old friends. Too much contact with the wrong sort of whites, probably. Peter said he had heard that cocaine dealers were working in some parts of the Amazon, but he didn't think any had infested the lower Napo. He'd seen no evidence of coca plantations, though he kept an eye out for them in his frequent flights over the region. If the *cocaineros* moved in, he would move out. They're dangerous.

Around Iquitos I found richer information on botanical medicines than I had hoped. Even living so frugally, I could no longer

fund any long trips to remote tribes, but Iquitos was home base for
several anthropologists studying those cultures, and they helped
me. Working in the sciences requires the ability to check for accuracy, and their evidence was generally pretty solid.

There were also the families who had lived there for more than a
generation. They almost always knew a lot of the old prescriptions,
though some of those most decidedly were not for me—like the
healing value of the first urine produced by a newborn infant.
Occasionally, however, what looked outlandish inexplicably turned
up a winner. Like the matter of the little red ants.

That had occurred during an earlier stay in Iquitos. My garden was
full of fire ants whose peculiarly painful stings put the place off limits
for any kind of open-air fun. I had sacrificed myself poking one kind
of poison after another down their holes, but they thrived on it.

One morning the gardener said, "Señora, if only we could get
some electric eels, the *pucacurus* would all go away."

I thought that was pretty funny. But the next Sunday, at the big
Belén market I saw a man with three small electric eels in a big
plastic bag of water, so I bought them. At least old Nemesio would
be pleased—unless he was embarrassed by being taken up on such a
story. I was sure he'd made it up; he loved to play the elder prophet.
When I gave them to him the next morning, he was delighted. He
cut them into chunks which he distributed all over the big garden.
The following day, red ants seemed unusually scarce, but there was
a drizzle and that could well have kept them home in their nice, dry
tunnels. The day after that, in brilliant sunshine, there was not an
ant to be found. Nor did any appear during the next three or four
weeks, or months, or years when I kept track. If anybody can come
up with a comprehensible reason for that, I would love to hear it.

I learned about some well-documented medicinals. Among the
best are two cures for hepatitis. Actually, I'd been told of one of
them long before, but thought the cure was given me by one of my
most reliable informants, I didn't trust it. It might be just a signa-
ture, an example of the ancient, worldwide belief that a plant cures
the thing it looks like. This one is a favorite condiment, and it dyes
anything it touches yellow, rather like turmeric. Its local name is
guisador, and it is sold in markets all over the country. Botanically it
is *Renealmia cf. breviscapa* Poepp. & Endl. Zingiberacae. I thought
the yellow coloring was probably the reason it was supposed to cure
jaundice.

My informant had told me about a young army conscript in the jungle post where he was sent for his year of service. The boy had such a severe hepatitis that the army doctor taking care of him said his death was only a matter of a day or two. Then a passing fisherman offered to cure him. From their kitchen garden he dug up some *guisador*, which is another of those rhizomes that look like small tubers. He made the patient swallow one finely chopped rhizome in a little water. It was the first thing the boy had been able to keep down in several days, and he also retained a second dose given him a few hours later. Improvement was noticeable almost immediately. In four days all yellow color was gone from his skin and eyes, medication was stopped, and he could eat even the food they get in army outposts.

I heard of no other cases until I returned this time to Iquitos, where I heard of several. One of them was Juanita's nephew Eduardo. He had been several days in an Iquitos hospital with a severe hepatitis and showed no improvement until Juanita intervened. She insisted on treating him with fresh *guisador* tubers from her garden, but her preparation was a little different; she used a "tea" made by steeping four grated rhizomes in boiling water. Eduardo got better in three days, and the hospital's daily analyses proved it. He went home five days after the first dose, and had no further trouble.

But that is not the only cure for hepatitis that the jungle offers. There are two others, equally good from what I have been able to learn. Both are the roots of palm trees, though not of the same genus.

One of them I have known for years; it is so widely accepted that it is sold, when they can get it, in markets as far away as Lima. This one is made with the roots of what is familiarly called *huasaí* or *wasaí*—*Euterpe edulis* (Palmae). This is a tall palm with a slim, cylindrical trunk that ends in a bouquet of feathery leaves. The healing agent is in the roots, some of which fan out on top of the soil at the base of the trunk. Six young and juicy roots are crushed and boiled in two or three liters of water, which is then strained and drunk. This is very highly recommended in many parts of the country, and is said to be an effective cure even for the dread hepatitis B. I have talked with a number of people who tell of being cured by it, even when the disease had advanced to a dangerous stage.

Daniel Fast, a Linguist who has lived many years with the

Ashuar, a remote Jívaroan tribe, says that they also use the roots of
the palm commonly called *ungurahui, Jessenia weberbaueri* (Palmae), in the same way. He tells of seeing the yellow eyeballs of a
very sick Ashuar boy regain their normal white within twenty-four
hours of taking the first dose of this one. They also use roots of
another palm, *Iriartea exorhyza*, locally known as *casha pona*. This,
too, is said to be successful in treating hepatitis B. When I was there
in January 1989, Daniel had been interpreting for Dr. Walter H.
Lewis, an ethnobotanist, and his wife, a dentist, Memory Elvin-
Lewis, who had gone into Ashuar territory to study the healing
practices of the tribe. Dr. Lewis, of Washington University and the
Missouri Botanical Gardens, is a scientist whose work I admire
enormously, though I have never had the good fortune to meet
him. He suggested to Dan that if these three genera of palm are so
good at curing hepatitis, others of this family ought also to be
investigated.

There is one plant whose properties might, I think, just possibly
make it one of the most important of all the healers in the rain
forest. It might meet a desperate need of present-day medicine if, as
it appears, it really does fortify and return to vigorous activity a
failing autoimmune system.

I first heard of it purely by chance. The little restaurant where I
often lunched was crowded, and the proprietor asked if he might
give the other seat at my table to a gentleman I had never met. I said
of course, and he brought over a pink-cheeked, very neat, and very
polite middle-aged man. I always talk to strangers, given a chance.
I've learned a lot that way. The man, Mario Arguellas, was a
friendly sort of person. When I said I was there because of my
interest in medicinal plants, his face lit up.

"But that's what saved me," he said. "I was dying of cancer, and
plant medicines saved me."

We immediately were friends. Telling me all about his remarkable recovery, he mentioned having the records of his illness from
the Hospital del Empleado in Lima. What luck! For once, I could
get some soundly documented evidence. People are all too ready to
add a little drama by insisting they were near death when they tell of
curing anything more serious than a hangnail. Since he had brought
up the records, I could explain that I'd studied in an American
medical school and would be interested in seeing how such things

were organized in Peru, and I could do it without sounding like a district attorney examining a defense witness.

He brought me the file the following Sunday. As I read it, I could feel my eyes bugging out. This man had to be dead! Medical journals sometimes describe inexplicable cases of spontaneous remission in a cancer case that has been diagnosed as terminal. Such things do occasionally occur—nobody knows why. But a case like this?

Nine specialists had attended Mario Arguellas, and I read the analyses they'd ordered. These reported, among other things, a severe cystitis, a generalized septicemia, and ten percent of cancer cells in the bloodstream. That's a massive metastasis. Terrible!

The tests had just been finished when, early one morning, two of the doctors came to his room and said they were sorry, but he would have to leave the hospital. Tomorrow they were all going on strike.

The hastily summoned friends who came to take him to their home were told that it didn't really matter where he was; he was dying. If he lasted as much as ten days more, they would be very much surprised.

Mario's friends knew a lot about plant medicine. They immediately started their own course of treatment. Among the plants they used were *chanca piedra* for the urinary infection—it helps with more than just kidney stones or gallstones—and a few drops of *sangre de grado* in a little water "to heal the blood." But the most important thing, he told me, was the plant *uña de gato*. They boiled twenty grams of the grated dried plant material in a liter of water, and he drank it throughout the day, every day.

His improvement was phenomenal. "In two weeks," he told me, "I was able to leave my bed."

The doctors' strike lasted thirty-one days. When it was over, he walked into the hospital. He enjoyed telling me about their amazement, but was a little disappointed that they hadn't thought he was a ghost.

Before long he went back to work. Doing what, I asked, and I got another surprise: Seven hours a day he taught ballet and classical Spanish dancing, including flamenco, for the Iquitos branch of the Ministry of Culture.

Those years of dance training I'd taken so seriously in my youth had taught me what stamina four or five hours of ballet required. But I didn't work at flamenco until much later, when I lived in Paris. I was studying with the corps de ballet of the Opéra Comique, so I was in pretty good shape when, on a trip to Barcelona, I decided to learn a little flamenco. I got a surprise. I have never known any exercise that demands such an output of energy as those prolonged *zapateòs*, the very fast stamping with both feet that sounds like loud castanets. That makes classical ballet feel like strolling through the park. And I was only twenty-two at that time.

Mario Arguellas was in his middle fifties. He told me he owed his good health to not smoking, not drinking, eating sensibly, and taking a daily dose of *uña de gato*, which he felt sure had protected him from any recurrence of the cancer.

I immediately started a search for the proper botanical identification. There are eight plants called *uña de gato* in Peru, and I wasn't able to get a specimen of whatever it was that had done the job. Mario got his supply from a man who sold it in Lima, already finely ground and packed in plastic bags. I knew only that the plant came from a place in the foothills of the jungle at an altitude of more than three thousand feet. Climate, in any country whose topography is as up-and-down as Peru's, is dominated by altitude; as a general rule, higher means colder, and different temperatures mean different species. That was a help. I began eliminating.

I could have saved a lot of time if I'd asked Dr. McDaniel, Adriana's boss, but I didn't know then that *uña de gato* was among the quantities of plants he had supplied to the anticancer research program of the National Institutes of Health. McDaniel later told me that Dr. Monroe Wall, working on *uña de gato*, reported that they were finding some very encouraging tumor-inhibiting properties in it when the Reagan Administration came into office and canceled the research program.

Mario's *uña de gato*, in some localities called *garabato casha* or *tambor huasca*, is *Uncaria tomentosa* (Rubiaceae). This is a woody vine which grows in the foothills, chiefly at altitudes between seven or eight hundred and twenty-five hundred meters. A very similar lowland species, known by the same set of local names, is *Uncaria guianensis*; it is abundant in lower altitudes of the Peruvian Amazon. It was *U. tomentosa* that cured Mario Arguellas, but *U. guianensis* that Dr. Wall studied. It appears that the two species are as nearly identical in medicinal properties as they are in appearance.

Some time later I learned that a man whose lung cancer was cured by *uña de gato* had, after continuing dosage, found that he could walk normally and even climb stairs, even though for years he had been badly crippled by arthritis. Then I got good evidence of its working wonders for diabetics. Could it be that this plant might perhaps be giving a tremendous boost to the immune system? I couldn't think of any other way of examining the diversity of its effects, its ability to eliminate so many problems that, as far as my limited knowledge let me guess, appeared to have only one thing in common: they were all degenerative diseases. In any case, I had not enough knowledge to make judgments in such a serious matter. And I knew nobody in Iquitos I could get the right kind of information from, so I put the matter aside.

Only very recently have I found any more extensive information on how some of these plants might work to benefit so many problems affecting different organs and functions. Lack of access to scientific publications is a handicap.

News media sometimes can be a useful source of information, though I'm afraid the pronouncements of "Madame Zuzu, the Mystical Seeress, No CODs," might be about as reliable as some of the more excitable publications. But now and then I come across one that I know has substance, like the story about several species of *tabebuia*. These are commonly called *pau d'arco* and *ipe* in Brazil, *siete cueros* in Columbia, and *tahuarí* or sometimes *palo de arco* in Peru. The species most abundant around Iquitos is the yellow-flowered *Tabebuia chrysantha*, Bignoniaceae, though the purple-flowered *Tabebuia obscura* can also be found here and there.

A clipping someone sent me from an unidentified slick publication says research on this botanical was done at the municipal hospital in San Andre, a suburb of São Paulo, Brazil, and gives glowing accounts of its success in treating leukemia and other types of cancer with more than one species of tabebuia. The tree's ability to cure arthritis and diabetes too is mentioned without specific data.

Any clipping is much more useful if the name and date of the publication it's cut from are given; if not, it is almost impossible to get more information from its contents.

Around Iquitos *Tabebuia chrysantha*, locally called *tahuarí* is well known, and praised as a means of controlling diabetes. I heard that one of the most important Peruvian businessmen keeps some of it in his desk in every office he has throughout the country. From gratitude for what it has done for his diabetes, he made a vow to have it always at hand to give to anyone who needs it. But its tumor-inhibiting properties have been less known here, though some of the Linguists report its startling success as a tumor or cancer cure in some of the tribes and in the Yarinacocha villages of Tushmo, San José, and Callao.

Peter Rachau, who has been with the Urarina tribe, has for several years been interested in native botanical medicines. He tells of the use of *tahuarí* also for liver and kidney disorders. And he has more accounts of *uña de gato*'s curing tumors, which may or may not have been malignant, in members of that tribe.

Peter attended an international congress of enthnobotanists interested in tribal medicinal plants in nearby Pucallpa a few months before I saw him in Yarinacocha. *Uña de gato* was one of the plants that was discussed, and several scientists gave reports of their research. Peter read me his notes.

An Italian doctor, Giaccarino Paolo Francesco, gave a long list of ailments for which it is used, and Peter quoted him: "One mechanism of its working is that it activates T-lymphocytes and macrophages." An unnamed Spanish doctor proved that it normalizes the immunoglobulins. Macrophages gobble up harmful particles or cells, and immunoglobins are proteins in the body's fluids that combat infections.

Another report stated that no toxicity had been found, even with such massive doses as one gram of evaporated essence of the active principle per kilo of body weight.

Later, when I got a very nasty infection, I decided to see what *uña de gato* could do to help my own immune system fight back. I had suffered the same problem some twenty-odd years earlier, and I learned then that it was the sort of localized but very stubborn infection that could only be cured by surgery, so I'd had the operation, which kept me in the hospital for a fortnight. Remembering the reports about how the plant boosted the activity of the body's own defense mechanisms, I started on a course of tetracyclines and added three doses daily of *uña de gato*. It worked beautifully. In only a week, the problem was gone, and it has not returned. I decided to continue taking it on general principles, but found one disadvantage, though some might consider it a boon. I have for years had white hair. Phyllis Manus, a Linguist friend, warned me that *uña de gato* sometimes turns gray hair back to its original color. My hair wasn't gray: it is white, and had been for a long time, so I didn't worry. After the infection was beaten, I kept on taking *uña de gato*. There was a lot of flu around, and it might help me avoid it. I did not get flu, but after another couple of months I began to notice an occasional dark hair showing up among the snowy ones that I've been so vain about. And just a few more, every week or so. That was disturbing, so I stopped taking the brew for a couple of months. But the dark hairs have kept right on. They probably are only a few each week, but lately one or two friends have noticed. I don't like that at all; a woman has a few things to be vain about when she's in her eighties. Recently I have learned of other plants which seem to work similarly for an equally unlikely variety of ills. I shall have to ask Dr. McDaniel for two of them and see if they will allow my hair to remain properly white.

XXXX

B<small>Y NOW</small> I had notes on hundreds of medicinal plants and a substantial amount of empirical evidence to help check the reliability of my data. I'd accomplished about as much as I could manage for now, if "accomplish" is the right word. I'm not sure. It has all been so much fun that on the rare occasions I've managed to be paid anything, I've had a slight, secret feeling of guilt. You wouldn't expect to be paid for an exciting, sometimes hilarious vacation, would you? And that was mostly what this work, especially the jungle part, felt like. But when I remember the shocking amount of money—just about all I ever had—I have put into getting that information, so much *quid* with no *pro quo*, guilt vanishes.

Now it was high time I faced the fact that the job was incomplete. It was all useless as long as I simply kept it to myself. I had to get to work and do a book, preferably in plain English rather than botanese, to make everything I've learned available to as many people as possible. That would be a lot less fun that getting the information, but after all, my purpose has always been to make known what is there and how it can help. Unless that is done, I might as well have stayed home and tried to get excited about bridge and golf, like my (late) family. I had to hope that if enough people knew it, science or industry would work on some of it, pick out the bugs, establish what was useful and then put it within reach of people who were hurting. I had to hope, too, that it might add a wisp to the growing weight of evidence that we must, for our own sakes, stop the destruction of the rain forests.

For the moment, the big difficulty was my lack of scientific names for a lot of the plants. Many of my specimens had never been checked at all, and I was not sure of the accuracy of a good part of the identifications I did have. But I thought I knew what to do about it.

My own observations and the opinions of others had convinced me that Adriana's boss, Dr. Sidney McDaniel, knew the flora of my particular working area more thoroughly than anybody else. I'd first been impressed by a telephone conversation. I asked if I had the right species name for a certain small herb and without a pause he answered, "No. If you got it around Iquitos it is almost certainly so-and-so. The species you named hasn't been found this far west. You have to go a little farther down the Amazon, almost to Leticia to find that one. The two species are closely related and look exactly alike except that the leaves of your plant have tiny stems and the other's leaves are stemless."

He did that sort of thing over and over, and checking always proved him right. For the book I obviously needed his help.

It was time to move back to the States for a while. I knew I'd come back to the jungle. I always do, but now I had to go stateside, find McDaniel, get his help, and start work on that book. It would probably mean moving to Mississippi in the Deep South, unknown territory to me. I have never gone along with the saying, "Better the devil you know than the devil you don't know." That makes for a very dull life. I'll take the devil I don't know anytime.

I phoned Dr. McDaniel. As I had hoped, he said he would do the identifications, and he could start whenever I got to Mississippi. But first I had a number of small matters to attend to in New York, so that's where I went. A lot of my specimens and most of my friends were there, and it was wonderful to be able to get at libraries and bookstores, good music and movies that were neither porn nor kung fu, which is about all Iquitos offers. So I dallied.

On other trips home I had noticed that the media now and then mentioned the rain forest's importance to world ecology. As a journalist I'd learned all about placing isolated "fillers" here and there when hard news was scarce. Very few people had seemed to pay much attention to warnings about how the great rain forests protect our environment and about the dangers that depleting them would bring. Only a few small groups seemed to find it interesting. But now things had changed.

It was a surprise to see a growing and lively interest in eliminat-

ing the more destructive kinds of development that were biting into
rain forests around the world and most especially in the Amazon
region. Best of all, the interest was no longer confined to an
educated elite. Think-tankers don't make much noise; it's the general public that has the power. Now I was hearing an occasional
mention of "greenhouse effect" and "soil erosion" even in such
unlikely places as supermarket lines and city buses.

Television programs about the Amazon were frequent. I even
saw a rerun of one of Jacques Cousteau's that my work and I were
shown in. Making it had been a delight. Captain Cousteau is one of
the best informed and most effective of all conservationists, and
people pay attention to his films. He also has as fast and funny a
sense of humor as I've ever encountered.

Newspapers and magazines now frequently publish strong stories about the jungle's role in preserving the environment and what
that means to our future. The contrast to earlier indifference is
striking. People are at last beginning to get an idea of how the
destruction of the forests can cut into our chances of having something left to drink and to eat, even enough oxygen to breathe, in the
coming century. I hope they will learn, too, that such destruction
does away with the raw material of medicines that not only can
make their lives longer but can make longer lives more worth living.

There are encouraging developments in that area, too. Interest in
the medical uses of plants had been noticeable when I was here
before, but now there is a big change. The interest is no longer
confined to plants of the old European tradition, things known and
used by our grandparents or their forebears. A few Asiatic things,
like ginseng, have been available for some time, but only recently is
news about the botanical medicines of primitive peoples being
featured by some of our most respectable publications and television programs. Some organizations are even beginning to give
them active attention. In the last year I have been called in for
consultation in various parts of the United States and even in
Europe. It's hard but satisfying work, and I love it, but it's greatly
slowed the writing of the book I must get done.

The economic advantages of preserving the rain forest have been
making news in good, solid, respected periodicals like the *New York
Times, Time* magazine, and *Newsweek* to mention only a few. Several
prestigious organizations—the New York Botanical Garden is
one—have finished studies proving that extraction makes smaller

profits than harvesting the fruits of the rain forest plants. They
show clearly that lumbering not only devastates surrounding areas
by eliminating the shade needed for regrowth of jungle plants, but
also earns the lumberman less money than the settler can make by
harvesting jungle fruits. Palm oil for kitchen use is a high-profit
example. The fruits containing it can be harvested from trees that
are already there by the thousands, and they require practically no
care, no work except the gathering of their fruits. This type of
production gives a steady income for years, and there is very little
capital investment. Nothing like that can be managed by cutting
trees that take decades to grow to a marketable size. Harvesting
also, the studies show, makes better profits than cattle raising,
which is a pretty hazardous and expensive business in the jungle.

Less publicity has been given to the economic advantage of
preserving the rain forests as a source of healing agents. The prices
of prescription drugs, according to published statistics, have increased 135 percent in the last ten years. That puts them just about
out of reach for people on small incomes.

One difficulty in promoting the study of jungle medicines lies in
the fact that this would probably be of more help to the general
public than to the pharmaceutical industry. It is practically impossible to patent a plant, but the processes of production can be
patented, and medicines of botanical origin still are proving profitable, as is shown by the sales of quinine, curare, digitalis, and similar
plant products. Wouldn't the preliminary research on substances
which have already been compounded and produced by nature be
less costly? Couldn't the first steps of any investigation of botanical
medicines use for initial studies a fairly simple extraction of the
active principle, the sort of thing that cures the natives? Wouldn't
that be a lot less expensive then the materials now used for most
research, substances produced by complicated laboratory processes?
The technicians and pharmacological chemists responsible for for-
mulating and providing those substances are skilled, highly paid
scientists. But with botanicals, nature does that part of it for free.

I wish the economic advantages of naturally occurring medicines
could get more publicity.

There are also some immediately encouraging developments.
Recently formed organizations are opening new vistas. Some of the
most urgently needed work is being done by Botanical Dimensions,
the nonprofit organization founded in 1985 by Terence and Kath-

leen Harrison McKenna. This foundation is, I believe, unique in its practical, wide range of activities. I think the most important thing they are doing is their work to preserve the gene pools of plants used as medicine by peoples of the tropical forests. It begins with collection of a large body of information about primitive medicinal practices. But to quote from *Plant Wise*, the organization's newsletter: "The data without the plants is merely anthropological information. The plants without the data are genetically preserved, but orphaned."

Many of those "orphans" are now being given a loving home on the big island of Hawaii, where Botanical Dimensions has bought a tract of rich, forested land. Here they are cultivating a steadily increasing collection of living plants, the little-known medicines used by inhabitants of the Amazon and the tropical rain forests of Asia, Africa, and Central America. This operation is succeeding beyond the most optimistic expectations; the plants thrive in Hawaii's cosseting climate.

In addition, Botanical Dimensions is working in California on a database which includes for each species a scientific illustration and description, the Latin and local names, geographical range, traditional uses, the results of any known chemical studies, etc. They hope eventually to make their software available to interested people and institutions.

Unlike the organizations which clog my mailbox with elegant printing, Botanical Dimensions spends everything it can get on producing rather than publicizing. That may be why they aren't better funded, but it certainly enables them to get a lot done. The only request I've ever had from them is for seeds of Amazonian plants, to be sent to them at the California address, P.O. Box 807, Occidental CA 95465—in case anyone who reads this should be interested. So many people are taking vacations in the Amazon, and while the bureaucratic complications governing international transport of any other plant materials are horrendous, there are no problems at all with dried seeds.

I'm in Mississippi now, but not, repeat not, connected in any way with Mississippi State University, although I've seen newspaper articles which say I am. They embarrass me. I would hate academic dignitaries to think I'm claiming a distinction to which I'm not entitled. The error is probably due to my being a research associate of the Institute for Botanical Exploration, which has a Mississippi State address at which I sometimes receive mail.

Identification of the plants I want to write about is practically completed, so I'll soon be moving to gentler climes, the sort of place I expected when I came to Mississippi. I had believed all the propaganda about the "balmy" Deep South. Just before Christmas the temperature here fell to three Fahrenheit degrees below zero. All those New Yorkers who congratulated me on moving into a balmy climate had been using that adjective as we did for my boarding-school roommate's great-aunt Lucy. The dear old lady brought us some beautifully packed "fudge" she had made herself— of rich, dark mud. She also made elegant mud pies until they moved her to a rest home.

Going back to the jungle now will not be like going back to a dear friend with some slow, wasting disease. True, the danger is not over, but there is steadily growing reason to believe that it is diminishing. I can now hope that it will, in time, be controlled, that at least some of the rain forest will be given effective protection, and that its healing gifts will gradually cease to be snubbed, and instead that they will be stripped of their age-old wrapping of intolerance and be carefully examined. Then some will surely be found worth using to free people everywhere, not just a few isolated groups, from sickness, from disfigurement, from pain and untimely death.

UÑA DE GATO
Uncaria guianensis, Rubiaceae

Paul E. Nace
Institute for Botanical Exploration

APPENDIX

IDENTIFICATION OF PLANTS MENTIONED

Page 28, Local name: *retama*; *Cassia reticulata* Willd. Caesalpinaceae (Leguminosae). This is the plant whose yellow flowers are credited with healing the cardiac edema of the engineer's mother, but I have been unable to find another instance of its use for this purpose. I do have several unverified accounts of its successful use for liver and kidney problems. It is reputed to be diuretic, but is chiefly prized for its value in curing such parasitic skin diseases as ringworm, mange, etc., by external application of crushed fresh leaves or pods of the beanlike fruit to the infected area.

Page 49: *Aysifera* is the Witoto name of the plant sometimes given babies to prevent adult obesity. I have not obtained the scientific name. After giving the original specimen to the pharmaceutical company, I didn't get another, because most of the tribe seemed to have scant respect for it, and so do I, for the following reasons: (1) It is hard to believe that a single dose given in infancy could prevent obesity for a lifetime. (2) I have never seen a really fat Indian in any Amazon jungle tribe; they don't appear to have the genes for obesity. (3) No member of the tribe except the extremely old or sick is exempt from the customary daily labor of hunting, fishing, land clearing, agriculture, housebuilding, etc., which gives the average person about the same amount of exercise as is required by a tennis or football star in training. And finally, (4) their diet includes very little fat. The fish and jungle animals which are their principal source of protein are invariably lean; constantly hunting or being hunted, the Witoto do a lot of running.

Page 50: Local name: *yanamuco*; *Neea parvifolia* Poepp. and Endl. Nyctaginaceae. This is the tree whose leaves blacken teeth and prevent caries. The local name is a mixture of Peru's two dominant languages, Spanish and Quechua, the language of the Inca Empire and lingua franca for parts of Peru's northern Amazon region. *Yana* is Quechua for "black," and *muco* is Spanish for "mucus."

Page 52: Local name: *ishango*, meaning, in English, "nettle"; *Urera carcassana* (Jacq.) Gaud. ex Grisch Urticaceae.

Page 52: Witoto name: *amuebe*; *Pluknetia volubilis* L. Euphorbiaceae. This is the twining shrub whose fresh leaves, made into a poultice, heal extensive infected third-degree burns without scarring.

Page 63–64: Local name: *insira* or *incira; Chlorophora tinctoria* (L.) Gaud. Euphorbiaceae. This is the tree whose sap removes teeth, whether carious or healthy, without pain or bleeding.

Page 103: Local name: *oje; Ficus insipida*, Moraceae. This is the tree whose sap is commonly used throughout the Amazon region for expelling intestinal parasites.

Page 107: Local name: *chanca piedra; Phyllanthus niruri, P. lathyroides, P. stipulatus*, Euphorbiaceae. All look very much alike, the difference being only in size, and all are effective in eliminating gallstones and kidney stones. *Chanca* means "shatter" in Quechua, and *piedra* is Spanish for "stone."

Page 131: Maria's hangover remedy remains unidentified because I have never found another tribe familiar with it and thus have not been able to get another specimen. It is apparently an Ocaina secret.

Page 190: Local name: *ayahuasca* or *ayawasca; Banisteriopsis caapi* Spruce, or *B. inebrians*, Malpighiaceae. These are the famous hallucinogenic vines used throughout the Amazon region by shamans.

Page 250: Local name: *piripiri; Cyperus corymbosus*, L. Cyperaceae.

Page 293: Local name: *sangre de grado; sangre de drago; Croton lechleri*, Eurphorbiaceae. This tree yields the hemostatic sap that accelerates wound healing.

Page 308: Local name: *torurco; Paspalum conjugatum* Berg., Gramineae. This is the grass whose juice cured the infected corneas of the settler on Río Tigre. This plant juice is also well known for healing eyes threatened with blindness by pterygium.

Page 334: Local name: *toé; Datura arborea (Brugmansia)* Solanaceae. This ornamental is dangerously narcotic.

Page 355: Local name in some parts of Peruvian Amazonia: *Cierra tu puerta; Mimosa pudica*, Mimosaceae (Leguminaceae)

The identity of all other plants mentioned accompanies their description in the text.

ACKNOWLEDGMENTS

I wish it were possible to express my thanks to all the people who have given me the help that has made this book possible. They are too many to mention here, but their names appear in these pages, and I can only hope that my appreciation will show through.

I cannot, however, forego mentioning my debt to members of the Summer Institute of Linguistics at Yarinacocha for their help, hospitality, and care. I especially want to express my thanks to Ted and Lillice Long, who have been like the family I wish I had, and also my first Linguist friends, the Riches, and to Ron and Phyllis Manus and George and Phyllis Woodward, all of whom have taken me into their homes and cared for me as though I really belonged. And I want to mention the pleasure I get from remembering long afternoons with Joyce Nies while she painstakingly interpreted details of the Piro pharmacopaia and culture, also my appreciation for the Fast family's many kindnesses and expert information on the Ashuar. I hope the value of Peter Rachau's generous help is clearly evident in the text.

I must also express my gratitude for all the personal kindness and professional help I received in Colombia from Dr. J. M. Idrobo and Señora María Jesús de Idrobo. And never shall I be able to give adequate thanks to Dr. Sidney McDaniel, of Mississippi State University and the Institute for Botanical Exploration. His indefatigable help has benefited me in so many ways. I must thank him for the days spent identifying hundreds of plants and teaching me about them. I am indebted to him not only for professional advice and teaching but also for the way he has aided my efforts to cope with the tiresome problems of daily life in an unfamiliar environment. I cannot imagine how I would have managed without his always kindly aid.

Printed in Great Britain
by Amazon